ÖZS-Sonderband 6
Talcott Parsons

Helmut Staubmann · Harald Wenzel (Hrsg.)

Talcott Parsons
Zur Aktualität eines Theorieprogramms

Österreichische Zeitschrift für Soziologie
Sonderband 6
Springer Fachmedien Wiesbaden GmbH

Die Deutsche Bibliothek – CIP-Einheitsaufnahme
Ein Titeldatensatz für diese Publikation ist bei
Der Deutschen Bibliothek erhältlich

Die Drucklegung wurde gefördert durch das Bundesministerium für Wissenschaft, Bildung und Kultur in Wien.

1. Auflage September 2000

Alle Rechte vorbehalten
© Springer Fachmedien Wiesbaden 2000
Ursprünglich erschienen bei Westdeutscher Verlag GmbH, Wiesbaden, 2000
Lektorat: Dr. Tatjana Rollnik-Manke

Der Westdeutsche Verlag ist ein Unternehmen der Fachverlagsgruppe BertelsmannSpringer.

Das Werk einschließlich aller seiner Teile ist urheberrechtlich geschützt. Jede Verwertung außerhalb der engen Grenzen des Urheberrechtsgesetzes ist ohne Zustimmung des Verlags unzulässig und strafbar. Das gilt insbesondere für Vervielfältigungen, Übersetzungen, Mikroverfilmungen und die Einspeicherung und Verarbeitung in elektronischen Systemen.

www.westdeutschervlg.de

Höchste inhaltliche und technische Qualität unserer Produkte ist unser Ziel. Bei der Produktion und Verbreitung unserer Bücher wollen wir die Umwelt schonen. Dieses Buch ist auf säurefreiem und chlorfrei gebleichtem Papier gedruckt. Die Einschweißfolie besteht aus Polyäthylen und damit aus organischen Grundstoffen, die weder bei der Herstellung noch bei der Verbrennung Schadstoffe freisetzen.

Druck und buchbinderische Verarbeitung: Rosch-Buch, Scheßlitz

ISBN 978-3-531-13468-0   ISBN 978-3-322-83346-4 (eBook)
DOI 10.1007/978-3-322-83346-4

Inhalt

ZUR WÜRDIGUNG PARSONS'
Helmut Staubmann / Harald Wenzel
   Talcott Parsons "revisited" 9
Renée C. Fox
   Talcott Parsons – Mein Lehrer 15

KONVERGENZEN – DIVERGENZEN
Talcott Parsons
   Das Konvergenzproblem in den europäischen Sozialwissenschaften
   an der Wende zum 20. Jahrhundert 33
Victor M. Lidz / Harold J. Bershady
   Convergence as Method in Theory Construction 45
Tamás Meleghy
   Über den hierarchischen Aufbau der Welt.
   Talcott Parsons' und Karl Poppers Theorien im Vergleich 107
Gerald Mozetič
   Talcott Parsons und die formale Soziologie 141
Dénes Némedi
   Parsons Reads Durkheim 157

BAUSTEINE DER THEORIE DES HANDELNS
Andreas Balog
   Theorie als "theoretisches System".
   Parsons' Beitrag zur soziologischen Theorie 175
Keith Doubt
   The Critique of Utilitarianism in *Structure* and *Gorgias* 203
Max Haller
   Zum Verhältnis von funktionaler, kausaler und historischer
   Erklärung bei Parsons. Eine kritische Betrachtung 221
Bryan S. Turner
   Scarcity of Means and Solidarity of Values. The Theory of Social Action
   in Talcott Parsons' General Sociology 239

ANWENDUNGEN DER THEORIE DES HANDELNS
Josef Langer
   Talcott Parsons' Kulturkonzept. Ein Zugang zum besseren Verständnis
   der Transformationsprozesse in Europa? 257
Jeremy Tanner
   The Body, Expressive Culture and Social Interaction.
   Integrating Art History and Action Theory 285

Zur Würdigung Parsons'

Talcott Parsons "revisited"
Helmut Staubmann/Harald Wenzel

Die Gegenwart der Sozialwissenschaften und insbesondere der Theorie des Handelns sei keine Zeit der Synthese, in der man sich der Konstruktion großer "geschlossener" Theorie-Systeme verschreiben könne, sondern eine, deren Fortschritt in der Kreativität, in intellektueller Fermentierung und in Efferveszenz spürbar sei. So jedenfalls lautet die Einschätzung der Situation, die Parsons am Ende der siebziger Jahre in mehreren seiner Schriften und Reden dieser letzten Periode seines Schaffens bekräftigt – zuletzt in den Schlusssätzen seines aus Anlass der Erneuerung seiner Doktorwürde an der Universität Heidelberg im Mai 1979 gehaltenen Vortrages, nur wenige Tage vor seinem Tod.[1] Dies ist eine durchaus doppeldeutige Diagnose zu diesem Zeitpunkt: Parsons Theorie dominierte schon lange nicht mehr die amerikanische Soziologie, wie sie es in den fünfziger Jahren zweifellos getan hat; in den siebziger Jahren ist Parsons' Theorie nur eine leiser werdende Stimme im Chor der Sozialtheorie. In Parsons' Diagnose liegt die Anerkennung dieser gewandelten Umstände: Es ist die Kreativität anderer, streitbarer und fruchtbarer Theorieansätze, die die Lebendigkeit der sozialtheoretischen Diskussion in den siebziger Jahren prägt. Doch Parsons – und das ist der weitere Sinn der Diagnose – schließt sich aus dieser Lebendigkeit nicht aus. Für ihn selbst ist der stetige Wandel theoretischen Denkens immer der Regelfall gewesen. Im späten Rückblick auf sein Werk *The Social System*, dem zweiten Opus magnum nach *The Structure of Social Action*, gesteht er z.B. freimütig zu, dass dieses Buch zum Zeitpunkt seines Erscheinens schon veraltet war, sein Denken sich damals schon neuen Horizonten zugewandt hatte. Jede Neuerung, die die Gestalt der Theorie nach ihrer Gründung veränderte – und es gab derer viele: die Psychoanalyse, das Gleichgewichtsmodell, die Kybernetik, die Genetik, die Austauschmedien, um nur einige herausragende zu nennen – , stellte Parsons vor das Problem, seine schon wieder veränderte Theorie auf Konsistenz und Kohärenz zu prüfen. Es sind deshalb die Fortschritte der Theorie, die ihn immer wieder zwingen, zu seinen Grundlagen zurückzukehren: insbesondere zu den Werken Emile Durkheims und Max Webers und zu scheinbar aufgegebenen Theo-

---

[1] Vgl. Parsons, Talcott: "On the Relation of the Theory of Action to Max Weber's ›Verstehende Soziologie‹". In: Wolfgang Schluchter (Hg.): *Verhalten, Handeln und System. Talcott Parsons' Beitrag zur Entwicklung der Sozialwissenschaften*. Frankfurt/Main: Suhrkamp 1980, S. 150-163 sowie die Vorworte und Einleitungen in: Ders.: *Social Systems and the Evolution of Action Theory*. New York: The Free Press 1977, ders.: *Action Theory and the Human Condition*. New York: The Free Press 1978.

riekonzepten wie dem der Mustervariablen. Allesamt stehen diese Rückbesinnungen unter dem Titel "revisited".

Dass Parsons keine hermetische "Übertheorie" der Sozialwissenschaften entwickelte, die die Natur menschlichen Zusammenlebens endgültig aufgeklärt und deren ewige Formen gefunden hat, sondern ein sich ständig veränderndes Gewebe, dessen Einheit er sich immer wieder in der Rückschau versichern mußte, scheint uns eindeutig zu sein. "Grand theory", als Schimpfwort für eine abgehobene soziologische Metaphysik geprägt,[2] ist heute kein Vorwurf mehr, um Parsons' Werk lächerlich zu machen.[3] Die Arbeit an großen Theoriesynthesen ist weiterhin nicht nur eine legitime Aufgabe, sie bestimmt gerade auch heute die Lebendigkeit der Disziplin, wie die Arbeiten von Anthony Giddens, Jürgen Habermas und Niklas Luhmann zeigen. Jeder Versuch einer Theoriesynthese nach Parsons, auch das ist klar, steht ungewollt oder gewollt in einem Bezug zu seinem Werk.

Aber beileibe nicht alle Bezugnahmen auf Parsons' Theorie – seien sie deklariert oder undeklariert – dienen der Erarbeitung einer großen Theoriesynthese. Was aber hält uns dann zur steten Rückkehr zu Parsons an? Dafür gibt es natürlich eine Menge besonderer Motive. Eine allgemeine Antwort könnte jedoch lauten: Die Qualität seiner Theorie als *klassische* Theorie. Parsons selbst hat exemplarisch vorgeführt, wie sich eine Disziplin bzw. eine Theorie ihrer Grundlagen vergewissert und wiedervergewissert, indem sie die Fiktion eines begründenden Anfangs, einen Ursprungsmythos schafft. Vor Parsons gab es doch noch gar keine klassische soziologische Theorie! Ob man die Klassiker soziologischer Theorie bloß formal als das Vorziehen des Alten, Bekannten, Reputierten vor dem Neuen, noch-nicht-Bewährten definiert[4] oder material mit einer bestimmten, z.B. normativen Auffassung sozialer Ordnung identifiziert – es geht immer um eine Vergewisserung, die sich in empirischer Validierung an der Realität allein nicht finden läßt. Was Parsons entdeckt hat und was wir seither anerkennen müssen, ist die postempiristische Eigenlogik theoretischer Entwicklungen in den Sozialwissenschaften. Auch wenn ihre empirischen Befunde korrekt sind, können Argumentationen, die auf ihnen aufbauen, mangelhaft sein, weil sie theoretisch nicht durchdacht sind. Theoretisches

---

2 Vgl. C. Wright Mills, *The Sociological Imagination*, NewYork: Oxford University Press 1967 (1959).
3 Vgl. Quentin Skinner, „Introduction: The Return of Grand Theory", in: Ders., *The Return of Grand Theory in the Human Sciences*, Cambridge: Cambridge University Press 1985, S.1-20.
4 Und schon das weist im Sinne von Mertons Matthäus-Effekt darauf hin, dass Klassiker in Zukunft zunehmend klassischer, d.h. berühmter und beachteter sein werden: Sie sind schon tot und können ihren eigenen Ruf nicht mehr schädigen. Vgl. Robert Merton, *Entwicklung und Wandel von Forschungsinteressen*, Frankfurt/Main: Suhrkamp 1985 (1973), S.147ff.

Durchdenken führt aber im Zweifelsfall immer zurück – und früher oder später landet man dann bei Parsons oder den Klassikern. Auch wenn man sich nur von ihnen absetzen, sie gerade nicht mehr als Orientierungsgröße benutzen will, erfordert das eine – oft zwischen den Zeilen ausgeführte – Begründung, warum nicht.

Die Frage ist heute also weniger: Hat uns Parsons noch etwas zu sagen? Sie lautet eher: Können wir es uns leisten, ihn zu ignorieren? Die in diesem Band versammelten Arbeiten zeigen, daß wir es nicht können. Um vorwärtszukommen müssen wir immer auch zurückgehen.

Anlaß für die Rückkehr zu Parsons war eine im Frühjahr 1999 veranstaltete Tagung am Institut für Soziologie der Leopold-Franzens-Universität Innsbruck. Sie stand unter dem Motto: *Talcott Parsons: Zur Aktualität eines Theorieprogramms*. Der vorliegende Band enthält einen Teil der dort präsentierten Beiträge und zwar jene, die sich primär mit der ersten Theoriephase Parsons' auseinandersetzen. Wir planen einen weiteren Band mit Beiträgen zum späten Parsons. Die Aufteilung der Aufsätze nach Bezug zu Theoriephasen war nicht ganz trennscharf vorzunehmen, sie ergab sich mehr oder weniger "induktiv" aus den vorgefundenen thematischen Naheverhältnissen. Neben den an der Tagung referierten Beiträgen wurden die für den vorliegenden Band erstellten Originalbeiträge von Keith Doubt, Josef Langer und Bryan S. Turner aufgenommen. Durchgängiges Motiv der in diesem Band vereinten Beiträge ist die Bezugnahme zum Erstlingswerk *The Structure of Social Action* und hier insbesondere auf die sogenannte Konvergenzthese. Ergänzt wird der vorliegende Band durch eine Erstveröffentlichung einer Parsons-Arbeit, in der er aus der Sicht seines Spätwerkes auf die Konvergenzthese zurückblickt, sowie um eine bereits im Amerikanischen veröffentlichte Erinnerung Renée Fox' an Talcott Parsons.

Renée Fox' lebendige Beschreibung ihrer freundschaftlichen Beziehung zu ihrem Lehrer ist eines der wenigen Dokumente, das zur Person Talcott Parsons existiert. Ihre Erinnerungen bringen uns die Persönlichkeit Parsons' näher, dessen intellektuelle Größe mit einer ebensolchen Tiefe an Empfindungsvermögen verbunden war und sich in einem hohen Verantwortungsbewußtsein in seinen fachlichen und privaten Beziehungen äußerte. Es sind gerade die Details und die "Momentaufnahmen" aus der alltägliche Lebensgestaltung, zu kulturellen Vorlieben, zur Herkunftsfamilie und der Bewältigung des beruflichen Alltags, die uns ein tieferes Verständnis des "unheilbaren Theoretikers", als welcher sich Parsons selbst bezeichnet hatte, ermöglichen.

Ein bisher unveröffentlichter Aufsatz von *Talcott Parsons* steht am Beginn einer Reihe von Beiträgen, die sich mit der Konvergenzthese beschäftigen. Das Papier wurde 1975 an einer Tagung der International Sociological Association vorgetragen. Darin bekräftigt Parsons seine Sichtweise von der Richtigkeit seiner in *The Structu-*

re of Social Action ausgeführten These und verteidigt sie gegen eine Reihe von kritischen Stellungnahmen. Aus der Perspektive seiner wissenschaftlichen Weiterentwicklung seit seinem Erstlingswerk bedürfe die Konvergenzthese vielmehr einer Erweiterung. Parsons nennt dabei die Psychoanalyse Sigmund Freuds, den Symbolischen Interaktionismus George Herbert Meads, eine Reihe von kulturanthropologischen Ansätzen, und nicht zuletzt das Werk von Jean Piaget.

Genau diese Aufgabe der Erweiterung der Konvergenzthese steht im Zentrum des Beitrages von *Victor M. Lidz* und *Harold J. Bershady*. Beide waren Schüler und Mitarbeiter Parsons'. Sie sehen die Bedeutung der Konvergenz für die soziologische Theoriebildung darin, daß sie eine analytische Methode des Theorienvergleichs darstellt, der für die Weiterentwicklung von Handlungstheorie eine grundlegende Bedeutung zukomme.

Drei weitere Beiträge befassen sich mit der Frage des Theorienvergleichs unter dem Aspekt der Konvergenz oder Divergenz zur Parsonsschen Handlungstheorie im Verhältnis zu den Werken einzelner Theoretiker. *Tamás Meleghy* greift das Thema der Kybernetik des Handlungssystems auf und kontrastiert es mit dem Modell hierarchischer Ebenen in Karl Poppers sogenannter Drei-Welten-Theorie. Dabei kategorisiert er zwei Typen von Ordnungsvorstellungen, die er als Hierarchie emergenter Steuerung bzw. als Hierarchie realer Phänomene bezeichnet. Sie sind zentral für die Frage der Definition von Soziologie und ihres Gegenstandsbereiches. Seine These lautet, daß sowohl Poppers als auch Parsons' Vorstellungen sich im Modell der Hierarchie emergenter Steuerungen bewegen. Da aber eine mit interdisziplinären Forschungen kompatible Soziologie nur in einem Modell möglich sei, dass beide Hierarchien verbinde, bedürften beide Theoriemodelle einer entsprechenden Ergänzung.

Die sogenannte formale Soziologie Georg Simmels hatte Parsons in Hinblick auf seine Konvergenzthese skeptisch beurteilt. An diese Einschätzung knüpfte sich eine kontroversiell geführte Diskussion, die *Gerald Mozetič* in seinem Beitrag durch einen Vergleich der methodologischen Prämissen der beiden Soziologien ergänzt. Beide Ansätze gehen in der Bestimmung von Soziologie und Sozialem von Abstraktionsnotwendigkeiten aus. Während jedoch die Simmelschen Abstraktionsebenen in funktionellem Rückbezug zu Tatsächlichkeiten gewählt seien, führe der analytische Realismus Parsonsscher Provenienz zu einer theoretisch nicht legitimierten Engführung der Soziologie auf den analytischen Aspekt der "common-value integration".

Dénes Némedi unterzieht Parsons' Lesart des Durkheimschen Werkes einer kritischen Überprüfung. Vor allem am Beispiel der Einarbeitung von Durkheims Religionstheorie in den Voluntarismus konstatiert er Umdeutungen, die die Authentizität Durkheims zwar oftmals verletzen, die aber für Parsons' Intentionen der Grundlegung einer von der Gesellschaftskritik der Gründergeneration emanzipierten "reifen" wissenschaftlichen Soziologie notwendig erscheinen. Parsons habe eine zentrale

Rolle gespielt in der Transformation der Soziologie als Modernitätskritik um der Jahrhundertwende in eine Theorie der Modernisierung, wie sie sich nach dem 2. Weltkrieg etablieren konnte.

Einzelne Aspekte oder "Bausteine der Theorie des Handelns" greifen die vier Beiträge des nächsten Abschnittes auf. *Andreas Balog* und *Max Haller* geht es um eine Korrektur in den methodologischen Prämissen Parsonsscher Handlungstheorie. Dessen analytischer Realismus vermenge konzeptuelle und empirische Komponenten, was den Voluntarismus zu einem "theoretischen System" (Balog) mache, in dem Erfahrungsaussagen aus apriorischen Annahmen abgeleitet würden. Für die soziologische Forschung habe dies eine Vermengung von funktionalen, kausalen und historischen Erklärungen (Haller) zur Folge.

Eine Art von historischer Konvergenz stellt *Keith Doubt* in seinem Vergleich der Kritik am Utilitarismus in Parsons' Voluntarismus und der Sokratischen Sophismus-Kritik in Platons Dialogen fest. Es ginge hier wie dort um Entscheidungen über die Kriterien des Handelns, deren Bruchlinie in der Anerkennung autonomer kultureller Phänomene wie der Wahrheit, der Werte, des Rechts etc. auf der einen Seite oder eines atomistischen Rationalitätskalküls auf der anderen Seite liege.

An Parsons' Utilitarismus-Kritik setzt auch der Beitrag von *Bryan S. Turner* an. Einen Schlüssel zum Verständnis der Entwicklung der Soziologie in der Ausdifferenzierung von der Ökonomie geben die beiden Konzepte Mittelknappheit und Solidarität zur Hand. Mittelknappheit als basaler Begriff des utilitaristisch-ökonomischen Modells werde wissenschaftsgeschichtlich in den natürlichen Gegebenheiten wie der biologischen Konstitution des Körpers verortet und müsse durch Solidarität-begründende Werte, dem Zuständigkeitsbereich der Soziologie, komplementarisiert werden. Dies impliziere jedoch eine problematische cartesianische Homo duplex Vorstellung, deren Korrektur im Rückgriff auf Spinoza ein besseres Verständnis des Gesellschaft-Umwelt-Verhältnisses ermögliche.

Im abschließenden Teil des Buches sind zwei Beiträge aufgenommen, die sich mit Fragen der Anwendbarkeit Parsonsscher Theorie beschäftigen. *Josef Langer* geht es im Rückgriff auf Parsons' Kulturkonzept um eine Vertiefung des Verständnisses der Transformationsprozesse in Europa und damit um eine Überwindung einer eindimensionalen, auf Fragen ökonomischer Integration reduzierten Problemsicht.

In *Jeremy Tanners* Beitrag geht es ebenfalls um Fragen der Parsonsschen Kulturtheorie. Die Vieldimensionalität des Handlungssystems und die darin implizierte spezifische Emergenz von Kultur ermögliche eine Überwindung der vorherrschenden reduktionistischen Ansätze in der Kunstsoziologie und in den in der Kunstgeschichte verwendeten Modellen. Er illustriert den Theoriegewinn an einer Fallstudie zur Entwicklung römischer Portraitkunst.

Zur Vieldimensionalität kulturellen Schaffens gehört auch die ökonomische Realität. Weder die Konferenz, noch die Publikation der Beiträge wäre ohne die Hilfe einer Reihe von Sponsoren zu verwirklichen gewesen. Für die finanzielle Unterstützung danken wir dem *Österreichischen Bundesministerium für Bildung, Wissenschaft und Kultur*, der *Tiroler Landesregierung* und der *Vorarlberger Landesregierung*, dem *Innsbrucker Universitätsfonds*, der *Österreichischen Nationalbank*, dem *Außeninstitut der Universität Innsbruck* und der *Wagnerschen Universitätsbuchhandlung*. Frau *Anna Maria Muigg* danken wir für die Erstellung der Druckvorlage.

Innsbruck – Berlin, im Juli 2000

Talcott Parsons – Mein Lehrer*
Renée C. Fox

Es war vor allem um bei Talcott Parsons zu studieren, dass ich mich entschied, mein Doktoratsstudium in Soziologie am Harvard Department of Social Relations zu absolvieren. Parsons gründete das Department of Social Relations, um sowohl eine interdisziplinäre als auch eine disziplinäre Ausbildung und Zusammenarbeit in Anthropologie, Individual- und Sozialpsychologie und Soziologie anzubieten. Während der Jahre meines Doktoratsstudiums (1949-1954) und durch all die 25 Jahre die daraufhin bis zu seinem Tod im Jahre 1979 folgten, war Talcott Parsons mein wichtigster Lehrer. Auch nach seinem Ableben behält er für mich diese Rolle.

Im Nachruf, der am 9. Mai 1979 in der *New York Times* erschienen ist, wurde Talcott Parsons als eine "überragende (intellektuelle) Gestalt" beschrieben, der "verantwortlich war für die Erziehung dreier Generationen" von SozialwissenschafterInnen. "Als er im Jänner 1973 emeritierte", stellte der Nachruft fest, kamen mehr als 150 seiner "ehemaligen und gegenwärtigen StudentInnen und KollegInnen zu einem ihm zu Ehren organisierten Festessen zusammen. Die ehemaligen StudentInnen umfassten eine Altersspanne von 23 bis 63 und kamen von so weit angereist wie etwa aus Deutschland oder Kalifornien". Was die Breite, Langlebigkeit und Tiefe von Talcott Parsons' Einfluss ausmacht, ist jedoch keineswegs selbstverständlich.

Um damit zu beginnen: er war keine physisch eindrucksvolle Person. Er war klein, mit kleinen Händen und Füßen, und einem vorstehenden Bauch, der die Knöpfe an den – oftmals gestreiften – Hemden auseinanderzog, die er in einfache Hosen gesteckt und mit unscheinbaren Krawatten trug, unter seinem begrenzten Vorrat von leicht zerknitterten Tweed Jacken, letztere gewöhnlich mit Zigarettenasche bestreut. Er wechselte diese für die Universität und die Lehre vorgesehene Kleidung mit Arbeitskleidung, wenn er Hausarbeiten rund um sein einfaches Landhaus in New Hampshire erledigte, das als "Die Farm" bezeichnet wurde; und zu zeremoniellen und formalen Anlässen trug er einen dunkelblauen Nadelstreifanzug, der wie auch immer tadellos gebügelt, irgendwie dieselbe Unförmigkeit annahm, die all seine andere Bekleidung charakterisierte. Im Alter von 48 Jahren, als ich ihn das erste Mal traf, hatte er feine, engelhafte Gesichtszüge und eine Glatze. Es war schwer sich ihn anders als glatzköpfig vorzustellen. Seine kleinen, graubraunen,

---

* Übersetzung: Helmut Staubmann. Der Aufsatz erschien unter dem Titel: *Talcott Parsons, My Teacher.* In: *The American Scholar*, Band 66, Nummer 3, Sommer 1997 und wird hier mit freundlicher Genehmigung der Zeitschrift und der Autorin abgedruckt. Copyright bei der Autorin.

mandelförmigen Augen waren weich und doch stechend, erkundend aber doch zurückhaltend; seine Nase war wohlgeformt; und über den Oberlippen seines breiten, dünnen Mundes hatte er einen gepflegten Schnurrbart, der, so wie die Glatze, ein intrinsischer Teil seiner Person zu sein schien. Auf eine unaufdringliche Art ähnelte er einigen seiner alt-amerikanischen kongregationalistischen Ahnen aus den Familienportraits, die er und seine Frau Helen mir einmal zeigten. Er hatte einen Stammbaum, der zurück reichte zu solch bemerkenswerten Vorfahren wie dem amerikanischen puritanischen Theologen und Prediger Jonathan Edwards.

Nach seiner Emeritierung in Harvard hat Parsons drei Jahre als Gastprofessor am Sociology Department an der University of Pennsylvania verbracht. Als er das erste Mal am Campus erschien, haben viele Studierende und auch Professoren-KollegInnen ihre Überraschung zum Ausdruck gebracht, wie klein, unscheinbar und gewöhnlich solch ein intellektueller Riese aussah. Sie hatten seine Erscheinung größer, glanzvoller und gebieterischer erwartet. Sie waren besonders überrascht durch sein scheues und keineswegs extravagantes Auftreten.

Talcott Parsons war ein sehr bescheidener und zurückhaltender Mann. Durch sein Temperament und seine Einstellung war an ihm nichts theatralisches. Er war kein fesselnder Vortragender, weder fähig noch darauf aus das Publikum einer Lehrveranstaltung oder ein anderes Auditorium durch Redekunst und elegante Gesten in den Bann zu ziehen. Wenn man etwas sagen kann, so war er der Pose und einem theatralischen Getue abgeneigt. Die einzige (freundlich vorgebrachte) Zurechtweisung, die ich mich erinnere je von ihm bekommen zu haben, war die Ermahnung "übertreibe nicht", aus einem Anlass heraus in dem er meinte, dass ich übertrieben dramatisch auf ein Ereignis oder eine Idee reagierte, die ich mit ihm diskutierte.

Parsons' Unterrichtsstil war assoziativ, manchmal frei in einem positiven Sinne. Für jene, die von solch einem brillianten Intellektuellen, großen Theoretiker und bedeutenden Soziologen erwarteten, dass er es verstehen würde, sein Wissen und sein Denken mit souveräner Logik und Anschaulichkeit zu vermitteln, konnte sein abschweifender Vortrag irritierend sein und sogar enttäuschend. Aber er war in seinen Vorlesungen, Seminaren und Diskussionsleitungen immer klar und konsequent darüber, was er vermitteln, ausarbeiten und erreichen wollte. Er war auch gut vorbereitet – üblicherweise in der Form von neuen, handgeschriebenen Notizen, die er für jede Unterrichtsstunde auf linierten gelben Blöcken zusammenstellte, während er am Morgen zu Hause in seinem Lieblings-Sessel seines Studierzimmers saß; im Hintergrund spielte oftmals leise klassische Musik.

Was Parsons in den Unterricht mitbrachte war eine komplexe Mischung eines sich über weite Bereiche spannenden Lernens in Biologie und Physik, der Medizin, Ökonomie, Anthropologie, Politikwissenschaft, Geschichte, Psychoanalyse, Philosophie und Religion zusammen mit Soziologie sowie eine eher private Beziehung zu Literatur, Musik und Kunst, verwoben mit Beobachtungen, Einsichten, und Fragen, die er genau so häufig aus seinen Alltagserfahrungen zog wie aus gelehrten Quellen. Diese frischen Ideen waren stimuliert durch seine tägliche Lektüre des *Boston Globe* und der *New York Times*; durch seine Wahrnehmungen während der Fahrt von seinem Haus in Belmont, Massachusetts nach Cambridge und dem Harvard Yard oder auf weiteren professionellen und persönlichen Reisen in andere Städte und Länder; und durch seine fortdauernden Konversationen, Diskussionen, der Korrespondenz, und was er seine "Sessions" nannte mit einem erstaunlich breiten und verschiedenartigen Netzwerk von Studierenden, Lehr- und ForschungsassistentInnen, KollegInnen, ScholarInnen und WissenschafterInnen, die er als MitarbeiterInnen in der Weiterentwicklung der Soziologie betrachtete. Dass er diese Arbeit als eine Berufung erachtete war unverkennbar – eine Berufung, die, wie auch immer ernsthaft – bar jeden Bombastes und zutiefst angenehm wirkte. ("Talcott hatte ein sehr gutes Leben gehabt indem er das tat was er am meisten zu tun wünschte", bekräftigte seine Frau in dem Brief, in dem sie mich über seinen Tod informierte).

Parsons' Unterricht war aufgelockert mit Geschichten, Erzählungen und Anekdoten. Sein Vergnügen an ihnen kam daher, dass sie aus dem realen Leben gegriffen waren, sie waren alltäglich aber doch denkwürdig, erfüllt durch menschliche Komödie, und vor allem, dass sie eine grundlegende theoretische Wahrnehmung oder einen Punkt, den er mitteilen wollte, lebendig veranschaulichten. Worauf sich seine Studierenden liebevoll als "Talcotts Geschichten" bezogen, waren intellektuelle Parabeln von folklorischer Bedeutung. "Viele von uns lernten Talcotts Anekdoten so wie Jus-Studierende ihre Fälle meistern, nämlich als Verkörperungen ernsthafter Prinzipien", hat der Soziologe Victor Lidz bezeugt. "Einige von ... uns meinen, dass wir unseren Studierenden theoretische Fragen nicht ausreichend erklärt haben, solange wir nicht die entscheidenden Anekdoten aus Talcotts Sammlung wiedererzählt haben".

Parsons' Leidenschaft für Soziologie und für soziologische Ideen führte ihn jenseits seiner natürlichen Beschränkungen. Oftmals, in seinem Universitätsbüro angekommen, oder bald nachdem er in ein Klassenzimmer gekommen war um zu unterrichten, erzählte er den Studierenden, AssistentInnen oder jüngeren KollegInnen überschwenglich über eine sehr produktive "Brainstorming"-Erfahrung die er in seinem Studierzimmer am gleichen Morgen gehabt hatte und über den konzeptionellen "Durchbruch", zu dem sie geführt haben könnte. Es gab in diesen Darstellungen nichts was nach Selbstlob oder Selbst-Beglückwünschung ausgesehen hätte. Was Parsons dafür vermittelte war seine kreative Begeisterung darüber, durch die dynamische Entwicklung ihres theoretischen Rahmens in den Fortschritt der Soziologie involviert zu sein. Manchmal, wenn er von einer soziologischen Idee oder einem Verbindungsglied in einer Kette von Gedanken besonders überzeugt war, wurde seine vehemente Ausführung von einem Pochen mit den Fäusten begleitet, das seinen Tisch oder Lesepult oder Konferenztisch zum Klappern brachte.

Gewöhnlich sprach Talcott auf eine ruhige, langsame Weise, unterbrochen von Gedankenpausen. Diese nachdenkliche Art des Sprechens trug zu einem gleichzeitig frustrierenden wie lustigen Vorfall bei, der sich 1967 zutrug, ein Jahr, das ich mit Forschungsarbeiten in Zaire zubrachte. Aus praktischen Gründen war es für mich notwendig mit Parsons über Vorkehrungen zu telefonieren, die für mich getroffen wurden, um nach Harvard zurückzukehren und am Department of Social Relations für einige Jahre zu unterrichten. Wegen des Zustandes des Telefonwesens in Zaire habe ich einige aufeinanderfolgende Tage im Zentralpostamt der Hauptstadt Kinshasa verbracht, bis mein Anruf durchkam und es mir gelang, ihn zu erreichen. Es war damals bei der Zairischen Vermittlung üblich in die Telefonate hinein zu hören (und manchmal sogar die Konversation mit eigenen Bemerkungen zu unterbrechen). Die bedächtige Art, in der Talcott sprach, unterbrochen durch längere Pausen, gab der Vermittlung den Eindruck, dass er zu Ende gesprochen hatte bevor das der Fall war; und so beschloss die Vermittlung unser Telefonat zu beenden. Es brauchte Tage wiederholter Besuche im Postamt in Kinshasa um die Konversation mit ihm wiederherzustellen.

Talcott hielt meinen Aufenthalt in Zaire nicht im geringsten für exotisch. Er betrachtete meine Forschung aus erster Hand in dieser zentralafrikanischen Gesellschaft und in Belgien, der europäischen Gesellschaft, die sie kolonialisiert hatte, als grundlegend für die Entwicklung der Art kulturübergreifender Perspektive, die er als konzeptionell und empirisch wesentlich für eine nicht engherzige Soziologie ansah. Er war überzeugt – und er überzeugte auch uns – dass man ohne diese Art kulturübergreifender Perspektive nicht klar die Umrisse der eigene Gesellschaft erkennen oder deren besondere Charakteristika wahrnehmen konnte.

Talcott Parsons widmete sein Buch *The Social System* (1951) seiner Frau in folgender Weise:

Für Helen

DEREN GESUNDER UND PRAKTISCHER
EMPIRIZISMUS LANGE EIN
UNENTBEHRLICHES GEGENGEWICHT
FÜR EINEN UNHEILBAREN THEORETIKER WAR

Er war in der Tat ein "unheilbarer Theoretiker", aber einer der – anders als die "völlig abstrakten Denker" als welcher er von einigen SoziologInnen karikiert wurde – den "Empirizismus" respektierte und schätzte. Er brachte die Theorie dazu, sich an empirische Forschung zu halten und empirische Forschung an Theorie, durch induktive als auch deduktive Denkweise. Sein ganzes intellektuelles Leben als Soziologe war der Entwicklung einer allgemeinen Theorie des Handelns gewidmet. Aber vom allerersten Anfang seines lebenslangen Bemühens an machte er klar, dass, wie er im Vorwort seines ersten Buches *The Structure of Social Action* – das chef d'oevre aller seiner publizierten Arbeiten – feststellte, nach seiner Meinung, "die Entwicklung eines Theoriesystems ohne Bezug auf die empirischen Probleme, für die es aufgebaut und verwendet worden ist, vorzunehmen ... zur schlimmsten Art von dialektischer Sterilität führen würde".

Wirkliche wissenschaftliche Theorie [schrieb er] ist nicht das Produkt leerer 'Spekulation', das Ausbreiten logischer Implikationen von Annahmen, sondern von Beobachtung, Denken und Verifikation, beginnend mit Tatsachen und fortwährend auf die Tatsachen zurückkehrend. ... Nur indem Theorie in dieser engen Verbindung mit empirischen Problemen und Fakten behandelt wird, ist irgend eine Art von adäquatem Verstehen möglich, sowohl wie sich die Theorie entwickelte, als auch der Bedeutung für die Wissenschaft.

Die angewandte Forschung, an der Talcott Parsons teilnahm, beschränkte sich auf drei Projekte: einer auf teilnehmende Beobachtung und auf Interviews basierende Feldstudie über medizinische Praxis, die er in den 40er Jahren durchführte, hauptsächlich im Raum Boston und in erster Linie in Verbindung mit dem Massachusetts General Hospital, insbesondere deren Chirurgie; eine 50er Jahre Studie über soziale Mobilität unter High School Knaben, auch im Raum Boston, in Zusammenarbeit mit dem Soziologen Samuel A. Stouffer und der Soziologin Florence Kluckhohn, unter Verwendung von Umfrage- und Feldforschungsmethoden, an der Studierende des Doktoratsstudiums (ich unter ihnen) teilnahmen; und in den späten 60er und frühen 70er Jahren, eine nationale Studie zu Fakultätsmitgliedern amerikanischer Colleges und Universitäten, die er mit dem Soziologen Gerald M. Platt durchführte, hauptsächlich durch eine Stichprobenerhebung. Das empirische Wissen und die Einsichten, auf die er sich bezog, um seine Theorie zu schaffen und die er in diese einverleibte, gingen allerdings weit über diese Forschungsprojekte hinaus. Sie kamen von seiner immensen Belesenheit in einem weiten Spektrum von Disziplinen; seinen persönlichen Erfahrungen, einschließlich einer psychoanalytischen Ausbildung, die er im mittleren Leben absolvierte und der Lehranalyse, der er sich im Zusammenhang damit unterzog; und, äußerst bedeutend, aus dem, was er durch seine aktive Eingebundenheit in die Forschung lernte, die von den Studierenden, die er gerade unterrichtete, von früheren Studierenden und von KollegInnen unabhängig durchgeführt wurde.

Beginnend mit den späten 40er Jahren und durch eine Zeitspanne von mehr als zwanzig Jahren hindurch, verwendete Talcott Forschungsmittel, um graduierte AssistentInnen anzustellen, mit dem Ziel der Erforschung "einer breiten Palette von Problemen in bezug auf amerikanische Werte, Sozialstruktur, soziale Probleme und Muster institutionellen Wandels". Dies war Teil dessen, was Victor Lidz als "einen relativ wenig bekannten aber sehr wichtigen Aspekt in Talcott Parsons' Arbeit" beschrieb: seine Hoffnung, "eine große interpretative Studie der amerikanischen Gesellschaft" zu schreiben. Durch ganze 30 Jahre hindurch lehrte Talcott in regelmäßigen Abständen auch einen allgemeinen Kurs über die amerikanische Gesellschaft für fortgeschrittene DiplomandInnen und DissertantInnen, in dem die von ihm unterstützte Forschung in Verbindung mit seiner theoretischen Analyse und deren Interpretation eine wichtige Rolle spielte.

Parsons ermutigte und förderte nicht nur unser Engagement für eigene Forschung, er war auch begeistert von der Möglichkeit, sie in ihrem Fortschritt zu begleiten. Nicht selten sah er Dinge von theoretischer Bedeutung in ihr, die seine StudentInnen überraschten. Wir waren erschrocken und ein wenig beschämt, aber sehr erfreut, wenn er verkündete, dass eine aus der Forschung stammende Beobachtung oder Einsicht von uns zum besonderen konzeptuellen "Durchbruch" beigetragen hatte, der sich in seinem Studierzimmer an jenem Tag oder in seinem Auto während er in sein Universitätsbüro fuhr, ergeben hatte.

Eine der bedeutendsten Erfahrungen, die ich als Dissertantin im Klassenzimmer hatte – vielleicht diejenige, die mir am meisten das Gefühl, eine aktive Soziologin zu sein vermittelte – war meine Teilnahme in einer Untergruppe eines Seminars über Sozialstruktur, geleitet von Talcott. Es war ein Ableger der Parsons/Stouffer/Kluckhohn Studie über die Klassenherkunft und soziale Mobilität von High School Schülern, und es war rund um einige der theoretischen Probleme organisiert, die Talcott in Verbindung mit dem überdachte, was letztendlich *The Social System* wurde. Im Vorwort dieses Buches, nahm Talcott Bezug auf die Wichtigkeit der "vielen Diskussionen, die eine Reihe von fähigen Studierenden" während des Schreibens gehabt hatte, indem er jede(n) einzelne(n) der sechs StudentInnen in diesem Seminar mit Namen in alphabetischer Reihenfolge hervorhob. Es erschien als eine überaus große Auszeichnung.

Die Lehrer-Schüler Beziehungen, die Talcott Parsons begründete, waren weder informell noch bar einer Hierarchie; gleichzeitig aber waren sie respektvoll und in großzügiger Weise auf Gegenseitigkeit beruhend. Er bot vielen von uns an, ihn anstatt mit Professor Parsons als Talcott anzusprechen. Wenn er in seinem Büro mitten am Vormittag ankam, war die Tür für uns immer offen für einen Besuch oder eine Diskussion (ein beispielhaftes Lehrerverhalten, dem ich durch meine ganze Karriere hindurch zu folgen trachtete). Und er lud zu so offenem intellektuellem Kommentar und Kritik von uns ein, dass er die Möglichkeit für Zusammenkünfte mit ehemaligen Studierenden und LehrassistentInnen schuf. Über einen Studenten, für den er große Bewunderung und Zuneigung hegte, vertraute er mir einmal an: "Nathan gibt mir manchmal das Gefühl, daß, wenn ich nur ein wenig klüger wäre, ich verstehen könnte was er mir zu erklären versucht!"

Parsons' Wertschätzung und Dankbarkeit gegenüber seinen Studierenden und den jüngeren SozialwissenschafterInnen, mit denen er arbeitete, wurden nicht nur in Vorlesungen, Zitationen und Fußnoten zum Ausdruck gebracht, sondern auch in der Form von Widmungen einiger seiner Bücher. Seine Widmung für *Sociological Theory and Modern Society* (1967), zum Beispiel, lautet:

DEM ANDENKEN AN
Kaspar D. Naegele
Aufmerksamer Beobachter, phantasievoller Theoretiker
Ein lieber Freund für ganz viele

Der Eintritt in den großen, generationenübergreifenden Zirkel von Talcott Parsons' Studierenden war jedoch kein elitäres Phänomen. Er war kein intellektueller Pförtner, der Studierende in seinen Umkreis primär auf der Grundlage von deren IQ oder deren Notendurchschnitt einließ. Was er von uns verlangte, war eine Verpflichtung auf Ideen und auf das Geistesleben, eine leidenschaftliche Bereitschaft und glühende Begeisterung, an der Entwicklung der Sozialwissenschaften und sozialem Denken teilzunehmen und dafür einen Beitrag zu leisten.

Dieses Gefühl der Hingabe und was Talcott als "Efferveszenz" bezeichnete, durchzog einen ethnografisch detaillierten Brief, den er mir am 12. November 1976 schrieb, während einer seiner drei akademischen Jahre, die er als Gastprofessor an der University of Pennsylvania unmittelbar nach seiner Emeritierung von seiner Professur in Harvard verbrachte. Ich war zu dieser Zeit Vorstand des Sociology Department und hatte in dieser Eigenschaft die Initiative ergriffen, ihn an die Universität zu bringen. An dem Tag jedoch, als er diesen Brief zusammenstellte, war ich vorübergehend für einen Forschungsaufenthalt in Belgien. "Ein Hauptpunkt" mir zu schreiben, stellte Talcott Parsons fest, bestand darin, mir "so etwas wie einen Bericht zu geben" über eine "Session" die er an der University of Pennsylvania hielt mit den Soziologen Harold Bershady, Victor Lidz und Robert Bellah über das "Paradigma der Conditio Humana", die er dabei war zu entwickeln. (Bershady und Lidz waren beide Mitglieder des Lehrkörpers und Bellah war aus Berkeley nach Philadelphia geflogen, um ein Papier an einer Tagung der Society for the Scientific Study of Religion zu präsentieren).

> Die Session ... war ein außerordentlicher Erfolg. ... Wir (hatten) am ... Sonntag einige Stunden zusammen, die darin bestanden, uns über einige Aspekte des Conditio humana Problems zu unterhalten. Wie ich mich erinnere, vereinnahmte ich ein gutes Stück der Zeit um gewisse Einsichten durchzugehen, die sich für mich ergeben hatten, insbesondere aus einer neuerlichen Lektüre eines guten Teiles der Arbeiten von Freud, und konzentrierte mich auf das Problem von gewissen Beziehungen zwischen dem Handlungssystem und dem Organismus, vor allem dem Organismus und dem Bezugs-Aktor. ...
>
> Als ich Bob am nächsten Morgen zum Frühstück traf, war er offensichtlich in einem efferveszenten Zustand. ... Er hatte am Abend zuvor, nachdem ich ihn verlassen hatte, und am nächsten Morgen über diese Dinge gegrübelt. Er hatte sogar einige neue Einsichten während unserer Konversation beim Frühstücks über die er Notizen auf die Speisekarte des Restaurants machte. Als wir uns dann im McNeil-Gebäude versammelten, platzte er einfach heraus. Wir waren in Deinem Büro zusammengekommen, aber er sagte sofort, er würde eine größere Tafel benötigen, die Harold in einem leeren Seminarraum im Parterre fand. Bob füllte sie sehr schnell mit Diagrammen und sagte, dass er nie ge-

ahnt hätte, dass er sich in 'Parsonianischen Formalismus' an diesem Punkt einlassen würde. Es waren alles Vierfelder Diagramme. Er begann ein Paradigma der primären Aspekte religiöser Orientierungen. ...

Vielleicht interessieren Dich die vier Kategorien. Seinem eigenen vorherigen Gebrauch und jenem von Tillich folgend verwendete er den allgemeinen Ausdruck 'letztbezüglich' und führte folgende Kategorien ein: A. letztbezügliche Handlungsinstanz; G. letztbezügliche Erfüllung; I. letztbezügliche Ordnung; und L. letztbezüglicher Grund. In der Anwendung auf den christlichen Fall stellte er interessanterweise Gott den Vater in die A-Box, Gott den Sohn in die G-Box, den heiligen Geist in die I-Box, und was er 'das Sein' nannte in die L-Box. Dann setzte er dies fort für die griechische Religion, für den Buddhismus, für den Judaismus, für den Konfuzianismus, für den Islam, und endete mit dem Marxismus.

Du kannst Dir wohl vorstellen, dass dies eine Atmosphäre einer wirklich hohen intellektuellen Begeisterung war. Wir alle kopierten hastig, was Bob auf die Tafel geschrieben hatte, und nach einer langen Diskussion, einschließlich vieler Interpretationsfragen was er mit diesem und jenem gemeint hatte, versprach er, dass er in der ... näheren Zukunft versuchen würde, eine Art diskursiven Entwurf zu verfassen. Wie leicht einsichtig, konnten wir dieses Niveau nicht für viele Stunden halten. Wir gingen zu Cohen and Kelly zum Mittagessen, und als wir zurückkehrten, konzentrierten wir uns für die verbleibende Zeit auf sein Paradigma des Marxismus in Beziehung zu dem von Harold und Victor vorgeschlagenen. ...

Ich habe mich weiterhin mit meinen eigenen Angelegenheiten abgemüht, viele davon peripher zu dem, was wir bei dem Treffen diskutierten. Ich denke, wenn Harold, Victor und ich nächste Woche zusammenkommen, sollten wir eine sehr gute Session haben.

"Es wird für die Anhänger der Handlungstheorie keine Überraschung sein", schrieb Parsons in dem Essay, den er später als *A Paradigm of the Human Condition* veröffentlichte, "daß der für diese Bemühungen gewählte Rahmen das vertraute Schema der vier funktionalen Kategorien darstellte, den wir auf vielfältige Weise durch zwanzig Jahre hindurch verwendeten". Und tatsächlich, jene von uns, die sich an den mitreißenden theoretischen Sessions, wie die beschriebene, beteiligten, fanden sich eingefangen in ein immerfort expandierendes konzeptuelles Universum, zusammengesetzt aus Vierfelder-Tabellen, die Speisekarten, ganze Blöcke linierten gelben Papiers und Räume voll mit Tafeln füllten. Sie führten uns manchmal an Orte, die gelegentlich genau so komisch wie auch kreativ waren – wenn wir uns zum Beispiel wiederfanden, Gott Vater, Gott Sohn und den Heiligen Geist in Parsonianische Quadranten einzupassen.

Unbeschadet seiner intellektuellen Begeisterung und Involviertheit hat Parsons klar anerkannt, dass seine vierfachen Konstruktionen und Metaphorik, wie der Modellbau in allen wissenschaftlichen Gebieten, seine Theorie und die Aspekte der Realität, auf die sie sich bezog, verdinglichten und symbolisch einige der Überzeugungen wie auch der kognitiven Ideen, auf denen sie basierten, zum Ausdruck brachten. Er lehrte uns, auch dies anzuerkennen.

Die Beziehung, die Parsons mit jedem von uns bildete, war nicht nur intellektuell, sondern auch sehr menschlich und in vielfacher Hinsicht väterlich. Obwohl jede(r) von uns ihre oder seine einzigartige Verbindung zu Parsons hatte, gab es ein Gefühl, in dem wir eine Art von Verwandtschaftssystem bildeten, in dem er das Familienoberhaupt war. Er wachte über unsere berufliche Entwicklung, freute sich über unserer Leistungen, unaufdringlich aber mit Bedacht verfolgte er die Geschehnisse, die sich in unserem persönlichen Leben ereigneten, verband uns untereinander und machte vielen von uns die Freude seine eigene Familie kennen zu lernen: seine Frau Helen, seine Töchter Anne und Susan und seinen Sohn Charles. (In meinem eigenen Fall wurde seine älteste mit mir gleichaltrige Tochter Anne, die brilliant Kulturanthropologie und Psychiatrie in ihren Arbeiten verband und die frühzeitig am 9. April 1964 im Alter von 33 Jahren verstarb, eine enge Freundin).

In einer Zeit, als viel weniger Frauen als Männer sich bildeten, um Soziologinnen oder Sozialwissenschafterinnen zu werden, war eine der Eigenschaften, die mich von den meisten von Parsons' Dissertanten unterschied, der Umstand eine Frau zu sein. Er ging auf die Tatsache, dass ich eine Frau war, ein, aber nicht auf eine Weise, die mich absonderte oder die mich auf irgend eine Art befangen machte. Er behandelte mich weder als "einer seiner Jungen" noch als eine im besonderen beliebte oder unbeliebte Person. Parsons' natürlicher Egalitarismus und seine Zuvorkommenheit gaben mir das Gefühl, dass er mich ernst nahm als eine werdende Soziologin, die er intellektuell wertschätzte und persönlich mochte.

Vier Erinnerungen:
- Die Erstsemestrigen-Arbeit, die ich für Parsons schrieb, war in einem Seminar über soziale Institutionen und deren Analyse in dem ich als eine beginnende Dissertantin inskribiert war. Das Papier, basierend auf meiner Geschichte als Kinderlähmungspatientin als ich 17 Jahre alt war, betonte die strukturellen Spannungen und Rollenkonflikte, die sich zwischen der Patientin, ihrer Familie, dem Physiotherapeuten und dem Orthopäden abspielten. Ich bekam ein sehr gut für meine Arbeit mit nur einem Kommentar darauf aus Talcott Parsons' eigner Hand: "Was für eine schreckliche Erfahrung!"
- Meine Doktorarbeit basierte auf den drei Jahren (1951-1954), die ich als teilnehmende Beobachterin zur Stoffwechsel-Forschungsabteilung eines der Harvard Medical School angeschlossenen Spitals zubrachte. Ich studierte die miteinander verschlungenen Probleme und Belastungen von Patienten und Ärzte dieser Station, deren gemeinsame Arten mit diesen Schwierigkeiten umzugehen und die tragisch-komische Gemeinschaft, die sie aus ihrer gemeinsamen Zwangslage heraus schufen. Aus Gründen, die zu komplex sind um sie hier wiederzugeben, war der Psychiater, der dem Team vorstand unter dessen Ägide ich diese Studie ausführte, verärgert über einige der Ergebnisse und über den "literarischen" Stil in dem sie verfasst waren. Nachdem er meine Dissertation, die ich ihm übermittelte, gelesen hatte, drohte er Maßnahmen an um mein Doktorat zu verhindern, wenn ich nicht zustimmen würde, meine Dissertation als vertrauliche Arbeit in der Harvard Bibliothek abzulegen, so dass sie nur für

LeserInnen unter eng definierten Bedingungen und durch ausdrückliche Genehmigung zugänglich gewesen wäre.

Da es für mich unmöglich war, mich vernünftig mit ihm darüber zu unterhalten, beschloss ich den Rat und die Hilfe von Talcott Parsons einzuholen. Seine unmittelbare Reaktion war verständnisvoll; aber er legte mir dringend nahe, zu versuchen die Probleme auf eine ruhige und reife Art durchzuarbeiten. Die weitere Diskussion jedoch überzeugte Parsons, dass in der Situation implizit Faktoren am Werk waren, die er "nicht-rational" genannt hätte, die es unwahrscheinlich machten, dass ich auf wirksame Weise selbst etwas machen könnte. Er stimmte ruhig zu, die Sache in die Hand zu nehmen und vereinbarte mit dem Psychiater, den er beruflich kannte, ein Mittagessen. Parsons machte dem Psychiater in freundschaftlicher aber unmissverständlicher Weise klar, dass er keine Zuständigkeit für meine Dissertation hatte und teilte ihm mit, dass sie vom Department of Social Relations als ein außerordentlich gutes Stück Arbeit betrachtet wurde, die es als Erfüllung der Anforderungen für das Doktorat annahm. Parsons machte auch klar, dass er dem Antrag des Psychiaters nicht zustimmen würde, den Bibliothekszugang für sie zu beschränken. Diese Zusammenkunft beim Mittagessen hat die Beziehung zwischen den zwei Männern nicht zerbrochen.

- Wenn ich in Parsons' Belmont Haus übernachtete – was ich periodisch nach meinem Studium machte – kam Parsons, ohne dass ich ihn darum bat, bevor ich zu Bett ging immer in mein Zimmer, um für mich die Fenster zu öffnen, ganz gleichgültig wie kalt das Wetter war, so dass ich sicher sein konnte, dass ich, wie er meinte, während der Nacht genügend gesunde, frische Luft zum Atmen hätte.
- Ein Brief, den ich 1976 von ihm erhielt, endete in folgender Weise:

Ich glaube nicht, dass ich je die Gelegenheit hatte, Dir meinen ganz speziellen Dank auszudrücken, für das, was Du getan hast, um meinen Gastaufenthalt an der University of Pennsylvania zu ermöglichen und ihn zu einer entscheidenden und interessanten Erfahrung zu machen. Ich hätte wirklich kaum auf eine schönere Art hoffen können, meine Arbeit in den ersten drei Jahren nach meiner formalen Emeritierung hier in Harvard, zu verankern. Es war aus meiner Sicht eine herausragende Erfahrung, deren Auswirkungen mich mein ganzes Leben lang begleiten werden. Wir waren lange zuvor sehr gute Freunde gewesen, aber dies besiegelte gewiß die Verbundenheit unserer Beziehung, wie es vielleicht durch nichts anderes möglich gewesen wäre. Helen schließt sich mir an.
Mit großer Zuneigung,
Talcott

Wie diese Vorkommnisse zeigen, drückte Talcott Parsons seine Gefühle oft auf wohlüberlegte, verhaltene, manchmal verlegene und oft verschlüsselte Art aus. Sowohl seine persönliche Schüchternheit als auch sein alter amerikanischprotestantischer Hintergrund formten, was er in der Diktion seiner Theorie seinen "affektiven" oder "expressiven" Stil genannt hätte.

Obwohl Talcott durch große musikalische Aufführungen (besonders durch das Boston Symphony Orchestra, für das er und seine Frau Jahresabonnements hatten) sichtlich an den Rand von Tränen bewegt war und offen sein Genießen der Kunst (besonders der Malereien der Holländischen und Flämischen Meister) zum Ausdruck brachte, war es durch machtvolle, nicht-verbale Bilder, durch die er viele seiner starken Gefühle kommunizierte. Der Soziologe Willy De Craemer erinnert sich lebhaft, dass, als er Dissertant war, Parsons' Stolz und Freude über sein gutes Abschneiden bei den Rigorosen zum Ausdruck brachte, indem er ihn in sein Büro nahm und die Tür hinter ihnen schloss, so dass er privat mit ihm die Reproduktion eines Brueghel Gemäldes, das da hing, teilen konnte – ein Kunstwerk, das aus De Craemers eigener Flämisch-Belgischer Kultur kam. Der Soziologe und Verleger Irving Louis Horowitz erzählte mir einmal, dass es durch die vertrauliche Art war, wie Parsons ihm den russischen Pelz, den er in der Sowjetunion während der Teilnahme an einer dort abgehaltenen Pugwash Konferenz am Höhepunkt des Kalten Krieges gekauft hatte, dass Parsons ihm vermittelte, wie bedeutsam er es erachtete an dieser Friedens-orientierten, Atomwaffenkontroll-Konferenz teilzunehmen. Und ich werde niemals die komprimierte Trauer vergessen, die in dem enthalten war, was Parsons an dem Tag des Begräbnisses seiner Tochter Anne sagte, als wir Seite an Seite auf der überdachten Veranda seines Belmont-Hauses standen und hinaus blickten auf einen schmerzlich schönen Juni Nachmittag und er eine leise Bemerkung machte über die außerordentliche Schönheit der Rosen, die in voller Blüte standen.

Rituale wie auch Symbole waren für Parsons wichtig. Er lehrte uns nicht nur sie anzuerkennen, zu analysieren und sie zu interpretieren, sondern auch sie besser zu verstehen und in unserem Leben auf sie zu reagieren. Das Leben, das er und seine Frau zusammen gestalteten, war organisiert und bereichert durch Alltags-Rituale, die beinhalteten, was sie an verschiedenen Tagen der Woche zum Frühstück vorbereitete; deren zeremonieller, wohl eingeschenkter Trunk vor dem Abendessen (ein großes Glas Bourbon und Wasser für Talcott); das Tischgebet an der Thanksgiving Tafel; und die jährliche Herstellung von "Apfel-Wein" im Herbst auf "der Farm" (in einem Jahr verbunden mit einem Satz denkwürdiger Ideen, erzeugt von Parsons, Stouffer und Florence Kluckhohn mitten in diesen Vorbereitungen, die fortan bekannt waren als die "Apfel-Wein Hypothesen").

Parsons' Beziehung zu Symbolen und Ritualen war eng verknüpft mit seiner grundlegenden Verbindung zur religiösen Dimension menschlicher Existenz. Er war der Sohn eines Kongregationalen Priesters, Edward S. Parsons, der zu der Zeit, als Talcott geboren wurde, ein "Heimat-Missionar" in Colorado Springs war (was erklärt, warum er dort sein Leben begann statt in New England, der Region seiner Vorfahren). Talcotts Vater, der auch ein Englisch-Professor war, wurde darauffolgend Präsident des Marietta College, ein protestantisches Kirchen-College in Ohio. Trotz seiner klerikalen Wurzeln war Talcott Parsons kein Kirchengeher, wie er offen zugab; und er neigte dazu, sich selbst als "ein in gewisser Weise rückfällig gewordener Protestant" zu bezeichnen. Aber er war beeindruckt und fasziniert durch die Allgegenwärtigkeit und Bedeutung von Religion oder deren "Äquivalent" über Zeit und Raum, Gesellschaften, Kulturen und Zivilisationen. Er hatte hohen Respekt für Männer (und Frauen) "der Geistlichkeit", wie er sie nannte, und für Laien aller religiöser Bekenntnisse, Überzeugungen und Traditionen. Sein Verpflichtetsein auf religiösen Pluralismus und auf Ökumene erstreckte sich "jenseits des Glaubens" um "Nichtglaube" und "Unglaube" genauso einzuschließen. Er erachtete es als eine besonders hohe Ehre an solchen Ereignissen wie dem First International Symposium on Belief teilzunehmen (abgehalten vom 22. bis 27. März 1969 an der Päpstlich Gregorianischen Universität in Rom unter der gemeinsamen Organisation des Vatikanischen Sekretariats für Ungläubige, der University of California in Berkeley und der Agnelli Foundation) und auf lokaler Ebene eingeladen zu werden, die St. Thomas Aquinas Vorlesungen am Jesuitischen Theologischen Seminar in Weston, Massachusetts zu halten. Die beiden jesuitischen Soziologen, die ihn zu den Aquinas Vorlesungen eingeladen hatten, waren über seine warme Zusage erfreut und erstaunt über die Bedeutung, die er diesem Ereignis zumaß.

Ich stimme der Aussage des Soziologen Roland Robertson zu, dass "das Thema der Religion ... Parsons' Werk durchdringt"; dass es "zunehmend zentraler zur gesamten Handlungstheorie wurde"; und dass seine "Beschäftigung mit Religion und verwandten Themen während der letzten Jahre seines Lebens expliziter wurden, ... und in seiner Spezifikation der analytischen Dimensionen der 'conditio humana' gipfelten".

Sein anhaltendes Interesse an Religion und die wichtige Rolle, die sie seiner Überzeugung nach in der modernen, zeitgenössischen Gesellschaft wie auch in traditionalen und historischen spielt, war nicht nur in seinen Schriften und in der Lehre zur Religionssoziologie offensichtlich. Es war auch ein Leitmotiv in seiner Behandlung von Familie und Verwandtschaft, Sexualität und Geschlechtsunterschiede, Alter und dem älter werden, der Wirtschaft und den Berufen, Wissenschaft und Magie, sozialen Klassen und Ungleichheit, Vorurteil und Diskriminierung, Faschismus und der Aufstieg des Nazismus in Deutschland, das Amerikanische Wertesystem, die Evolution von Gesellschaften und die globale Ordnung, und, vielleicht vor allem, in dem was er über Gesundheit, Krankheit und Medizin und über Sterblichkeit und Tod dachte, schrieb und lehrte.

Parsons hatte persönlich und intellektuell einen Sinn für die Meta-Bedeutung und das Mysterium des menschlichen Organismus und dessen Lebenszyklus, wie auch für das "Sinnproblem", das sich durch das menschlich Gute und Böse stellt und durch die mit der menschlichen Existenz verbundenen Ungewissheiten und Unglück, Leiden und Tragödie und durch die Diskrepanzen zwischen Tugendhaftigkeit, Anstrengung und dem Resultat menschlichen Strebens. Sein Gefühl von Tragik war komplex und tief. "Menschliche Geschichte ist kein Moral-Stück, in dem die Guten belohnt und die Bösen bestraft werden ", erklärte er am römischen Symposium über die Kultur des Unglaubens, "sondern ein Kampf für Erlösung, Aufklärung, Fortschritt oder Gemeinschaft, in der viele, eigentlich die meisten der Mitglieder in tragische Konflikte und Dilemmata verstrickt waren und sind". Im Angesicht der Tragödie und seiner Unergründlichkeit war Parsons außerordentlich stoisch, mitfühlend und leidensfähig. Alle diese Einstellungen kommen in einem Brief zum Ausdruck, den er mir über den Tod bei einem Autounfall einer jungen Tochter eines seiner früheren Studenten schrieb:

> Soweit ich es sehe war es ein reiner Unfall, am Heimweg von einer Party, aber das macht es nicht erträglicher ... Diese Dinge sollten nicht passieren, aber manchmal tun sie es, und irgendwie muss der Rest von uns weiterleben. In diesem Geist war es angenehm, Deine detaillierte Beschreibung Deiner aktiven und komplizierten Tätigkeiten in Belgien zu bekommen...

Parsons' Zustimmung zu meinen "Tätigkeiten" in Belgien war auf sein Gefühl der Berufung zu soziologischer Arbeit bezogen. Für ihn war sie eine aktive Bejahung: eine Art zu leben, weiter zu leben und Sinn aus dem Unergründlichen zu beziehen, was Trost brachte.

Diese Erinnerungen an Talcott Parsons, meinem Lehrer, wären nicht vollständig ohne Bezug auf die Sphäre, wo er und ich unsere bedeutendste intellektuelle Beziehung hatten – im Bereich der Medizinsoziologie, einem Fach, das er zu etablieren half.

Parsons' Herkunftsfamilie hatte eine starke medizinische wie auch eine klerikale Tradition und in seiner Jugend hat Parsons ernsthaft in Erwägung gezogen Arzt zu werden. Er behielt ein lebenslanges Interesse an Biologie, die er um ihrer selbst willen schätzte und wegen ihrer Beziehung zur Medizin und aus der er wertvolle konzeptuelle Einsichten ableitete, die zur Entwicklung seiner Theorie der sozialen Handlung beitrugen. Die Harvard Physiologen Walter B. Cannon und Lawrence J. Henderson nahmen eine prominente Stellung unter den von Parsons geschätzten Kollegen und persönlichen Bekanntschaften ein. Deren Sichtweise der elementaren Bestandteile, Strukturen und Prozesse lebender Organismen und deren Homöostase hatte einen besonderen Einfluss auf Parsons' Theorie, besonders in seiner früheren, struktur-funktionalen Phase. Er verfolgte eifrig die revolutionären Änderungen, die in Molekular- und Zellbiologie sich während seiner Lebenszeit ereigneten, beginnend mir der Entdeckung der DNA Doppelhelix durch Watson und Crick im Jahre 1953. Dank der Freundlichkeit von Helen Parsons habe ich ein Exemplar der zweiten Ausgabe von Watsons Lehrbuch *Molecular Biology of the Gene* in meinem Besitz, 1971 von Parsons gekauft, das er durch die gesamten 602 Seiten sorgfältig mit Unterstreichungen und an vielen Stellen mit Anmerkungen versah. "Schön!" schrieb Parsons an den Rand einer Passage (auf Seite 179), die lautete:

... die Anordnung (von Aminosäuren in Proteinen) kann nicht durch den Rückgriff auf für jede Aminosäure in einem Protein spezifische Enzyme erreicht werden, aus folgendem Grund heraus. Solch eine Einrichtung würde so viele ordnende Enzyme erfordern wie es Aminosäuren im Protein gibt; aber da alle bekannten Enzyme selbst Proteine sind, würden noch zusätzliche ordnende Enzyme notwendig sein um die Enzyme zu synthetisieren. ... Dies ist ganz klar eine Paradoxie, wenn wir nicht eine phantastische miteinander verbundene Reihe von Synthesen annehmen, in der ein gegebenes Protein abwechselnd viele verschiedene enzymische Besonderheiten haben kann. ... In der Tat, unser ganzes Wissen weist auf eine entgegengesetzte Schlußfolgerung, von einem Protein, einer Funktion.

Und an den Anfang von Watsons Kapitel "The Concept of Template Surfaces", notierte Parsons die Parallelen, die er zwischen dem sah, was er als die funktionalen Erfordernisse sozialer Systeme erachtete - nämlich Adaption (A), Zielerreichung (G), Integration (I) und latente Strukturerhaltung (L) - und den Eigenschaften, die Watson als jene identifizierte, von der die Fähigkeit einer Zelle zu wachsen und zu teilen abhängt. Parsons' Anmerkungen lauten:

    L - DNA-RNA
    I - Enzyme
    G - Energie (ATP)
    A - Membrane

Parsons studierte diesen Text so genau, dass er sogar einen typografischen Fehler auf Seite 27 ausbesserte, wo der Nachname des Biologen Thomas Hunt Morgan versehentlich mit einem *e* statt mit einem *a* geschrieben war.

Diese Aspekte von Parsons' persönlicher und intellektueller Biographie, seine Ausbildung in Psychoanalyse, die Ergebnisse seiner Feldstudie medizinischer Praxis im Raum Boston, sowie der Einfluss, den Bronislaw Malinowskis Analyse von Magie, Wissenschaft und Religion und Lawrence J. Hendersons Formulierung von "Arzt (Ärztin) und Patient(in) als ein soziales System" auf ihn hatten, das alles floß in seinen Entwurf ein, welcher zu einem Grundlagen-Dokument der Medizinsoziologie wurde. Das war Kapitel 10 seines Buches *The Social System* mit dem Titel "Social Structure and Dynamic Process: The Case of Modern Medical Practice". "Es wird vielleicht dem/der Leser(in) bei der Wertschätzung der empirischen Bedeutung der von uns entwickelten abstrakten Analyse der grundlegenden Elemente des sozialen Systems und deren Beziehungen untereinander ... hilfreich sein", stellte Parsons in seiner Einleitung zu diesem Kapitel fest, wenn "wir versuchen viele der Fäden der vorangegangenen Diskussion in einer extensiveren Analyse einiger der strategischen Merkmale eines wichtigen Subsystems der modernen westlichen Gesellschaft zusammenzubringen. Für diesen Zweck haben wir die moderne medizinische Praxis gewählt. Dieses Gebiet war der Gegenstand eines langfristigen Interesses von Seiten des Autors, weswegen er auf diesem Gebiet über eine größere Beherrschung des empirischen Materials verfügt als in den meisten anderen".

Die Tatsache, dass Parsons während meiner Anfangsjahre als Dissertantin in die Ausarbeitung dieses Kapitels vertieft war, hat mein Schicksal als Soziologin bestimmt. (Ich "übertreibe" nicht, Talcott, wenn ich diese Aussage treffe!) Die gerade gemachten Erfahrungen als Kinderlähmungs-Patient hatten wahrscheinlich meine Empfänglichkeit für dieses Gebiet soziologischer Forschung erhöht. Ich war gründlich beeinflusst von den Ideen, die Parsons über die Bedeutung von Gesundheit, Krankheit und Medizin für das Funktionieren einer Gesellschaft, deren kulturelle Bedeutung und deren Beziehung zum menschlichen Lebenszyklus, dem Leiden und dem Tod hatte; über Kranksein als eine soziale Rolle; über die emotionale Bedeutung der Arztrolle aufgrund der existentiellen Bedeutung von Krankheit und die physischen und psychischen Intimitäten, die die medizinische Arbeit beinhaltet; und durch Parsons' besonderen Nachdruck auf die Grenzen und Unwägbarkeiten, die der Medizin eigen sind, ganz gleichgültig auf welcher Stufe wissenschaftlicher Entwicklung sie sich auch befindet; die Frustrationen und Spannungen, die sie für den Arzt/die Ärztin und den Patienten/die Patientin mit sich bringen und der "ritualisierte Optimismus" – den er als eine Form wissenschaftlicher Magie betrachtete – den ÄrztInnen und PatientInnen unter diesen Umständen entwickeln als eine Art nicht nur zurechtzukommen, sondern ihr Zutrauen zu erhöhen.

Talcott förderte meine Ausbildung in medizinischen Angelegenheiten, indem er die Seminararbeiten erleichterte, die ich am Boston Psychopathic Hospital (nun euphemistischer bekannt als das Massachusetts Mental Health Center) machte, wie auch die Forschung, die ich an der Psychiatrie des Massachusetts General Hospital durchführte. Er gab mir auch die Chance der Teilnahme an der Untersuchung der biochemischen und psychologischen Effekte von "Stress auf den Menschen", 1951 organisiert von den metabolischen und psychiatrischen Abteilungen des Peter Bent Brigham Spitals. Unter diesen Vorzeichen führte ich meine Dissertationsforschung über die soziale Welt durch, wie sie von ärztlichen Forschern und Patienten der Ward F-Second geschaffen wurden, was in der Folge mein erstes publiziertes Buch wurde, *Experiment Perilous*.

Talcott verfolgte mit großem Interesse aber ohne Aufdringlichkeit die Entwicklung meiner Dissertation. Als ich mit einer mündlichen Präsentation dieser in Entwicklung befindlichen Arbeit für das Department of Social Relations an der Reihe war, lud er einige herausragende medizinische Akademiker dazu ein, einschließlich den Professor für Psychiatrie, der sein Analytiker gewesen war.

Nicht lange danach wurde Talcott gebeten einen Artikel für ein Spezialheft des *Journal of Social Issues* über Familie und Verwandtschaft beizutragen. Er entschied sich, "Illness, Therapy, and the Modern Urban American Family" zu schreiben. Aufbauend auf meine Beiträge zu seinem Seminar über Sozialstruktur, und seinem

Wissen was ich aus meiner Forschung über Ward F-Second gelernt hatte, lud er mich zum gemeinsamen Abfassen des Artikels ein, was ich machte – in einer Zusammenarbeit, die gleich, gegenseitig und ohne Spannung war, wie sie auch nur zwischen einem Lehrer und einer Studentin denkbar sein konnte. Der Artikel wurde 1952 veröffentlicht, während meines zweiten Jahres im Doktoratsstudium. Es war meine erste gedruckte soziologische Arbeit; und es hat meine Karriere gefördert.

An die 44 Jahre später ist die Quelle des Lehrens, der Forschung und des Schreibens in der von mir betriebenen Medizinsoziologie und die Themen die sich dabei durchziehen noch immer mit Bezug auf und geschuldet den Einsichten und Konzepten, die Talcott Parsons mir übermittelte und den Gelegenheiten zu lernen, die er mir ermöglich hatte, als ich eine Dissertantin war.

Die bleibende Bedeutung der Art von Lehrer, wie es Talcott Parsons war, liegt in dem was er als die "unvergeßliche Erfahrung intellektueller Efferveszenz" bezeichnete und die er seinen StudentInnen verschaffte. Durch die Übertragung eines solchen Funkens von einer Generation zur nächsten wird die intellektuelle und menschliche Vitalität eines Faches sichergestellt. "Mit dieser Bemerkung im Geiste eines relativen und vorsichtigen intellektuellen Optimismus, aber eben doch eindeutig eines Optimismus, scheint es angemessen, diese lange und komplizierte, und wie ich hoffe, nicht verwirrte Analyse zu einem Abschluß zu bringen" schloss Talcott Parsons in "A Paradigm of the Human Condition", einer der letzten Essays, die er publizierte. "Der nunmehrige Abschluß, jedoch", fuhr er fort, "ist auch der Beginn einer neuen Phase der Erkundung dieser Probleme". Dies ist die Essenz des Erbes, das ich von Talcott Parsons erhalten habe. Ich hoffe, dass ich einigermaßen erfolgreich war, es denen weiterzugeben, die ich unterrichtet habe.

Konvergenzen – Divergenzen

Das Konvergenzproblem in den europäischen Sozialwissenschaften an der Wende zum 20. Jahrhundert
Eine Kritik aus der Retrospektive[1]
Talcott Parsons

Zentral für mein erstes, 1937 veröffentlichtes Buch, *The Structure of Social Action*[2], war die These der Konvergenz der vier annähernd zur selben Epoche gehörenden Autoren, deren Schriften den Kern des Buchs ausmachen: Alfred Marshall als Vertreter der "neueren" ökonomischen Theorien, Vilfredo Pareto, Emile Durkheim und Max Weber. Diese Konvergenz ist erst kürzlich von Whitney Pope in Frage gestellt worden – in erster Linie in bezug auf Durkheim.[3] Pope behauptet, dass Durkheim nichts zu tun hatte mit dem, was heute die "Theorie des Handelns" genannt wird und dass nur meine Fehlinterpretation von Durkheims Werk dessen Einschluss in die erwähnte Konvergenzthese stützen kann. In einer langen Fußnote am Ende seines Artikels geht Pope jedoch einen Schritt weiter und stellt in Frage, ob Weber in die These der Konvergenz eingeschlossen werden kann, wobei er behauptet, dass Weber primär eine Theorie der ökonomischen und politischen Interessen formuliert habe, nicht aber eine Theorie der Werte und der gesellschaftlichen Integration.[4] In einer demnächst erscheinenden Diskussion seines Artikels in der *American Sociological Review* habe ich Popes Vorwürfe energisch zurückgewiesen.[5] Es scheint jedoch

---

[1] [Vortragsmanuskript verfasst Juli 1974 für die Tagung zur Geschichte der Soziologie der International Sociological Association in Toronto, August 1974, übersetzt von Harald Wenzel. Editorische Anmerkungen und Ergänzungen sind in eckige Klammern gestellt. Wir danken den Archiven der Harvard University für ihre Unterstützung. Courtesy of the Harvard University Archives]

[2] Talcott Parsons: *The Structure of Social Action*. New York: McGraw-Hill 1937.

[3] Whitney Pope: *Classic on Classic: Parsons' Interpretation of Durkheim*. In: *American Sociological Review*, 38 (4), 1973, S.399-415.

[4] Vgl. dazu die lange Fußnote am Ende des Artikels von Pope (1973). [Anmerkung 8, S.413f.]

[5] [Die Debatte über Parsons' Konvergenzthese wurde in folgenden weiteren Arbeiten fortgeführt: Jere Cohen: *Moral Freedom Through Understanding in Durkheim*. In: *American Sociological Review*, 40 (1), 1975, S.104-106; bei der von Parsons erwähnten Replik handelt es sich um: Talcott Parsons: *Comment on 'Parsons' Interpretation of Durkheim' and on 'Moral Freedom Through Understanding in Durkheim'*. In: *American Sociological Review*, 40 (1), 1975, S.107-111; weitere Beiträge der Debatte waren: Whitney Pope: *Parsons on Durkheim. Revisited (Reply to Cohen & Parsons)*. In: *American Sociological*

gerade bei einer Tagung zur Geschichte der Soziologie angebracht, eine Bestandsaufnahme mit Blick auf den Status dieser Angelegenheit zu unternehmen.

Weit davon entfernt, mir den Irrtum meiner vor siebenunddreißig Jahren entwickelten Perspektive plausibel zu machen, hat mich Popes Kritik im großen und ganzen in der Auffassung bestärkt, dass diese ursprüngliche These triftig war. Und in der Tat ist die Literatur, in der die These in Frage gestellt wird, eindeutig nicht besonders beeindruckend. In dem Kommentar, auf den ich mich gerade bezog, habe ich die primären Gründe darzulegen versucht, warum ich Popes Position für verwundbar halte. Ich sollte deshalb kurz auf einige Aspekte der damals in jenem Buch vorgebrachten Konvergenzthese eingehen und dann etwas zur Erweiterung des damals explizit behandelten Autorenkreises sagen.

Zunächst sollte ich eine kurze Stellungnahme zur ursprünglichen Konvergenz der vier Autoren geben. Erinnern wir uns: Diese Autoren waren unterschiedlicher nationaler Herkunft, jeder von ihnen nahm seinen Ausgangspunkt von ganz unterschiedlichen intellektuellen Traditionen und Problemformeln. Es wurde damals dargelegt, dass Marshalls Beitrag erheblich beschränkter war als die Beiträge der anderen drei Autoren, weil Marshall im wesentlichen ein Wirtschaftswissenschaftler war, dessen "Soziologie" nur einen residualen Status in seinem Werk einnahm, und weil er dem utilitaristischen Denken am nächsten war, dessen Unzulänglichkeiten eine grundlegende Orientierungsprämisse der anderen drei Autoren war. Nirgendwo in seinem Werk entfaltet Marshall eine radikale Kritik des Utilitarismus.

Es sollte auch hervorgehoben werden, dass die Perspektive, von der aus ich mich auf den Konvergenzbeweis zubewegte, ihren Brennpunkt im Problem des Status der ökonomischen Theorie und ihren allgemeinen Beziehungen zu anderen Aspekten des sozialen Systems auf der einen, des allgemeinen Handlungssystems auf der anderen Seite hatte. Diese Umstände waren besonders dabei wichtig, den Stellenwert von Paretos Werk in dieser Studie zu bestimmen. Da Pareto sehr viel bestimmter die Entwicklung einer eigenständigen ökonomischen Theorie in Angriff genommen hatte als dies bei Durkheim und Weber der Fall gewesen war, hatte er – und dies bildet einen Kontrast zum Vorgehen Marshalls – ausdrücklich den Versuch

---

Review, 40 (1), 1975, S.111-115; Jere Cohen, Lawrence E. Hazelrigg, Whitney Pope: *De-Parsonizing Weber: A Critique of Parsons' Interpretation of Weber's Sociology*. In: *American Sociological Review*, 40 (3), 1975, S.221-241; Whitney Pope, Jere Cohen, Lawrence E.Hazelrigg: *On the Divergence of Weber and Durkheim. A Critique of Parsons' Convergence Thesis*. In: *American Sociological Review*, 40 (4), 1975, S.417-427; Talcott Parsons: *On 'De-Parsonizing Weber'*. In *American Sociological Review*, 40 (5), 1975, S.666-670; Jere Cohen, Lawrence E. Hazelrigg, Whitney Pope: *Reply to Parsons*. In: *American Sociological Review*, 40 (5), 1975, S.670-674].

unternommen, diese ökonomische Theorie durch eine sehr viel allgemeinere Theorie der Gesellschaft zu ergänzen.6

Es war jedoch nicht die Ökonomie als solche, sondern der allgemeine Bezugsrahmen, innerhalb dessen sich die anglo-amerikanischen Wirtschaftswissenschaften entwickelten, nämlich der Utilitarismus, der sich als primärer Zugangspunkt zum Konvergenzproblem erwies, so wie ich es in *The Structure of Social Action* zu begreifen lernte. Bei Pareto war der Status dieses Problems relativ explizit, speziell in seiner Behandlung der Ideen der Ophelimität (ein Begriff, den er selbst prägte) und der Nützlichkeit.7 Ganz eindeutig konnte Weber nicht als ein utilitaristischer Theoretiker eingestuft werden, stellte man die besondere Perspektive in Rechnung, in der er kulturelle Glaubensüberzeugungen und Werte in ihrer Auswirkung auf die ökonomischen wie auch auf andere Aspekte des sozialen Handelns behandelte. Für mich war in gewissem Sinn sein Essay über die Ethik des asketischen Protestantismus ein entscheidendes Dokument.8 Durkheim andererseits befasste sich nie ausdrücklich mit den Wirtschaftswissenschaften, sondern zog die utilitaristischen Auffassungen nur als Kontrastfolie für die Entwicklung seiner eigenen Konzeption heran, speziell für den Begriff der organischen Solidarität. In diesem Zusammen-

---

6   Es ist interessant, dass eine relativ unbekannte Stellungnahme Max Webers vor kurzem ins Englische übersetzt wurde und in einer texanischen Zeitschrift veröffentlicht werden wird. In dieser Stellungnahme akzeptiert Weber ganz explizit die Version ökonomischer Theorie, die in England zu seiner Zeit entstanden war, speziell in Gestalt der Arbeiten Marshalls, aber auch der in Österreich entstandenen Arbeiten Karl Mengers und des in der französischsprachigen Welt entwickelten Werks von [Léon] Walras, dem Vorgänger Paretos in Lausanne. In seiner Stellungnahme grenzte Weber seine eigene Position explizit von jeder Version dessen ab, was in Deutschland oft "institutionalistische Ökonomie" genannt wurde, insbesondere von den Arbeiten Werner Sombarts und – in einem anderen Zusammenhang, natürlich – von der marxistischen Ökonomie. Ich hebe diesen Punkt hervor, weil sich die Ökonomie und die Soziologie als Wissenschaftsdisziplinen seit meiner Arbeit an *The Structure of Social Action* voneinander abgelöst haben. Nur sehr wenige Soziologen sind sich der herausragenden Bedeutung der historischen Bande dieser Disziplinen bewusst. [Bei der von Parsons hier erwähnten Übersetzung handelt es sich um Max Weber: *Die Grenznutzenlehre und das 'psychophysische Grundgesetz'*. In: ders., *Gesammelte Aufsätze zur Wissenschaftslehre*. Tübingen: Mohr 1973, S.384-399 (1908). Die Übersetzung erschien als *Marginal Utility and 'The Fundamental Law of Psychophysics'*. In: *Social Science Quarterly*, 56 (1), 1975, S.21-36].
7   Talcott Parsons: *Pareto's Approach to the Construction of a Theory of the Social System*. In: *Proceedings of the Convegno Internazionale su Vilfredo Pareto*, der von der Academia die Lincei in Rom vom 25. bis 27. Oktober 1973 ausgerichtet wurde. [Roma: Accademia Nazionale dei Lincei 1975].
8   [Vgl. Max Weber: *Die Protestantische Ethik und der Geist des Kapitalismus*. In: ders., *Gesammelte Aufsätze zur Religionssoziologie*, Tübingen: Mohr 1920, S.17-206 (1904/1905)].

hang ist Durkheims Werk *Über soziale Arbeitsteilung* am bedeutendsten, da hier diese polemische Bezugnahme sehr auffällig ist.[9]

Es erscheint mir nicht notwendig, die Gründe meiner Konvergenzthese auf dem Hintergrund des utilitaristischen Denkens und seiner positivistischen Abarten weiter zu erläutern. Wenn sie auch keine Zurückweisung bedeutete, so bedeutete die Konvergenzthese doch vor allem eine Skepsis, ob die traditionelle Betonung dessen, was viele deutsche Autoren um die Jahrhundertwende *Realfaktoren*[10] nannten, für die Bestimmung sozialer Ereignisse und menschlichen Handelns im allgemeinen angemessen waren. Dieser Begriff bezieht sich vornehmlich auf das, was man heute ökonomische und politische Interessen nennt. Ihnen gegenüber stehen einerseits die Faktoren gesellschaftlicher Integration, andererseits der Einfluss kultureller Komponenten im Bereich der Glaubensüberzeugungen und Werte.

Was die Autoren und ihre Werke betrifft, die den Kern von *The Structure of Social Action* bilden, bin ich nach dieser langen Zeit, nach nun weitaus umfangreicherer theoretischer Arbeit und nach wiederholten, intensiven Visiten bei den Autoren mehr denn je vom Bestand und der Bedeutsamkeit ihrer Konvergenz überzeugt.

Ich sollte nun den Erweiterungsprozess der Konvergenzthese über die ursprünglichen vier Autoren hinaus umreißen. In diesem Zusammenhang sollte ein Wort zum Status des Werks von Karl Marx gesagt werden. Im Rahmen der Ausarbeitung der Konvergenzthese der vier Autoren in *The Structure of Social Action* habe ich auch kurz Marx diskutiert. Ich betrachtete Marx jedoch nicht ernsthaft als erstrangigen Kandidaten für eine umfassende Analyse in diesem Buch. Für diese Entscheidung gab es zwei elementare Gründe. Der erste Grund bezieht sich auf die Generationszugehörigkeit von Marx: Die vier Theoretiker, mit denen ich mich befasste, gehörten ein und derselben Generation an; Marx jedoch gehörte zu einer früheren Generation, er starb z.B. 1883, noch einige Jahre bevor die ersten der in meinem Buch diskutierten Werke erschienen. Der zweite Grund besteht darin, dass Marx, obwohl er ein tiefes Verständnis der "Geschichtsphilosophie" entwickelte, im Grunde nicht zu derselben Entwicklungslinie gehörte.[11] Es ist Alexanders Grundüberzeugung, dass Marx die Überwindung des utilitaristischen Dilemmas nicht gelang, wohingegen die anderen Autoren, auf verschiedenen Wegen und in unterschiedlichem Maß,

---

9 Émile Durkheim: *Über soziale Arbeitsteilung*. Frankfurt/Main: Suhrkamp 1988 (1893), Buch I, Kapitel 7 und Buch II, Kapitel 1 und 2.
10 [Im Original deutsch].
11 Vgl. dazu das gerade fertiggestellte und noch nicht veröffentlichte Manuskript der Dissertationsschrift von Jeffrey Alexander (University of California, Berkeley, Department of Sociology), in der – wie ich meine – die bisher angemessenste Darstellung von Marx' Denken in diesem Sinne gegeben wird. [Vgl. Jeffrey Alexander: *Theoretical Logic in Sociology. Volume Two. The Antinomies of Classical Thought: Marx and Durkheim*, London: Routledge & Kegan Paul 1982].

diese Aufgabe lösten. Dies ist der zweite Grund, warum ich Marx nicht als vollwertigen Konvergenztheoretiker behandelte, doch das Buch war schon sehr lang geworden und es war deshalb fraglich, ob es das Gewicht der Analyse eines fünften Autors in voller Länge hätte tragen können.

Von Bedeutung ist ferner, dass ich insbesondere mit bestimmten Entwicklungen in der Beziehung zwischen ökonomischer und soziologischer Theorie befasst war, die – wie oben schon erwähnt wurde – die Gelegenheit gaben, Alfred Marshall in die Analyse einzuschließen. Sowohl Pareto wie auch Weber passten ganz eindeutig in diesen Teil meines Projekts, Durkheim lag hier etwas ferner, passte jedoch auch definitiv dazu. Keiner von ihnen vertrat die Marxsche Linie in bezug auf den Charakter der Wirtschaft und auf ihre Rolle in den umfassenderen sozialen und Handlungssystemen. In den letzten Jahren ist es zu einer auffälligen Mode geworden, Marx, Durkheim und Weber zusammenzubringen. Dies verdankt sich offenbar der Prominenz neo-marxistischen Denkens in der jüngsten Zeit, zugleich fügt es sich jedoch in einen theoretischen Komplex, dessen Auswahl der Grundvariablen durch eine andere Selektivität charakterisiert ist als diejenige, die ich akzentuierte – und an die ich mit wichtigen Modifikationen auch weiter anschließe.

Der Kreis der Konvergenztheoretiker wurde über die Jahre erweitert, um eine Zahl von Autoren und intellektuellen Bewegungen aufzunehmen, die für die vier Autoren von *The Structure of Social Action* im Grunde zeitgenössisch waren. Unter denjenigen, denen ich ernsthaft Aufmerksamkeit schenkte, war die früheste und für meine intellektuelle Entwicklung wichtigste Einflussfigur Sigmund Freud. Ich begann mit einer ernsthaften Lektüre von Freud auf die Empfehlung von Elton Mayo hin,[12] als das Manuskript von *The Structure of Social Action* in seinen Grundzügen gerade fertiggestellt war. Wie ich schon im Vorwort zur zweiten Ausgabe jener Arbeit angemerkt habe, hätte ich hier wohl einen Fall gehabt, der von seiner Substanz her eindeutiger als Marx eine umfassende Analyse im Buch verdient hätte. Die Analyse der theoretischen Beiträge Freuds zu dem, was ich heute die Theorie des Handelns nenne, ist eine komplizierte Angelegenheit, und Freud selbst nahm substantielle Änderungen an seiner Theorie im Verlauf seiner langen, produktiven Karriere vor.

Aus der Retrospektive betrachtet kann zurecht behauptet werden, dass Freuds Beiträge für das Verständnis der nicht-rationalen Komponenten menschlicher Motivation die wichtigsten waren – ein Problem, für das ich durch drei der vier Autoren in *The Structure of Social Action* in hohem Maß sensibilisiert wurde: durch Pareto, Durkheim und Weber, insbesondere durch den erst- und den letztgenannten. Dies

---

[12] Vgl. Talcott Parsons: *Die Entstehung der Theorie des sozialen Systems: Ein Bericht zur Person*. In: ders., Edward Shils, Paul F. Lazarsfeld: *Soziologie – autobiographisch*, Stuttgart: Ferdinand Enke/Deutscher Taschenbuch Verlag 1975 (1970), S.1-68.

fiel mir besonders vor kurzem bei einer Wiederbegegnung mit Freuds Werk auf,[13] die die erneute, vollständige Lektüre seines ersten großen theoretischen Werks, der *Traumdeutung*, und die Ausarbeitung eines kurzen Artikels dazu beinhaltete. Wiederum war ich enorm beeindruckt vom theoretischen Raffinement dieses Buches und von den Kontinuitäten, die Freud trotz wichtiger Änderungen über sein ganzes, intellektuell produktives Leben hinweg aufrechterhielt. Natürlich war Freud in erster Linie ein Psychologe und kein Soziologe, und der soziologisch orientierte Interpret hat deshalb beträchtliche Modifikationen an vielen Formulierungen Freuds vornehmen müssen. Nichtsdestoweniger behaupte ich, dass die Übereinstimmung mit den Auffassungen insbesondere von Freuds Spätwerk ausnehmend groß ist. Schließlich sollte angemerkt werden, dass Freud keinesfalls ein einfältiger "Antirationalist" war, sondern gerade die Tatsache, dass er die nicht-rationale Motivation mit in hohem Maße rationalen Methoden wissenschaftlicher Forschung analysierte und dass die therapeutischen Ziele der psychoanalytischen Therapie eine erhebliche Stärkung des kognitiven Elements implizierten, macht klar, dass er mit dem grundlegenden Anspruch auf die Synthese dieser Komponenten auftrat und nicht als Parteigänger des einen Elements im Gegensatz zum anderen.

Eine der wichtigsten Grundlagen der Konvergenz auf der Seite Freuds betrifft die Internalisierung der normativen Kultur in der Persönlichkeit des Individuums. Dies wurde besonders klar und deutlich bei Freuds Einführung des Begriffs des Über-Ichs und seiner Rolle in der Persönlichkeitsentwicklung. Schon sehr früh war ich von diesem wichtigen Konvergenzpunkt zwischen Freud und Durkheim beeindruckt – ich meine hier den Durkheim von *Erziehung, Moral und Gesellschaft*.[14] Genau dieser Konvergenzpunkt wurde etwas später auf eine ganze Bewegung – und nicht nur auf einen individuellen Beiträger – erweitert, die spezifisch amerikanisch war. Ich denke, ihre wichtigste Einzelfigur war George Herbert Mead, der als Lehrer weit über die Rezeption seiner zeitlebens veröffentlichen Werke hinaus einflussreich war. Unter seiner Mentorschaft wurde dieser Einfluss von W. I. Thomas an der University of Chicago weiter ausgearbeitet, und eine davon relativ unabhängige Version entwickelte sich im Werk von Charles Horton Cooley an der University of Michigan. Diese Bewegung ist in jüngerer Zeit als Theorie des "Symbolischen Interaktionismus" bezeichnet worden. Mir scheint, dass sie sich gut in die Konvergenzthese auf der Ebene der allgemeinen Theorie einpasst, wobei ihre besonders engen Beziehungen, wie ich schon sagte, zu Freud auf der einen, zu Durkheim auf der anderen Seite festzuhalten sind. Ich glaube nicht, dass diese Bewegung als eine

---

[13] Talcott Parsons: *The Interpretation of Dreams by Sigmund Freud*. In: *Daedalus*, 103 (1), 1974, S.81-86.
[14] Émile Durkheim: *Erziehung, Moral und Gesellschaft. Vorlesung an der Sorbonne 1902/1903*. Frankfurt/Main: Suhrkamp 1984 (1925).

eigenständige Schule betrachtet werden sollte, wie dies oft und durchaus in einem antagonistischen Verhältnis zur "Theorie des Handelns" geschieht.

Eine dritte sehr wichtige Erweiterung des Kreises der Konvergenztheoretiker betrifft eine Bewegung, bei der die Identifikation spezifischer Urheber schwerer fällt. Die Fundamente dieser Entwicklung wurden von der Sozial- und Kulturanthropologie gelegt, die derselben Generation zugehört. Insbesondere der Kontakt mit Malinowski als Lehrer vermittelte mir für die Arbeit an *The Structure of Social Action* wichtiges Rüstzeug. In der einflussreicheren Britischen Schule war es jedoch eher die Gruppe um Radcliffe-Brown, die sich ohne weiteres in die Konvergenztradition einordnen ließ. Dies wird besonders daran deutlich, wie stark sich Radcliffe-Brown an Durkheim orientierte. Auf der amerikanischen Seite war A. L. Kroeber ein wichtiges Mitglied jener Generation; unter den Angehörigen einer jüngeren Generation war es ein mir nahestehender Kollege, Clyde Kluckhohn. Unter den Forschern, die der Profession der Anthropologen zugehören, haben auf unterschiedlichen Wegen David Schneider und Clifford Geertz bemerkenswerte Beiträge geliefert, wie dies auch bestimmte Mitglieder der Britischen Gruppe getan haben, vor allem Evans-Pritchard und Firth in meiner Generation und solche Autoren wie Edmund Leach und Max Gluckman in einer jüngeren Generation. Natürlich gibt es hier komplizierte Fragen nach der Beziehung all dessen zum Werk von Levi-Strauss und anderen. Mir scheint, dass der wichtigste Beitrag, der nicht einer einzelnen Person zugerechnet werden kann, in der Klärung der Beziehungen zwischen dem, was ich Kultursysteme nenne, und sozialen Systemen liegt.

Schließlich denke ich, dass auch das Werk von Jean Piaget in diesem Kontext erwähnt werden sollte. Auf die Bedeutung seines Frühwerks wurde ich in der Zeitphase der Ausarbeitung von *The Structure of Social Action* aufmerksam. Sein bemerkenswertes Buch, *Das moralische Urteil beim Kinde*,15 wurde in den frühen dreißiger Jahren veröffentlicht. Piaget blieb für mein Interesse an Konvergenz jedoch bis vor relativ kurzer Zeit peripher; eine wichtige, vor der Veröffentlichung stehende Arbeit von Victor und Charles Lidz hat seine Relevanz jedoch plötzlich erhöht.16 Ohne viel Zeit auf die Darstellung dieses Ansatzes zu verwenden möchte ich doch bemerken, dass die Autoren die These vertreten, dass Piagets Psychologie der kognitiven Entwicklung sich dazu eignet, der Theorie des Handelns als eine Analyse der Struktur des primär adaptiven Subsystems inkorporiert zu werden – des "Verhaltenssystems" wie es die Gebrüder Lidz nennen. Sie plazieren es damit in der

---

15 Jean Piaget: *Das moralische Urteil beim Kinde*. Frankfurt/Main: Suhrkamp 1973 (1932).
16 [Charles W. Lidz, Victor Meyer Lidz: *Piagets Psychologie der Intelligenz und die Handlungstheorie*. In: Jan J. Loubser, Rainer C. Baum, Andrew Effrat, Victor Meyer Lidz (Hg.): *Allgemeine Handlungstheorie*. Frankfurt/Main: Suhrkamp 1981, S.202-327 (1976)].

Position, an die ich in den letzten Jahren den "Verhaltensorganismus" gestellt habe. Von der Stichhaltigkeit ihres Arguments bin ich überzeugt.

Bevor ich zwei weitere beeindruckende Fälle hier aufführe, die den Kreis der Konvergenztheoretiker erweitern, möchte ich hier einen kurzen Kommentar zur Bedeutung einer bestimmten Entwicklung innerhalb der Theorie des Handelns abgeben, wie sie nach der Formulierung von *The Structure of Social Action* erfolgt ist. Erst kürzlich erfolgte, neuerliche Begegnungen mit den Werken von Durkheim und Pareto[17] haben für mich die Bedeutung bestätigt, die in der Interpretation ihrer Arbeiten der Unterscheidung zwischen dem sozialen System im engeren, analytischen Sinn und dem allgemeinen Handlungssystem zukommt, für das speziell die Unterscheidung zwischen dem kulturellen und dem sozialen System wichtig ist. Dieses Problem tritt hervor, wenn man in den Werken der beiden Autoren die Verwicklungen in der Bedeutung des von ihnen häufig verwendeten Begriffs "Gesellschaft" aufzuklären versucht.[18] Bei beiden Autoren können sich die allgemeineren Bedeutungen auf das beziehen, was ich und verschiedene Kollegen das allgemeine Handlungssystem genannt haben – und nicht auf Gesellschaft in einem analytischen Sinn. Ich meine, dass die These der Konvergenz dieser beiden Autoren untereinander und mit den übrigen Autoren, die ich hier erörtert habe, erheblich gestärkt werden kann, wenn man die Analyse in diese Perspektive bringt – etwas, was Pope klarerweise nicht tut.[19]

Die theoretischen Entwicklungen, die zu diesen Veränderungen geführt haben, haben sich über eine Reihe von Jahren erstreckt. Wichtige Meilensteine auf diesem Weg waren der Band *Toward a General Theory of Action*[20] und die Essaysammlung *Working Papers in the Theory of Action.*[21] Von besonderer Bedeutung sind hier zwei Begriffe. Der erste ist der Begriff eines Vier-Funktionen-Schemas, wobei unterstellt ist, dass nicht nur Handlungssysteme, sondern lebende Systeme generell in den Begriffen der vier Grundkategorien Anpassung, Zielerreichung, Integration und

---

17 Talcott Parsons: *Durkheim on Religion Revisited: Another Look at the Elementary Forms of the Religious Life.* In Y. Glock, P. E. Hammond (Hg.): *The Scientific Study of Religion: Beyond the Classics?* New York: Harper & Row 1973, S.156-180. Siehe auch meinen Kommentar zu Whitney Pope: *Classic on Classic.* A.a.O. [Talcott Parsons: *Comment on 'Parsons' Interpretation of Durkheim' and on 'Moral Freedom Through Understanding in Durkheim'.* In: *American Sociological Review*, 40 (1), 1975, S.107-111], sowie Talcott Parsons: *Pareto's Approach to the Construction of a Theory of the Social System.* A.a.O.
18 Robert N. Bellah (Hg.): *Emile Durkheim on Morality and Society.* Chicago: The University of Chicago Press 1973.
19 Vgl. Pope: *Classic on Classic.* A.a.O.
20 Talcott Parsons (Hg.): *Toward a General Theory of Action.* Cambridge/Massachusetts: Harvard University Press 1951.
21 Talcott Parsons, Robert F. Bales, Edward A. Shils: *Working Papers in the Theory of Action.* New York: The Free Press 1953.

Strukturerhaltung analysierbar sind. Ich bin davon überzeugt, dass diese Kategorien für die Theorie der organischen Biologie genauso grundlegend sind wie für die Theorie des Handelns. Von diesem Gesichtspunkt aus wird Gesellschaft zu einem besonders herausragenden Fall im Rahmen des integrativen Subsystems eines allgemeinen Handlungssystems. Es sollte sowohl von kulturellen Systemen wie auch von solchen Systemen unterschieden werden, die sich im Kern auf das menschliche Individuum beziehen – in gegenwärtiger Terminologie also: vom Persönlichkeits- bzw. vom Verhaltenssystem.

Die erste der beiden Erweiterungslinien, auf die ich mich hier beziehe, betrifft die Art und Weise, wie die Theorie des Handelns mit einer grundlegenden Entwicklung in der Wissenschaftstheorie in Beziehung gesetzt werden kann – der Kybernetik. Der ursprüngliche Begründer dieses Feldes war – wie man weiß – der Mathematiker Norbert Wiener.[22] Einige ihrer frühesten Anwendungen fand die Kybernetik im Bereich der Ingenieurwissenschaften, insbesondere in der Entwicklung des Computers. Ihre Anwendungen in der Biologie waren jedoch schon früh genauso grundlegend. Tatsächlich gab die Kybernetik eine breitere theoretische Erklärungsgrundlage für Phänomene, die durch die Arbeiten von Claude Bernard und W. B. Cannon Prominenz erlangten und die alle durch die Fähigkeit von Organismen zur Selbstregulierung charakterisiert waren.[23] Bernard und Cannon befassten sich mit höheren Organismen, aber seit ihren Forschungen ist klar geworden, dass kybernetische Prinzipien auch auf mikrobiologischer Ebene gültig sind.[24] In der Tat beruht die sensationelle Entwicklung der Mikrogenetik definitiv auf dieser Art von Perspektive. Das Gen ist ein Kontrollelement, das die Synthese derjenigen organischen Verbindungen kontrolliert, die für den Aufbau der lebenden Zelle konstitutiv sind.

Allmählich wurde es evident, dass die vier primären funktionalen Kategorien des Handlungssystems in einer hierarchischen Ordnung kybernetischer Kontrolle arrangiert werden konnten. Die unterste Stufe in dieser Ordnung nahmen adaptive Strukturen und Prozesse ein. Diese werden auf der nächsten Ebene vom zielorientierten Verhalten lebender Systeme kontrolliert, und zwar sowohl auf dem Niveau des Organischen wie auch auf dem Niveau des Handelns. Oberhalb der Zielerreichungsebene finden wir die Ebene der Integration, die natürlich zum Teil deswegen notwendig ist, weil komplexe Organismen multiple und nicht nur einfache Ziele haben. Schließlich erreichen wir die höchste Ordnungsebene in diesem Kontrollbe-

---

[22] Norbert Wiener: *Kybernetik. Regelung und Nachrichtenübertragung in Lebewesen und in der Maschine.* Düsseldorf: Econ 1963 (1948, [2]1961).
[23] Vgl. Claude Bernard: *An Introduction to the Study of Experimental Medicine* (übers. von Henry Copley Greene). New York: Dover Publications 1957 (1865), Walter B. Cannon: *The Wisdom of the Body.* New York: W. W. Norton & Co. 1932.
[24] Vgl. J. D. Watson: *Molecular Biology of the Gene.* New York: W. A. Benjamin [2]1970.

zugsrahmen: das, was wir die Strukturerhaltungsfunktion genannt haben. Eine besonders charakteristische Eigenschaft der Strukturerhaltungskomponenten ist ihre relative Isolation gegenüber kurzfristigem Änderungsbedarf, wie er typischerweise auf niedrigeren kybernetischen Ebenen operiert.

Mir scheint, dass die Theorie der Kybernetik ganz klar zum sogenannten Handlungsparadigma passt, das zweifellos auch ein theoretisches Schema darstellt, das es mit im kybernetischen Sinn sich selbst regulierenden Systemen zu tun hat. Ich hoffe, es ist deutlich geworden, dass die Theorie der Kybernetik eine wissenschaftliche Entwicklung mit sehr hohem Allgemeinheitsgrad ist, ihre Anwendung auf Phänomene des Handelns wie im Fall vieler anderer Anwendungen, z.B. auf organische Systeme, als Anwendung auf eine spezielle Gruppe von Erscheinungen gelten sollte.

Die letzte Erweiterung des Kreises der Konvergenztheorien, die ich erwähnen möchte, betrifft die Konvergenz zwischen den theoretischen Schemata der organischen Biologie einerseits und der Theorie des Handelns andererseits in bezug auf Begriffsbildung und logische Struktur. Dies ist eine komplizierte Geschichte und nur einige Marksteine sollen deshalb hier erwähnt werden. Ein ausnehmend guter Ausgangspunkt ist die von Bernard und Cannon stammende Vorstellung selbstregulierender Eigenschaften des individuellen Organismus, die Cannon *Homöostase* nannte. Dies ist natürlich eine spezielle Form des allgemeineren wissenschaftlichen Gleichgewichtsbegriffes, die jedoch spezifische Charakteristika aufweist, unter denen die Erhaltung differentieller, interner Bedingungen des jeweiligen Systems gegenüber der Umwelt, in der dieses System lebt, besonders auffällt. Bernard hat in diesem Zusammenhang den Begriff der inneren Umwelt eingeführt, die stabiler ist als die äußere Umwelt. Ich meine, dass direkte Parallelen zur inneren Umwelt des Organismus für eine Vielzahl von verschiedenen Handlungssystemen ermitttelt wurden. Ein solcher Begriff scheint mir besonders für die Interpretation des Durkheimschen Denkens, speziell in seinen späteren Phasen, relevant zu sein. Der Begriff eines ökonomischen Marktes jedoch ist im wesentlichen der Begriff einer inneren Umwelt der Wirtschaft, die sich gegenüber anderen Aspekten des sozialen Systems differenziert hat.

Ein zweites Konvergenzzentrum liegt weniger auf der Ebene des individuellen Organismus als auf der Ebene der Spezies und der evolutionären Beziehungen der Spezies untereinander. Darauf wurde ich zuerst durch den Biologen Alfred Emerson aufmerksam gemacht, der davon sprach, dass Symbole, die von Handlungstheoretikern normalerweise als kulturelle Komponenten begriffen werden, im Vergleich mit den Genen auf der Ebene der organischen Spezies parallele Funktionen haben. Beide sind relativ isoliert von den selektiven Zwängen ihrer Umwelten und konstituieren eine der zentralen Grundlagen – vielleicht *die* zentrale Grundlage – der Kontinuität der Systemstruktur und der von Generation zu Generation weitergegebenen Systemeigenschaften.

Ausgehend von diesen beiden primären Bezugspunkten der Homöostase des individuellen Organismus und der besonderen Rolle der transgenerationalen Vererbungskomponente können wir unsere Aufmerksamkeit zwei weiteren außerordentlich wichtigen Parallelen widmen, obwohl hier die Entwicklung noch nicht weit gediehen ist. Da ist erstens die Parallele zwischen dem Begriff der Spezies, wie er von Ernst Mayr in seiner Studie *Populations, Species and Evolution* formuliert wird,[25] und dem Begriff der Gesellschaften, wie er im Bezugsrahmen des allgemeinen Handlungssystems verstanden wird, das außerdem noch die Subsysteme der Kultur, der Persönlichkeit und des Verhaltens einschließt. Die Theorie des Handelns beschränkt sich auf die Humanevolution und es besteht Konsens in der Biologie, dass es nur eine humane Spezies gibt. Was in einer Gesellschaft organisiert ist, ist deshalb nicht die Spezies Mensch als ganze, sondern eine differenzierte Population innerhalb dieser Spezies. Das ist natürlich ein organisches System, aber eine Gesellschaft ist auch mehr als das, insofern sie auf nicht-organischen Ebenen die drei Hauptkriterien erfüllt, die Mayr für Spezies aufstellt. Damit meine ich, dass sie klar unterscheidbare Grenzen zwischen Mitgliedern und Gruppen zieht, die der Gesellschaft zugehören und solchen, für die das nicht gilt – ein Kriterium, das wie ich meine analog zu Mayrs Begriff der reproduktiven Isolation bzw. der reproduktiven Gemeinschaft ist. Menschliche Gesellschaften erreichen dies zum Teil dadurch, dass sie die Reproduktion regulieren, aber auch durch andere Methoden wie z.B. durch die Kontrolle der Migrationsbewegungen und durch Vergabe von Staatsbürgerschaften. Zweitens ist eine Gesellschaft zu Mayrs Begriff einer "ökologischen Gemeinschaft" analog, insofern sie eine territoriale Basis hat, innerhalb der ihre normative Ordnung mehr oder weniger effektiv durch politische, rechtliche oder andere Mechanismen kontrolliert wird. Drittens gibt es – wie ich gerade schon erwähnt habe – ein Element der Kontinuität über lange Zeitphasen. Für organische Systeme spricht Mayr in diesem Zusammenhang von einem "Genpool",[26] bei Gesellschaften würden wir, Alfred Emersons Vorschlag folgend,[27] von kultureller Tradition sprechen.

Ähnliche Parallelen können meiner Meinung zwischen dem Prinzip der natürlichen Selektion ausgearbeitet werden, wie es sich in der biologischen Theorie seit Darwin herauskristallisiert hat, und dem Prozeß der Institutionalisierung im Bereich des Handelns. Ich will diese theoretische Übereinstimmung an dieser Stelle nicht weiter erläutern, aber ich halte es für sehr naheliegend, für sie einzutreten.

---

[25] Ernest Mayr: *Populations, Species and Evolution*. Cambridge/Massachusetts: Harvard University Press 1970.
[26] Vgl. Mayr: *Populations*. A.a.O.
[27] Vgl. Alfred Emerson: Homeostasis and the Comparison of Systems. In: Roy R. Grinker, Sr. (Hg.): *Towards a Unified Theory of Human Behavior: An Introduction to General Systems Theory*. New York: Basic Books 1956 [S.147-163].

Schließlich möchte ich noch ein Wort zum Evolutionsbegriff verlieren. Die Handlungswissenschaften haben eine Entwicklungsphase durchgemacht, in der eine ziemlich naive Aneignung der Theorien organischer Evolution unter dem Etikett des "Sozialdarwinismus" populär war und die dann zu einer Gegenreaktion dergestalt führte, dass die Legitimität eines solchen theoretischen Vorgehens generell zurückgewiesen wurde. Eine weiterentwickelte, verbesserte Theorie des Handelns und ein besseres Verständnis des Wesens organischer Evolution hat meiner Meinung nach den Weg freigemacht, um auch auf diesem Gebiet Konvergenz zu attestieren und soziokulturelle Evolution als wesentlich kontinuierlich mit organischer Evolution und als Gegenstand einer gleichermaßen für beide Bereiche geeigneten theoretischen Analyse zu begreifen.

Anders als Whitney Pope das behauptet, ist die ursprüngliche Konvergenzthese, wie ich sie in *The Structure of Social Action* behauptet habe, weit davon entfernt, in sich zusammenzufallen, ganz im Gegenteil. Das an der grundlegenden Entwicklungstendenz meines Denkens zu zeigen, war das Ziel dieser Arbeit. Die ursprüngliche Konvergenzthese besteht meiner Auffassung nach nicht nur weiter fort, sie kann weit über die ursprünglich von mir gesetzten Grenzen hinaus in der Entwicklung der Wissenschaften vom menschlichen Handeln und in Beziehung zur Kybernetikbewegung und zu parallelen Entwicklungen der biologischen Theorie erweitert werden. Sie erweist sich als ein Beispiel einer sehr viel breiteren theoretischen Entwicklung in der Wissenschaft, als dies jene von uns, die in früheren Entwicklungsphasen mit ihr zu tun hatten, sich jemals vorstellen konnten.

Convergence as Method in Theory Construction
Victor M. Lidz/Harold J. Bershady

Parsons' Early Theory of Social Action

For several decades, critical evaluation of Talcott Parsons' *The Structure of Social Action* (1937) has focused on the so-called convergence argument. Critics have argued that, contrary to Parsons' claims that Max Weber, Emile Durkheim, Vilfredo Pareto, and Alfred Marshall had all developed social theories emphasizing normative order, the works of these theorists were in historical fact rooted in such radically different intellectual traditions that they could not possibly have reached similar conclusions about the nature of human society and social relationships. Most discussion has concentrated on the differences between Weber and Durkheim. Weber is portrayed as a leading exponent of German historical scholarship on economic and social institutions and thus a methodological individualist, whereas Durkheim is represented as a descendent of Rousseau, Montesquieu, and Comte, hence as a positivist in the French collectivist tradition. Marshall was the leading politically liberal utilitarian economist in the Britain of his time. Pareto is harder to characterize. He was both Italian and Swiss, an engineer and economist as well as sociologist. In his political writings, he was conservative and, in a tradition descending from Machiavelli, focused on issues of power. Yet, he aspired to formalize his sociological ideas in a way continuous with his economic writings, and his conception of society emphasized abstract system concepts.

Thus, it has been suggested that hardly any four thinkers of the turn from the 19th to the 20th century could have been less alike. In the face of these well-documented differences, Parsons' view that the four scholars converged on a common theory has been treated as historically insupportable. The most favorable view is that the convergence argument may have some idiosyncratic justification within Parsons' own convoluted schema, but little if any value to the broader discipline.

Against this common view, we will argue that the convergence theme is more than an interpretive argument in *The Structure of Social Action*. For Parsons, it was a method of theory construction that he used first in creating the conceptual framework for his early masterpiece and then continued to use throughout his career. We will clarify the method of convergence that played a creative part in all of Parsons' major theoretical innovations. In the present article, we will review the foundational role it played in *The Structure of Social Action*. In doing so, we will show that most of the criticisms of the "convergence argument", despite the accuracy of their historical observations, fail to address the central questions of *The Structure of Social*

Action. We will also survey the use Parsons made of the convergence method in his later theoretical work that extended the scope of his theory through more than forty years of scholarship. This part of our discussion will help to clarify the ingredients of convergence as a general method. In conclusion, we will argue that convergence is a powerful analytic method for generating and systematizing theoretical formulations in sociology[1].

Convergence as Method

In sociology, many conceptual schemes have captured aspects of social life and dealt with them in creative ways. However, each has dealt with social phenomena selectively, leaving important aspects untreated. When taken together, these schemes are not compatible, as can be seen by comparing, for example, the utilitarianism of Spencer and the collectivism of Durkheim, the historicism of Dilthey, and the system theory of Pareto. Insofar as each of the well-established schemes has yielded genuine insight, Parsons insisted, its categories should not be abandoned. To be sure, the schemes should be critiqued, their respective claims assessed, and the differences resolved. The starting point toward conceptual coherence and general theory is critique – criticism, but also appreciative analysis – of the underlying frameworks of previously established social knowledge. This was, in sum, the program of *SSA*: to move from critique of prior theories to a fresh categorial synthesis.

In *SSA*, Parsons used what he called the method of convergence (*Ibid*, Chapter XVIII) to produce a categorial synthesis. He identified the chief underlying categories of analysis in the theories of several leading European thinkers of the previous generation. He selected these specific figures because each had worked insightfully, and within a different intellectual tradition, on the relations of the economy to social institutions more broadly. He then devised a small, yet more comprehensive, set of categories in order to establish common terms for comparing their works (*Ibid*, Chapter II). The new set of categories were employed to synthesize the contributions of all these thinkers into richer, empirically more adequate knowledge. To establish the value of this result, Parsons demonstrated that none of the original

---

[1] In a second article, we will continue our argument about the importance of the convergence method. Our focus will be on the continual transformation of the basic conceptual scheme of the theory of action in Parsons' later scholarship. We will argue that, by utilizing the convergence method to draw on new sources of ideas, Parsons transformed the basic striucture of his system of theory. Our second article will explicate the specific ways in which the convergence method figured in these large and technical changes. Our conclusion will be that the convergence method is a fruitful tool that can still be helpful in resolving impasses between different schools of thought in soeiology.

thinkers, due to the limitations of their respective theories, could have developed the more comprehensive knowledge. The limitations of their theories were due to systematic blindspots ("residual categories", see *Ibid*, pp. 16ff) or areas relevant to their work, but overlooked in their respective conceptual schemes.

The convergence method, as Parsons used it, was distinctly cosmopolitan. He examined the works of four figures who stood at the apex of scholarly traditions in their respective nations: Alfred Marshall in the British tradition of utilitarian individualism (*Ibid*, Chapter, IV; Marshall, 1925); Vilfredo Pareto in the Italian tradition of realist social thought as well as in utilitarian and systematic economics (*Ibid*, Chapters V-VII); Emile Durkheim in the French tradition of collectivist thought (*Ibid*, Chapters VIII-XII); and Max Weber, who represented but also transcended the frameworks of German idealism and historicism, (*Ibid*, Chapters XIII-XVII). By identifying categories shared in the works of these diverse thinkers, Parsons revealed that there were common elements of understanding that had roots in practically all of the major social scientific traditions of Western civilization. At a deep and unrecognized level, this shared core of understanding unified modern European social thought. Having identified this shared core, Parsons was able to illuminate areas in each of the four national traditions that had previously been hidden. His own scheme was formulated as a way of eradicating the blindspots (residual categories) of these previous schools of thought. Parsons thus claimed to have explicated a basis for generalizing knowledge that had previously been encapsulated within separate traditions (*Ibid*, Chapter XVIII).

In Parsons' interpretations of the theories of his predecessors (Parsons, 1937; see also Parsons, 1967, Chapters 1-3, and 6), each account was connected to each of the others in terms of an abstract scheme. This scheme was essentially the one he also used to establish the groundwork of a universal theory. His interpretive claims rested on the idea that this scheme articulates problems central to all social scientific theory. He argued that in applying this scheme to his predecessors' theories he was able to cut to primary issues in their theoretical systems. Moreover, this scheme provided him with a common grid for comparing theories developed within divergent traditions (Gould, 1981). His interest in restating the formulations of his predecessors in full historical individuality was, thus, secondary. Although he dealt at considerable length with historical materials, his purpose was not to write intellectual history. The appropriate standard for assessing Parsons' discussions of his predecessors is not whether he captured the details of their formulations with greater historical veracity than other accounts, but whether the terms of his analytical grid yield greater insight into the ways in which the particular sociological theories are constructed. The value of Parsons' treatments lies in their explication of the structure of social theories as instanced in the works of several masters. By this standard, Parsons' secondary treatments have continuing theoretical importance even though they need correction on historical details (*cf.* Schluchter, 1989; Besnard, ed., 1983).

Despite his focus on developing his own analytical scheme, Parsons' use of the convergence method was not mechanically superimposed upon readings of his predecessors. His treatments of Durkheim and Weber in *SSA*, and of Freud in later writings (Parsons, 1951, 1964; Parsons and Bales, 1955), show that he made painstaking efforts to understand fundamental theories, their logical structures, and empirical insights. He subjected what he took to be the leading theories of the previous generation to unremitting critique of an intensity and scope that perhaps only Marx's *Grundrisse* (1973) had previously attained in the history of social thought. At the same time, he eschewed the role of partisan of any of these traditions and squarely faced their limitations. His chief concern in *SSA* was to explore inconsistencies and contradictions both within and between the traditions. He compared the potentials of theories within each tradition, balanced their respective advantages and shortcomings, and attempted to optimize the scope and precision of his newly proposed theory. He designed *SSA* as an essentially pan-Western product, a resolution of dialogues between major Western traditions of thought. As Habermas has said (1981), "..no one else among the productive theorists of society has conducted a continuing debate with the classics of our discipline with equal intensity and persistence to build on received tradition." In establishing grounds for discourse that would enable scholars of diverse backgrounds and perspectives to participate with one another in common learning, Parsons stood out sharply against both the pragmatic distrust of formal theorizing that predominated in America and the nationalistic patterns of thought that limited European social science of the 19th and early 20th centuries (*cf.* Mannheim, 1953).

As Parsons made clear, his primary formulations were not yet substantive, but foundational and constitutive (Parsons, 1937, Chapters XVIII and XIX). They articulated a set of categories designed to coordinate knowledge of all social phenomena. Their primary purpose was to establish a *frame of reference* for theorizing about, as well as for empirical studies of, innumerable social settings (*Ibid*, Chapters XVI through XIX). In this respect, the categories were intended to define universal aspects of social phenomena. Specific theories, when developed within the frame set forth by the categories, would clarify the relations among these aspects for any particular empirical case or, indeed, class of empirical materials.

As Mark Gould (1981) has emphasized, the categorial scheme as a whole can also be used to evaluate the scope of other theories. Social theories that, in their own terms, failed to encompass one or another category were necessarily partial and inadequate. It should then be possible to use the categories and the relations among them to redirect and broaden inquiry. Indeed, after assessing a theory as partial and in need of redirection, Parsons often used his own categorial set to suggest how that theory could be synthesized with others into a single scheme of greater generality and coherence. A striking instance of this kind of critique was Parsons' treatment of the utilitarian framework. He demonstrated it to be inherently limited and in need of supplementing by categories drawn from the idealistic and collectivistic traditions (Parsons, 1937, Chapters II through IV).

Parsons hoped that the conceptual scheme he was developing would be capable of supporting an indefinite number of specialized theories designed for particular research projects and fields of study, such as the sociology of medicine (Parsons, 1951, Chapter X), social stratification (e.g., Parsons, 1954, Chapter XIX), deviance and social control (Parsons, 1951, Chapter VII), economic institutions (Parsons and Smelser, 1956), education (Parsons and Platt, 1973), and politics (Parsons, 1969, *passim*), among many others. He understood that sociology cannot be theoretically simple, but requires a variety of conceptual materials, differing in substantive concern, level of generality, and form of synthesizing data. The abstract quality of the categories he devised was intended to accommodate a plurality of empirical fields and interests in sociology. In all this, his overriding methodological intention was empirical, to provide a foundation that would coordinate the procedures and findings of all sociological research (*cf.* Bourricauld, 1981; for the most comprehensive overview and critique, see Alexander, 1983).

Parsons' premise in the *SSA* is that the entire domain of meaningful social action should be expressed through a single conceptual framework. He reasoned that all the social sciences – economics, psychology, political science, anthropology, and various interstitial disciplines as well as sociology – must come to terms with common phenomena of social life. Such qualities of human conduct as its symbolic mediation, goal directedness, involvement in social interaction, normative constitution, sentimental or affective quality, engagement with the practical circumstances of time and place, and voluntaristic "openness" to choice and decision-making are problematic for all these disciplines and for every study carried out within them. A firm foundation can be established for sociology and the other social sciences only by dealing directly with these essential qualities of human relationships. His general theory of action attempted to grasp these realities and place them at the center of social scientific attention (Parsons, 1937, Chapter XIX; Parsons, 1986b [*circa* 1939]). A sociology developed on that basis will share a foundation with the other social sciences and, hence, be logically and substantively related to them.

Because of this conviction, Parsons moved back and forth throughout his career between addressing sociology as a separate discipline and addressing a broader range of the social sciences (Parsons, 1937; Parsons and Shils, 1951b; Parsons, 1964 and 1967, Chapter 6; Parsons and Smelser, 1956). A properly founded sociology, he believed, will deal with a number of issues of fundamental importance to all social science. Throughout his career, he sought to clarify his views on these issues of general significance in terms that might broadly affect social science and promote favorable interchange between sociology and related fields. To understand his work, one must appreciate that he had major nonsociological concerns, yet recognize that these concerns are closely related to sociology.

Categories and Convergence

Parsons dated the origins of his methodological views to his studies of Kant, first as an undergraduate at Amherst and then as a doctoral student in Heidelberg (Parsons, 1977, Chapter 1). At Amherst, his intellectual outlook was profoundly influenced by a year-long course on Kant, concentrating on *The Critique of Pure Reason* (1930). Kant demonstrated for him that scientific knowledge cannot be developed from sheerly empirical materials, as Hume and many others had claimed, whatever the genuine importance of experimentation and observation. From the outset of his career, Parsons had an understanding of the importance of categories in coordinating and giving meaning to empirical data. This perspective was consolidated when, at the University of Heidelberg, he took part in Karl Jaspers' seminar on Kant. Jaspers' influence came to be part of an immersion in Neo-Kantian methodology (Weber, 1949/1922; Windelband, 1901/1892; Rickert, 1986/1902) that was central to Parsons' education in Heidelberg.

From the time he arrived in Heidelberg in 1925, Parsons was strongly affected by the writings of Max Weber, then deceased for five years, but still an intellectual force at the university. *The Protestant Ethic and the Spirit of Capitalism* (1930/1903-04) had an immediate impact, but he soon immersed himself in Weber's methodological writings, the *Gesammelte Aufsaetse zur Wissenschaftslehre* (1922) and sections of *Wirtschaft und Gesellschaft* or *Economy and Society* (1968/1925). Weber's methodological works directed him to the writings of Heinrich Rickert (1902), Ernst Troeltsch (1922 and 1931/1911), Werner Sombart (1913 and 1916), Gustav Schmoller (1904 and 1923/1900), Wilhelm Windelband (1892), Wilhelm Dilthey (1883), Karl Mannheim (1929), and others who addressed the nature of knowledge of human conduct, social institutions, culture, and history. He acquired a broad understanding of the German Neo-Kantian movement of the late 19th and early 20th centuries, including the important debates over the characteristics of historical, economic, and socio-cultural objects, such as the famous *Methodenstreit* between Schmoller and Karl Menger (1963). The major issues addressed in these debates led him to concentrate on the Neo-Kantian philosophers and methodologists, such as Windelband (*op. cit.*), Rickert (*op. cit.*), von Schelting (*op. cit.*), and to a degree some of the phenomenologists, including Husserl (1900-1901) and Schutz (1967/1932). Although hardly uncritical of the Neo-Kantian perspectives, Parsons identified particularly with Weber's methodological writings, which he perceived to have reached a depth of analysis unparalleled in the works of any other social scientist.

When Parsons first arrived at Harvard in 1927 as an instructor in economics, his professional identity was that of a German-trained historical social-economist. Since his undergraduate days at Amherst, he had studied the American institutionalist school (Parsons, 1977, Chapter 1). However, his major training, gained in Heidelberg, had been in the German schools of historical economics. His interests, too, had shifted to center on German scholarship, which he believed had achieved a greater depth of understanding than the American and English. The doctoral thesis he had submitted to the faculty at Heidelberg addressed the theories of capitalism in Marx, Sombart, and Weber against a background of other German scholarship (Parsons, 1991/1928-29, Chapter 1). His longer term intellectual ambitions were inspired largely by Weber's project, in *Economy and Society*, of developing general categories for the analysis of socio-economic life, with a focus on the institutions of modern, Western, capitalistic civilization, but applicable as well to many civilizations and historical epochs (Weber, 1968/1925).

Although Parsons' interests were historical and comparative, he sided with the generalists on each of the controversies that divided the Neo-Kantian schools over the nature of social scientific knowledge. He rejected the "ideographic", historicist views he attributed to Windelband (*op. cit.*), Dilthey (*op. cit.*), and others. Despite Dilthey's identification with the slogan, "Back to Kant!," Parsons also viewed him as overly influenced by "mystical!" Hegelian traditions of historicism (Parsons, 1966, p. 115; 1977, p. 236; also personal communication). Because historicist scholars aspired to immerse themselves in the unique social and cultural phenomena of each of the epochs they studied, Parsons believed they were in effect creating a separate kind of understanding for each epoch. Some scholars heralded the historicist program as promising to yield a richness of human understanding that, when a great many studies were brought together, would be truer to the varieties of human life (Droysen, 1882; Cassirer, 1950; *cf.* for a more recent work, Gadamer, 1975). Parsons, however, with his commitment to the development of generalizing modes of analysis, believed this would result in a fragmentation of the understanding. He valued the diversity of human experience and was appreciative of many examples of "historicist" scholarship, but was intellectually frustrated by inconsistencies among their conceptual schemes, whether explicit or implicit. For example, he cited the "striking methodological formulation of Ranke" that the task of the historian is to restate the past "wie es eigentlich gewesen ist", but then argued that this methodology "can scarcely be said to have created a school of theory in social matters – it rather issued in a negation of theory in general" (Parsons, 1937, p. 477).

Although Parsons' interpretations of the historicists are selective and misleading, his critique led to forceful conclusions. In his view, the historicist methodology yields congeries of knowledge that are totally relativistic, that is, framed in terms limited to given settings. These congeries might cumulate, permitting groups of specialized scholars to become cultivated in the materials of increasing numbers of epochs, civilizations, and various of their aspects – the art or politics of Greek and Roman antiquity, the religion and philosophy of classical China and India, the dynamism of the Renaissance, the class structure and upheaval of Revolutionary France, and so forth. However, an integrated and generalizing body of knowledge, which would allow for systematic comparisons across settings, would in principle be impossible in the historicist program, as Parsons construed it. Parsons believed that in demonstrating the indispensability of generalized concepts for any and all scholarship, Rickert (1986/1902) and Weber (1922) had articulated a definitive answer to the relativism of the historicists, particularly, in his view, Dilthey. Consistent with this understanding, Parsons emphasized the generalizing components of Weber's methodology and comparative studies. Where he criticized Weber, it was for the 'historicist' quality of certain ideal-typical constructs with their insufficient connections to generalizing concepts (Parsons, 1937, Chapter XVI; Parsons, 1947).

In adapting to the intellectual scene at Harvard, Parsons neither accepted nor rejected the predominant neo-classical economics. He saw in its abstract formulations an opportunity for theoretical integration with the Weberian analytic on which his own interests were based. In his view, neo-classical economics and Weberian theory shared an interest in generalizing concepts for integrating knowledge of large domains of human social life (Parsons, 1991/1928-29, Chapter 1; Parsons, 1937, Chapter XVI). Parsons was well aware that Weber had given a place to theories of marginal utility in his own schema for the analysis of economic institutions. Nevertheless, Weber's scheme and neo-classical marginal utility theories were based on radically different premises and categories of analysis. Parsons was sensitive to the implications of these differences. He understood that each theory stated essential insights into social and economic life and believed that both were necessary to substantive understanding. However, given his Kantian training, he saw that the categorial schemes of these two inconsistent and conflicting bodies of theory were random with respect to one another. Other scholars who were aware of this situation, such as Schumpeter (1934) and Frank Knight (1947), who had also translated Weber's *General Economic History*, 1950/1923, tended to accept neo-classical theory while bracketing the importance of German historical economics as background knowledge without direct theoretical application. But Parsons viewed this conflict between schemas as a crisis in social scientific knowledge. He formulated his intellectual problem as that of joining conceptual elements drawn from two schemes of different origins, focus, and scope. In this respect, he undertook early in his career to develop a framework more general than either the neo-classical economics or the Weberian theory.

As Camic (1991) has noted, Parsons in his early essays presented his larger task as an integration of the neo-classical and institutional perspectives. But it is also important to recognize that Parsons' ambition was even greater, and that it focused on the Weberian analytic. Indeed, his commitment to reworking the Weberian scheme preceded his later project of integrating elements from Marshall, Pareto, and Durkheim with Weber. One way to understand the convergence theory presented in

SSA is to view it as having evolved from Parsons' planned revision of Weber's historical and social-economic framework (Parsons, 1991).

In starting to develop a general framework, Parsons, with his neo-Kantian training, was cognizant of the underlying epistemological issues. Yet, he maintained that the social sciences with their empirical interests are not branches of philosophy, but disciplines of a different kind. The primary interests of the social sciences are in gaining knowledge of the phenomena of social life; the primary interest of epistemology is in clarifying the meaning and structure of such knowledge. Parsons thus did not turn directly to philosophical epistemologies, but sought a non-philosophical, though philosophically informed, foundation for social science.

He, therefore, sought models among practicing scientists engaged in advancing the knowledge of empirical disciplines. He did not adopt the view common among positivists that sociology, as a fledgling science, must follow in the paths of more highly developed sciences, e.g., physics, chemistry, or biology (Parsons, 1937, Chapter II). The differences in subject matter between the social and the natural sciences were in his view too great to admit of direct imitation, as was often proposed in his generation of scholars. Many positivists – for example, William Ogburn (1922) and later George Lundberg (1939) – argued that the social sciences could not develop until they had devised techniques of measurement comparable to those of physics. While not disputing the value of measurement, Parsons emphasized the *conceptual* sources of the coherence of the natural sciences even in matters of measurement. His Kantian studies had persuaded him that the most refined procedures of measurement could not by themselves yield an integrated body of knowledge. The content of sociology – motives, symbols, interpersonal relationships, cultural patterns, normative orders, appreciative standards, and so forth – requires radically different methods of observation and recording. As Weber, above all, had made clear to Parsons, the grasp of social phenomena requires methods of *Verstehen*, which often cannot be accommodated in procedures for the direct measurement of behavior (Weber, 1949/1922).

Parsons' understanding of the role of theory in the natural sciences was influenced in particular by the philosopher Alfred North Whitehead and the physiologist Lawrence J. Henderson, both senior figures at Harvard in the 'twenties' and 'thirties'. Whitehead and Henderson held independent views of the nature of science, but agreed on many points. Parsons began to assimilate their teachings several years before the publication of *SSA* and continued to use them, with modifications, to the end of his life. Although their views of the relationship between conceptual schemes and scientific facts was similar to the Kantian analysis, Whitehead in particular examined changes of conceptual schemes in historical perspective, thereby achieving a new understanding of processes of organization and reorganization of scientific knowledge.

Whitehead's influence on Parsons centered on the conception of a frame of reference. This idea was for Parsons the key element in Whitehead's treatment of the growth of science in *Science and the Modern World* (1925). Whitehead held that innovations in frames of reference are the most important source of creativity in science. The great innovators of science – Galileo, Copernicus, Kepler, Lavoisier, Newton, Darwin, Einstein – altered the ways of thinking in their fields by establishing new frames of reference. New frames of reference change kinds of abstraction and organization of facts, definitions of scientific problems, and hence issues to be addressed in the formulation of theories. Whitehead emphasized that the truly innovative frames of reference in the history of science have an organic character. Their conceptual elements have been intimately tied to one another to yield a theoretical unity. It is through this organic quality that scientists have been able to perceive relationships among varied empirical phenomena.

Newton's achievement, for example, was to place motions of everyday objects (the falling apple or the flying musket ball) and the motions of heavenly bodies (stars, planets, or comets) in one frame of reference where they could be explained by the same laws of motion. The formula $F=ma$ and Newton's other laws derive their general yet precise meanings from the underlying frame of reference that abstracts the qualities of mass, acceleration, and force from all physical bodies, heavenly or mundane. Without this new and sharply defined frame of reference, the laws of motion could not have been formulated. Once the Newtonian frame of reference had been established, many new fields in physics and chemistry emerged as areas of disciplined empirical investigation during the 17th, 18th, and 19th centuries. The reach of science, both empirically and theoretically, grew immensely through these developments. Yet, since one generalized frame of reference provided the foundation for physico-chemical science throughout this period, consistency with the Newtonian laws of motion became an overriding criterion of validity for contributions in all of the emerging specialties. The creative import of the Newtonian frame of reference lasted at least until the emergence of the new, still more generalized frame of reference that permitted formulation of the relativity theory. Part of the import of Einstein's achievement is that it displaced the Newtonian frame of reference as the conceptual foundation for all physical science.

From Whitehead's discussion, Parsons learned that frames of reference play a vital if often latent role in shaping the sciences (Parsons, 1937, 1961b). In their routine work, most scientists take their frames of reference for granted, presuming the truth of their premises and not questioning whether alternative ways of conceptualizing knowledge are possible. This tendency to take categories for granted is an element of what Kuhn (1970) calls "normal science". As Kuhn observed, there are advantages for the scientist investigating particular phenomena *not* to be distracted by questions about well established underlying premises and concepts. However, this is only the case once a workable frame of reference is in use. In the absence of an integrated frame of reference, coherent and determinate thought about the relationships among observed phenomena is never possible. Indeed, the very definition of the phenomena to be observed is ambiguous. Parsons found this insight consistent with Kant's epistemological analysis of Newtonian mechanics, even though Whitehead presented it in somewhat different terms.

Whitehead's discussion convinced Parsons that developing a frame of reference is necessary for a workable scientific discipline. A field that aspires to become a science yet proceeds to empirical studies without a coordinating categorical scheme is doomed to remain a non-science frustrated by intellectual anomie. As one such study after another is carried out, the practitioners of the discipline will eventually learn, Parsons believed, that the findings of these studies cannot be compared in precise ways and will never cumulate into an integrated body of knowledge. Despite the practical value of many of its empirical studies, the sociology he encountered in the 1920s and '30s was barren of the conceptual means to become an authentic scientific discipline. To move beyond its "pre-scientific" condition, sociology needed to clarify its characteristic modes of abstraction (Parsons, 1937, Chapter 1).

Clarifying modes of abstraction for the social sciences requires careful definition of the *distinctive* characteristics of social phenomena. Moreover, Parsons was convinced, sociology needed to develop sets of categories to synthesize these modes of abstraction into a coherent frame of reference. With the guidance of such a frame of reference, it would become possible for empirical studies to yield genuinely cumulative knowledge of social phenomena (*Ibid*). In arguing this point, Parsons did not dispute the necessity of better techniques of empirical observation and measurement. A developed science in his view requires its own empirical technology, typically embracing a variety of specific procedures (*Ibid*. See also, Parsons, 1986a). The effective development of such technology, however, requires a clear conception of the field of phenomena to be studied.

These insights into the conceptual requirements of scientific knowledge provided the guiding notion for *SSA* as well as for many of Parsons' later works. Sociological theory for him became a technical enterprise aiming at precise formulations even as it retained a very broad scope. His expectation was that other sociologists would use the results of his work as resources for their empirical investigations in many specialized fields. He fully acknowledged a division of labor among sociologists and did not expect that more than a small minority would engage in his sort of theoretical work. He offered the *SSA* to clarify sociology's orientation to social phenomena, guide its conceptualization of empirical studies, and facilitate its integration of research findings (Parsons, 1937, Chapter XIX).

A rarely appreciated implication of Parsons' methodological work concerns the role of the sociological theorist. Most sociologists had seen the theorist as a figure who states the broad conclusions of research, but Parsons emphasized the theorist's role in laying a groundwork for research. Theorists are specialists in developing the broad outlooks that orient research to its subject matter and provide technical evaluation of alternative conceptual schemes. The theorist's resources for making such evaluations consist in critical mastery of the various perspectives that have been developed in the history of sociology and related disciplines. Through critical readings of a broad range of conceptual materials, the theorist gains insight into the potential issues and findings of studies. It thus becomes possible for the theorist to construct propositions that will apply across a number of empirical domains or specialties and yet be supported by a common framework. The theorist creates conditions for researchers to work within a particular area with an expectation that their studies will have the support of other findings and have implications for other specialties.

Lawrence J. Henderson studied the physiology of blood and, through an interest in fatigue, had collaborated with Roethlisberger, Dixon, and Mayo in their studies of worker productivity (Mayo, 1933). He had also developed an interest in Pareto's sociology, both for its political conservatism and its general systems theory, with the parallels to his own ideas on homeostatic systems in physiology (Henderson, 1928, 1935). When Parsons began to study Pareto and develop interests in systems theory, intellectual exchange with Henderson followed.

Henderson espoused a methodological proposition that Parsons quickly found persuasive: a scientific fact is not a phenomenon, but a statement *about* phenomena in terms of a conceptual scheme (Henderson, 1932; Parsons, 1937, Chapter 1). Parsons likely noted an affinity with the Kantian theory of knowledge. But Henderson presented this conception of fact as a working scientist, not as a philosopher, and his achievements in the laboratory (e.g., Henderson, 1928) enhanced the idea's authority for Parsons. In Parsons' understanding, an implication of Henderson's conception is that a fact, as a statement, has two closely related aspects. First, a statement of fact refers to actual phenomena in the external world. When we claim a fact is valid, we are making a judgment based on methodical tests that the statement correctly characterizes some quality of the empirical world. It follows that facts in a science evolve with methodologies: what appears valid at one time may not pass scrutiny later (Parsons, 1937, Chapter 1; cf. Kuhn, 1970). Second, a fact is part of a body of knowledge, a larger set of statements from which it derives some of its meaning. Facticity does not derive directly from the phenomena of reference alone, but is embedded in concepts that guide observation, selection, and ordering of phenomena. These conceptual processes are prerequisite to any statement about the qualities of phenomena. In this sense, facts are never utterly concrete, but always abstractions from the empirical world (Parsons, 1937, Chapter 1).

A statement of fact is a mix of concept and observation; it cannot exist without either element. For Parsons, it was of paramount importance that the basic unit of scientific knowledge, the fact, cannot exist without a conceptual element. The most stringently empirical research cannot be conducted without the guidance of concepts. When concepts are made explicit and rationally ordered, the observational process can become systematized and focused. Without conceptual ordering, empirical research flounders, as if blind (*Ibid*; see also, Parsons, 1986a). To emphasize this dependence of empirical research on concepts, Parsons often said that "Facts cannot speak for themselves." Facts require a broader conceptual and theoretical context to shape their meaning and significance. This understanding of the nature of empirical science, fortified by Henderson's notion of fact, became the starting point for Parsons' social scientific methodology.

Henderson's emphasis on the conceptual element of empirical knowledge, for Parsons, complements Whitehead's treatment of frames of reference as the key source of progress in scientific knowledge. Parsons thus underscored that fruitful changes in concepts yield *new facts* as certainly as novel empirical observations. The *implications* of new concepts also generate scientific interest in finding new phenomena and creating new facts or even new domains of fact (Parsons, 1937, Chapter XIX). In later years, Parsons cited the "double helix" conception of DNA as an example. As soon as the double helix idea was formulated, molecular biologists grasped its potential for explaining how genetic materials replicate and investigations of many hitherto unimagined facts about gene systems were started. Forty odd years later, the domain of facts opened to research by this fundamental conceptual shift continues to expand vastly. The Mendelian genetics of the period before the pivotal Watson-Crick article now appears primitive. In citing the productivity of the Watson-Crick model, Parsons emphasized that previously impenetrable areas were opened to empirical investigations producing great riches of new fact.

From this methodological understanding of the importance of conceptual schemes, Parsons set out to explicate the set of concepts that can define social action as a unified field for disciplined investigation. Following Weber and other neo-Kantian methodologists, he believed from the outset that this field differs from the ones studied by physicists, chemists, biologists, and even behaviorists. He understood that human actors are physical entities, that action typically involves motion, that relationships among individuals require communication in physical media, and that institutions are generally embodied in material artifacts, ranging from buildings to written documents (Parsons, 1937 Chapters 2 and 19; Parsons, 1978, Chapter 15). Yet, he viewed social relationships and processes of social action as constituted essentially of meanings, in contrast to the material objects and relationships dealt with in the natural sciences. The study of these entities and relationships in a frame of reference that treats them sheerly (or even mainly) in material terms cannot produce knowledge of the properties of social action. If the *social* features of human conduct are to be captured, meaningful entities such as symbolic relationships, beliefs, motives, sentiments, expectations, and normative constraints must be placed at the center of the frame of reference (Parsons, 1937, Chapter, 19; Parsons and Shils, 1951b; Parsons, 1951, 1961a, 1964, 1967, 1977, 1978; Parsons and Platt, 1973).

Parsons' early insight into the differences between the social and natural sciences convinced him that sociology neither should nor could develop by substantive emulation of physics, chemistry, biology, and related disciplines. He made no claim to be offering a completed scheme for the study of meaningful social action – only to be outlining an elementary theoretical structure for synthesizing social action as an autonomous domain of facts. He knew that a well developed theory lay far in the future and would depend on the accumulation of a vast body of empirical research (Parsons, 1937, Chapter XIX).

Frames of Reference and Social Action

The epigraph of the *SSA* is a quotation from Max Weber that can be translated: "Every thoughtful reflection on the fundamental elements of meaningful human conduct is closely tied to the categories 'ends' and 'means'". This maxim encapsulated for Parsons the nature and purposes of the frame of reference he sought to formulate. *Meaningful human conduct is a master category*, the most general characterization of the domain of sociological study. Parsons committed himself to this overriding orientation consistently throughout his career. He also believed that Weber's proposition was entirely correct: all human action, everywhere and always, involves ends and means (Parsons, 1937, Chapter II, XVI, XVII), and they are irreducible elements of action. Where ends and means are absent, there is no true action, although there may be some form of passive human existence, "instinctual" behavior, or reflex devoid of meaning (Parsons, 1937, Chapter II). Ends and means are categories of universal application. The social scientist is well advised to seek out ends and means as part of studying any and all instances of human conduct.

Yet, Parsons was acutely aware that "ends" and "means" are only a partial formulation of a frame of reference. They are not a sufficient set of categories for a frame of reference because they are incapable of capturing many meaningful qualities of social action. Weber emphasized that relationships between "ends" and "means" permit representation of rationally planned action, but exclude from analysis features of traditional, affectual, or charismatic grounds of action (Weber, 1968/1925). He also argued that the demand to be rational cannot be explained in terms of a means-ends relation, but only by reference to a source of value and legitimation (*Ibid*). Rationality is a constituent of human social action, but its own foundation is not rational. The foundation of rationality consists of values that assert its importance and legitimacy. In brief, this is the analytic basis of Weber's famous thesis that economically rational capitalism and modern scientific vocations have their source in the religious ethic of ascetic Protestantism (Weber, 1930/1903-04).

Parsons believed that Weber's exposition of the action frame of reference, although far-reaching, did not yield an integrated scheme of categories (Parsons, 1937, Chapter XVII; Parsons, 1947). Weber developed many insightful concepts that capture particular qualities of social action. "Ends" and "means" were related to affectual, traditional, and charismatic sources of legitimacy, to ascetic and mystical orientations to the world, to corporate group, power and authority, types of bureaucracy, and patrimonial domination, to collegiality, and to class and status group, to mention only some of the categories (Weber, 1968/1925). Weber's categories are defined at many different levels of abstraction and related to one another in complicated, largely schematic, and only partly specified ways. They provide fruitful guidance for empirical studies in many sociological specialties, yet have not fostered unification of the discipline. Many scholars have been left in a quandary over how the categories may be organized. One consequence has been many divergent theoretical and methodological paths have been taken in the name of Weberian scholarship. The works of Reinhard Bendix (1960), Hans Gerth and C. Wright Mills (1953), Edward A. Shils (1975), and Wolfgang Schluchter (1989) reflect the scope of this divergence.

Weber's interests in comparative sociology led him to concentrate on the ways in which a distinctive category or set of categories can open up understanding of particular historical settings. Many of his discussions of categories end in lists of subtypes, some intended as general concepts, others applying only to narrowly defined historical conditions (Weber, 1968/1925, Part One). His discussion of subtypes of patrimonial authority – for instance, patriarchalism or sultanism – have this characteristic (*Ibid*, p. 231ff). These type categories were devised in part to analyze a limited range of historical epochs. Used only for this purpose, they could have no direct application to historical situations whose features are in contrast to the more general type. Patriarchalism and sultanism, for example, have only peripheral application in the study of modern, Western bureaucracies. Weber therefore incorporated his type concepts into more abstract sets of concepts, so that they would articulate with general theoretical frameworks. Sultanism, to continue with that example, is a form of patrimonial authority and stands in contrast with some other forms, but in common with all of them involves a pervasive tension between centralization and decentralization of the control of resources. In framing the category around this tension, Weber made the type of sultanism applicable not only to the authority systems of medieval Islam, but also to the dynamics of other centralized, absolutist political orders, including Moghul India or Imperial China (*Ibid*, p. 232; Weber, 1951, p. 138ff; Weber, 1958, p. 63ff).

Many of Weber's concepts are empirical types whose formulation depends on the scope of the institutions under examination. The number of these concepts and the relations among them are thus left open. Weber did not present his categories as logically exhaustive. The question of whether additional concepts are needed to analyze the domains to which they apply did not even arise as a matter of theoretical principle. In these respects, Weber's scheme appeared to Parsons as not fully developed and systematically organized (Parsons, 1937, Chapter XVI and Parsons, 1947). Parsons' epigraph on ends and means pointed not only to the ideal of generalized categories, but also to a shortcoming in Weber's treatment. When abstracted from his perceptive empirical discussions, Parsons argued, Weber's categories were only a partially ordered list, not a genuinely integrated framework. The fundamental difficulty lay less in the concepts and categories themselves than in the fragmentary structure of relationships among them.

Despite his immense respect for Weber, Parsons resolved early in his career to construct a more methodical scheme of basic categories. In his early writings, he deliberately sacrificed refinement and detail in elaborating concepts. Instead, he adopted a strategy of thoroughly and systematically justifying each category. He settled on a handful of categories and tried to demonstrate that each is universal and necessary to all well-formed sociological theory (Parsons, 1937, Chapters I, II, XVII, and XIX; Parsons, 1949b, preface to the second edition). His goal was to establish constant reference points for all theoretical work in the social sciences. At this juncture, certainty, clarity, and logical closure were paramount. Development of a richer, more refined theory was postponed (Parsons, 1986b\circa 1939).

Parsons' strategy in theory development can be clarified by comparing it to Weber's. Against the comparatively atheoretical historicist school, Weber used type concepts to organize his empirical studies and generalize their results. Because of this strategy, he was called an historian by the sociologists and a sociologist by the historians. The historical dimension was, indeed, of such importance that he assessed type concepts by their ability to capture and give meaning to historical materials. His strategy was thoroughly neo-Kantian, partly influenced by Rickert (*op. cit.*). Weber insisted that it is not possible to grasp historical materials without more general concepts; in particular it is not possible to compare "historical individuals" without sets of concepts for delineating contrasts. Parsons fully agreed with Weber on these points, but also asked how the concepts themselves can be organized into a larger scheme. Without methodical organization, concepts cannot carry stable significance or anchor the development of knowledge for an entire discipline (Parsons, 1937, Chapter XVI). Weber shifted the focus of historical knowledge from ever more specialized information about particular situations to type concepts that transform the information into organized understanding of historical individuals. Parsons' goal was to shift theoretical focus from developing and justifying particular concepts to *organizing* concepts into a single, coherent framework. His primary concern was to systematize categories of analysis to an extent and in a manner that Weber did not attempt. In this, Parsons followed a Whiteheadian as well as neo-Kantian agenda and sought to raise social scientific theory to a new level of generality, rigor, and coherence (Bershady, 1973; Lidz, 1986).

The Categories of Social Order I: The British Utilitarians

Parsons held that the historic "problem of order", as treated by Hobbes and his successors in British social thought, posed the most radical issue for social theory (Parsons, 1937, Chapter III), one more fundamental than any addressed by the philosophers of antiquity. The classical authors, e.g., Plato, Aristotle, Cicero, or Augustine, had concentrated on the qualities of authority and political order in the *polis*, republic, or church. Hobbes shifted attention to the ability of individuals to live with one another as members of civil society. Hobbes lived in times of revolution and feared radical political change. In *The Leviathan*, he proposed a way of recreating order in tumultuous times (Hobbes, 1928/1651). Unlike the ancients, he did not seek to revive an old order, but to impose a new one. Instead of reconstructing a traditional monarchy, he proposed creating an absolute ruler, the Leviathan. Fully acknowledging the difficulties of civil life under unrestrained authority, he claimed that subjects of the Leviathan would be thankful to reap the benefits of security.

For Hobbes, the key point is that individuals must choose either to live in society or to forego its protections. For Parsons, the key point is that Hobbes cut directly to the essential issue: he did not take social order in any form for granted, but treated it as the creature of human actors, requiring theoretical explanation (Parsons, 1937, Chapter III). He thus demonstrated that the ability of individuals to establish and maintain orderly relations is problematic for social theory as well as civil society. Parsons argued that this was a new starting point for social theory, placing all of modern social thought in Hobbes' debt (*Ibid*; Parsons, 1967, Chapter 6).

Since Hobbes, social order has been understood as not given with life itself, but as created and sustained through institutions and relationships. In whatever degree order is present or absent, it is a social fact that requires explanation. Order is a variable of social life, and to the extent it is absent, life becomes, in Hobbes' famous phrase, "solitary, poor, nasty, brutish, and short" (Hobbes, p.65; *cf.* Parsons, 1937, p.90). Without order, there is no society; with order, continuing social life comes into being, even if it is at times precarious. How social order is created, of what it consists, and how it can be explained are root questions (Parsons, 1937, Chapter III). Although Parsons saw the fundamental status of the problem of order, he was opposed to unrestrained authority of any kind and rejected the idea of the Leviathan.

Locke's theory of the social contract is often viewed as a more reasonable and less authoritarian solution to the problem of order. But Parsons adamantly reject it because, in explaining the assent of individuals to the creation and maintenance of civil society, Locke assumed a natural harmony of interests (*Ibid*). Locke's version of the social contract followed from principles of mutually understood advantage from exchange (Locke, 1924/1690). He gave the example of two Indians, in a state of nature in the wilds of America, who both benefit when they agree to exchange meat from a deer hunted by one for the fur of a beaver trapped by the other.

In portraying the social contract that established civil society as an elaborate exchange of this kind, Parsons argued, Locke actually evades the problem of social order. Unexplained is why the deer hunter does not advance his interest by taking the beaver fur through force or cunning; or, vice versa, why the trapper does not simply steal the deer meat. Similarly unexplained is why some actors do not seize dominant positions in civil society by imposing oppressive social contracts on others. The idea of a natural harmony of interests cannot address phenomena of oppression and inequality that are typically embedded in the foundations of social order (Parsons, 1937, Chapter III). Even though Locke's emphasis on civil society was closer to his own liberal outlook, Parsons considered Hobbes' treatment of the problem of order to be better formulated and more fruitful as a point of departure for social science.

In Parsons' estimation, Locke established the main foundation for utilitarian social thought, including most of British and American economic theory following Adam Smith (1937/1776). With partial exceptions of Ricardo and Marshall, Parsons held, the utilitarian tradition in economics reified Locke's idea of a natural harmony of interests in its understanding of the market. Utilitarians have emphasized the advantages accruing to civil society through workings of the 'invisible hand' of the market, while giving less attention to the market's dependence on such practical institutions as the law, formal organization, the authority of the state, and entrepreneurial subcultures (*Ibid*). Economic theory is often formulated in apparently universal terms, with little recognition of the few historical circumstances in which close approximations to a free and competitive market have existed. The growth of technical economics from Adam Smith to the 20th century was, Parsons argued, limited at nearly every point by a failure to address the problem of social order squarely (Parsons, 1937, Chapter IV; Parsons, 1991, Chapters 8, 16, 17, and 18). Even when figures such as John Stuart Mill commented on the workings of force and fraud in economic life, or conditions such as slavery, their observations remained residual to a theory of markets as the free interplay of independent interests (Parsons, 1961c, pp. 85-97). The market was consistently interpreted as a mechanism enabling different interests to serve one another rather than a social institution in its own right, embodying, like any other social institution, constraints and inequalities as well as freedoms.

Despite reservations about the reach of utilitarian thought, Parsons appreciated its concern to develop a theory of human relationships as on-going processes. The French and German schools by contrast were static in their portrayals of everyday social relationships (*Ibid*; Parsons, 1967, Chapter 6). Continental theories considered dynamic factors when comparing entire societies or analyzing how one historical epoch becomes transformed into another. But scholars whose thought was framed strictly in the French or German traditions did not examine the routine workings of social institutions or interpersonal relationships as dynamic matters. Marx (1976) was oriented to British as well as German and French thought, and thus is a major exception (*cf.* Parsons, 1937, pp. 488-495; Parsons, 1961c; Parsons, 1967, Chapter 6)

From study of neo-classical economics early in his career, Parsons came to value the process schema of utilitarian thought. However inadequate its understanding of social order, utilitarian theory framed the analysis of everyday relationships as a give and take of individual actors. Parsons resolved to include this focus in his own frame of reference (Parsons, 1937, Chapter XIX). As presented in *SSA*, *The Social System*, and in many later works, Parsons' theory always centered on dynamic processes of interaction and social relationships.

The Categories of Social Order II: The German School

In Parsons' view, the 18th century continental thinkers transformed the notions of the social contract that, for the British, had centered on issues of political order. This was apparent from his studies of the German Enlightenment and its 19th century aftermath. Kant was the key figure in this development. His teachings built upon Rousseau's recasting of the theory of social contract. But, whereas Rousseau (1950/1762) had elevated the General Will as a basis for resolving social and political conflict, Kant invoked duty to follow moral law as clarified by Reason (Kant, 1956/1788). In his notion of duty, Kant located the crucial dilemmas of community life in the moral conscience of the individual. His theory was individualistic in the sense that its stoicism called upon each individual to respond independently to the ethical imperative to act in the light of impersonal, universal, Reason. As compared to Rousseau's idea of the General Will, Kant's doctrine did not convey a strong sense of how individuals are constrained by the collective morality of their social milieu. Yet, Kant's historical understanding was more refined than Rousseau's in assessing the dependence of autonomous consciences on the cultural orders that determine the content of Reason, morality, and duty. There was in Kant's thought a constant tension between the actual world and the moral world of duty in the light of Reason (Kant, 1930/1781). Morality, for Kant, is the lever for betterment of the human condition.

Certain of Kant's successors further elevated the moral sphere to the central position in the coordination of human conduct and affairs (Windelband, 1892; Collingwood, 1956; Cassirer, 1950; Habermas, 1968; Gadamer, 1975; Schnadelbach, 1984). In Hegel's reaction to Kant's dualism, Reason and morality are absorbed in the Spirit (Geist), an all-encompassing concept that transcends several dichotomies that Kant had carefully maintained, namely, between subject and object, noumenal and phenomenal, religious and rational, the real and the ideal (Hegel, 1967/1807). For Hegel, human understanding and moral enlightenment will be joined and attain certitude and completion when, after a long historical process, they merge with the Absolute Spirit. Hegel's philosophy of history imparted a new orientation to historical studies, namely, to search out the forms assumed by the Spirit in different peoples, epochs, and institutions (Hegel, 1950/1831-32). Hegel had essayed, for example, the contributions of Greek antiquity to the development of the spirit, and the insights and intellectual coherence of his account spurred interest in understanding Hellenic culture's contributions to the civilization of the European peoples. Indeed, Hegel's philosophy spurred the emergence of history as a major academic undertaking first in Germany, with new methods of interpreting documents and artifacts and new areas of specialization.

The human studies arose in Germany through gradual refinement and differentiation of both Kantian and Hegelian concepts (Cassirer, 1950; Schnadelbach, 1984). Separate fields of philosophical, historical, political, aesthetic, philological, legal, economic, and theological scholarship, and various subtle mixtures of them, were created around different combinations of the notions of Reason, Spirit, morality and law, civil society, art, historical conditions, and Critique. These concepts became sufficiently structured in intellectual terms, increasingly distinct from religious, metaphysical, and philosophical underpinnings, that they could frame new academic disciplines. Yet, in the post-Hegelian setting, historical scholarship occupied the central position in human studies. History became the task of elucidating the Spirit in each of its embodiments – in archival documents, works of art, archeological remains, language, law, scientific knowledge, philosophy, or religion. Knowledge of the plenitude of the Spirit gained through the cumulation of methodical, reasoned scholarship was believed to cultivate the mental and moral capacities of scholars and readers (the educational ideal of *Bildung*) and thus to facilitate human progress. History framed in this light became itself an uplifting and civilizing endeavor shared by the educated community. For the generations following Hegel, the intellectual disciplines that investigated social institutions and their cultural products were predicated on an ideal of humanizing and elevating civilization, no longer, as for the British philosophers, on an effort to establish a given social order. Mundane subjects were invested with meaning and legitimated as topics of investigation, but their interpretation was mediated by the notion of Spirit and thereby raised to transcendental import (Gadamer, 1975). In this high-flown attitude, there was generally a lack of attention to the "merely" practical conditions of everyday social life. Despite its exalted status, academic scholarship in the German tradition developed a certain cloistered, other-worldly quality.

To be sure, the Hegelian legacy was not entirely unified. Among the left Hegelians, of whom the young Marx became the *enfant terrible*, the intellectual's duty came to be defined as criticizing all historical forms of the Spirit in order to elevate the human condition (Marx, 1964). All actual social life was understood as riddled with profanities that prevent realization of the human Spirit and potential. The ties to life and experience as they have heretofore been actualized must be opposed and overcome in order to point humanity toward its spiritual perfection. Such neo-Hegelian premises have animated the entire German Marxist tradition down to the Frankfurt School, including Adorno, Marcuse, and even its last authentic heir, Habermas (Jay, 1973). By contrast, the Hegelian trend that predominated in the universities tended to glorify the achievements of past civilizations and epochs and to rest content as expositors of those achievements. Their teachings frequently had a conservative cast and were tied to the socio-political regimes of their times. These scholars were often self-conscious of their roles as civil servants and educators of future generations of elevated status groups (Bendix, 1978; Krieger, 1957). Treitschke represents the nationalistic and xenophobic tendency of such scholarship, whereas Weber's teacher, Theodor Mommsen (1958), exemplifies the more rationalistic and scholarly potential of historicism. Recent great exponents of this historicist tradition of scholarship, committed to its rational potential, have been Eric Voegelin (1956-87) and Hans-Georg Gadamer (op. cit.).

The development of social and historical scholarship in Germanic countries brought animated controversies over method. Figures as diverse as Ranke, Droysen, Windelband, Dilthey, Simmel, Rickert, Weber, Troeltsch, Husserl, Meinecke, Scheler, Lukács, Heidegger, Mannheim, and Schutz entered the fray (Cassirer, 1950; Gadamer, *op. cit.*; Schnadelbach, *op. cit.*; Oakes, 1977, 1980, 1986). Their works are not truly interpretable without attention to the implicit and often explicit Kantian and Hegelian overtones. A product of the controversies was an explicit, refined methodology for interpreting historical events, artifacts, documents, figures, and cultural constructs that did not exist in the scholarship of other nations. The later contributions of Dilthey (1954/1904; 1989/1883; 1996) and Simmel (1977 and 1980), in particular, grounded these methods with a degree of philosophical sophistication that had no parallel in scholarship elsewhere. Today, this entire tradition of thought, conventionally referred to as hermeneutics, has affected scholarship throughout the West. Hermeneutic scholarship provides methods not only for understanding meanings created by actors, but also for understanding the subjective orientation of actors. In the light of this scholarship, actors are seen as bearing a personal cultivation and as connected to the culture and traditions of their times and places (Troeltsch, 1922). Their conduct is treated as a meaningful outcome of an interaction between the personal and the socio-cultural. Actors are viewed as inherently creative and unique individuals, yet engaged in conduct that is understandable to others. The hermeneutic method is an effort to clarify the ways in which actors are understandable to one another, and especially to scholars who study them (Gadamer, *op. cit.*).

Although sympathetic to much of German scholarship, Parsons, with his ascetic and pragmatic cast of mind, tended to distrust the hermeneutic dimensions of German historicist thought, which he thought too mystical and overly influenced by Hegel. Even when drawn into elements of the historicist tradition, as in his appreciation of Max Weber's *verstehende* methodology, his interpretations emphasized the neo-Kantian foundations and downplayed the hermeneutic influences (Parsons, 1937 and 1967, Chapters 2, 3, 5, and 6). Parsons did not, in fact, fully understand the methodological contributions of such figures as Dilthey, Simmel, and Troeltsch, whose works were significantly related to the problems of the historicist school.

The Categories of Social Order III: The French School

In trying to respond to the full range of sociological frameworks developed by the preceding generation, Parsons turned to Emile Durkheim as an exemplar of the French tradition (Parsons, 1937, Chapters VIII through XI). In Parsons' understanding, the key contribution of French thought was to portray social life as a reality *sui generis*, sustained through a coherent and collectively sanctioned moral order. From Montesquieu and Rousseau through Durkheim and the 20th century structuralists, French theorists have characterized social life as effective in constraining the individual's conduct (*Ibid*; 1967, Chapter 6). Such control is achieved through the workings of laws, informal morality, precepts of tradition, and sanctions of the sacred – in short, through normative order (Parsons, 1937, Chapters X and XI). The reality of collectivities, occupational groups, communities, social classes, nations, and entire civilizations emerged far more forcefully for French scholars than for English or German. As Parsons noted (1967, Chapter 6), even Marx first developed his sharp sense of the social reality of class from his study of French authors during his time in Paris.

The French contribution to *SSA* is mediated mostly through Durkheim. Because Durkheim was thoroughly steeped in French philosophy and social thought, however, Parsons' discussion of his writings in effect addresses characteristics of the whole tradition. Durkheim followed the thinkers of the French Enlightenment – Montesquieu, Diderot, Condorcet, Voltaire, and especially Rousseau – who espoused a collectivist Rationalism (Peyre, 1960; *Cf.* Lukes, 1972). The *philosophes* emphasized not the individual who acts in the light of Reason to advance self-interest, but the cultural standards of Reason that orient members of society collectively. For them, Reason became the touchstone for reworking society – a powerful solvent of old traditions and a ground for building new institutions (Cassirer, 1951; Gay, 1966). They also adapted the model of system embedded in Newton's mechanics to the understanding of society. Society was seen as a coherent entity whose parts are lawfully regulated and hence subject to manipulation in light of general laws (Gay, 1969). A major theme in the political thought of the *philosophes* was that Laws of Nature determine the ideal forms of the organization of society. Reason provides access to these Laws, enabling members of society to obtain authoritative guidance in reshaping institutions handed down by tradition. On this basis, the *philosophes* proposed reforms of law, politics, family relationships, agricultural practices, relations among social classes, community life, trade relationships, educational institutions, and, indeed, society as a whole.

The secular rationalism of the *philosophes*, tending toward radical reform or revolution, prompted a conservative reaction in defense of the Old Regime. As early as the late 17th century, Bishop Bossuet defended Catholic tradition, the social position of the Church, the monarchy, and privileges of aristocracy, including the entailment of land (Gay, *op. cit*.). Yet, the conservative ideology embraced a collectivist perspective no less than did the *philosophes*. Its argument for the Old Regime invoked the value of an established social order as a whole, legitimating each of its major institutions as necessary to maintenance of civilization. The tension between the two schools of thought came to a head in the Revolution, when Reason triumphed over Tradition and brought about what was both applauded and feared as a total overturn. In the aftermath of the Revolution, however, a conservative reaction articulated by Louis de Bonald and Joseph de Maistre initiated a more influential school of thought (Levy-Bruhl, 1924). Their conservativism benefited from official sponsorship down through the period of The Second Empire. Despite official disfavor, such figures as Saint Simon, Proudhon, and Comte revitalized the Revolutionary tradition in the form of positivism. The resulting dialectic between left and right ideologies brought social analysis to new prominence, perhaps especially in the writings of Tocqueville and later Comte (Aron, 1965). The reality of religion, law, normative orders, social classes, and not least collective sentiment in the make-up and functioning of society was illuminated in a way that had escaped English and German scholarship (Parsons, 1967, Chapter 6).

When Durkheim studied at the Ecole Normale during the early years of the Third Republic, most of the faculty were sympathetic to the liberal tradition of the Enlightenment, yet strived to define a ground for philosophical and social understanding independent of ideologies (Lukes, *op. cit*.; Peyre, *op. cit*.). The writings of Fustel de Coulanges, Durkheim's teacher in ancient history, partook of this effort, as did his neo-Kantian teachers in philosophy, Renouvier and Boutroux. When Durkheim began to think of himself as a sociologist, he also assimilated the views of Comte, despite his mentors' objection to use of a non-academic source. By amalgamating French neo-Kantianism with the social thought of the French left, Durkheim laid the foundation for academic sociology and anthropology in France. He emphasized methodology and logical demonstration and insisted that sociology be an empirical discipline (Durkheim, 1984 and 1950). From Renouvier, he adopted a view of academic inquiry as encompassing all of civilization. Transposed from philosophy to sociology, this outlook entailed a broadly comparative perspective. From Boutroux and Coulanges, he learned respect for the historical dimensions of the present, particularly the traditions of Western thought and institutions deriving from Classical antiquity (Durkheim, 1977). From Comte, he derived confidence that society is an autonomous milieu whose study is fatefully important for human betterment (Durkheim, 1984, p.23). With Rousseau, he stressed the moral dimensions of education and social reform, particularly secularization of educational institutions. He became an eloquent spokesman for the ideals of the Third Republic and won sponsorship from the Ministry of Education (Lukes, *op. cit.*). His talent as an academic politician enabled him to legitimate sociology's role in university curricula and create opportunities for his students (Clark, 1973).

The distinctive perspective of Durkheim's sociology is best apprehended through his concept of the collective conscience or consciousness. Better than any other concept in sociology, the collective conscience captures the central reality of moral-normative regulation of conduct and relationships (Parsons, 1937, Chapters X and XI; Parsons, 1978, Chapter 10; Wallwork, 1972; Bellah, 1973). The collective conscience highlights the social origin and import of moral belief and conviction. It stipulates the moral terms of every social relationship. It establishes normative standards for every aspect of social life and ensures that normative constraint affects all human judgment and human action. Durkheim emphasized the reality of the collective conscience in all of his work, noting its externality and constraining qualities in his early writings, its part in the shaping of social institutions in his middle period, and the intensity of collective sentiments in his last writings (Bellah: *op. cit.*). The central tenet of his teaching is that the collective conscience is the natural atmosphere of social life, and sociology must begin with the study of this atmosphere, its complex makeup, and its manifold effects. Every problem in the social sciences can be addressed with the concept of the collective conscience; collective consciences epitomize what Marcel Mauss (1954) later called "total social phenomena".

Parsons' critique of Durkheim fastened on implications of the concept of collective conscience (Parsons, 1937, Chapters VIII to XII). Although several implications emerged in the course of Durkheim's career, Parsons argued that a first and basic insight came with the analysis of the non-contractual or institutional elements of contract (*Ibid*, Chapter VIII) and the resulting radical critique of Spencer's theory of contract. Parsons held that, in demolishing the utilitarian premises of Spencer's theory, Durkheim established a radically different basis for understanding social relationships. He demonstrated that institutional regulation, such as that imposed by the legal system and the courts independently of any agreement, is necessary for any and all contractual relationships to be viable. If there were no institutional regulation, the terms of contracts could not be interpreted or enforced, and parties could not rely upon contracts to protect their interests. Moreover, third parties and the public also rely on institutional constraints on the types and scope of contracts to protect their interests. Contracts of employment must be limited so that they do not legitimize slavery and other degrading work situations or conspiracies against the public welfare. In sum, true contracts cannot exist without the institutional supports that Durkheim called the "noncontractual elements of contract". As Parsons insisted, these institutional factors fall outside the utilitarian frame of reference with its focus on self-interest and agreements reached through the reciprocal pursuit of interests. The utilitarian perspective leaves residual the fact that contracts are products of institutions. The freedom of contract that Spencer and others extolled can be achieved only through methodical reshaping of institutional constraints, not by their elimination. Eliminating such constraints yields a profound anomie, not a workable freedom (Durkheim, 1984).

In his early work, Durkheim analyzed the institutional structures that sustain solidarity in European industrial societies. These societies had undergone economic and social changes of previously unknown complexity and rapidity. Their stability and integrity were much in doubt (Durkheim, 1951). Durkheim followed Spencer in emphasizing the growth of social differentiation and, with it, "organic solidarity" constituted by the interdependence of differently specialized parts. Unlike Spencer, he argued that the interdependence of differentiated parts of society requires regulation by common institutions. He maintained that the solidarity among specialized parts arises not only from their practical interdependence, but also from their shared normative order. Just as contracts are not viable without non-contractual institutions, organic solidarity is not possible without a solidarity based on shared commitment to common rules of conduct, i.e., "mechanical solidarity" (Durkheim, 1984, Book I, Chapters II through VII). The more that a society's institutions share a commitment to common rules or normative orders, the more they are like one another and participate in mechanical solidarity. Durkheim acknowledged that organic solidarity had grown rapidly in European societies, but also insisted that the mechanical solidarity of shared commitment and sentiment is still an essential social force. The two aspects of solidarity are not in a zero-sum relationship; they often grow together and in coordination (Durkheim, 1984, Book III, Chapter I and Preface to the Second Edition).

In contrast to Spencer and the utilitarians, who believed that common structures evaporate before the forces of modern individualism, Durkheim placed at the core of sociological understanding the analysis of the normative orders on which the *reality* of mechanical solidarity depends. He held that organic solidarity and individualism are important features of modernity, but that they rest on cultural and normative foundations. Where Spencer wrote rapturously of individualism and individual freedom, Durkheim wrote soberly of the "cult of the individual", emphasizing that modern individualism entails religious-like beliefs supported by socially imposed obligations to respect individuals and to act individualistically (Durkheim, 1984,

Book II, Chapters III to V). Parsons saw in Durkheim's perception of Protestant communities as centers of the "cult of the individual" a parallel to Weber's emphasis on the Protestant ethic as a source of modern individualism (Parsons, 1937, pp. 710-714). For Parsons, this empirical insight opened a path to his analysis of the convergence in categories of thought between Weber and Durkheim.

Durkheim's discussion of the "cult of the individual" in modern societies reveals how both social and individual dimensions of human experience are shaped by normative culture. To fulfill their need to communicate with one another, individuals must share categories for coordinating their mental lives. The categories that organize the interior thoughts and feelings of individuals have their source in a collective conscience. The reality of the collective conscience can be felt in the sentiments of the individual, seen in the culturally patterned gestures of the body, and experienced in the interdictions that support rules of personal behavior (Durkheim, 1995, Introduction and Book One, Chapters Seven through Nine). This reality can be observed in everyday activities as well as in the aspirations, hopes, and principles that guide personal conduct over the life course. Durkheim's studies of education illuminate the crucial part played by the moral authority that teachers inculcate in their students (Durkheim, 1961). The content of an intellectual discipline cannot be conveyed until students have learned through the agency of the teacher to perceive and respect the methodical demands of knowledge. Once they have internalized, identified with, and mastered a discipline, they gain freedom in its use. Learning is in essence a moral endeavor for the student, as research is for the mature scholar.

Durkheim's recognition that social organization is a real entity independent of individuals gave society an objective status that opened new possibilities for comparative study. His comparative studies focused on the distinctive characteristics of each collective conscience in various societies and historical epochs (Durkheim, 1977; Bellah, 1973). He also sought to understand how normative orders are embodied in institutions that regulate everyday social relationships – religion, law, families, the professions, education, civil institutions, etc. – and how these institutions are affected when normative orders change. In *The Evolution of Pedagogical Thought in France* (1977), he analyzed several periods of cultural and moral transformation, including Greek antiquity, early Christianity, Medieval scholasticism, the Renaissance and Counter-Reformation, and the Enlightenment, that shaped the high culture and institutional order of modern France. While the immediate subjects of Durkheim's lectures were French pedagogical institutions, his underlying interest was the growth of a distinctive French society as a variant of European civilization. The heart of his analysis was an elucidation of the French collective conscience as it emerged through this series of cultural transformations.

The scope of Durkheim's comparative sociology is best appreciated by considering the writings of his protégés, who applied the same mode of analysis to other civilizations and epochs. Other than studies of aboriginal peoples of Australia and other tribal societies (Durkheim, 1995; Durkheim and Mauss, 1963), Durkheim's writings concentrated on France. However, his comparative perspective informed Granet's writings on China (Granet, 1934, 1958, 1975) Bougle's work on the Indian caste system (1971), Hubert's writings on the Celts (1966 and 1972), and Mauss's (Hubert and Mauss, 1964; Mauss, 1954; Mauss, 1972; Mauss, 1979) and later Dumezil's (1970), Levi-Strauss's (1969a, 1963a, 1963b, 1966), and Dumont's (1980, 1986) anthropological studies with a focus on the part of normative order in creating and sustaining social institutions. A similar focus is also evident in many of the great works of the contemporary French school of social and comparative history.

In *The Elementary Forms of the Religious Life*, Durkheim sought to explicate basic and universal forms of social life. He sought anthropological materials that would enable him to identify a social order comprised of, in essence, the panhuman elements of community. In early anthropological field reports from Australia (Spencer and Gillen, 1969/1904; Strehlow, 1907), he believed he had found peoples who were bearers of such an elementary way of life. His reanalysis of these reports demarcated fundamental components he believed present in every human society. While anthropologists have criticized his judgment that Australian aboriginal societies were simple (e.g., Stanner, 1963; Warner, 1964), Durkheim's primary interest was in identifying principles of social life that are as fully applicable to Parisians as to aborigines.

Durkheim proceeded along two related lines, analyzing both common beliefs and common practices or rituals. Of common beliefs, Durkheim emphasized the categories that give shape to the entire domain of shared culture (Durkheim, 1995, Introduction and Book I, Chapter I). In elementary societies, the categories of sacred and profane, with their many dimensions of contrast, provide the fundamental structure from whose terms normative order emerges (*Ibid*, Book II, Chapter VII and IX). In giving honor and respect to beliefs deemed sacred, members of society commit themselves to ideals, principles, and values that guide their conduct and relationships, and permit them to cooperate (*Ibid*). Everyday relationships and activities occur within the profane sphere where decisions are made on the basis of expediency or pragmatic rationality. But unless everyday activities are oriented to the sacred through a normative order, they lack concerted, enduring moral guidance. A major theme of *The Elementary Forms* is to elaborate the complexity of *even* an elementary system of sacred beliefs – of encompassing ideals that contrast, and yet also articulate, with the profane (*Ibid*, Conclusion).

Durkheim's treatment of the sacred also emphasizes its embodiment in social relationships through ritual practices (*Ibid*, Book III). The sacred is believed dangerous and all who enter its orbit unprepared are vulnerable to destruction, whether by illness, accident, storm, or vengeance of the offended. Ritual is a means of contacting the sacred in a prepared, controlled, and safe manner (*Ibid*, Book III, esp. Chapter V; *cf.* Stanner, 1963). Rites begin with a preparatory phase in which members of the community withdraw from the profane world and ready themselves for contact with the sacred and its dangers. In a central phase, the sacred parts of the ritual take place, often as dramatic embodiment of mythic events, as when Christian communion reenacts elements of the Last Supper. Ritual is then completed by acts that enable the participants to withdraw from the sacred and return without harm to the profane world.

Ritual forms are constituted around cycles of approach to, engagement with, and withdrawal from the sacred that Durkheim held to be a universal of "religion" (*Ibid*, Book III, Chapters III and V). These cycles represent the need to maintain the separation of the profane from the enormous power of the sacred. The central phase of ritual is the prototypical occasion when members of a community relate directly to symbols of deep beliefs and shared commitments. Ritual is thus a phenomenon of passion, enthusiasm, and shared sentiment, a way of showing respect for the awesome qualities of the sacred and all objects, persons, and ideals connected with it. Durkheim saw ritual as providing structure for participants, but also as an occasion for concentrated social creativity (*Ibid*, Book III, *passim*). All who participate in an authentic ritual process experience the creation and/or *re*creation of the social ideals and mutual commitments on which the solidarity of the community is founded. Among the aboriginal peoples of Australia, the annual ritual gatherings of many bands (*corrobboris*) were occasions of social renewal accompanied by the strongest feelings and sentiments (*Ibid*; *cf.* Stanner, 1963). At times they also produce radical social change when ritual innovation yields new beliefs, rules of conduct, and relationships of social solidarity. Durkheim likened such *corrobboris* to the French Revolution with its effects on all subsequent French history (1995, pp. 215-16).

Parsons (1937, Chapters X through XII) was attracted to the constancy as well as depth of Durkheim's analytic focus. Durkheim's framework captures the vitality of collective life and its immediate effects on members of society. He and his school – Mauss (1954, 1972, 1979a and b), Bougle (1971), Granet (1934, 1958, 1975), Hubert (1966, 1972), Davy (1922), Halbwachs (1958, 1980), and others – used this framework in many empirical studies that illuminate societal organization in different civilizations and historical epochs. In this respect, Durkheim's theory provided a more direct model than Weber's for Parsons' interest in achieving a universal and substantive theory. When Parsons turned to non-utilitarian solutions to the theoretical problem of order, it was Durkheim's critique of Spencer that provided the crucial guide toward a new conceptual scheme (Parsons, 1937, Chapters VIII, XII, and XVIII).

Parsons' formulations, however, were based on a methodology of analytical realism, which is in sharp contrast to Durkheim's social realism. Analytical realism maintains that aspects of reality can be captured authentically through carefully developed abstractions. Categories, hypotheses, and laws can reveal elements of reality, but can never capture reality as a whole. While Durkheim held that social knowledge is organized through categories, he also maintained that certain universal categories and practices – such as, the sacred and profane, rite, collective conscience, and sentiment – capture essences of social life. Concepts such as the collective conscience were intended to represent the fullness of the reality of the moral-normative life that exists in all societies. Parsons' conception of normative order is much more qualified. Durkheim's collective conscience weaves together qualities of sentiment, moral authority, bindingness, and solidarity that Parsons addressed separately through a complex series of analytic concepts. Parsons' analytical approach yielded a more refined theory of the institutionalization of normative order, but did not capture the integrated reality of the many qualities of normative order.

A Strategy for Integrating Social Knowledge

In *SSA*, Parsons argued that the 'problem of order' posed by Hobbes did not receive satisfactory resolution until the generation of social thinkers that included Weber, Durkheim, Pareto, and Marshall late in the 19th century. Only in the writings of that generation were there materials for an adequate foundation of social scientific thought. He presented the *SSA* as a consolidation and systematization of this foundation (Parsons, 1937, Chapter XIX). The core of Parsons' effort was to draw together the traditions of social thought that had led his predecessors to formulations that could resolve the problem of order. The principal themes of these different traditions, reviewed above, must be kept in mind in order to understand his synthesis.

In centering the discussion of *SSA* on Durkheim and Weber, Parsons faced a quandary. Both figures had backgrounds in Kantian teachings, but developed different methodological principles. Durkheim emphasized universal coordinates of social life as a basis for his categories of analysis. Weber, by contrast, believed that many concepts and levels of analysis are essential to sociological understanding. He did not exclude other perspectives and theories to the same degree as Durkheim, and he left his own concepts less systematized. Weber's methodology surpassed Durkheim's in the attention it gave to the orientation of the scholar, the ways in which the scholar's civilization, historical situation, social role, sense of scholarly duty, learning, and social and political values contribute to the formation of knowledge (Weber, 1922). Contrary to Durkheim's Comtean insistence on the primacy of sociology, Weber drew from many disciplines – economics, law, history, political science, religious studies, anthropology, and philology as well as sociology – in order to understand different aspects of social life. Far more than for Durkheim, social knowledge was for Weber relative to the particular scholarly apparatus that synthesizes it, even though he emphasized the universality of a schema of proof. Parsons found both outlooks compelling and was thus taking on a task of synthesizing elements of methodologies that, taken as wholes, are irreconcilable.

Parsons had the insight that Whitehead's contributions to methodology suggested a way of integrating Weber's and Durkheim's perspectives. In the *SSA*, and for the remainder of his life, Parsons called his methodology analytical realism and said that it derived from Whitehead (Parsons, 1937, p. 29ff; Parsons, 1977, Chapter 1; cf. Lidz, 1986; Wenzel, 1986). This methodology stressed the frame of reference as crucial for the creation of knowledge. Parsons understood in general terms the importance of empirical observation and procedures for validating factual knowledge. Yet, he emphasized that knowledge can be synthesized only within the terms, implicit or explicit, of a conceptual scheme. Moreover, without a well defined conceptual scheme, "empirical knowledge" cannot integrate the reality it tries to represent, but leaves it fragmented. The progress of a science toward more penetrating and comprehensive understanding depends critically on methodical elaboration of a central frame of reference. Parsons never suggested that this is the only element involved in scientific progress, but argued that it is essential.

Parsons held his methodology to be a kind of realism because it posits a knowable empirical reality. In the social sciences, the reality consists of meanings that have psychological, social, and cultural elements, whose actual qualities can be captured ever more fully by further development of the frame of reference (Parsons, 1949b, Preface). The methodology is also analytical in that the reality captured in a body of knowledge is always relative to a specific frame of reference. As he frequently said in his lectures and seminars, knowledge always captures only aspects of reality, not the reality of the world in its diffuse fullness. An analytical apparatus, a frame of reference, selects the aspects of the reality to be investigated and establishes the modes of abstraction in whose terms knowledge can be formulated. A frame of reference defines the parameters of the reality to be studied and how it can be studied. It may also define relationships with other forms of disciplined knowledge that address different aspects of the world and typically rest upon different techniques of investigation.

On this methodological foundation, Parsons set out to develop a new frame of reference. Adopting a Weberian term, he called it the frame of reference of social action. He thus signaled that his frame of reference would be broader than those proposed for sociology alone by Durkheim and others. He examined with some care, first at the end of the *SSA* (Chapter XIX) and then in a number of other writings (Parsons and Shils, 1951b; 1977, Chapter 1), the relationships between the frame of reference of social action and the conceptual schemes employed in other disciplines, ranging from economics to psychology to political science to anthropology. The main line of continuity in his work is the effort to elaborate, refine, extend, and critique this frame of reference.

The Problem of Order

As noted, Parsons regarded the Hobbesian problem of order as the root question for social thought. His focus on the 'problem of social order' is analogous to Kant's starting point for a theory of knowledge (Bershady, 1973). Kant observed that complexly ordered knowledge exists. His question was, how is such knowledge possible? Parsons observed that social life is ordered, not chaotic. He did not mean that social life is perfectly ordered, nor that it is equally ordered in all times and places. Hobbes had demonstrated that social order is problematic: an ordered society is no more intrinsic to human nature than the "war of each against every". The question for Parsons was: how is social order possible? The answer to this question, he believed, would provide the basis for formulating a master analytical scheme for understanding social life. Because the Hobbesian problem of social order is so radical, a correct solution to it should prove no less radical in its analytic and empirical implications.

Parsons first found a solution to the problem of order in Weber's demonstration that the whole complex of modern, Western, highly rationalized institutions had derived historically from the Calvinist religious ethic of inner-worldly asceticism (Parsons, 1937, Chapter XIV). Modern rationalism does not exist simply as a result of the aggregation of acts designed as rational by independent actors. It cannot be understood without attention to the underlying normative culture that has stressed methodical choices of ends and means. When people act rationally, whether in conducting a scientific study, budgeting expenditures for an organization, or assessing a proposed political policy, they typically do so because they are *obligated* to act rationally. Self-interest and rational calculation do not explain their conduct. Norms that embody a moral demand to be rational are essential to each of these situations. Weber did not address the theoretical implications of his argument directly at the level of universal elements of social action, but his typology of the orientations of action emphasized that *Zweckrationalitaet* (purposeful rationality) is never self-sufficient (Weber, 1968, p. 24ff). A purposefully rational orientation must be animated by a more fundamental mode of orientation, affectual, charismatic, or value-grounded (*Wertrationalitaet*). For Parsons, this formulation, in combination with the empirical findings of Weber's comparative studies, justified extremely broad conclusions about the indispensability of normative categories.

Weber's emphasis on religious ethics and Durkheim's emphasis on the legal frameworks of contract deeply sensitized Parsons to the importance of normative culture. In trying to systematize the implications of Weber's and Durkheim's inquiries, he focused on the conception of normative order and argued that the category of norms is necessary for understanding how actors choose ends and means appropriate to various situations. Norms are standards of conduct that transcend the interests and outlooks of any one person (Parsons, 1937, Chapter XVIII). They constrain the choices of ends and means for actors engaged in a common situation. More than this, the constraint of norms enables independent actors to coordinate with one another in their choices of ends and means. Norms establish certain standards of conduct as obligatory in all forms of relationship, whether exchange, domination, conflict, friendship, or others. Norms provide individuals with the grounds for defining expectations of the ends each may pursue as well as the means each may use to attain ends. Norms intrinsically involve judgments of right and wrong, and of legitimacy, justifiability, validity, propriety, and decency. These issues are universal to human conduct. Specific standards of conduct vary in indefinitely many ways by time, place, culture, and social setting. Yet, every human community comes to terms with these irreducible moral-normative problems (*Ibid*).

Like Weber and Durkheim, Parsons initially concentrated on analyzing rational types of action as social institutions – e.g., economic production, exchange, and investment, scientific investigation, legal procedure, and civil administration. All three took this tack in reaction to the positivism and utilitarianism that had long treated individual rational action as prototypal of human conduct. Once they had toppled positivistic and utilitarian explanations with their emphasis on norms, they were freed to examine non-rational areas of human activity. Instead of deprecating non-rational conduct as a vast domain of error and confusion, as had Comte (1875-77) and the positivists, they could perceive the dignity of religious beliefs or feelings, community sentiments, aesthetic appreciation of the arts, and love relationships.

Drawing on the works of Weber, Durkheim, and their schools, Parsons argued that the same *categories* of ends, means, and norms provide analytic access to non-rational as well as rational conduct (Parsons, 1937, Chapter XVIII). Even though the particular ends, means, and norms vary in substance by type of conduct, every kind of human action involves the same *categories* (*Ibid*, Chapter XIX). Parsons sharply attacked every effort to bifurcate human conduct into separate domains of the rational and the non-rational, one worthy of close study, the other beneath disciplined understanding (*Ibid*, Chapters II, V, and XIX; Parsons, 1951; 1964, *passim*; Parsons and Platt, 1973; Parsons, 1978, Chapters 10-12, 15). In Parsons' view, the immense variety of the non-rational forms of action had, before Weber and Durkheim, been left residual to social science, despite their observable prominence in social life.

The Action Frame of Reference

We are now in a position to understand the significance that Parsons saw in the dictum he quoted from Max Weber at the start of *SSA*: "Every thoughtful reflection on the fundamental elements of meaningful human conduct is closely bound up with the categories of 'end' and 'means'." Parsons sought to develop a set of categories that would have the fundamental and universal quality that Weber had attributed to ends and means. His aim was to formulate a specific set of concepts to serve as a frame of reference to guide the development of an entire social scientific theoretical system. Given the scope of his ambitions, the theory would necessarily be complicated and require an extended period to develop, but it would take shape within the analytical domain demarcated by the frame of reference and its categories.

The categories would also provide stable measures for evaluating alternative theoretical formulations (*cf.* Gould, 1981). They would facilitate appraisals of the strengths and weaknesses of specific theories, indicate how shortcomings might be overcome with particular revisions, and suggest how residual issues might be addressed. A stable frame of reference, Parsons believed, is necessary for determining which of a number of possible formulations might best contribute to the development of a unified theoretical system (Parsons, 1937, Chapter XIX; see also Parsons, 1961a).

Parsons' emphasis on categories follows from the methodology of analytical realism. The basis of all well formed empirical knowledge is a firm and constant mode of abstraction. A particular mode of abstraction can be stabilized only through clear and explicit concepts or categories. To accomplish stable abstraction, Parsons proposed a small set of categories to anchor the entire development of a theory of social action: ends, means, norms, and conditions. In doing so, he deliberately sacrificed refinement of the frame of reference in order to gain a certain and constant focus on essential characteristics of the social world. His primary claim was that each of the four categories is necessary to any adequate social theory (*Ibid*). He did not claim the list of categories to be exhaustive in the sense that no additional comparably necessary categories could or would be devised. Indeed, a few years later, he proposed additional categories and thus altered the frame of reference (Parsons, 1986/circa 1939).

In the *SSA* itself, Parsons attempted to incorporate the understanding of human action in the traditions represented by Weber, Durkheim, Pareto, and Marshall within an apparently simple, but carefully ordered, scheme of concepts. No one had previously thought to conceptualize social action in this manner, and the multidimensional depth of his framework has a subtlety that is still not widely appreciated. Parsons endeavored to construct nothing less than the *ground* of all possible valid theories of human conduct. Aware that he had not captured all characteristics of social action in this early formulation, he emphasized that it was still preliminary and schematic. He maintained that this first categorical set did *not* constitute a substantive theory, only a foundation for a future theory (Parsons, 1937, Chapter XIX). His main concern was to establish a general frame of reference that could accommodate and integrate an indefinitely wide range of theoretical formulations addressing problems across the entire range of the social sciences. Yet, he argued that each of four categories is universal to and necessary for empirical knowledge of the social world. Critics have depreciated the schema by treating it as a simplistic theory. And, of course, if four variables were the sum and substance of a theory, the scheme would be utterly simplistic. What critics have not perceived is the logically *pretheoretical* status of Parsons' scheme (Bershady, 1973).

Although Parsons did not aim to develop a substantive theory in the *SSA*, he attended to the empirical implications of his categories. He methodically surveyed the empirical evidence for Pareto's, Durkheim's, and Weber's theories (Parsons, 1937, Chapters VII, VIII-XI, and XIV-XV). His hundreds of pages of discussion of these materials – in quantity most of the book – demonstrated the indispensability of each of the categories he had adopted from his predecessors. He was clear about his purposes and noted their scientific limitations as well as insisting on their critical importance for the progress of sociological research.

The Categories

Parsons argued that every instance of social action is structured by four kinds of elements: ends, means, norms, and conditions. Without all four, there is no true action; wherever there is action, all four must be present. But each element is stated as a general concept, which may be concretized in indefinitely many ways. From Parsons' historical and sociological reading, he was aware of the vast diversity among the actual elements that have structured social action in different times, places, cultures, and epochs. He used the term categories to underscore the highly generalized way in which he conceptualized the basic elements of action.

Ends

Ends is a category that Parsons took over from utilitarianism and the metatheory underlying neo-classical economics (Parsons, 1937, Chapters II and III). As a category, ends represent a traditional theme in social thought, and well before the *SSA* were accepted across a wide range of 'rationalistic' orientations in economics, political science, and sociology, such as that of Max Weber. Yet, as Parsons observed, the anti-intellectualistic orientations in social science, especially the behaviorist psychology of Watson and later Skinner (1938), assimilated ends to 'mere' conditions of action (see Parsons, 1937, p. 79ff). In opposing the scientism of anti-intellectual orientations, he emphasized the importance of the purposive quality of social action. Parsons portrayed the actor as striving to achieve goals that serve to orient his or her conduct. Whether the actor is aware of these goals, takes them for granted, or positively represses them from consciousness is variable. The actor, nevertheless, has intentions. Without an intention, explicit or implicit, the individual's movement is automatic, not truly action. Breathing and digestion are generally such automatic processes, and in Parsons' treatment they stand outside of action. The category of ends thus demarcates a boundary between action and mere behavior. Parsons was adamant that action, not behavior, was the crucial empirical domain for understanding the organization and operations of society, institutions, and everyday social relationships (Parsons, 1937, 1986/circa 1939, 1951, 1961a, 1978, Chapter 15).

Ends refer to desired states of the relationship between actor and situation or environment (Parsons, 1937, 1951, 1961a, Parsons and Platt, 1973). An end represents for the actor some change in his or her relationship to the setting. With an end in mind, an actor is able to mobilize energy and resources to achieve this change. Without an end, the actor has no criterion for selecting means and his or her conduct becomes undirected. The behavior then lacks the intentionality essential to action. Parsons insisted that goal-direction is a distinctive quality of action and ends can be identified in every instance of social action.

The ends that motivate an actor are not always simple and obvious. Actors pursue many ends in the course of their daily routines. In given settings, they may pursue a number of ends simultaneously. A person at dinner may want to satisfy his or her hunger and also enjoy eating fine food, being present in an attractive restaurant, being seen in a prestigious place, and meanwhile engaging in lively conversation. Such a person will make choices to satisfy each of these goals, and their interconnection may become apparent in the decision-making, for example, if a restaurant with excellent food is too noisy for good conversation, lacks ambience, or is in a neighborhood that lacks prestige. Goals may differ in the scope of the intended changes in an actor's relations with his or her settings, in the number of other actors involved in their pursuit, and in the length of time projected for their attainment. The policies of a nation-state often entail goals that require the coordination of vast resources, the engagement of many citizens, and years or decades to accomplish (Parsons, 1969, Chapter 13). Many subordinate goals may have to be established and appropriate hierarchies maintained among them. Courses of action are taken to achieve subordinate goals, but their larger significance is to facilitate reaching the primary goal. An entire regiment may provide logistical support in a battle as a step toward winning a war, and a particular soldier's goal may simply be to drive a truck from Point A to Point B.

The crux of Parsons' rejection of behaviorism was that it assimilates the ends of action into the conditioning forces of the environment. In doing so, behaviorism portrays the individual and the process of behavior in truncated, passive terms. The individual is conceived as incapable of directing his or her own conduct and changing his or her relationship to the environment. Behaviorism also represents the individual as lacking in the judgment to choose among goals and courses of conduct; the "actor" is a result of conditioning processes to which he or she responds in a rigidly determined fashion.

Parsons also dissented from versions of positivism that make opposite assumptions about ends. Following Halevy (1960/1901-1904), he argued that, while utilitarian positivism emphasizes the importance of ends, it gives no account of their organization. The utilitarian positivists do not address the consistency of the various ends of a given actor across time, place, and social situation. Moreover, utilitarians lack the terms to investigate whether the ends of persons who interact as members of the same community are meaningfully related. Given their view of actors as able to make choices, and as potentially effective in changing social situations, utilitarians' conception of ends as without organization (or random) precipitates, Parsons argued, the theoretical problem of order (Parsons, 1937, Chapter III). Actors who are effective but whose ends are not organized will necessarily be uncoordinated and potentially in conflict. Not only will their conduct be uncoordinated, but so too will their relationships, and with disastrous consequences. Parsons, like Halevy, held the utilitarian actor to be a theoretical fiction because neither persons nor communities can exist without ordering of ends.

Parsons' analysis thus led him to examine the ordering of ends. He emphasized that ends are developed in a context of constraints, which are principally normative (Parsons, 1937, Chapter IX). Normative constraints entail standards for judging which ends are permissible and which are preferable (*Ibid*, Chapter X). They provide standards of choice that establish priorities among ends and thus transcend specific ends. They work to coordinate ends among independent actors, groups, institutions, and whole communities (*Ibid*, Chapter XIV and XV). The goals of actors typically reflect broad normative orders of the social systems in which they are involved, even entire societies. Yet, goals are not reducible to normative order. Although shaped by norms, ends relate to the changing settings and life-circumstances that actors encounter in their practical activities (*Ibid*, Chapter VXII and XIX).

Goals are particular to individuals and groups in a way that norms are not. However, actors cannot always state their ends. An actor's goals in a given situation may be part of a hierarchy of goals that pertain to many activities over extended periods. A goal may be shared with others and pursued over a variety of situations and relationships (Parsons, 1951 and 1964). Goals may shift in salience from situation to situation in the flow of an actor's routines. Awareness of goals typically fluctuates as an actor moves from one situation to the next. There are times when any actor is uncertain of the ends of his or her on-going conduct. An individual may become aware only in retrospect of goals (or elements of them) that he or she had actually pursued at some past time.

In Parsons' later work, goals are discussed in relation to the broad problem of motivation. He observed that for specific goals to be pursued in a sustained way, they must have a steady place in an actor's system of motivation (Parsons, 1951, Chapter VI). Energy is allocated among the various goals that an actor pursues in the many settings in which he or she is involved. Motivational energy must be organized in some degree or the actor's conduct will lack direction and continuity. Following the lead of Weber (Weber, 1930) and Schumpeter (1934; 1950), he took particular interest in motivation for entrepreneurial innovation. In the cultural context of modern capitalism, many actors value the 'bold spirit' of the entrepreneur and attribute transcendental significance to success in business. Such actors often allocate extraordinary personal energy to business enterprise and work vigorously to attain monetary success. A huge number of specific ends derive significance over a person's career from the overarching goal of success in business. The energy that a successful entrepreneur expends to attain specific ends depends largely on the value that his or her motivational system attaches to the overarching goal (*cf.* Parsons' discussion of the so-called profit motive in 1951, pp. 243-248). But however great the actor's reserves of energy, they are not endless. The concentration of energy on the goal of success in business typically reduces energies available to other activities. It is often noted that, compared to others, successful entrepreneurs have little time for family, friends, community activities, and artistic appreciation (Parsons and Bales, 1955, Chapter 1). Similar observations are made about 'driven' professionals. To be sure, despite the emphasis on entrepreneurship in modern capitalist societies, many individuals remain motivationally averse to taking risks and avoid roles in which they must exercise leadership or place their capital in jeopardy.

To sustain goals over time, Parsons emphasized, requires institutional supports. For the modern entrepreneur, the business corporation typically offers a "ladder" of entrepreneurial roles with progressively greater responsibilities and rewards (Parsons, 1951, *loc. cit.*). The corporation provides many of the means of institutional success: a fund of capital, a trained work force, entrepreneurial colleagues, and established modes of production (Parsons and Smelser, 1956). The entrepreneur who works in the corporation, moreover, may gain respect from family, church, civic and community associations in addition to coworkers who directly share his or her goals. The motivation to pursue difficult goals is strengthened when supportive values and norms are widely shared. Under such conditions, the motivation itself becomes a routinely available resource of the community and entrepreneurship becomes widespread (*Ibid*; Parsons, 1971, Chapters Five and Six). Parsons contrasted the modern economy in which entrepreneurship is rather ordinary with early capitalism in which only exceptionally motivated individuals became entrepreneurs (*Ibid*). He concluded that "the institutional integration of motivation" – not simply the motives of individuals – generates and stabilizes socially valued goals (Parsons, 1951, Chapter VI and VII).

Parsons' treatment of ends and motivational structures must be distinguished from the conception of objective interests that has figured in a number of social scientific theories, including those of Marx, Weber, and Mannheim (Marx, 1976/1867; Weber, 1968, vol. 1; Mannheim, 1936/1929). The idea of objective interests is that certain social positions, independent of their actual incumbents, entail the pursuit of particular ends as practical necessity. Capitalist employers use a variety of measures to hold down labor costs. One can attribute the goal of holding down labor costs to the *position* of capitalist employer independent of whatever individuals occupy that position and regardless of their actual motives. Marx warned against reducing the objective interests attaching to the role of capitalist to the personal motives of individual capitalists (*Ibid*). As his concept of the "institutional integration of motivation" makes clear, Parsons understood that the interests of actors are affected, though not determined, by objective social constraints. However, he did not adopt the conception of objective interests as a key to understanding the motives of actors. Rather, his concern was to understand the subjective motivations of actors within the context of often complicated social constraints.

A crucial issue of Parsons' schema concerns the interpretation of the subjective ends of the actor. The observer/analyst requires a method for understanding the subjective motivation of the actual persons under study. Weber's method of *Verstehen* is thus built directly into basic elements of the theory of action. Although Parsons never attempted to go beyond Weber's formulations of the *verstehende* method, a number of his students, including Garfinkel (1967), Geertz (1973), Bellah (1970, 1975, 1983) Fox (1959, 1979, 1994), Lidz (1979, 1981, and 1984), and others, have addressed issues of social or interpersonal interpretation.

Means

Like ends, Parsons adapted the category of means from utilitarian thought. He agreed with the utilitarian conception that means are simply things that can be used to attain ends. Any object or service can function as means if viewed by some actor as a resource for attaining some end or ends. Actual means differ in number and scope of ends that can be attained through their use. Some objects (money in particular) can be used to acquire a vast range of concrete resources for use as means to a variety of ends. Given the wide range of ends that actors typically pursue, they invariably experience the means available to them as insufficient to achieve *all* of their ends. Not only are means scarce for all actors, but all actors perceive them to be such. Scarcity of means is a universal of social life. All actors must decide how to allocate the scarce means they control among their ends. As Adam Smith (1937/1776) and his followers since the 18th century have argued, economic markets foster the rational allocation of resources among ends. But as Durkheim (1984/1893) and his school observed, not all means to all ends can be made available through the market without offending crucial human values.

Critics of the utilitarians, notably Marx (1964, 1973/1857-58, 1976/1867), have emphasized that markets, as allocative mechanisms, are affected by the reality that some actors control greater means than others. To understand a society's allocative processes, actors must be stratified or classed by types and amounts of means (wealth, knowledge, prestige) they control. All historical societies have had classes and status groups whose relations are based substantially on differential control of resources. Radical changes in relations among classes or status groups precipitate vast changes in the uses of resources and the ends that may be achieved. Structural change in a system of social action affects the relations of means to ends (*cf.* Weber, 1968/1925).

The utilitarian perspective emphasizes that creation of new means expands human capabilities for achieving ends. Since the time of Adam Smith, to understand the Industrial Revolution has been a major concern of utilitarian thinkers. They have argued that a vast growth of resources benefits actors who control the new means. Smith's topic, however, was the wealth of nations, not specific social classes, and he emphasized that under certain conditions, society as a whole benefits. Many points of view have informed debates over the social conditions under which not only 'capitalist classes' but a broader range of groups may or may not benefit. Parsons participated in some of these debates (Parsons, 1960, 1969). His discussion of Weber's writings in *SSA* shows the importance he attributed to these issues from early in his career and the complexity of the factors he believed necessary to explain growth in economic production.

Parsons' begins his discussion of means and ends by recognizing that the status of entities as ends or as means depends on actors' relations to them (Parsons, 1937, Chapters II through IV and XVIII). For the art lover who purchases a painting to enjoy its aesthetic values, the money so used is a means; for the dealer who sells the painting, the money received is an end and the painting merely a means. Yet, the dealer, too, may understand and appreciate the painting's aesthetic values and, in other contexts, regard it as an end. Ends and means are always relative to situated plans of action. Parsons concluded, more radically than any of his predecessors, even Weber, that means and ends are analytic categories. In the *SSA*, the distinction between ends and means is *not* a result of concrete classification. No entity is either end or means except in relation to a situation and course of action. Only in relation to a projected course of action does an entity become end or means, and then its status may change with the plan of action. The art lover may die and his heirs may market his prized painting for mere cash.

With this relativistic conception of ends and means, Parsons quickly saw that there are many modes of evaluating both ends and means. From Smith to the neoclassical economists, utilitarians had construed utility as the fundamental principle for evaluating the relationship of means to ends (Samuelson, 1973) and tended to treat all other principles as residual. Means were evaluated in terms of utility, cost, and efficiency for attaining specific ends. In contemporary sociology, rational choice theorists (James S. Coleman, 1990, for example) construe social relationships as means by which actors try to maximize their own advantage or satisfaction. This conception portrays social relations as analogous to the utilities that economic actors aim to maximize in the neo-classical theory. Like neoclassical economics, rational choice theory reduces important qualities of social phenomena to 'mere' means, and thus significant aspects of social facts (ends, norms, values, affect, sentiment) become residual to theoretical reflection.

The French school of positivism, as noted, considered Reason to be the fundamental and universal principle of evaluation. This orientation did not yield the technical apparatus of utilitarian economics or even the pleasure-pain calculus of Bentham's (1948/1780) utilitarian political theory. From Rousseau (1950/1755) to Comte (1875-77), however, Reason proved a powerful solvent of traditional social relationships. All social institutions became mere means to be altered as deemed necessary to achieve rational human order. This was a truly revolutionary idea, and through the influence of Rousseau reverberates even in contemporary thought, particularly Marxism.

Although positivism is a diverse intellectual movement, both the British utilitarians and French rationalists conceived the ends and means of social action rigidly. The utilitarian positivists ignored other principles that relate means to ends, such as, passion, social solidarity, beauty, tradition, or the sacred. The rationalistic positivists considered these principles, but absorbed them into a single standard, Reason, for ordering means to ends. In both frameworks, the empirical variability of relations between ends and means in social life was left residual *(cf.* Parsons, 1967, Chapter 6). By contrast with both forms of positivism, Parsons proposed that ends and means are related along many dimensions of evaluation, not simply the dimensions of utility, economic value, efficiency, personal advantage, Reason, or, indeed, Science. His analysis of the limitations in the treatment of ends and means in both traditions of positivism led him to attempt a more abstract and generalized conception. He thus developed a conception of means and ends as analytic categories rather than concrete entities. This conception enabled empirical investigation to encompass the full *variability* of means and ends relations that can be observed in social situations (Parsons, 1937, Chapter XVIII). He held that a theory of social action must address all such variability, not reify any particular mode of relationship between means and ends.

Parsons' understanding of the relation of means to ends opened a variety of issues to empirical investigation. With Weber, he saw that means-ends relationships differ radically from one society or historical epoch to the next (Parsons, 1937, Chapters XIV and XV). For example, differences between Medieval Catholicism and post-Reformation Protestantism in the *means* of obtaining a conviction of one's salvation are differences between sacraments and hard work. Although rooted in theological issues, these differences affected common beliefs about the significance of everyday work as means. Parsons could then ask how such differences in means-ends relationships occur and how they evolve over time (*Ibid*). He could further observe, with Weber and Marx, that control of means is unevenly distributed among members of society, as are ends pursued (1954, Chapter XV). His later analytical theory of social stratification emphasized the differential control and uses of means – including wealth, power, knowledge and expertise, and personal influence – among status groups (Parsons, 1954, Chapter XIX; Parsons, 1969).

His analytical rather than concrete treatment raises the question of how the relations of means to ends are regulated. In his theory, there is no intrinsic structure to the relationship between the two, as utilitarians had postulated for utility and rational positivists for Reason. In Parsons' theory, many principles provide regulation, but each does so only in certain classes of situation. The resulting theoretical questions are: what is the ordering among the many principles? What prevents, or at least limits, conflict among them? This is where Parsons confronts the Hobbesian problem of social order in its analytically elemental form. His introduction of the category of norms addresses the potential for disorder in the relation of means to ends.

Norms

By including norms in his categorial scheme, Parsons diverged sharply from his utilitarian predecessors, in whose thinking norms are at the farthest remove. The direct source for his treating norms as a basic constituent of social life was Durkheim's critique of Spencer and the utilitarian tradition. Weber's writings on comparative social institutions were a key background. The crux of Parsons' convergence argument is that Durkheim and Weber both demonstrated normative orders to be essential to any and all social life. This part of the convergence argument concerns specifically (and only!) the abstract level of categories, and is focused on one essential point: norms are among the categories necessary for understanding social action.

In his treatment of norms, Parsons brought Durkheim and Weber's analyses to a new logical point. Both had empirically showed the ubiquity and importance of normative elements in social life, but neither had formulated norms as a category at the level of generality that Parsons was proposing. Parsons' proposal revealed the force of Durkheim's and Weber's arguments in breaking through utilitarian and positivist frameworks. The resulting conceptual scheme was designed to make the empirical variability of ends and means accessible to social scientific understanding – across civilizations, historical epochs, religious movements, social classes, etc.

Following Halevy (1960/1901-04), Parsons held that the utilitarians treated ends as random, varying from actor to actor in an arbitrary and unexplained manner. Utilitarian explanations addressed causes and empirical patternings of ends simply through narrative histories. Given their individualistic premises, utilitarians could not in principle address the ways in which the ends of one actor relate to the ends of other actors in the same situation (Parsons, 1937, Chapter II, particularly Note B; Chapter XVIII).

The basic shortcoming of utilitarian thought, Parsons argued, is an inability to resolve the 'problem of social order'. The utilitarian discussions are in principle limited by their focus on the rational use of means by actors whose ends are treated as given. In the utilitarian view, an actor can exchange means with others or use others as means to his or her own ends, but such decisions are postulated to be acts of individuals. There is no clear recognition of shared standards or constraints, including law and tradition, that shape selections of ends by all actors in a situation (Parsons, 1937, Chapter III).

Law, tradition, and other shared sources of ends vary empirically by community, class, religion, and historical epoch. An adequate solution of the problem of social order requires a frame of reference that explicitly directs investigation to empirical relationships between the ends of actors and the normative patterning of those ends. Social scientific categories must guide empirical study to relationships among ends, means, and norms. The theorist's task is to formulate possible relations among these entities and explain particular social orders in this multidimensional framework. The workings of the economic market, power and authority, class and status cannot be explained simply in terms of individualistic pursuit of self-interest and rational choices of means. Any and all social relationships are patterned by normative institutions as well as by means and ends, and hence require description, analysis, and explanation in these terms.

In *SSA*, Parsons cast norms as a summary category pointing to a large and diverse domain. His discussion of Weber in particular makes clear that he understood much of the complexity of normative domains (Parsons, 1937, Chapters XIV, XV, and XVII). He was aware of Weber's distinction between the evaluative and rule components of norms. He understood that complex societies need extensive, highly organized systems of norms, including religious belief systems, legal systems, and specialized structures, such as codes of professional ethics. He also appreciated that there are many informal norms, such as standards of etiquette, that regulate everyday interaction. By setting aside many of the complexities, and representing the entire normative domain with one category, Parsons defined norms on the same level of generality as ends and means, in essence adding an element to Weber's motto about ends and means. He thus included norms along with ends and means in a radical revision of the process framework that the utilitarians had developed. In this revised framework, the *process* of social action involves, as for utilitarians, choosing means to pursue ends, *but* choices of both ends and means are limited by norms that actors are morally compelled to observe (Parsons, Chapter XIX).

Although Parsons drew heavily on Weber and Durkheim to establish the category of norms, his scheme in the *SSA* preserved qualities of the utilitarian process analysis. The secondary literature has emphasized Parsons' radical differences from utilitarian theory, but his scheme also differs sharply from French structuralism and German idealism/historicism. The French tradition from at least Rousseau's concept of the General Will through Comte and Durkheim down to 20th century structuralism and post-structuralism concentrates on analyzing the principles that determine relationships in society. The structuralist tradition has generally treated issues of process as residual. Structuralists have even implied that once structural principles are determined, there is no need to address process (see, for example, Levi-Strauss, 1969a/1949, 1963a, 1963b, 1966) and the attention of Anglo-American social scientists to choices of means and ends is a waste of energy. A frame of reference that focuses on norms as well as ends and means is, to the structural rigorist, a distraction.

Scholars in the German idealistic-historicist tradition since Kant have, like Parsons, endeavored to clarify patterns of meaning. Their conceptual schemes have focused on explication of the cultural orientations (*Geist*, spirit or ethos) of peoples or epochs, treated as "historical individuals". In their premises, cultural orientations of such historical individuals guide the judgment of persons whose conduct is largely shaped by their consciences. Analysis thus concentrates on the normative guidance of conscience, not on such practical and material matters as situated choices of ends and means. In this approach, the notion of situation and the process of interaction are entirely residual. The emphasis on explicating moral orientations of *Geist* or *Kultur* in a particular historical individual depreciates, or even precludes, the task of constructing a generalized schema applying to all epochs and societies (Parsons, 1937, Chapter XIII). While Parsons' understanding of norms was informed by the idealistic-historicist perspective, his schema retained the notions of situation, social interaction, and choice of ends and means from the utilitarian process framework.

In contrast to utilitarianism, structuralism, and idealism/historicism, Parsons conceptualized norms as an analytic category that refers to an indefinite number and variety of actual elements of normative orders, not to any actual concrete norms or normative orders. Conceiving norms in this way, Parsons refrained from endorsing or privileging any particular normative content. His categorial scheme stipulates that normative contents operate in every instance of social action. The scheme leads the investigator to determine what normative elements are active in the situation under study and how they affect conduct. In this respect, the analytical category of norms points to a real element *constitutive* of social life and action. Parsons' basic premise is that without the presence of a normative element, there can be no ongoing social action. As with the categories of ends and means, norms are presented in the mode of Whiteheadian analytical realism.

As Parsons well knew, norms are not simple, inflexible, self-executing rules. They are not learned once and then followed passively forever, but are standards that guide judgment in making choices of ends and means. In all situations, the applicable norms are indefinitely numerous, more or less clearly defined, and more or less complicatedly related to one another. As Harold Garfinkel and other ethnomethodologists later emphasized, dilemmas of understanding and choice are present on every occasion of social action (Garfinkel, 1967; Cicourel, 1968 and 1974; Button, editor, 1991). In dealing with the nuances of a new situation, an actor must first select among indefinitely many institutionalized normative elements that regulate aspects of complex social situations. By combining and adapting these standards into a coherent definition of the situation, the actor projects a concrete understanding of how to act. The judgment to resolve ambiguities and conflicts of normative standards is thus a routine resource for social action, even if ordinarily taken for granted. Yet, as Parsons stressed, for an actor's judgment to be effective, it needs access to previously established normative structures appropriate to the situation. In thus defining a situation, an actor implicitly takes responsibility for the legitimacy of his or her conduct (cf. Parsons, 1951, Chapters VI and VII). The legitimacy of the definition of the situation is in principle always open to question by others, including actors animated by conflicting interests and/or normative outlooks. Effective judgment entails anticipating possible challenges to the normative grounds of one's conduct.

With the place of normative orders in the action frame of reference clarified in *SSA*, Parsons later analyzed institutional orders in terms of functional dynamics. In *The Social System*, he presented a processual theory of the institutionalization of normative orders. Social interaction was treated in terms of an equilibrium theory with the stability of a relationship depending on the parties' commitment to common generalized norms, their development of reciprocal expectations for one another's conduct, and their abilities to sanction each other in support of their respective expectations. Parsons applied this dynamic model to various types of social situation – parent-child interaction (Parsons, 1951, Chapter VI), doctor-patient relationships (*Ibid*, Chapter X), buyer-seller markets, and so forth – as well as to various societies, American, European, Indian, Chinese, and Japanese (*Ibid*, Chapter V). Above the level of dynamics of interaction in Parsons' model operate institutional forces that establish and maintain the content of specific normative orders over time. Such institutional structures as the laws of contract, stock markets, banks, courts, families, business enterprises, political parties, churches, schools, professional practices, and universities emerged through complicated historical developments. Parsons emphasized that the fate of all of such institutions depends upon functional dynamics of their relationships with one another. He noted that business enterprises have been changed by the forces of religious ethics, family institutions have changed in adaptation to the demands of business enterprises on employees, patterns of voting in political elections have changed in response to evolving status and class systems, and so forth. Yet, the compatibility of different institutions in a given society was not, in his view, merely a fortuitous result of their ongoing interplay, nor was it due simply to the domination of certain institutions over others. Parsons held that widely shared cultural values imbued practically all institutions in a society with specific principles of orientation (*Ibid*, Chapters III and IV). Functionally differentiated institutions pursue the same cultural principles, but are adapted to realizing them in separate domains of activity. The differences in the ways similar institutions are organized across societies, e.g., German and Italian factories, American and Japanese families, English and Russian universities, reflect differences in cultural values.

In his late work, Parsons suggested that the distinctive normative pattern of a society can be viewed as analogous to the unique genetic pattern of a living species. Just as a genome controls the molecular processes that produce a functioning organism, so a normative order regulates the processes of social control through which institutions are coordinated (e.g., Parsons, 1967, Chapter 5). This analogy was more than a loose "organic" metaphor; it encapsulated an emphasis on social control and regulation that had been central to Parsons' thought from early in his career. It provided a new insight into the need for precise analysis of normative orders and the processes of social control.

Conditions

Parsons' discussion of the category of conditions in *SSA* was fleeting in comparison to his treatment of ends, means, and norms. He insisted that conditions are a basic category of the action schema, but did not attempt a systematic classification of them in his early work. Conditions are for Parsons factors over which the actor cannot control and which limit or constrain what the actor can do. In his few examples, conditions consist of such things as biological forces underlying drives and motives, the hereditary make-up of an actor, the species characteristics of humans, and the material setting of action (Parsons, 1937, Chapters II, III, V, and XVIII). At one level of conditions are the physical realities of space and time. This includes the physical location of action and the physico-chemical characteristics of objects in the setting. Actors are also part of a biosphere of other species, from microorganisms to large mammals, that affect human life and activity. Social institutions over which particular actors have no control in their given situations also condition specific courses of action. The Marxian idea of the conditions of production is a forceful example.

Another conditioning element is the architecture that creates spaces for human interaction, e.g., the Roman Forum, a football field, the stock exchange, or the living room of a middle class house. In such instances, many of the conditions of action may also serve as means. However, the categories of conditions and means are *analytically* distinct. As noted, ends and means are often distinguishable only in their relations to particular courses of action; the same holds true for means and conditions. Structures built as means often function as conditions for the subsequent conduct of actors.

Because conditions did not receive the sustained discussion given to the other elements of the action frame of reference, it has often been argued that Parsons' treatment of them was perfunctory. Alexander (1983), in particular, has argued that Parsons' understanding of the impact of conditions in shaping human society did not approach the depth and intensity of Marx's. Parsons largely passed over such Marxian categories as the forces, conditions, and relations of production and eschewed an emphasis on material factors. As compared even with Weber, he sharply limited the role of class analysis in understanding the trajectories of social change (although he did emphasize social status, status groups, and status hierarchies). Nor did Parsons give more than scant attention to ecological variables or, indeed, developments in ecological theory. He largely ignored the "Chicago School" writings on urban areas as factors affecting social order and life chances.

Inadequately appreciated by Alexander and ignored by other critics – Gouldner (1970), in particular – is that, from the mid-'fifties onward, Parsons developed a more generalized analytical treatment of conditions. The basis of this development was his view, held consistently from his early work, that conditions must not be viewed concretely, but analytically: conditions are a *category* that shapes or frames *aspects* of *all* of human action. The cybernetic theory that Parsons created in the 'fifties and 'sixties formulates this analytical view of conditions in the most general terms possible (Parsons, 1961a). The cybernetic hierarchy deals with the interaction of conditional and informational elements of action. All concrete entities are treated as mixtures of conditional and informational elements (Parsons, 1966, Chapter 2). Informational elements are treated as controlling in the cybernetic sense, but conditional elements are treated as setting the limits within which control operates. Every course of action in every situation has diverse conditioning as well as controlling elements. Parsons outlined some of the general patterns of relationships between controlling and conditioning factors. Of present importance is not the details of these relationships, but Parsons' stress on the universal presence and activity of conditioning factors. A basic difference from Marxist and other materialist views is that he did not reduce conditions to a few factors. From his perspective, the Marxian emphasis on the "material" factors of forces and relations of production amounts to misplaced concreteness. Indeed, Parsons emphasized that there are non-material (informational) elements in the forces and relations of production (see especially Parsons, 1954, Chapters XV and XIX). His more general perspective on conditions opened up the possibility of investigating without the bias of materialist presuppositions just what factors are conditioning in any given social setting.

Throughout his career, Parsons consistently acknowledged that conditions are an essential category. In his interpretations of Freud (Parsons, 1964, Chapters 1 through 4), his insightful treatment of the Id is an important counterweight to his better known emphases on the Superego. In his adaptation of Norbert Wiener's cybernetics (Wiener, 1948), his focus on factors of control was always balanced by recognition that conditioning factors are equally fundamental. As a category, conditions are coordinate with control. Indeed, control is a meaningless concept without understanding of the constraints imposed by conditions. In Parsons' late formulations, the cybernetic hierarchy is based on an entirely analytical distinction between control and conditions. The same entities that are controlling when analyzed with reference to certain matters, are conditioning for others (Parsons, 1966, especially Chapter 2). Political authority that is controlling of the allocation of economic resources is typically itself a condition of the operation of the legal system (Parsons, 1969, Chapters 13 through 15). Only in his last work, however, did Parsons bring this analytical conception of the cybernetic hierarchy to bear on the question of the conditioning elements for all of the action system. In *A Paradigm of the Human Condition* (Parsons, 1978, Chapter 15), he attempted a general classification of the kinds of conditioning factors and the variety of their relations to the processes of action. This major development was based on Parsons' career-long conviction that conditions have categorial status in the action frame of reference and that the implications of that status can be clarified only through radical reformulation of established ideas.

Relationships Among the Categories

In the *SSA*, the four categories were not submitted as a list, but as an ordered set. Means only take their significance in a particular course of action from the ends to which they are related. Norms set limits on the ends actors may legitimately pursue and restrict the selection of means to be used in attaining them. Conditions limit the range of feasible actions, hence, the sorts of ends actors will choose to pursue and means they are able to utilize under given circumstances. Thus, in any empirical system of action, there is an inherent tension between the ideal elements of a normative order and the circumstantial elements of the conditions. As Parsons portrays it, action arises in the effort to transform the circumstantial toward the ideal – or at least to stave off the degradation of ideals by the pressure of changing conditions.

Parsons demonstrated that the categorial set proposed in the *SSA* constitutes a coherent frame of reference by exploring the theoretical consequences of removing any one or more of the categories (Parsons, 1937, Chapter XVIII). Without the category of norms, the theory of action reverts to utilitarianism and the problem of order becomes insoluble. Without the category of conditions and attention to process relationships between ends and means, the theory of action turns into idealism – or, as we have noted, structuralism. Without the categories of norms and ends, action theory reduces to behaviorism. The coherence of the frame of reference depends on an integration of the four coordinate categories. This principle stood as a guide for the next phase of Parsons' work.

Since Parsons' principal concern was to highlight categories essential to social action at all times and places, he deliberately limited the categories proposed in *SSA* to a simple set. He knew that the elementary set of categories he had formulated was not yet adequate to ground a system of theory that would be useful for a wide range of empirical analyses. As he began to develop a theory within the action frame of reference, he concentrated on representing the relationships among all four categories.

By the summer of 1939, Parsons had begun to add specificity and detail to the conceptual scheme of *SSA*. In a lengthy manuscript, "Actor, Situation and Normative Pattern; An Essay in the Theory of Social Action", not published in his lifetime, but used in his teaching for a decade, Parsons introduced a new emphasis on relationships between the actor and the *objects* of his action (Parsons, 1986/circa 1939). The essay created a category of the situation to stand for the setting (including conditions) in which an actor engages specific objects. Parsons also introduced distinctions among three dimensions of the actor's relationships with physical or social objects: cognitive, affective, and telic – derived, as he noted, from Kant. The cognitive dimension refers to the actor's practical knowledge of objects in his situation – and to his or her efforts to gain knowledge – as a basis for relating the use of means to ends. The affective dimension refers to the actor's involvement and attachment to particular objects. Affective relations with objects are closely bound up with the meaning of ends for the actor. The telic dimension refers to the actor's judgment in determining the normative significance of courses of action and the normative standards to be applied in the situation. This dimension relates situated action to the normative traditions of the society. The distinctions among these three dimensions moved Parsons toward a more differentiated analysis of the process of action than the simple scheme of means-ends-norms-conditions permitted. In thus opening up his analytical scheme, Parsons took the first steps on a long path of conceptual revision and elaboration that extended to his last writings.

Convergence as Method

To this point, we have tried to demonstrate that "convergence" in *SSA* was less an argument about a common normative emphasis in the works of, principally, Weber and Durkheim and, secondarily, Pareto and Marshall than it was Parsons' original method of theory construction. What, then, is the method of convergence? First of all, convergence was a method in Parsons' efforts to develop his own theoretical system. It was not merely a commentary on the works of Weber, Durkheim, and others, nor even a conclusion of such commentary. In *SSA*, convergence was a procedure used to define the basic categories that enable the social scientist to conceptualize the object domain of social action. In part, Parsons accomplished this by analytic critique of the writings of several leading figures of the previous generation of social scientists. We have emphasized that Parsons' readings of his predecessors was neither historical recounting nor epistemological analysis. Elements of both entered his discussions, but his consistent focus was on critical assessment of the conceptualization of social objects. In clarifying the categories that organized his predecessors' theories, he was able to reach conclusions about what categories are essential to any and all social scientific thought. The resulting conclusions were more generalized and systematic than any formulations his predecessors themselves had achieved. He then validated his conclusions about essential categories by using them to highlight limitations in the works of his predecessors and others. He thus established that his categories for the action frame of reference (ends, means, norms, conditions) are not only substantive concepts for defining social objects, but also basic measures for comparing and evaluating social theories.

Parsons regarded his conclusions about the essential categories of social theory in two ways. In one perspective, he held emphatically that each of the categories was necessary to any future social theory. No theory that omitted any one of the four categories could be theoretically or empirically adequate. Omitting one or more of the categories would result in a truncated and basically flawed characterization of the social object. Empirical analyses carried out with such a schema would necessarily have large gaps and ineluctably lead to false or partial understanding. In a complementary perspective, however, Parsons viewed the categorical scheme of *SSA* as preliminary and open to elaboration and revision. He understood that as a frame of reference for social scientific analysis it was a simple starting point. He anticipated that it would be changed and developed in his later work and the works of others. In this sense, it is an error to consider the *SSA* as a conclusion; it is a beginning, a prolegomenon, to any future theory of social action.

As Parsons proceeded to develop the theory of social action, he relied at a number of turning points on convergence as an analytical method for advancing the scope and technical precision of his thought. Although convergence is a method of broad importance for social science, it is clear in retrospect that it was also a distillation of Parsons' personal talent for technical, intensive, abstract, and generalizing critique of theoretical systems. Convergence thus figured centrally in the elaboration and systematization of the theory of action from the late 1940s to the end of Parsons' life. Although it is widely understood that Parsons reworked the theory of action several times after the late 1940s, it has not been appreciated that he relied on the method of convergence to accomplish these developments and that this method is one of the keys to understanding the continuity in his work.[2] In order to highlight the status of convergence as a general method, we now forecast several themes that we will examine in a future essay.

Although we have seen that Parsons started reformulating the theory of action in the late 1930s, the first major codification of change occurred in the system theory of the early 1950s. As has often been noted, the main conceptual shift was from the unit act (with its categories of ends, means, norms, and conditions) to the system of action. In his new conception of the social system, Parsons emphasized not unit acts, but relationships among actors and the institutions that stabilize such relationships. This emphasis was derived through a convergence process. Parsons saw in the homeostatic theories in physiology associated with W. B. Cannon (1932) and L. J. Henderson (1928, 1935) a convergence with Pareto's conception of system. The implication was that social systems could also be conceptualized in terms of equilibria and functions. In *The Social System* (1951), Parsons began to explore the ways in which social relationships are maintained in equilibria through interaction. He also examined ways in which social relationships and institutions are affected by the functional needs of societies and other social systems for adaptation and integration.

In the same period, Parsons intensively studied Sigmund Freud and psychoanalytic theory. He reached the conclusion that, in relation to the central role of the Oedipus Complex in the development of personalities, the Superego is a chief concept in Freud's thought. The insight followed that the Superego's prescriptions, proscriptions, taboos, rules, ideals, and, indeed, the mechanisms of repression were the equivalent for the personality of Durkheim's collective conscience for society (1964, Chapter 1). Parsons proposed that the Superego and the normative order of society held the same moral content, but were differently specialized to the needs of persons and social systems. A result of this recognition of convergent theories was that Parsons reformulated the theory of action to encompass personality as well as social systems.

Parsons was dissatisfied with the limited explanatory value of functional theories based on varying and unmethodical lists of functional needs. By 1953, he sought to establish a systematic foundation for the concept of social function. At that time, he collaborated with R. F. Bales, who had developed a set of sixteen apparently exhaustive categories for analyzing the contributions of interaction to group processes. Together, Parsons and Bales ordered the sixteen categories into four generalized dimensions of social process and relationships (Parsons, Bales, and Shils, 1953). Formulation of the four dimensions was facilitated by recognition of a convergence

---

[2] In our next article, we will examine the role played by the method of convergence in these developments.

between Bales' interaction process categories and Parsons' own treatment of social interaction in *The Social System*. Soon the four dimensions became the four function paradigm, which provided the basis for a formal theory of the relations among functions in systems of action (*Ibid*).

Parsons almost immediately endeavored to use the four function theory to define subsystems of society and the relations among them. In conceiving of these relations, Parsons applied the process perspective he had adapted from utilitarian thought and, in *The Social System*, reformulated as normatively regulated exchanges of expectations and sanctions. In *Economy and Society* (Parsons and Smelser, 1956), Parsons proposed that the equilibrium processes of supply and demand in economic markets are special cases of his more general model of interaction. Parsons and Smelser then extended this recognition of convergence to, in the first instance, Keynes' treatment of the double market relationship between households and business firms (1936). One market or set of interactions involves the exchange of labor for wages; a second market or set of interactions involves the exchange of finished goods for consumer spending. In the second instance, they proposed that Wassily Leontieff's input-output analysis of market exchanges could be generalized to understanding all the relationships between the economy and other subsystems of society. Later, Parsons generalized this insight even further and proposed that all social processes could be treated as inputs and outputs between functionally differentiated units of society (Parsons 1961b, 1975). The key to these changes was Parsons' perception of the convergence between his earlier processual treatment of interaction and the supply and demand dynamics of Keynesian economics.

From his earliest work, Parsons emphasized the regulating role of normative elements in social interaction. In the 1950s, he had entered a phase of his work in which he attempted to achieve more generalized and abstract formulations. In this phase, he encountered the writings of Norbert Wiener on cybernetics (Wiener, 1948). Wiener was a special sort of positivist who used certain fields of mathematics to improve mechanisms of information control and feedback in social communication. Wiener's idea of cybernetics is epitomized in his example of the steering mechanism of a ship: it is weaker than the engine, but can nevertheless control the ship's direction of travel (Wiener, 1948). The cybernetic theory was written at a high level of generalization, but was basically an applied, practical proposal. Wiener's own understanding of its application to human affairs was rather simplistically positivistic (Wiener, 1954). Parsons, by contrast, saw a broad convergence between Wiener's idea of cybernetic control and his own emphasis on normative regulation. By contrast to Wiener's practical concern, however, Parsons adapted the cybernetic idea to clarification of the most general processes of regulation in systems of social action. The key insight that he derived from Wiener's mathematical demonstration is that in stable systems factors higher in information are needed to regulate factors higher in energy. Parsons related this principle to Freud's insight that the relationship of the id to the ego is analogous to a horse and rider. For Parsons, the ego's control over the id in a well functioning personality is an instance of processes of cybernetic control in action systems (Parsons, 1961a and b; 1964; 1973; 1978). Parsons proceeded to generalize cybernetic concepts to all elements of the action system, which he then analyzed in terms of differing mixes of information and energy. He proposed that a hierarchy exists with cultural factors at the apex, then social factors, then personality factors, and finally mental factors at the base (Parsons, 1968; 1973). However, this hierarchy has an obverse dimension: factors greater in energy are more difficult to control and may more readily break through the regulatory relationships, or even overturn them (Parsons, 1973). As a category, conditions are coordinate with control. Control is meaningless without understanding of the constraints imposed by conditions. Indeed, in his late formulations, the cybernetic hierarchy is based on an entirely analytical distinction between control and conditions. The same entities that are controlling when analyzed with reference to certain matters, are conditioning for others (Parsons, 1966, especially Chapter 2). For example, political authority that controls the allocation of economic resources is typically itself a condition of the operation of the legal system (Parsons, 1969, Chapters 13 through 15).

In the late 1960s and early 1970s, Parsons tried to reformulate his ideas from the 1950s on relationships among psychological, social, and cultural systems. A goal of the reformulation was to apply both the four function paradigm and input-output schema to dynamic analysis of these relationships (Parsons, 1977, Chapter 10; Parsons and Platt, 1973). He proposed that four categories of subsystem of social action could be defined: cultural systems, social systems, personality systems, and the behavioral organism as system. The new term, behavioral organism, referred to the whole organism of the individual actor viewed analytically as a system of capabilities to behave, or implement action. Lidz and Lidz (1976), however, argued that the concept of behavioral organism violates Parsons' controlling definition of social action as a system constituted of meaningful entities. They proposed that Piaget's psychology of intelligence be taken as a resource for conceptualizing the fourth subsystem of action. Piaget's writings described a system of cognitive schemata that are meaningful in character and address a general type of psychological process that Parsons' theories had left residual. Parsons (1978, Chapter 15) was quick to recognize the convergence between Piaget's and his own works and accept the proposal to characterize the fourth subsystem as a system of cognitive mind.

Parsons' reliance on the convergence method was not infallible. In the 1960s, he undertook an evolutionary theory of comparative institutional analysis based on convergence with the Darwinian theory (Parsons 1966, 1971). His approach was radically different from the ethnocentric, often racially biased, "evolutionary" formulations of Herbert Spencer, William Graham Sumner, and others of the late 19th and early 20th centuries. Although he emphasized the special adaptive capacities of modern Western societies, he followed Weber rather than Spencer in also highlighting the sophistication of the ancient civilizations of Greco-Roman antiquity, India, China, and Islam (Parsons, 1966). He also sought to replace the heavily ideological notions of "survival of the fittest" that figured in Spencer's and Sumner's writings with sociological analogues of Darwinian natural selection. Moreover, his approach also contrasts with recent formulations in sociobiology. He did not emphasize selective advantages in reproduction that may accrue to specific populations from particular institutions or forms of behavior. Nor did he hypothesize that such institutions or forms of behavior might be heritable and directly linked to specific genes. Rather, he argued that specific institutional patterns tend to give entire societies "adaptive advantages" over other societies in their environments, advantages that may lead to more efficient use of resources, more effective organization, firmer institutions of solidarity, and greater openness to cultural development (*Ibid*).

In his evolutionary writings, Parsons developed an elaborate typology of primitive, archaic, historic, and modern societies and civilizations based on levels of adaptive advantage (Parsons, 1966 and 1971). He distinguished between higher and lower levels of differentiation and institutional complexity within each of these broad types. He discussed institutional variations found at each level due to differences in basic cultural premises and social values. He also highlighted processes of institutional change by which particular societies had changed from one type of society to another or by which they had regressed from higher to lower types. Despite the scope of his comparative institutional analysis, however, Parsons failed to demonstrate a sociological analogue of natural selection. His entire "evolutionary" scheme thus amounted to a complex typology without the unifying conception of change and stability that characterizes the Darwinian theory of speciation. At root, we believe, Parsons' endeavor to create a theory of social evolution followed from a category error: biological systems are characterized by natural selection, but systems of social action change through historical processes. Again, the category error is a violation of the criterion that systems of action are meaningful in character.

Conclusion: The Method of Convergence

As we have seen, convergence was a basis of the argument in the *SSA* that set the main parameters for the theory of action. Convergence continued to figure in nearly all of Parsons' later work and played a major role in the changes and elaborations he introduced over 40 years. Most of the time, the convergence method produced successful results, enabling Parsons to assimilate the insights of other systematic thinkers into the theory of action and thus to increase its reach and technical rigor. To conclude, we wish to schematize the chief features of the convergence method.

The prospects for convergence arise from efforts of different theories or even whole schools of thought to address similar problems. The problems may be broad, as Parsons discerned in the categories that Marshall, Pareto, Durkheim, and Weber used to analyze the institutions of modern capitalist societies. Or they may be more specific, as in the similarity between Durkheimian conception of repressive moral rules and the Freudian conception of the repressive superego. The similarity may be more apparent to an observer than to one of the original theorists. Thus, it was Parsons who perceived the broad applicability of cybernetic concepts, which Wiener had proposed with narrower positivist intentions.

Convergence itself begins with conceptual analysis of theories to be compared. Parsons was especially concerned with frames of reference and therefore all of his comparisons dwelled on categorial schemes. He analyzed the categories used in each theory, the relationships among the categories, and the contribution of each category to the understanding of the objects under study. Every theory has ways of characterizing the objects it seeks to understand. The objects and their qualities are defined by use of substantive categories. Parsons' analysis concentrated precisely on the substantive categories, and was thus purely scientific rather than epistemological. His overriding concern was on the capacity of conceptual schemes to capture basic qualities of social action and establish frameworks for fruitful theorizing. He critiqued strengths and weaknesses of utilitarian, rationalist, idealistic, and other frameworks in their capacities to synthesize social action. Because Parsons set the contribution to understanding of social action as the measure of theories, his critiques of Hobbes, Locke, Rousseau, Marx, Weber, and other figures differ substantially from the critiques of philosophers and historians.

The next step in the convergence method, as Parsons used it, was to outline the differences and similarities in the categories of a set of theories. By evaluating the contributions of each category, it becomes possible to plan the synthesis of new combinations of categories. The aim is to create a new frame of reference that extends understanding and is also coherent. The new frame of reference should then be compared with its forerunners to ensure that it actually expands the capacity for understanding. Parsons himself highlighted the removal of residual areas as a standard for demonstrating the analytic superiority of a new frame of reference. In Parsons' experience, reformulation of categorial schemes typically took several iterations before yielding results that could withstand repeated critical assessment. He often invited the help of students and colleagues in critiquing his provisional formulations.

Finally, the convergence method requires empirical use and evaluation of the proposed categorial scheme. We have seen that *SSA* reviews the extensive empirical writings of Durkheim and especially Weber. Parsons' goal in reviewing these materials was to demonstrate the necessity of each category in the action scheme, especially norms. In fact, his early categorial scheme of ends, means, norms, and conditions was justified by the essential contribution of each category to the empirical understanding of basic features of social action. A number of Parsons' early essays explore the empirical potential of his action schema, although this aspect of their significance has not always been perceived because they also address specific substantive problems (Parsons, 1949a).

Use of the convergence method as a procedure for understanding the theory of action opens up three issues that have previously been obscured – not totally, but to a degree that has limited understanding. The first issue has been addressed in the present essay and concerns the construction of the theory of action. Our discussion of the convergence method permits us to see in greater depth the historical process by which Parsons synthesized the theory of action. The second issue concerns the ways in which Parsons continued to use the convergence method in his theory.[3] The third issue is that the convergence method also enables us to evaluate relationships between the theory of action and other theoretical frameworks in the social sciences. We believe that over the longer term this aspect of the convergence method has the potential to open additional paths for revision of the theory. We believe it is yet possible to draw selectively from other traditions and domains of social scientific thought to extend and develop the theory of action as a general analytical frame of reference. Indeed, innovation gained in this manner would be the most direct emulation of the *methodology* that Talcott Parsons devised in *The Structure of Social Action*.

References

Alexander, Jeffrey C. (1983): *Theoretical Logic in Sociology.* Volume Four: *The Modern Reconstruction of Classical Thought: Talcott Parsons*. Berkeley, CA: University of California Press.
Aron, Raymond (1965): *Main Currents in Sociological Thought*. Two volumes. New York: Basic Books.
Bellah, Robert N. (1970): *Beyond Belief; Essays on Religion in a Post-Traditional World*. New York: Harper and Row.
Bellah, Robert N. (1973): Introduction to *Emile Durkheim on Morality and Society*. Edited by Robert N. Bellah. Chicago: University of Chicago Press.

---

[3] This will be explored in more detail in our succeeding essay. Again, our claim will be that tracing-the uses of the convergence method historically helps lay out the conceptual structure of the theory. This critical approach enables us to go beneath Parsons' claims to abstract generality in the logical make up of the theory and to identify categorial and substantive weaknesses in its structure. We anticipate that this approach will yield a new critical standpoint on the theory in its late stages of development.

Bellah, Robert N. (1975): *The Broken Covenant; American Civil Religion in a Time of Trial*. New York: Seabury Press.
Bellah, Robert N. (1983): "The Ethical Aims of Social Inquiry," In Norma Haan, Robert N. Bellah, Paul Rabinow, and William M. Sullivan, editors, *Social Science as Moral Inquiry*. New York: Columbia University Press.
Bendix, Reinhard (1960): *Max Weber; An Intellectual Portrait*. Garden City, NY: Doubleday.
Bendix, Reinhard (1978): K*ings or People*. Berkeley, CA: University of California Press.
Bentham, Jeremy (1948): *An Introduction to the Principles of Morals and Legislation*. New York: Hafner. Reprint of revised edition of 1823. First edition, 1780.
Bershady, Harold J. (1973*): Ideology and Social Knowledge*. Oxford: Basil Blackwell.
Bougle, Celestin, (1971): *Essays on the Caste System*. Cambridge, U.K.: Cambridge University Press.
Button, Graham, ed. (1991): *Ethnomethodology and the Human Sciences*. Cambridge: University of Cambridge Press.
Camic, Charles (1991): "Introduction" to *Talcott Parsons; The Early Essays*. Edited by Charles Camic. Chicago: University of Chicago Press.
Cannon, W. B. (1932): *The Wisdom of the Body*. New York: Norton.
Cassirer, Ernst (1950): *The Problem of Knowledge: Philosophy, Science, and History Since Hege*l. Three volumes. New Haven: Yale University Press. First published in German, 1906 through 1920.
Cassirer, Ernst (1951): *The Philosophy of the Enlightenmen*t. Princeton, NJ: Princeton University Press. First published in German, 1932.
Cicourel, Aaron V. (1968): *The Social Organization of Juvenile Just*ice. New York: Wiley.
Cicourel, Aaron. V. (1974): *Cognitive Sociology; Language and Meaning in Social Interaction*. New York: Free Press.
Clark, Terry N. (1973): *Prophets and Patrons: The French University and the Emergence of the Social Sciences*. Cambridge, MA: Harvard University Press.
Coleman, James S. (1990): *Foundations of Social Theory*. Cambridge, MA: Harvard University Press.
Collingwood, R. G.. (1956): *The Idea of History*. New York: Oxford University Press.
Comte, Auguste (1875-77): *The System of Positive Polity or Treatise on Sociology Instituting the Religion of Humanity*. Four volumes. London: Longmans. First published in French, 1851-54.
Davy, Georges (1922): *La Foi Juree: Etude sociologique du probleme du contrat, la formation du lien contractuel*. Paris: Alcan.
Dilthey, Wilhelm (1954): *The Essence of Philosophy*. Chapel Hill, N.C.: University of North Carolina Press. First published in German in 1904.
Dilthey, Wilhelm (1989): Selected Works. Vol. 1: *Introduction to the Human Sciences*. Edited by Rudolf A. Makkreel and Frithjof Rodi. Princeton, NJ: Princeton University Press. First published in German as *Einleitung in die Geisteswissenschaften* in 1883.
Dilthey, Wilhelm (1996a): Selected Works. Vol. 4. *Hermeneutics and the Study of History*. Edited by Rudolf A. Makkreel and Frithjof Rodi. Princeton, NJ: Princeton University Press.
Dilthey, Wilhelm (1996b): Selected Works Vol. 5. *Poetry and Experience*. Edited by Rudolf A. Makkreel and Frithjof Rodi. Princeton, NJ: Princeton University Press.
Droysen, Johann Gustav (1882): *Grundriss der Historik*. Leipzig. Velt.
Dumont, Louis (1979): *Homo Hierarchicus*. Revised edition. Chicago: University of Chicago Press.

Dumont, Louis (1970): *Religion, Politics, and History in India;* Collected Papers. The Hague: Mouton.
Dumont, Louis (1977): *From Mandeville to Marx; The Genesis and Triumph of an Economic Ideology.* Chicago: University of Chicago Press.
Durkheim, Emile (1950): *The Rules of Sociological Method.* New York: Free Press. First published in French in 1895. French in 1897.
Durkheim, Emile (1961): *Moral Education; A Study in the Theory and Application of the Sociology of Education.* New York: Free Press.
Durkheim, Emile (1977): *The Evolution of Educational Thought; Lectures on the Formation and Development of Secondary Education in France.* London: Routledge and Kegan Paul. First published in French in 1938.
Durkheim, Emile (1984): *The Division of Labor in Society.* New York: Free Press. First published in French in 1893. First English edition, 1933.
Durkheim, Emile (1992): *Professional Ethics and Civic Mor*als. London: Routledge. First English edition, 1957.
Durkheim, Emile (1995): *The Elementary Forms of Religious Life.* New York: Free Press. First published in French in 1912. First English edition, 1915.
Durkheim, Emile and Mauss, Marcel (1963): *Primitive Classification.* Chicago: University of Chicago Press.
Fox, Renee C. (1959): *Experiment Perilous; Physicians and Patients Facing the Unknown.* New York: Free Press.
Fox, Renee C. (1979): *Essays in Medical Sociology; Journeys into the Field.* New York: Wiley.
Fox, Renee C. (1994): *In the Belgian Chateau; The Spirit and Culture of a European Society in an Age of Change.* Chicago: Ivan R. Dee.
Gadamer, Hans-Georg (1975): *Truth and Method.* New York: Continuum. First published in German in 1960.
Garfinkel, Harold (1967): *Studies in Ethnomethodology.* Englewood Cliffs, N.J.: Prentice-Hall.
Gay, Peter (1966):.: *The Enlightenment: An Interpretation* Volume I: *The Rise of Modern Paganism.* New York: Vintage.
Gay, Peter (1969): *The Enlightenment: An Interpretation.* Volume II: *The Science of Freedom.* New York: Norton.
Geertz, Clifford (1973): "Thick Description: Toward an Interpretive Theory of Culture," in *The Interpretation of Cultures; Selected Essays.* New York: Basic Books.
Gerth Hans H. and Mills, C. Wright (1953): *Character and Social Structure.* New York: Oxford University Press.
Gould, Mark (1981): "Parsons versus Marx: 'An Earnest Warning...'" *Sociological Inquiry,* 51 (3-4): 197-218.
Gouldner, Alvin W. (1970): *The Coming Crisis of Western Sociology.* New York: Basic Books.
Granet, Marcel (1934): *La Pensee Chinoise.* Paris: La Renaissance du Livre.
Granet, Marcel (1958): *Chinese Civilization.* New York: Meridian Books.
Granet, Marcel (1975): *The Religion of the Chinese People.* New York: Harper and Row.
Halevy, Elie (1960): *The Growth of Philosophical Radic*alism. Boston: Beacon. First published in French in three volumes, 1901-1904.
Halbwachs, Maurice (1958): *The Psychology of Social Class.* New York: Free Press. First published in French, 1955.

Halbwachs, Maurice (1980): *The Collective Memory.* New York: Harper. First published in French in 1950.
Hegel, Georg Wilhelm Friedrich (1950): *The Philosophy of History.* New York: Dover. First published posthumously in German from lectures of 1831-32.
Hegel, Georg Wilhelm Friedrich (1967): *The Phenomenology of Mind.* New York: Harper. First published in German in 1807.
Henderson, L. J. (1928): *Blood: A Study in General Physiology.* New Haven: Yale University Press.
Henderson, L. J. (1932): "An Approximate Definition of Fact," in *University of California Publications in Philosophy*, vol. 14: 179-199. Reprinted in *L. J. Henderson on the Social System*, edited by Bernard Barber. Chicago: University of Chicago Press, 1970.
Henderson, L. J. (1935): *Pareto's General Sociology: A Physiologist's Interpretation.* Cambridge, MA: Harvard University Press.
Hobbes, Thomas (1928): *The Leviathan.* London: J.M. Dent and Sons, Ltd. First published in 1651.
Hubert, Henri (1966): *The Rise of the Celts.* New York: Biblo and Tannen. First published in French in 1934.
Hubert, Henri (1972): *The Greatness and Decline of the Celts.* New York: Benjamin Blom. First published in French in 1934.
Hubert, Henri and Mauss, Marcel (1964): *Sacrifice: Its Nature and Function.* Chicago: University of Chicago Press. First published in French in 1898.
Husserl, Edmund (1900-1901): *Logische Untersuchungen.* Two volumes. Halle: Max Niemeyer.
Jay, Martin (1973): *The Dialectical Imagination.* Boston: Little, Brown.
Kant, Immanuel (1930): *Critique of Pure Reason.* London: G. Bell and Sons. First published in German in 1781.
Keynes, John Maynard (1936): *The General Theory of Employment, Interest, and Money.* London: Macmillan.
Knight, Frank (1947): *Freedom and Reform; Essays in Economics and Social Philosophy.* New York: Harper and Row.
Krieger, Leonard (1957): *The German Idea of Freedom.* Boston: Beacon Press.
Kuhn, Thomas S. (1970): *The Structure of Scientific Revolutions.* Second edition, enlarged. Chicago: University of Chicago Press. First edition, 1962.
Levy-Bruhl, Lucien (1924): *History of Modern Philosophy in France.* Chicago: Open Court. First published in French.
Lidz, Victor (1976): Introduction to Part II: General Action Analysis. In Jan J. Loubser, Rainer C. Baum, Andrew Effrat, and Victor Lidz, editors. *Explorations in General Theory in Social Science*, volume one. New York: Free Press.
Lidz, Victor (1979): "Secularization, Ethical Life, and Religion in Modern Societies," in Harry M. Johnson, editor, *Religious Change and Continuity.* San Francisco: Jossey-Bass.
Lidz, Victor (1981): "Conceptions of Value-Relevance and the Theory of Action," in *Sociological Inquiry*, vol. 51, (3-4), pp. 371-408.
Lidz, Victor (1984): "Television and Moral Order in a Secular Age," in Willard D. Rowland, Jr. and Bruce Watkins, editors. *Interpreting Television: Current Research Perspectives.* Beverly Hills, CA: Sage.
Lidz, Victor (1986): "Parsons and Empirical Sociology," in *The Nationalization of the Social Sciences*, edited by Samuel Z. Klausner and Victor Lidz. Philadelphia: University of Pennsylvania Press.

Lidz, Charles W. and Lidz, Victor (1976): "Piaget's Psychology of Intelligence and the Theory of Action," in *Explorations in General Theory in Social Science*, volume one, edited by Jan J. Loubser, Rainer C. Baum, Andrew Effrat, and Victor Lidz. New York: Free Press.
Locke, John (1924): *Two Treatises on Civil Government*. London: J.M. Dent and Sons. First published in 1690.
Lukes, Steven (1972): *Emile Durkheim; His Life and Work*. New York: Harper and Row.
Lundberg, George Andrew (1939): *Foundations of Sociology*. New York: Macmillan.
Mannheim, Karl (1936): *Ideology and Utopia; An Introduction to the Sociology of Knowledge*. London: Routledge. First published in German in 1929.
Mannheim, Karl (1953): *Essays on the Sociology of Knowledge*. Edited by Paul Kecskemeti. New York: Oxford University Press.
Marshall, Alfred (1925): *The Principles of Economics*. London: Macmillan.
Marx, Karl (1973): *Grundrisse; Introduction to the Critique of Political Economy*. Translated with a foreword by Martin Nicolaus. New York: Vintage Books. Translation of manuscripts written in German in 1857-58.
Marx, Karl (1976): *Capital*. Vol. 1, Introduced by Ernest Mandel, translated by Ben Fowkes, New York, N. Y., Penguin Books. First published in German in 1867.
Mauss, Marcel (1954): *The Gift; Forms and Functions of Exchange in Archaic Societies*. London: Cohen and West.
Mauss, Marcel (1972): *A General Theory of Magic*. New York: Norton
Mauss, Marcel (1979a): *The Seasonal Variations of the Eskimo*. London: Routledge and Kegan Paul
Mauss, Marcel (1979b): *Sociology and Psychology:* Essays. London: Routledge and Kegan Paul.
Mayo, Elton (1933): *The Human Problems of an Industrial Civilization*. New York: Viking.
Menger, Carl. 1963. *Problems of Economics and Sociology*, translated by Francis J. Nock, edited and introduced by Louis Schneider. Urbana: University of Illinois Press.
Mommsen, Theodor (1958): *The History of Rome*. New York: Meridian Books. First published in German in 1854-56.
Oakes, Guy (1977): "Introduction" to *Georg Simmel, The Problems of the Philosophy of History*. Translated and edited by Guy Oakes. New York: Free Press.
Oakes, Guy (1980): "Introduction" to *Georg Simmel, Essays on Interpretation in Social Science*. Translated and edited by Guy Oakes. Totowa, NJ: Rowman and Littlefield.
Oakes, Guy (1986): "Introduction" to *Heinrich Rickert. The Limits of Concept Formation in Natural Science; A Logical Introduction to the Historical Sciences*. Abridged edition, edited and translated by Guy Oakes. Cambridge: Cambridge University Press.
Ogburn, William F. (1922): *Social Change, With Respect to Culture and Original Nature*. New York: Viking.
Parsons, Talcott (1937): *The Structure of Social Action*. New York: McGraw-Hill.
Parsons, Talcott (1947): "Introduction" to *Max Weber, The Theory of Social and Economic Organization*. Translated by A.M. Henderson and Talcott Parsons. Edited with an introduction by Talcott Parsons. New York: Oxford University Press.
Parsons, Talcott (1949a): *Essays in Sociological Theory: Pure and Applied*. New York: Free Press.
Parsons, Talcott (1949b): *Structure of Social Action*. Second edition. New York: Free Press.
Parsons, Talcott (1951): *The Social System*. New York: Free Press.
Parsons, Talcott (1954): *Essays in Sociological Theory*. Revised edition. New York: Free Press.

Parsons, Talcott (1960): *Structure and Process in Modern Societies.* New York: Free Press.
Parsons, Talcott (1961a): "General Introduction," in Talcott Parsons, Edward A.Shils, Kaspar D. Naegele, and Jesse R. Pitts, editors. 1961. *Theories of Society; Foundations of Modern Sociological Theory.* Two volumes. New York: Free Press.
Parsons, Talcott (1961b): "An Outline of the Social System," In Talcott Parsons, Edward A. Shils, Kaspar D. Naegele, and Jesse R. Pitts, editors. *Theories of Society; Foundations of Modern Sociological Theory*, two volumes. New York: Free Press.
Parsons, Talcott (1961c): "Editorial Foreword" to Part One, Section A. "The Interpretation of Action in the History of Social Thought," in Talcott Parsons, Edward A.Shils, Kaspar D. Naegele, and Jesse R. Pitts, editors. *Theories of Society; Foundations of Modern Sociological Theory.* Two volumes. New York: Free Press.
Parsons, Talcott (1964): *Social Structure and Personality.* New York: Free Press.
Parsons, Talcott (1966): *Societies; Evolutionary and Comparative Perspectives.* Englewood Cliffs, NJ: Prentice-Hall.
Parsons, Talcott (1967): *Sociological Theory and Modern Society.* New York: Free Press.
Parsons, Talcott (1968): "Durkheim," *International Encyclopedia of the Social Sciences.* New York: Macmillan
Parsons, Talcott (1969): *Politics and Social Structure.* New York: Free Press.
Parsons, Talcott (1971): *The System of Modern Societies.* Englewood Cliffs, NJ: Prentice Hall.
Parsons, Talcott (1975): "The Present Status of Structural-Functional Theory in Sociology," in Lewis A. Coser, editor. *The Idea of Social Structure; Papers in Honor of Robert K. Merton.* New York: Harcourt, Brace, Jovanovich.
Parsons, Talcott (1977): *Social Systems and the Evolution of Action Theory.* New York: Free Press.
Parsons, Talcott (1977b): *Evolution of Societies.* Englewood Cliffs, NJ: Prentice Hall.
Parsons, Talcott (1978): *Action Theory and the Human Condition.* New York: Free Press.
Parsons, Talcott (1986a): "Social Science: A Basic National Resource," in Samuel Z. Klausner and Victor Lidz, editors. *The Nationalization of the Social Sciences.* Philadelphia: University of Pennsylvania Press. Manuscript written circa 1948.
Parsons, Talcott (1986b): *Aktor, Situation und normative Muster; Ein Essay zur Theorie sozialen Handelns.* Translated, edited, and with an introduction by Harald Wenzel. Frankfurt: Suhrkamp. Manuscript written in English circa 1939 entitled "Actor, Situation and Normative Pattern; An Essay in the Theory of Social Action."
Parsons, Talcott (1991): *The Early Essays.* Edited and with an introduction by Charles C. Camic. Chicago: University of Chicago Press.
Parsons, Talcott and Bales, Robert F. (1955): *Family, Socialization and Interaction Process.* New York: Free Press.
Parsons, Talcott, Bales, Robert F. and Shils, Edward A. (1953): *Working Papers in the Theory of Action.* New York: Free Press.
Parsons, Talcott, and Platt, Gerald M. (1973): *The American University.* Cambridge, MA: Harvard University Press.
Parsons, Talcott and Shils, Edward A., eds. (1951a): *Toward A General Theory of Action.* Cambridge: Harvard University Press.
Parsons, Talcott and Shils, Edward A. (1951b): "Values, Motives, and the Theory of Action," in Parsons and Shils. Editors. 1951. *Toward A General Theory of Action.* Cambridge: Harvard University Press.

Parsons, Talcott, Shils, Edward A., Naegele, Kaspar D. and Pitts, Jesse R., eds. (1961): *Theories of Society; Foundations of Modern Sociological Theory*. Two volumes. New York: Free Press.

Parsons, Talcott and Smelser, Neil J. (1956): *Economy and Society*. New York: Free Press.

Peyre, Henri (1960): "Emile Durkheim; The Man, His Time, and His Intellectual Background," in Kurt Wolff, editor, *Essays on Sociology and Philosophy by Emile Durkheim et al.* New York: Harper.

Rickert, Heinrich (1986): *The Limits of Concept Formation in Natural Science; A Logical Introduction to the Historical Sciences*. Abridged edition, edited and translated by Guy Oakes. Cambridge: Cambridge University Press. First published in 1902 as *Die Grenzen der naturwissenschaftlichen Begriffsbildung*.

Rousseau, Jean Jacques (1950): *The Social Contract and Discourses*. Translated with an introduction by G. D. H. Cole. New York: E. P. Dutton. *The Social Contract* was first published in French in 1762, the *Discourse on the Origin and Foundation of Inequality among Men* in 1755.

Samuelson, Paul A. (1973): *Economics*. Ninth edition. New York: McGraw-Hill. First edition 1948.

Schelting, Alexander Von (1934): *Max Webers Wissenschaftslehre*. Tuebingen: J.C.B. Mohr.

Schluchter, Wolfgang (1989): *Rationalism, Religion, and Domination; A Weberian Perspective*. Translated by Neil Solomon. Berkeley, CA: University of California Press.

Schmoller, Gustav (1904): *Ueber einige Grundfragen der Sozialpolitik und der Volksvirtschaftslehre*. Second edition. Berlin: Dunker und Humblot. Previous editions 1874 and 1897.

Schmoller, Gustav (1923): *Grundriss der allgemeinen Volkswirtschaftslehre*. Second edition in two volumes. Munich: Dunker und Humblot. First edition 1900-1904.

Schnaedelbach, Herbert (1984): *Philosophy in Germany, 1831-1933*. Translated by Eric Mathews. Cambrige: Cambridge University Press.

Schumpeter, Joseph A. (1934): *The Theory of Economic Development; An inquiry into Profits, Capital, Credit, Interest, and the Business Cycle*. Translated by Redvers Opie. Cambridge, MA: Harvard University Press.

Schumpeter, Joseph A. (1950): *Capitalism, Socialism, and Democracy*. Third edition. New York: Harper and Brothers. First edition, 1942.

Schutz, Alfred (1967): *The Phenomenology of the Social World*. Translated by George Walsh and Frederick Lehnert. Evanston, IL: Northwestern University Press. First published as *Der sinnhafte Aufbau der sozialen Welt* in 1932.

Simmel, Georg (1977): *The Problems of the Philosophy of History*. Translated and edited by Guy Oakes. New York: Free Press. Translated from the German edition of 1907.

Simmel, Georg (1980): *Essays on Interpretation in Social Science*. Translated and edited by Guy Oakes. Totowa, NJ: Rowman and Littlefield.

Skinner, B. F. (1938): *Behavior of Organisms*. Cambridge, MA.: Harvard University Press.

Smith, Adam (1937): *The Wealth of Nations*. New York: Modern Library. First published in 1776.

Sombart, Werner (1913): *Der Bourgeois: Zur Geistesgeschichte des modernen Wirtschaftsmenschen*. Munich: Dunker und Humblot.

Sombart, Werner (1916): *Der moderne Kapitalismus. Historisch-systematische Darstellung des gesamt-europaeischen Wirtschaftslebens von seinen Anfaengen bis zur Gegenwart*. Second edition, four volumes. Munich: Dunker und Humblot.

Spencer, Baldwin and Gillen, F. J. (1969): *The Northern Tribes of Central Australia*. Oosterhout, The Netherlands: Anthropological Publications. First published in 1904.

Stanner, W.E.H. (1963): *On Aboriginal Religion*. Sydney: Oceania Monographs.
Strehlow, Carl (1907): Die Aranda- und Loritja-*Staemme in Zentral-Australien*. Two volumes. Frankfurt: J. Baer.
Troeltsch, Ernst (1922): *Der Historismus und Seine Probleme*. Volume III of "Gesammelte Schriften." Tuebingen: J.C.B. Mohr.
Troeltsch, Ernst (1931): *The Social Teachings of the Christian Churches*. Two volumes. New York: Harper Torchbooks. Originally published in German in 1911.
Wallwork, Ernest (1972): *Durkheim: Morality and Milieu*. Cambridge, MA: Harvard University Press.
Weber, Max (1930): *The Protestant Ethic and the Spirit of Capitalism*. Translated by Talcott Parsons. New York: Charles Scribner's Sons. Originally published in German in 1903-04.
Weber, Max (1949): *The Methodology of the Social Sciences*. Translated and edited by Edward A. Shils and Henry A. Finch. Previously published in *Gesammelte Aufsaetze zur Wissenschaftslehre*, 1922. New York: Free Press.
Weber, Max (1950): *General Economic History*. Translated by Frank H. Knight. New York: Free Press. First English language edition, 1927; first published as *Wirtschaftsgeschichte* in 1923.
Weber, Max (1951): The *Religion of China; Confucianism and Taoism*. Translated and edited by Hans H. Gerth. New York: Free Press. 1951. Previously published in *Gesammelte Aufsaetze zur Religionssoziologie*, three volumes, 1920-21.
Weber, Max (1958): *The Religion of India; The Sociology of Hinduism and Buddhism*. Translated and edited by Hans H. Gerth and Don Martindale. New York: Free Press. Previously published in *Gesammelte Aufsaetze zur Religionssoziologie*, three volumes, 1920-21.
Weber, Max (1968): *Economy and Society*. Three volumes, edited by Guenther Roth and Claus Wittich. New York: Bedminster Press. First published in German in 1925 as *Wirtschaft und Gesellschaft*, edited by Marianne Weber.
Weber, Max (1975): *Roescher and Knies; the Logical Problems of Historical Economics*. Translated with and introduction by Guy Oakes. New York: Free Press. First published in German in 1903 and 1906.
Weber, Max (1981): "Some Categories of Interpretive Sociology," translated by Edith Graber, in *The Sociological Quarterly*, 22 (Spring, 1981) 145-180.
Wenzel, Harald (1986): "Einleitung des Herausgebers: Einige Bemerkungen zu Parsons' Programm einer Theorie des Handels," in *Talcott Parsons: Aktor, Situation und normative Muster; Ein Essay zur Theorie sozialen Handelns*, translated, edited, and with an introduction by Harald Wenzel. Frankfurt: Suhrkamp. Manuscript written in English circa 1939 entitled "Actor, Situation and Normative Pattern; An Essay in the Theory of Social Action."
Whitehead, Alfred North (1925): *Science and the Modern World*. New York: Macmillan.
Wiener, Norbert (1948): *Cybernetics*. Cambridge, MA: M.I.T. Press.
Wiener, Norbert (1954): *The Human Use of Human Beings; Cybernetics and Society*. Garden City, NY: Anchor Books.
Windelband, Wilhelm (1901): *A History of Philosophy*. Second edition in translation, translated by James H. Tufts. New York: MacMillan. First published in German as *Geschichte der Philosophie*. 1892.

Über den hierarchischen Aufbau der Welt
Talcott Parsons' und Karl Poppers Theorien im Vergleich
Tamás Meleghy

Einführende Bemerkungen

Die Erscheinungen dieser Welt sind zahlreich und vielfältig. So gibt es Freude, Schmerz, Pflanzen, Tiere, Naturgesetze, religiöse Wahrheiten, wissenschaftliche Theorien, Gesetze, Verordnungen, Steine, Hunger usw. Zahlreiche Philosophen haben hinter all dieser Vielfalt eine natürliche Ordnung vermutet und waren bemüht, diese zu erkennen und zu rekonstruieren.[1] Die Frage, die Soziologen in diesem Zusammenhang bewegte, war, wo innerhalb einer solchen Ordnung ihr Gegenstand, die sozialen Erscheinungen, zu lokalisieren war.[2]

Die vorgeschlagenen Ordnungen lassen sich im Wesentlichen in zwei Grundtypen einteilen. Beide Typen sind hierarchischer Natur.

Beim ersten Typus geht man von der Idee aus, dass die Welt aus Teilchen – Atomen besteht; manche dieser Teilchen bleiben zusammen, verklumpen sich und bilden größere Einheiten. Diese größeren Einheiten sind dann die Elemente wieder größerer Einheiten usw.

Das Prinzip, nach dem diese Ordnung konstruiert ist, lässt sich als "Teil und Ganzes" bezeichnen. Die Elemente der jeweils höheren Stufe werden aus den Elementen der jeweils darunter liegenden Stufe gebildet oder zusammengesetzt. Ich bezeichne eine solche hierarchische Ordnung als *"Hierarchie der realen Phänomene"* oder Hierarchie 1. Art.

Eine solche hierarchische Ordnung sieht etwa folgendermaßen aus: subatomare Teilchen, Atome, Moleküle, organische Großmoleküle, lebende Zellen, Organe,

---

[1] Nach Gottfried Wilhelm Leibniz sieht die Stufenordnung des Seins folgendermaßen aus: unorganische Materie – Pflanze – Tier – Mensch – Engel – Gott (vgl. Sombart 1956, S. 101); Nicolai Hartmann unterscheidet anorganisches, organisches, seelisches und geistiges Sein (vgl. Wolf 1986, S. 254, Solms 1956); bei Gerhard Vollmer treffen wir auf folgende Stufenordnung: reale Systeme – chemisch reagierende Systeme – lebende Systeme – Systeme mit Bewusstsein (vgl. Vollmer 1988, S. 225, Engel 1990, S. 61).

[2] Vgl. z. B. Comte 1974, S. 25ff., Spencer 1961, S. 139f., Mauss 1989, S. 149f. sowie Wiese 1955, S. 101ff.

Organismen, Gruppen von Organismen, Gesellschaften, Gruppen von Gesellschaften.[3]

Der zweite Typus Ordnung gründet auf der Erkenntnis, dass auf bestimmten Stufen der Hierarchie 1. Art vollkommen neuartige Phänomene erscheinen, die den realen Phänomenen dieser und der darüber liegenden Stufen ganz und gar neue Qualitäten verleihen.[4] So taucht auf der Ebene der lebenden Zelle (Hierarchie 1. Art) ein vollkommen neues Phänomen auf, das man als vitales Prinzip bezeichnete,[5] heute spricht man von genetischer oder biologischer Steuerung. Einige Stufen (Hierarchie 1. Art) höher, spätestens bei den Wirbeltieren, lässt sich wiederum das Erscheinen eines neuen Phänomens, eines wenn auch noch primitiven Bewusstseins, ausmachen. Das primitive Bewusstsein – die physiologische Grundlage dafür liefert die Herausbildung des Zentralnervensystems – mit dem Vermögen, Wohlbehagen und Schmerz zu empfinden, ist eine neue Steuerungsart, im Dienste der aktuellen Verhaltensanpassung. Noch höhere Steuerungsarten sind Sinn, Institutionen und Wissen. Letztere Steuerungsarten sind nach heutigem Wissensstand nur beim Menschen voll ausgebildet.[6]

Das Prinzip, nach dem diese 2. Ordnung konzipiert ist, lässt sich als *"Hierarchie emergenter Steuerungen"* bezeichnen: Das, was geschehen soll, wird durch die Steuerungen der jeweils höheren Ebene bestimmt; das, was prinzipiell geschehen kann, wird durch die Steuerungen der jeweils niedrigeren Ebene vorgegeben.

Dieses Prinzip lässt sich am Beispiel der Beziehung der beiden unteren Steuerungsebenen folgendermaßen erläutern: Durch das Hinzutreten der höheren, biologischen, Steuerung werden die Steuerungen auf der niedrigeren Ebene nicht etwa außer Kraft gesetzt. Es geschieht in einem Organismus nichts, das gegen die Gesetze der unbelebten Natur verstoßen würde. Diese Gesetze geben den prinzipiellen Möglichkeitsspielraum vor, was überhaupt geschehen kann. Was von diesen prinzipiell gegebenen Möglichkeiten aber realisiert wird, bestimmt die höhere Steuerung: das genetische Programm. Dabei muss aber betont werden, dass das aktive Element der höheren, hier der genetischen Steuerung zukommt. Sie gibt an, was geschehen soll.

---

[3] Vgl. Bertalanffy 1990, S. 34ff., Elias 1983, S. 230, Riedl 1987, S. 113-167, Meleghy 1993, S. 26f. und Meleghy 1997, S. 295ff.
[4] Man spricht in diesem Zusammenhang häufig auch von Emergenz. Auf die Diskussion dieses Begriffes möchte ich mich hier aber nicht einlassen. Vgl. dazu Vanberg 1972, 1975, 250ff. sowie Meleghy 1997, S. 564ff.
[5] Bertalanffy bezeichnet die Vorstellung "im Keim, und in ähnlicher Weise in sonstigen Leistungen des Organismus, wirke ein von den physikalisch-chemischen Naturkräften grundsätzlich verschiedener Faktor, der die Geschehnisse in Vorausschau des Zieles, des herzustellenden typischen Organismus, ausrichtet" als "Vitalismus" (Bertalanffy 1990, S. 19f.). Vgl. auch Bertalanffy 1990, S. 6 ff.
[6] Vgl. Lorenz 1977, Maturana und Varela 1987.

Die Steuerungen der tieferen Ebene entscheiden nur darüber, ob das, was geschehen soll, auch geschehen kann. Ich bezeichne eine solche hierarchische Ordnung als Hierarchie der Steuerungen oder Hierarchie 2. Art.[7]

Diese hierarchische Ordnung sieht etwa folgendermaßen aus: Naturgesetze (und Randbedingungen), genetische Programme, Bewusstsein (Sinn), Institutionen und Wissen.

Diese zweite hierarchische Ordnung ist weniger geläufig als die erste. Offensichtlicher ist die Ordnung, die sich als Ausdruck der Hierarchie der Steuerungen innerhalb der natürlichen Welt ergibt. Durch das Hinzutreten höherer Steuerungen entstehen innerhalb der Welt Phänomenenbereiche oder Ebenen mit jeweils grundlegend neuen Qualitäten. Solche Phänomenenbereiche oder Ebenen sind: physikalisch-chemische Systeme, biologische Systeme, biologische Systeme mit Bewusstsein und biologische Systeme mit einem höheren *sinngesteuerten* Bewusstsein.[8]

Dabei erhalten die einzelnen Ebenen ihre Einheit durch das Vorherrschen einer besonderen Steuerungsart. Der Bereich, den wir als die unbelebte natürliche Welt bezeichnen (physikalisch-chemische Systeme), gewinnt seine Einheit dadurch, dass die Vorgänge in ihm durch allgemeine (Natur-) Gesetze und von besonderen Umständen (den Randbedingungen) gesteuert werden; der Bereich, den wir als die belebte Natur bezeichnen (biologische Systeme), erhält wiederum seine Einheit dadurch, dass die in ihm ablaufenden Prozesse durch ein biologisches oder genetisches Programm gesteuert werden; kennzeichnend für Systeme mit Bewusstsein ist wiederum die Steuerung durch psychologische Gesetze und Bewusstseinsempfindungen; im Zusammenhang mit der Herausbildung der beschreibenden Sprache entsteht schließlich die Welt des spezifisch menschlichen Bewusstseins, die Welt der sinngesteuerten Handlungen, die Welt der Normen und Institutionen und die Welt des externen objektiven Wissens.

Möglicherweise gibt es neben diesen beiden hierarchischen Ordnungen auch noch andere, die nach einem ganz anderen Prinzip konzipiert wurden. Die mir bisher bekannten Entwürfe lassen sich aber entweder zu dem ersten oder zu dem zweiten Typus zuordnen, oder, was häufig anzutreffen ist, sie repräsentieren eine Mischung aus diesen beiden Grundtypen.

Wie sollten wir bei der Beurteilung von konkreten Entwürfen, hier bei den Entwürfen von Karl Popper und Talcott Parsons, verfahren? Ich schlage vor, dass wir dafür drei Kriterien heranziehen sollten:

1. Ist die betreffende hierarchische Ordnung durchgehend nach einem einheitlichen Prinzip konstruiert?

---

[7] Vgl. Meleghy 1993, S. 27f., Meleghy 1997, S. 324ff. und Meleghy 1998, S. 229ff.
[8] Vgl. Meleghy 1997, S. 326f.

2. Lässt sich der eigene Gegenstandsbereich, in diesem Fall der Gegenstandsbereich der Soziologie, innerhalb der betreffenden Ordnung deutlich lokalisieren?
3. Nützt die betreffende hierachische Ordnung der interdisziplinären Kommunikation oder behindert sie diese?[9]

Ich werde in diesem Aufsatz folgendermaßen vorgehen:
Erstens werde ich anhand der hierarchischen Ordnungen von Auguste Comte und Emile Durkheim zeigen, dass die beiden von mir referierten Grundtypen hierarchischer Ordnungen – die Hierarchie der realen Phänomene und die Hierarchie der Steuerungen – bei der Konzeption der Soziologie von Anfang an eine wichtige Rolle gespielt haben und auch für manche Kontroversen innerhalb des Faches verantwortlich waren. Zweitens werde ich Poppers und Parsons' Entwürfe referieren und ihre Gemeinsamkeiten und Differenzen untersuchen. Drittens werde ich diese beiden Konzepte anhand der oben dargestellten Kriterien bewerten und einen Vorschlag zur Lösung der Probleme der beiden Entwürfe präsentieren.

Auguste Comte und Emile Durkheim und die Hierarchie 1.und 2. Art

Comtes Auffassung von der Soziologie war eingebettet in sein System der Wissenschaften. Die abstrakten oder theoretischen Wissenschaften und deren Objektbereiche bilden ihm zufolge eine natürliche Ordnung. Die fünf grundlegenden theoretischen Wissenschaften sind: Astronomie, Physik, Chemie, Biologie und Soziologie. Die Gegenstandsbereiche dieser fünf Wissenschaften umfassen nach Comte alle Phänomenenbereiche.[10]

Zu dieser Ordnung der Wissenschaften gelangt Comte, indem er die einzelnen Disziplinen mit Hilfe der Kriterien Einfachheit und Allgemeinheit in eine Rangordnung bringt.

Die einfachsten und allgemeinsten, d. h. alle anderen Bereiche mitbestimmenden, Erscheinungen sind die Himmelskörper und deren Bewegungen. Mit diesen Phänomenen beschäftigt sich die Physik der Himmelskörper oder Astronomie. Sie ist daher die einfachste und allgemeinste Wissenschaft.

Bereits komplexer und spezifischer (weniger allgemein) sind die anorganischen Stoffe und Vorgänge auf der Erde. Mit diesen Phänomenen befasst sich die "Physik der Erde" (Comte 1974, S. 25). Die Vorgänge in diesem Bereich gliedern sich wie-

---

[9] Will man diese drei Kriterien mit Namen belegen, so bieten sich folgende Bezeichnungen an: 1. interne Konsistenz, 2. sachliche Adäquanz und 3. externe Kompatibilität.
[10] Dieser Sachverhalt wird von Comte auch als enzyklopädisches Gesetz bezeichnet (vgl. Fuchs-Heinritz 1998, S. 146f.).

derum in zwei Klassen: in die Klasse der mechanischen und in die Klasse der chemischen Vorgänge, wobei die mechanischen Vorgänge einfacher und allgemeiner sind als die chemischen. Die zuerst genannten Vorgänge bilden den Gegenstandsbereich der Physik, die zuletzt genannten Erscheinungen dagegen den Gegenstandsbereich der Chemie.

Noch komplexer und spezifischer sind die organischen Erscheinungen auf der Erde. Der Erforschung dieses Bereichs widmet sich die allgemeine Lebenswissenschaft oder organische Physik. Auch in diesem Bereich gliedern sich die Erscheinungen in zwei Klassen: zu der ersten Klasse zählen die Vorgänge bei den individuellen Organismen, zu der zweiten Klasse die Wechselwirkungssysteme individueller Organismen oder der "soziale Organismus".[11] Mit den Vorgängen der ersten Klasse befassen sich die Biologie im engeren Sinne und die Physiologie, mit den Vorgängen der zweiten Klasse die soziale Physik oder Soziologie.[12]

Erscheinungen und Vorgänge, die die neue Wissenschaft soziale Physik oder Soziologie untersucht, sind bei Menschen besonders augenfällig. Eine gesellige Natur und damit soziale Erscheinungen[13] weisen nach Comte aber auch viele andere Organismen auf. Die organische Physik oder Soziologie ist daher nach Comte die Wissenschaft aller sozialer Erscheinungen, und solche gibt es sowohl (oder insbesondere) bei Menschen als auch bei Tieren.

Und die Humansoziologie, so Comte, könnte viel von der Tiersoziologie lernen, "insbesondere dann, wenn die Vergesellschaftung der Tiere, die man jetzt noch so wenig kennt, besser beobachtet sein wird" (Comte 1974, S. 107). Die ausschließliche Beobachtung von menschlichen Sozietäten und die strikte Ablehnung von Vergleichen mit Tiervergesellschaftungen beruht nach Comte auf dem immer noch herrschenden Einfluss der theologischen und metaphysischen Philosophie.[14]

Comtes beide obersten Stufen der Hierarchie der Gegenstandsbereiche sind offensichtlich nach dem Prinzip der Hierarchie 1. Art "Teil und Ganzes" konzipiert. Gegenstand der Biologie im engeren Sinne sind die individuellen Organismen, Ge-

---

[11] Diesen Ausdruck benützt Comte für die Kennzeichnung der Wechselwirkungssysteme lebender Organismen in Gruppen, Verbänden und Gesellschaften wiederholt (vgl. Comte 1974, S. 83, S. 88, S. 149).

[12] Diese beiden Vorgänge oder Bereiche werden von Comte folgendermaßen charakterisiert: "Die eine bezieht sich auf das *Individuum*, die andere auf die *Gattung*, namentlich wenn sie geselliger Natur sind. Deshalb gilt diese Einteilung hauptsächlich für den Menschen. ... Darauf beruht die weitere Einteilung der organischen Physik in Biologie und Soziologie" (Comte 1974, S. 25f.).

[13] Mit sozialen Erscheinungen sind hier die Wechselwirkungen individueller Organismen in Gruppen, Verbänden und Gesellschaften gemeint.

[14] "Wenn aber die Soziologie erst von dem positiven Geist geleitet sein wird", schreibt Comte, "wird man erkennen, wie nützlich der Vergleich des Menschen mit den Tieren ist und namentlich mit den höheren Säugetieren" (Comte 1974, S. 107).

genstand der Soziologie oder sozialer Physik sind dagegen die Wechselwirkungssysteme derselben. Folgerichtig fällt nach Comte auch das Studium der Tiervergesellschaftungen in den Aufgabenbereich der Soziologie.

Auch bei Durkheim erhielt die Soziologie ihren Platz innerhalb des Systems der Wissenschaften. Diese lassen sich nach ihm folgendermaßen anordnen: physikalisch-chemische Wissenschaften, Biologie, Psychologie und Soziologie (vgl. Durkheim 1961, S. 188 f.). Diese Vorstellung von der Hierarchie der empirischen Wissenschaften beruht bei ihm auf der Idee, dass die Welt selbst einen hierarchischen Aufbau aufweist. Mit den vier Ebenen der empirischen Wissenschaften korrespondieren nach Durkheim innerhalb der realen Welt: physikalisch-chemische Systeme, biologische (lebende) Systeme, psychische Systeme (Systeme mit Bewusstsein) und soziale Systeme (Gesellschaften).

Die Gesellschaft ist nach Durkheim ein System miteinander wechselseitig verbundener Individuen.[15] Das System, das menschliche Individuen miteinander bilden, ist aber ihm zufolge ein besonderes. Es unterscheidet sich von den Systemen, die subhumane Organismen miteinander bilden, grundlegend. Sie besteht im Wesentlichen aus Ideen. Sie ist anders ausgedrückt, eine geistige Wesenheit.[16]

Wie lassen sich die von Durkheim gemeinten geistigen Wesenheiten oder Ideen, die der menschlichen Gesellschaft ihre eigene Wirklichkeit verleihen, charakterisieren? Diese sind nach Durkheim Phänomene, die 1. vom Standpunkt des individuellen Bewusstseins betrachtet, einen externen Charakter haben und 2. die Fähigkeit besitzen, auf das Bewusstsein einen mehr oder weniger starken Druck auszuüben (vgl. Durkheim 1961, S. 105 f.).

Diese Typen des Verhaltens und des Denkens werden von Durkheim als soziale Tatsachen (faits sociaux) oder Institutionen bezeichnet. Diese haben moralischen Charakter. Diese moralischen Phänomene bilden nach Durkheim den eigentlichen Gegenstand der Soziologie: "Die Soziologie kann definiert werden als die Wissenschaft von den Institutionen, deren Entstehung und Wirkungsart" (Durkheim 1961, S. 100).

Worauf es bei der menschlichen Gesellschaft letztlich ankommt, ist also ein Spezifikum, etwas, was Tiergesellschaften nicht kennen.

---

[15] "Kraft dieses Prinzips ist die Gesellschaft nicht bloß eine Summe von Individuen, sondern das durch deren Verbindung gebildete System" (Durkheim 1961, S. 189).
[16] "Denn eine Gesellschaft besteht nicht einfach aus der Masse von Individuen, aus denen sie sich zusammensetzt, aus dem Boden, den sie besetzen, aus den Dingen, derer sie sich bedienen, aus den Bewegungen, die sie ausführen, sondern vor allem aus der Idee, die sie sich von sich selber macht" (Durkheim 1984, S. 566).

Durkheims und Comtes Vorstellungen von der Ordnung der Wissenschaften sind beinahe identisch.[17] Soziale Systeme repräsentieren in beiden Ordnungen die höchste Stufe, und die Soziologie ist in beiden Ordnungen die Krönung der Wissenschaften. Es kann dabei leicht übersehen werden, dass Comtes sozialer Organismus und Durkheims soziales System recht unterschiedliche Typen von Phänomenen darstellen. Erstere sind Wechselwirkungssysteme biologischer Organismen (welcher Art auch immer), letztere dagegen sind die externen normativen Produkte der Wechselwirkungssysteme menschlicher Individuen (und nur dieser).

Diese Institutionen, externe moralische und kognitive Tatsachen, sind besondere Elemente innerhalb der Hierarchie 2. Art. Sie haben ihren Ort oberhalb der Steuerung (des individuellen Bewusstseins) durch psychologische Gesetzmäßigkeiten und Bewusstseinsempfindungen. Durkheims beide obersten Stufen der Hierarchie der empirischen Wissenschaften – Psychologie und Soziologie – sind also nach dem Prinzip der Hierarchie der Steuerungen oder Hierarchie 2. Art konzipiert.

So ist die Identität der beiden Ordnungen ein scheinbarer. Comtes sozialer Organismus – ein Phänomen der Hierarchie 1. Art – wurde durch Durkheim durch institutionalisierte normative und kognitive Muster, oder kurz Institutionen – ein Phänomen der Hierarchie 2. Art – ersetzt. Die Betrachtung der Tiergesellschaften wird so aus der Soziologie ausgeschlossen.[18]

So spielten die beiden hierarchischen Ordnungen – Hierarchie 1. und 2. Art – bereits in der Gründungsphase der Soziologie eine wichtige Rolle. Comtes Entwurf der Soziologie beruhte auf der Idee der Hierarchie 1. Art: Teil und Ganzes, und schloss, wie wir gesehen haben, die Tiersozietäten in den Gegenstandsbereich der Soziologie ein. Durkheims Konzeption der Soziologie wurde dagegen von der Idee der Hierarchie 2. Art oder Steuerungshierarchie bestimmt. Die charakteristischen sozialen

---

17 Durkheim betrachtet nur die Vorgänge auf der Erde. So kommt in seiner Ordnung die Astronomie nicht vor. Dafür fehlt bei Comte die Ebene psychischer Phänomene und damit korrespondierend die Wissenschaft Psychologie. Psychische Phänomene sind, seiner Meinung nach, einerseits eng an körperliche Vorgänge gebunden und werden daher zweckmäßigerweise gemeinsam mit diesen von der Biologie untersucht, andererseits sind sie als Vorgänge, die die Entwicklung des menschlichen Geistes betreffen, gesellschaftliche Vorgänge und daher Aspekte des sozialen Organismus und sollten daher in der Soziologie behandelt werden (vgl. Fuchs-Heinritz 1998, S. 166f.).

18 Diese Konsequenz der Durkheimschen Soziologie wird von Marcel Mauss ganz deutlich ausgesprochen: "Wenn man mir eines Tages auch nur entfernte Äquivalente von Institutionen in den Tiergesellschaften zeigt, werde ich mich verneigen und sagen, dass die Soziologie die Tiergesellschaften berücksichtigen muss. Doch man hat mir noch nichts dieser Art gezeigt. Und bis es soweit ist, kann ich mich durchaus in der Humansoziologie einquartieren. Also der erste Unterschied: Die Psychologie ist nicht nur die Psychologie des Menschen, während die Soziologie im strengen Sinn Humansoziologie ist" (Mauss 1989, S. 150).

Phänomene waren für ihn Institutionen, also Erscheinungen, die Tiergesellschaften nicht kennen. Damit wurden die Sozietäten von nicht menschlichen Organismen aus dem Gegenstandsbereich der Soziologie ausgeschlossen.

Die auf diese Weise erfolgte Transformation der Soziologie durch Durkheim und seine Schüler wurde von Comtes geistigen Erben nicht widerspruchslos hingenommen. Fausto Squillace, ein Verfechter der Durkheimschen Position, erwähnt in seinem 1911 erschienen Buch "Die Soziologischen Theorien" den "lange(n) Streit, der zwischen den Soziologen in diesem Punkt herrscht(e) " (Squillace 1911, S. 38).[19]

Diese Auseinandersetzung ist längst abgeschlossen. Durkheims Schüler haben den Sieg davongetragen. Die Idee des "sozialen Organismus" ist in der Soziologie in Vergessenheit geraten. Allerdings, wie gesagt, innerhalb der Soziologie, und man kann hinzufügen, innerhalb der sogenannten "Sozialwissenschaften". Denn Biologen, seien diese von ihrer Spezialisierung her Botaniker, Zoologen, Anthropologen, verstehen auch heute noch unter sozialen Systemen genauso wie Comte die Wechselwirkungssysteme individueller Organismen, seien diese nun Pilze, Pantoffeltierchen oder Menschen.[20]

Diese beiden verschiedenen Bedeutungen "sozialer Phänomene" bei Sozialwissenschaftern und Biologen, hinter denen sich, wie wir gesehen haben, zwei grundlegend verschiedene Konzeptionen sozialer Phänomene (Hierarchie 1. und 2. Art) verstecken, sind dafür verantwortlich, dass heute Biologen und Sozialwissenschaftler gewöhnlich aneinander vorbeireden. Der ursprünglich intradisziplinäre Streit ist so zu einem interdisziplinären Missverständnis geworden.

---

[19] Squillace führt auch die wichtigsten Kontrahenten in diesem Streit an: Für den Einschluss von Tiergesellschaften in den Gegenstandsbereich der Soziologie waren Ribot, Siciliani, Boccardo, De Marinis. Die gegenteilige Meinung wurde vertreten von Schaeffle und von Guarin de Vitry (vgl. Squillace 1911, S. 38).

[20] So gehen z. B. die Projektwerber der Studien "Zur Soziologie und Ökologie der Hopfenbuchen-Bestände Kärntens und einiger benachbarter Länder" und "Mikroklimatische und pflanzensoziologische Untersuchungen in der Ebentaler Schlucht (Zwanzgerber-Bach-Schlucht) bei Klagenfurt" ("FWF", Fonds zur Förderung der wissenschaftlichen Forschung, Info 4, Nov. 1991, S. 6) offensichtlich davon aus, dass es auf den von ihnen untersuchten Gebieten irgendwelche soziologisch relevanten sozialen Phänomene (Phänomene der innerartlichen Koppelung oder Abgestimmtheit) gibt, wohl aber kaum davon, dass es sich bei diesen sozialen Phänomenen gleichzeitig um normative Phänomene handelt. Vgl. auch den Band: Biologie des Sozialverhaltens, Heidelberg: Spektrum der Wissenschaft 1988 (Deutsche Ausgabe von Scientific American), in dem sich Untersuchungen über das Sozialverhalten von zahlreichen Tierarten finden.

Karl Poppers und Talcott Parsons' hierarchische Ordnungen im Vergleich

Nach Karl Popper weist die Welt eine hierarchische Ordnung auf. Er spricht in diesem Zusammenhang von drei Welten. Er nimmt aber innerhalb der einzelnen Ebenen zusätzliche Differenzierungen vor, sodass man mit gleicher Berechtigung auch von fünf Welten sprechen könnte.[21] Poppers hierarchische Ordnung sieht folgendermaßen aus: Die unterste Ebene bilden die physikalisch-chemischen Erscheinungen.[22] Oberhalb dieser Welt 1 im engeren Sinne (hier gekennzeichnet als Welt 1a) liegt die Welt der biologischen Phänomene (Welt 1b).[23] Eine Stufe darüber ist die Welt der psychischen Zustände und Erfahrungen (Welt 2) angesiedelt.[24] Die obersten Ebenen der Hierarchie bilden die beiden Abteilungen der Welt 3. Poppers Welt 3 ist ein menschliches Produkt, ein Erzeugnis des Menschen. Abteilung 3a ist die Welt der Normen, der Vorschriften und der Institutionen,[25] Abteilung 3b ist die Welt der "objektiven Gedankeninhalte" (Popper 1979, S. 264), "die Welt der logischen *Gehalte* von Büchern, Bibliotheken, Informationsspeichern, von Datenverarbeitungsanlagen und ähnlichem" (Popper 1973, S. 88).

Wie hängen Poppers 3 (fünf) Welten zusammen? Welche Eigenschaften weist diese hierarchische Struktur auf? Ich werde an dieser Stelle auf drei Eigenschaften dieser Struktur eingehen. Diese Eigenschaften sind: 1. mögliche Kausalbeziehungen, 2. hierarchische Struktur und 3. plastische Steuerung.

---

[21] Obwohl Popper in diesem Zusammenhang von einer Drei-Welten-Theorie spricht, ist er keineswegs der Ansicht, dass es wirklich nur drei Welten gibt: "Ich bin nicht der Auffassung und behaupte hier nicht, dass wir unsere Welten nicht anders oder auch gar nicht abzählen könnten. Wir könnten insbesondere mehr als drei Welten unterscheiden. Mein Ausdruck 'die dritte Welt' gilt lediglich der Bequemlichkeit" (1973, S. 124).

[22] Popper bezeichnet diese Welt als die "Welt der physikalischen Zustände" (Popper 1973, S. 174) oder auch die "Welt der 'Dinge' – der physikalischen Objekte" (Popper 1979, S. 264).

[23] Nach Popper bestehen lebende Strukturen zwar aus physikalisch-chemischen Entitäten und Prozessen; sie sind aber nicht auf diese reduzierbar (vgl. Popper 1979, S. 259f.).

[24] Obwohl diese Welt 2 ein Produkt der materiellen Welt 1 ist, ist sie nicht mit dieser identisch oder auf sie reduzierbar. Genauso, wie Gesetze und Theorien menschliche Produkte sind und trotzdem weder mit den Menschen identisch noch irgendwie auf Menschen reduzierbar sind (vgl. Popper 1973, S. 278).

[25] "Diese sozialen Institutionen bestimmen den eigentlichen sozialen Charakter unserer sozialen Umwelt. Sie bestehen aus allen jenen sozialen Wesenheiten, die den Dingen der physischen Welt entsprechen. Eine Gemüsehandlung oder ein Universitätsinstitut oder eine Polizeimacht oder ein Gesetz sind in diesem Sinn soziale Institutionen. Auch Kirche und Staat und Ehe sind soziale Institutionen, und gewisse zwingende Gebräuche, wie zum Beispiel in Japan Harakiri" (Popper 1970, S. 121f.).

Charakteristisch für diese Struktur ist 1., dass immer nur zwei benachbarte Welten oder Ebenen unmittelbar oder kausal aufeinander einwirken können[26]. So können Phänomene der natürlichen Welt 1a, wie z. B. Hitze, Kälte, Nässe, Trockenheit oder Druck, unmittelbar auf biologische Strukturen (Welt 1b) einwirken. Das gilt auch umgekehrt, biologische Strukturen üben auf die sie umgebende unbelebte Natur auf vielfältige Weise eine kausale Wirkung aus.[27] Die subjektive Welt 2 kann dagegen nicht unmittelbar auf die unbelebte Natur einwirken, sie benötigt dafür die Vermittlung der organischen Strukturen der Welt 1b. Und auch umgekehrt: Die Erscheinungen der unbelebten natürlichen Welt 1a können nur durch die Vermittlung der organischen Strukturen der Welt 1b eine Wirkung auf die Erscheinungen der 2. subjektiven Welt ausüben.

Und die Kette der Vermittlungen wird umso länger, je höher wir innerhalb der hierarchischen Struktur emporsteigen. Normen und Institutionen (Welt 3a) können unmittelbar auf die Phänomene der 2. subjektiven Welt einwirken. Durch die Vermittlung der 2. Welt, der organischen Strukturen der Welt 1b, können sie aber auch die Erscheinungen der unbelebten Natur beeinflussen. Ideen, objektive Wissensbestände im Sinne von Inhalten von Aussagen, können nur mittels der normativen Struktur einer Sprache (Welt 3a) Zugang zur 2. subjektiven Welt finden.[28] Ideen können aber durch die Vermittlung der Phänomene der normativen Welt 3a, der Welt 2, der Welt 1b durchaus auch auf die unbelebte Natur einwirken. Die auf diese Weise entstandenen Phänomene werden als Artefakte bezeichnet. Diese sind Bestandteile der von Menschen geschaffenen materiellen Kultur.

Charakteristisch für diese Struktur ist 2., dass die einzelnen Ebenen eine hierarchische Ordnung bilden. Damit ist zunächst nur gemeint, dass die höheren Ebenen ohne das Vorhandensein der darunter liegenden Ebenen nicht existieren könnten. Die unteren Ebenen bilden sozusagen die Basis für die höheren Welten.

Biologische Strukturen (Welt 1b) werden aus den Stoffen der unbelebten Natur (Welt 1a) gebildet. Die unbelebte Natur ist die Trägerin oder die Basis der biologi-

---

[26] "Die drei Welten hängen so miteinander zusammen, dass die ersten beiden und die letzten beiden aufeinander wirken können. Die zweite Welt, die Welt der subjektiven oder persönlichen Erfahrungen, steht also mit jeder der beiden anderen Welten in Wechselwirkung. Die erste und die dritte Welt können nicht aufeinander wirken, außer durch das Dazwischentreten der zweiten Welt, der Welt der subjektiven oder persönlichen Erfahrungen" (Popper 1993, S. 174).

[27] Als ein Beispiel kann hier die Veränderung der Atmosphäre der Erde durch die Stoffwechselausscheidung der Pflanzen angeführt werden.

[28] Unter objektivem Wissen versteht Popper externalisierte, d. h. sprachlich formulierte, besser noch veröffentlichte Aussagen. Diese können kritisch diskutiert werden und auf Grund der kritischen Diskussion verändert oder auch verworfen werden. Objektivität ist nicht gleich Wahrheit. Auch falsche Behauptungen können im oben bestimmten Sinne objektiv sein (vgl. Popper 1993, S. 132ff.).

schen Welt 1b. Die biologische Welt ist wiederum die Trägerin oder die Basis für die Welt der psychischen Erscheinungen. Diese Welt 2 könnte ohne das Vorhandensein biologischer Strukturen (Welt 1b) und einer unbelebten materiellen Basis nicht existieren. Die Welt der Normen und Institutionen ist ein Produkt des menschlichen Bewusstseins. Sie wird von der Welt 2 getragen. Letztere könnte, wie wir gesehen haben, ohne eine biologische, und diese ohne eine unbelebte natürliche Basis, nicht existieren. Phänomene der Welt der objektiven Gedankeninhalte könnten schließlich ohne eine normative Basis (normative Struktur der menschlichen Sprache) nicht existieren. Diese wird ihrerseits getragen von der 2. Welt, welche wiederum von der biologischen Welt, welche wiederum von der unbelebten natürlichen Welt getragen wird.

Charakteristisch für diese Struktur ist 3., dass sie ein System plastischer Steuerungen darstellt. Unter plastischer Steuerung versteht Popper "eine Steuerung mit Rückmeldung" (Popper 1973, S. 265) oder Rückkopplung. Die Idee der plastischen Steuerung umfasst mindestens vier Aspekte, die hier anhand der Beziehung des Bewusstseins (Welt 2) zum biologischen Organismus (Welt 1b) erläutert werden.

1. Der Organismus macht nicht immer genau das, was das Bewusstsein will. Der Körper ist ein recht widerspenstiges Instrument. Man denke nur an die zähen Bemühungen, die notwendig sind, bis man ein Musikinstrument relativ anständig spielen kann (vgl. Popper 1973, S. 279).

2. Die Beziehung ist eine Interaktionsbeziehung. Wir (d. h. unser Bewusstsein) können auf Grund unserer erfolglosen Versuche lernen, dass wir uns mehr anstrengen müssen, wenn wir unsere Ziele tatsächlich erreichen wollen (z. B. ein erstklassiger Geigenspieler zu werden); oder, dass wir auf Grund unserer Beschränkungen (des körperlichen Vermögens) unsere Ziele abändern oder aufgeben müssen (vgl. Popper 1973, S. 278 f.).

3. Das Bewusstsein wird von der biologischen Basis entlastet: Probleme, an deren Lösung das Bewusstsein anfangs mit voller Hinwendung arbeitete, so etwa beim Spielen einer relativ schweren Passage eines Musikstückes, werden später ohne Beteiligung des vollen Bewusstseins ausgeführt. Das Bewusstsein wird für die Wahrnehmung von neuen Aufgaben freigehalten. Die Steuerung des bereits Erlernten wird von der biologischen Basis übernommen.[29]

4. Das Bewusstsein greift nur ein, wenn es notwendig ist, d. h. z. B. dann, wenn größere Abweichungen von einem wie auch immer gearteten Sollwert vorkommen.

---

[29] Karl Popper drückt diesen Sachverhalt folgendermaßen aus: "Es spricht also alles dafür, dass der Geist, das Bewusstsein, im Haushalt der höheren Organismen unerlässlich ist, und für die Notwendigkeit, gelöste Probleme und 'erlernte' Situationen in die Physis, in den Körper zurücksinken zu lassen – vermutlich, um den Geist, das Bewusstsein, für neue Aufgaben frei zu machen" (Popper 1979, S. 280).

So wird etwa beim aufrechten Stehen die Körperstellung durch unzählige Muskelbewegungen aufrechterhalten. Die Kontrolle erfolgt normalerweise auf der biologischen Ebene ohne Beteiligung des Bewusstseins. Das Bewusstsein greift nur dann lenkend ein, wenn es auf Grund von einer größeren Abweichung vom Sollwert (von der aufrechten Stellung) alarmiert wird.[30]

Die Vorstellung, dass die Welt einen hierarchischen Aufbau aufweist, ist ein konstitutives Element der strukturfunktionalistischen Systemtheorie Talcott Parsons'. Die hierarchische Struktur, die Parsons beschreibt und analysiert, ist eine Hierarchie von Systemen.

Systeme entstehen, indem bestimmte Bereiche der Welt gegenüber der übrigen Welt sich abgrenzen. Durch diese Abgrenzung entsteht die Differenz zwischen System-Innenwelt und System-Umwelt (vgl. Jensen 1976, S. 46).

Kennzeichnend für Systeme ist darüber hinaus eine gewisse innere Ordnung. Die Elemente eines Systems stehen untereinander in relativ stabilen Beziehungen. Die Relationen der Elemente bilden ein mehr oder weniger geordnetes Muster in der Zeit. Das Bestehen eines Systems in der Zeit ist kein Zufall sondern die Leistung der relativ stabilen Beziehungen zwischen ihren Komponenten. Das Muster der relativ stabilen Beziehungen zwischen den Elementen wird als Struktur,[31] die Leistung eines solchen Musters für die Erhaltung des Ganzen wird als Funktion,[32] und das abgegrenzte Aggregat selbst wird als System[33] bezeichnet.

An dieser Stelle sollten wir einige Unterscheidungen einführen. Man unterscheidet 1. theoretische und empirische Systeme. Theoretische Systeme[34] bestehen aus Begriffen und deren Beziehungen. Innerhalb von empirischen Wissenschaften – zu denen nach Parsons die Soziologie zählt – sollten die Termini eines solchen Systems

---

[30] "Bewusstseinszustände oder Folgen von Bewusstseinszuständen können als Steuerungs- oder Fehlerbeseitigungs-Systeme arbeiten: in der Regel handelt es sich um die Ausschaltung (einsetzenden) Verhaltens, das heißt (einsetzender) Bewegung. Unter diesem Gesichtspunkt ist das Bewusstsein einfach eine von vielen zusammenwirkenden Arten der Steuerung" (Popper 1973, S. 277f.).

[31] "Eine Struktur ist eine Reihe von verhältnismäßig stabilen Beziehungsmustern zwischen Einheiten" (Parsons 1968, S. 54).

[32] Der Begriff Funktion weist in diesem Zusammenhang auf eine teleologische Beziehung hin: "Ein Prozess oder eine Reihe von Bedingungen können entweder zur Erhaltung (oder Entwicklung) des Systems 'beitragen', oder aber sie sind 'disfunktional', d. h. sie beeinträchtigen die Integration, die Wirksamkeit usw. des Systems" (Parsons 1968, S. 38).

[33] "Ein System ist ein geordnetes Aggregat in einer fluktuierenden Umwelt" (Parsons 1976, S. 73).

[34] "Ein theoretisches System, so wie es hier verstanden wird, ist eine Gesamtheit allgemeiner Begriffe, die logisch interdependent sind und einen empirischen Bezug haben" (Parsons 1968, S. 31).

zudem empirischen Bezug haben, d. h. sie sollten auf Beobachtungstatsachen bezogen werden können.

Die gerade diskutierten Begriffe Struktur, Funktion und System sind ein Beispiel für ein theoretisches System. Diese drei Begriffe stehen untereinander in einem logischen Zusammenhang und können für die Beschreibung und Analyse von empirischen Zusammenhängen benützt werden.[35]

Ein empirisches System[36] besteht dagegen aus einer Reihe von miteinander zusammenhängenden empirischen Erscheinungen – also aus dem, was man bei der Anwendung eines theoretischen Systems beschreibt und analysiert.

Beschreiben und analysieren wir mittels der Begriffe und Aussagen der strukturfunktionalistischen Systemtheorie (theoretisches System) einen biologischen Organismus, z. B. ein Haushuhn, so ist das, was mittels der Begriffe und Aussagen des theoretischen Systems beschrieben wird (die strukturellen und funktionalen Aspekte des Systems Haushuhn) ein empirisches System.

Wissenschaftliche Beschreibungen und Analysen sind mit anderen Worten Rekonstruktionen empirischer Zusammenhänge (Systeme) mittels theoretischer Konstruktionen (theoretischer Systeme).

Wir können 2. zwischen empirischen und konkreten Systemen unterscheiden.[37] Konkrete Systeme bilden eine Unterabteilung von empirischen Systemen. Der Gegenstand einer wissenschaftlichen Beschreibung und Analyse kann entweder eine reale, raum-zeitlich lokalisierbare Einheit sein oder sich lediglich auf bestimmte

---

[35] Dabei geht man davon aus – und das ist die Grundannahme der Systemtheorie –, dass in der Welt tatsächlich Phänomene existieren, die als Systeme gedeutet werden können.

[36] Verwendet man ein theoretisches System – also ein System von Begriffen bei der Beschreibung von empirischen Erscheinungen, so beschreiben sie etwas. "Dieses 'Was', nämlich die miteinander zusammenhängenden empirischen Erscheinungen, welche den Gegenstand der Beschreibung und Analyse für eine wissenschaftliche Untersuchung bilden, sind es, die wir als empirisches 'System' bezeichnen" (Parsons 1968, S. 33).

[37] Es wäre auch möglich, hier von der Unterscheidung abstrakter und konkreter Systeme zu sprechen. Man würde empirische Systeme, die keine konkreten Systeme sind, also als abstrakte Systeme bezeichnen. Das wäre aber unüblich. Bei Stefan Jensen kommen die beiden Pole des Gegensatzpaares konkret – abstrakt als Bestandteile zweier verschiedener Unterscheidungen vor. Konkrete Systeme bilden bei ihm eine Unterabteilung von empirischen Systemen. Empirische Systeme sind entweder konkrete Systeme (z. B. ein raumzeitlich gegebener Organismus) oder eben nicht (z. B. die strukturalen und funktionalen Aspekte eines konkreten Organismus) (vgl. Jensen 1976a, S. 28). Abstrakte Systeme werden von ihm empirischen Systemen gegenübergestellt. Lokalisiert man empirische Systeme auf der elementaren Ebene (Ebene der Dinge und deren Beziehungen), so können abstrakte Systeme auf der Meta-Ebene lokalisiert werden. Abstrakte und empirische Systeme stehen in demselben Verhältnis wie Beschreibung und Gegenstand der Beschreibung und Analyse und Analysegegenstand (vgl. Jensen 1976a, S. 27).

Aspekte einer solchen Einheit beziehen. Im ersten Fall haben wir es mit konkreten, im zweiten Fall mit abstrakten Systemen zu tun.

Beispiele für konkrete empirische Systeme sind ein Haushuhn und die Einheit Hühner eines Hühnerstalls, Beispiele für abstrakte empirische Systeme sind die strukturalen und funktionalen Aspekte der realen Einheit Haushuhn und der realen Einheit Hühner eines Hühnerstalls.

Die bisher diskutierten Unterscheidungen – theoretische und empirische Systeme, sowie konkrete (empirische) und nicht konkrete (empirische) Systeme – entstanden durch die geistige Beschäftigung mit der Welt. Welche Systembildungen werden aber im Objektbereich der menschlichen Wirklichkeit selbst von Parsons unterschieden? Parsons unterscheidet zunächst einmal Systembildungen auf vier hierarchisch angeordneten Ebenen. Die unterste Ebene bilden physikalisch-chemische Systeme, eine Ebene höher werden biologische Systeme angeordnet, wieder eine Ebene höher werden Handlungssysteme lokalisiert, die oberste Stufe bilden schließlich die sogenannten telischen Systeme.[38]

Im Zentrum des Interesses von Parsons steht nun dasjenige System, welches von menschlichen Handlungen[39] gebildet wird. Die Entstehung von Handlungssystemen erfolgte nach Parsons auf einer relativ späten Stufe der Evolution. Handlungssysteme werden von motivierten, intentionalen, sinn-gesteuerten Verhaltensakten menschlicher Individuen gebildet, sie erschöpfen sich aber nicht in diesen. Handeln in Kollektiven wirft zwei verschiedene Fragen auf. Die eine Frage zielt ab auf den subjektiven Sinn des Handelns für den Handelnden, die zweite Frage dagegen auf die objektiven Merkmale und Folgen der Verkettung von intentionalen Akten innerhalb eines sozialen Kollektivs (vgl. Parsons 1968, S. 53).

Keine Bestandteile von Handlungssystemen sind die unter diesen liegenden physikalisch-chemischen und organischen Systeme, soweit diese nicht in Handlungssysteme integriert sind. Diese Systeme gehören zur Umwelt von Handlungssystemen. Zur Umwelt von Handlungssystemen gehören darüber hinaus die bereits erwähnten telischen Systeme. Telische Systeme bilden in dieser Hierarchie, wie wir gesehen haben, die oberste Stufe. Die menschliche Existenz wirft Fragen nach dem Sinn des Seins, nach den letzten Werten usw. auf. Diese Ideen und Ideensysteme sind kulturelle Repräsentationen von Objekten oder Dingen einer nichtempirischen transzendenten Wirklichkeit.[40]

---

38 Von telos, gr. Ziel. Vgl. Staubmann 1999, S. 152.
39 Handeln ist eine besondere Art des Verhaltens. Handeln ist keine Reaktion auf innere oder äußere Reize, Handeln ist motiviertes, sinn-gesteuertes menschliches Verhalten.
40 Die in den Religionen thematisierten "Dinge" der "letzte(n) Realität" (Parsons 1972, S. 14) sind in genau dem Sinne Bezugs- und Referenzobjekte dieser Aussagensysteme, wie die in den naturwissenschaftlichen Theorien thematisierten "Dinge" Bezugs- und Re-

Handlungssysteme weisen verschiedene Bezüge auf. Es lassen sich kulturelle, soziale, psychische und physikalische Bezüge von Handlungssystemen unterscheiden. Handlungen haben 1. Sinn, Handlungssysteme sind Sinnsysteme; Handlungen konstituieren 2. soziale Zusammenhänge, Handlungssysteme sind soziale Systeme; Handlungen sind 3. Ergebnisse psychischer Prozesse, sie sind Äußerungen menschlicher Psychen; Handlungen sind 4. konkrete Verhaltensakte, welche von biologischen Organismen (Mensch als biologischer Organismus) ausgeführt werden. Mittels der vier genannten Bezüge lassen sich analytisch, d. h. durch Abstraktion, vier verschiedene Subsysteme des allgemeinen Handlungssystems unterscheiden: Kultursystem, Sozialsystem, Persönlichkeitssystem und Verhaltensorganismus.[41]

Handlungssysteme werden von Parsons mittels der Kategorien der strukturfunktionalistischen Systemtheorie beschrieben und analysiert. Diese besondere Zugangsweise lenkt die Aufmerksamkeit einerseits auf die strukturalen, d. h. relativ festen und dauerhaften Komponenten des Systems. Andererseits wird durch den gewählten Ansatz der Aspekt der Leistung oder Funktion der einzelnen Subsysteme thematisiert.[42]

Das hier charakterisierte allgemeine Handlungssystem ist ein theoretisches System. Es ist ein spezifisches System von Begriffen und deren Beziehungen. Beschreibt man mittels dieses theoretischen Systems einen Handlungszusammenhang, so ist das, was diese Beschreibung beschreibt, ein empirisches, aber kein konkretes System. Gegenstand dieser Beschreibung ist nicht etwa eine konkrete Einheit, z. B. ein sozialer Wechselwirkungszusammenhang handelnder Individuen, sonder lediglich die strukturalen und funktionalen Aspekte eines solchen Handlungszusammenhanges.[43]

Beginnen wir mit Sozialsystemen. Die Leistung oder die Funktion dieses Subsystems ist die Integration der Elemente des Handlungssystems.[44] Die Handlungen

---

ferenzobjekte dieser Theorien sind. In beiden Typen von Aussagensystemen wird auf "Dinge" in der Umwelt von Handlungssystemen hingewiesen.

[41] Die vier Subsysteme des Handlungssystems sind, wie Parsons betont, keine "konkreten Seinseinheiten" (Parsons 1972, S. 12). Sie sind mittels Abstraktion gewonnene "analytische Konstruktionen" (Parsons 1972, S. 12).

[42] Parsons drückt diesen Sachverhalt folgendermaßen aus: "Die Unterschiede zwischen den vier Handlungssubsystemen sind rein funktionaler Natur. Sie richten sich nach den vier Hauptfunktionen, die wir allen Handlungssystemen zuweisen, nämlich: Normenerhaltung, Integration, Zielverwirklichung und Anpassung" (Parsons 1972, S. 12).

[43] "Man darf übrigens bei der Betrachtung dieser Aspekte nicht aus den Augen verlieren, dass nicht etwa die konkreten Verhaltensabläufe zu den Handlungssystemen rechnen, sondern allein deren sinnhafte Regelung durch bestimmte Handlungsschemata" (Jensen 1976a, S. 66).

[44] "Das vorrangige Integrationsproblem eines Handlungssystems ist die Koordination seiner Teileinheiten, in erster Linie also menschlicher Individuen, obwohl zu bestimmten Zwe-

der Einheiten müssen aufeinander abgestimmt werden; sie müssen zu einem koordinierten Ganzen zusammengefügt werden. Die wichtigste strukturale Kategorie in diesem Zusammenhang ist die soziale Rolle.[45] Andere strukturale Komponenten des Sozialsystems sind Werte, Nomen und Kollektive (vgl. Parsons 1972, S. 15, 1976, S. 177). Sämtliche strukturalen Komponenten des Sozialsystems sind normativer Natur. Die Struktur des Sozialsystems besteht, mit anderen Worten, "aus institutionellen Mustern (patterns) normativer Kultur" (Parsons 1976, S. 168).

An zweiter Stelle betrachten wir kulturelle Systeme. Die Leistung oder die Funktion dieses Subsystems ist die Normenerhaltung und der kreative Normenwandel.[46] Es geht dabei einerseits um die Legitimierung der innerhalb des Sozialsystems institutionalisierten Muster normativer Kultur,[47] andererseits um die schöpferische Erneuerung und Neustrukturierung dieser Muster.[48] Die Legitimierung der Gesellschaftsstruktur erfolgt nach Parsons letztlich immer auf religiöser Grundlage.[49] Gemeint ist damit dasjenige Sinnsystem, welches die Beziehungen des Sozialsystems zur letzten Wirklichkeit (als Umwelt des Handlungssystems) thematisiert. Kulturelle Systeme sind Sinn- oder Bedeutungssysteme. Sie liefern "Interpretationsschemata, die das Geschehen auf einen gemeinsamen Sinn hin auslegen" (Jensen 1976, S. 34). Die festen, d. h. strukturalen Elemente von Sinnsystemen sind, wie Parsons sich ausdrückt, "die von ihnen benutzten besonderen Symbolgruppen sowie

---

cken auch Gesamtheiten als Akteure behandelt werden können. Daher schreiben wir dem sozialen System hauptsächlich Integrationsfunktion zu" (Parsons 1972, S. 12).

[45] "Im Handlungssystem geht es dabei um die Koordination und Steuerung von Interaktionen, wobei der soziologische Grundbegriff der sozialen Rolle am treffendsten diesen Sachverhalt zum Ausdruck bringt. In den Rollen wird festgelegt, wer welche Aufgaben im Rahmen eines Kollektivs auf Grund einer bestimmten Position zu übernehmen hat. Man denke etwa an Berufsrollen im Rahmen eines Betriebes. Dieses Subsystem des Handlungssystems entspricht damit dem *sozialen System*" (Staubmann 1999, S. 158).

[46] "Normenerhaltung und schöpferischen Normenwandel sehen wir als Hauptaufgabe des kulturellen Systems an" (Parsons 1972, S. 12).

[47] "Keine normative Gesellschaftsordnung kann *aus sich selbst* legitimiert werden, sodass gebilligte oder missbilligte Lebensweisen in sich richtig oder falsch sein und vor keinerlei Fragen stellen könnten. " Sie wird auch niemals hinreichend durch Funktionsnotwendigkeiten der unteren Kontrollebenen legitimiert – etwa dadurch, dass Dinge in einer ganz *bestimmten* Weise getan werden müssten, weil Stabilität oder Überleben des Systems in Frage stünden" (Parsons 1976, S. 128).

[48] Das Problem der Legitimierung betrifft natürlich auch die dynamischen Aspekte der Sozialstruktur, d. h. auch den kreativen Normenwandel.

[49] Parsons führt in diesem Zusammenhang aus, "dass ein Legitimationssystem stets auf denjenigen Begründungszusammenhang bezogen und sinnhaft durch ihn bedingt ist, dem die Ordnung aller Beziehungen zur 'letzten' Wirklichkeit (ultimate reality) entspricht. Mit anderen Worten", fügt er hinzu, "seine Begründung ist in irgendeinem Sinne immer religiöser Art" (Parsons 1976, S. 129).

die Bedingungen ihrer Anwendung, Erhaltung und Veränderung" (Parsons 1972, S. 12).[50]

Wir betrachten an dritter Stelle Persönlichkeitssysteme. Persönlichkeitssystemen wird von Parsons die Funktion der Zielerreichung oder Zielverwirklichung zugeordnet.[51] Persönlichkeitssysteme bestehen nach Parsons aus internalisierten Elementen normativer Kultur. Die kulturellen Muster werden den Individuen in einem sozialen Interaktionszusammenhang im Rahmen von Sozialisierungsprozessen vermittelt. Die internalisierten Kulturinhalte des Handlungssystems sagen den Individuen, welche Ziele erstrebenswert und welche Mittel der Zielerreichung legitim sind. Die internalisierten Kulturmuster, gemeinsam mit dem Bedürfnis nach Belohnung und Befriedigung motivieren das Handeln und stellen sicher, dass die für das Funktionieren des Handlungssystems notwendigen Leistungen erbracht werden.[52] Die Struktur der Persönlichkeit wird von denjenigen erworbenen Kulturmustern gebildet, welche beständig sind, welche ihre Muster in der Zeit bewahren.[53]

Schließlich betrachten wir an vierter Stelle den Verhaltensorganismus. Dem Verhaltensorganismus wird innerhalb des Handlungssystems von Parsons die Funktion der Adaptation oder Anpassung zugeordnet.[54] Mit Verhaltensorganismus bezeichnet Parsons dasjenige Subsystem des Handlungssystems, welches die physischen Aspekte des Erlebens und Handelns steuert. Dazu zählen einerseits die von

---

50 An anderer Stelle spricht Parsons von " 'patterns of meaning' ", also von "Werten, Normen, organisiertem Wissen und Glauben sowie expressiven 'Formen' " (Parsons 1976, S. 165).
51 "Die Zielverwirklichung fällt als Hauptaufgabe der Persönlichkeit des Individuums zu. Das Persönlichkeitssystem ist die *Haupttriebkraft* von Handlungsprozessen und somit auch der Erfüllung kultureller Prinzipien und Anforderungen. Auf der Ebene der Belohnung als Motivationsfaktor ist die Optimierung von Gratifikation und Befriedigung der Persönlichkeiten das Ziel aller Handlung" (Parsons 1972, S. 13).
52 "Der Fokus der Zielorientierung liegt für das Sozialsystem in seiner Beziehung als System zu den Persönlichkeiten der beteiligten Individuen. Er betrifft daher nicht die Bindung an die Werte der Gesellschaft, sondern die Motivation, notwendige Beiträge zum Funktionieren des Systems zu liefern, diese 'Beiträge' variieren entsprechend den jeweiligen Erfordernissen" (Parsons 1976, S. 175).
53 " 'Persönlichkeit' sind also diejenigen Handlungsmuster, die vom einzelnen Individuum aufgrund von Lern- und Erfahrungsprozessen zu einem System von Selektion von Erlebnis- und Verhaltensschemata geordnet und als identisches System in der Zeit bewahrt werden" (Jensen 1976a, S. 48).
54 "Wir begreifen den Verhaltensorganismus als das Subsystem der Anpassung, als Ort der primären menschlichen Fähigkeiten, die den anderen Systemen zugrunde liegen. Er umfasst eine Reihe von Bedingungen, denen sich das Handeln anpassen muss, und beinhaltet den primären Mechanismus der Wechselbeziehung zur physischen Umwelt, hauptsächlich durch die Aufnahme und Verarbeitung von Informationen im zentralen Nervensystem sowie durch Bewegungen, die den Anforderungen der physischen Umwelt entsprechen" (Parsons 1972, S. 13).

Parsons im zentralen Nervensystem lokalisierten Programme der Wahrnehmung, andererseits die von Parsons gleichfalls im zentralen Nervensystem lokalisierten Programme, die die psychischen Verhaltensimpulse (das Bewusstsein) in Bewegungen des Körpers umsetzen.[55] Diese Programme verknüpfen das Handlungssystem mit den physiologischen und anatomischen Aspekten des Organismus und mit der übrigen "natürlichen" (d. h. physikalisch-chemischen und organischen) Umwelt des Handlungssystems. Anpassung oder Adaptation meint sowohl die durch die Leistung des Verhaltensorganismus mögliche Resonanz des Handlungssystems auf externe Erfordernisse als auch das gleichfalls erst auf Grund der Leistung des Verhaltensorganismus mögliche Eingreifen des Handlungssystems auf die physikalisch-chemische Umwelt des Systems.[56] Die Struktur des Verhaltensorganismus besteht aus wenig lernbereiten, zum Teil angeborenen, festen Programmen.

Wie hängen die beschriebenen vier Subsysteme des Handlungssystems und diese mit den Umwelten des allgemeinen Handlungssystems zusammen? Ich werde an dieser Stelle drei Aspekte dieser Zusammenhänge behandeln. Diese drei Aspekte sind: 1. mögliche Beziehungen, 2. hierarchische Struktur und 3. plastische Steuerung.[57]

Zunächst einmal soll festgehalten werden, dass nach Parsons die vier beschriebenen Subsysteme des Handlungssystems eine hierarchische Ordnung, und zwar von oben nach unten angeordnet, in folgender Reihenfolge bilden: Kultursystem, Sozialsystem, Persönlichkeitssystem und Verhaltensorganismus.

Diese vier Ebenen umfassende Struktur kann zudem noch durch die zwei Umwelten des Handlungssystems, nach oben durch die "transzendente Wirklichkeit" und nach unten durch die organische und physikalisch-chemische Umwelt, ergänzt werden.

---

[55] "Das oben eingeführte Konzept des 'Verhaltensorganismus' ist das eines kybernetischen Systems, das sich im Wesentlichen im zentralen Nervensystem befindet und mit mehreren Zwischenmechanismen arbeitet, um die Stoffwechselvorgänge des Organismus und das Verhalten der körperlichen Analogien, etwa die Bewegungen der Gliedmaßen, zu steuern" (Parsons 1976, S. 171).

[56] "Ähnlich verhält es sich mit dem Begriff der 'Adaptation'. Auf der Ebene des allgemeinen Handlungssystems bezieht sich dieser Begriff auf die Strukturbildungen, die zwischen der konkreten physischen Umwelt und den Handlungssystemen entstehen und die Funktion der wechselseitigen Anpassung erfüllen. Solche Strukturen müssen sich notwendig zunächst auf die organische Basis des Handelns beziehen, also auf das Organismussystem" (Jensen 1976a, S. 47).

[57] Die Auswahl dieser Momente ist natürlich nicht zufällig. Ich betrachte an dieser Stelle nur solche Aspekte, die auch im Zusammenhang mit Poppers drei (fünf) Welten behandelt wurden. Mir geht es hier darum, die Gemeinsamkeiten der beiden Strukturen herauszuarbeiten. Auf die Differenzen der beiden Konzepte werde ich an späterer Stelle eingehen.

Charakteristisch für diese hierarchische Struktur ist 1., dass nur unmittelbar benachbarte Ebenen direkte Beziehungen untereinander aufweisen, oder anders ausgedrückt, unmittelbar aufeinander einwirken können. Diese Einwirkungen oder Beziehungen werden von Parsons nicht als kausale Ursache-Wirkungs-Zusammenhänge sondern als systemische (entsprechend dem Modell offener Systeme) Input-Output-Beziehungen gedacht.

Betrachtet man die nach Parsons möglichen unmittelbaren Einwirkungen zwischen den insgesamt sechs Ebenen von unten nach oben, so ergibt sich folgendes Bild: Die "natürliche", d. h. organische und physikalisch-chemische Umwelt des Handlungssystems weist unmittelbare Beziehungen zum Verhaltensorganismus auf, dieser steht in unmittelbarer Beziehung zum Persönlichkeitssystem, das Persönlichkeitssystem steht in unmittelbarer Beziehung zum Sozialsystem, das Sozialsystem steht in unmittelbarer Beziehung zum Kultursystem, und das Kultursystem weist direkte Beziehungen zur "letzten Realität" auf. Beziehungen zwischen zwei nicht unmittelbar benachbarten Ebenen dieser Hierarchie sind immer durch die dazwischenliegenden Ebenen (Subsysteme) vermittelt.

So steht nach Parsons die "natürliche" Umwelt des Handlungssystems in keiner unmittelbaren Beziehung zur Persönlichkeit oder zum Sozialsystem. Das Sozialsystem und die Persönlichkeit können nur durch die Vermittlung des Verhaltensorganismus auf die natürliche Umwelt einwirken oder von dieser Impulse empfangen.[58]

Ähnlich gibt es nach Parsons keine unmittelbaren Beziehungen zwischen der "letzten Realität", der zweiten Umwelt des Handlungssystems und dem Persönlichkeits- oder Sozialsystem. Was nach Parsons auf die Persönlichkeiten wirkt, sind kulturelle Objekte. Die Beziehung zwischen Persönlichkeit und "letzter Realität" ist immer eine durch das Kultursystem vermittelte.[59]

Charakteristisch für diese Struktur ist 2., dass die einzelnen Ebenen eine hierarchische Ordnung bilden. Bei Parsons sind mit der Idee der Hierarchie zwei verschiedene Aspekte verknüpft. Von unten nach oben betrachtet, handelt es sich bei dieser Hierarchie um eine Hierarchie der ermöglichenden und zugleich beschränkenden Bedingungen, oder mit Parsons' Worten ausgedrückt, um eine "Hierarchie der konditionellen Faktoren" (Parsons 1976, S. 154). Zu den konditionellen Fakto-

---

[58] "Weder die einzelne Persönlichkeit noch das Sozialsystem haben irgendwelche direkten Beziehungen zur physischen Umwelt, diese Beziehungen sind vollständig durch den Organismus vermittelt, als Bindeglied zwischen Handeln und Wirklichkeit" (Parsons 1976, S. 279f.).

[59] "Die Objekte, die Persönlichkeiten und Sozialsysteme erkennen und sonst direkt erfahren, sind in unserer Terminologie kulturelle Objekte: humane Artefakte in fast dem gleichen Sinn wie die Objekte empirischer Kognition. Die Beziehungen von Persönlichkeiten und Sozialsystemen zur letzten 'nichtempirischen Realität' sind also in einem grundlegenden Sinn *vermittelt* durch das Kultursystem" (Parsons 1976, S. 280).

ren rechnet Parsons den für das Bestehen und Funktionieren des Systems notwendigen Energiezufluss. Ausgangsbasis für die Hierarchie der konditionellen und energetischen Bedingungen ist die "natürliche Umwelt". Die in der natürlichen Umwelt gegebenen Bedingungen müssen entweder für die Zwecke des Systems kontrolliert werden, oder, soweit das nicht möglich ist, das System muss sich an die gegebenen Bedingungen anpassen.[60]

Von oben nach unten betrachtet handelt es sich bei dieser Hierarchie wiederum um eine "Hierarchie der steuernden Faktoren" (Parsons 1976, S. 154). Im Sinne einer Hierarchie der Steuerungen, oder wie Parsons sich ausdrückt, "im *kybernetischen* Sinne" (Parsons 1976, S. 129), bildet innerhalb des Handlungssystems das Kultursystem die höchste Instanz.[61] Von hier aus wird das Handlungssystem mit Information versorgt (vgl. Parsons 1976, S. 154).

Charakteristisch für diese Struktur ist 3. eine besondere Art der Steuerung. Das Handlungssystem wird, wie wir gerade gesehen haben, vom kulturellen Subsystem gesteuert. Im kybernetischen Sinne ist das kulturelle Subsystem die höchste Instanz. Darunter liegen, und zwar in dieser Reihenfolge, das Sozialsystem, das Persönlichkeitssystem und der Verhaltensorganismus. Die physiologischen und anatomischen Aspekte des physischen Organismus werden wiederum vom Verhaltensorganismus gesteuert.

Ich werde an dieser Stelle drei Aspekte dieser Steuerungshierarchie behandeln.

1. Die Steuerung erfolgt mittels wechselseitiger Durchdringung oder Interpenetration. Die Subsysteme besitzen nach Parsons "Bereiche" oder "Zonen", die strukturelle Elemente aufweisen, die gleichzeitig beiden benachbarten Subsystemen angehören.[62] Die Struktur des Sozialsystems besteht "aus institutionalisierten Mustern (patterns) normativer Kultur" (Parsons 1976, S. 168), und die Struktur der Persön-

---

[60] "Im konditionellen Sinne ist die Ausgangsbasis die Umwelt (d. h. die Menge der konkreten materiell-energetischen Bedingungsfaktoren, eben die 'konditionellen' Bedingungen). Soweit die physischen Faktoren durch die kybernetisch höheren Systeme nicht kontrolliert werden können, müssen wir uns ihnen anpassen oder menschliches Leben hört auf. Die Abhängigkeit des Menschen von Sauerstoff, Nahrung, erträglichen Temperaturen usw. sind vertraute Beispiele" (Parsons 1976, S. 129).

[61] "Die Subsysteme des allgemeinen Handlungssystems bilden eine hierarchische Folge solcher Steuerungsinstanzen für das Verhalten von Individuen oder Organismen. Der Verhaltensorganismus ist der Verbindungpunkt des Handlungssystems mit den anatomisch-physiologischen Merkmalen des physischen Organismus und sein Berührungspunkt mit der physischen Umwelt. Das Persönlichkeitssystem wiederum steuert die Persönlichkeiten seiner beteiligten Mitglieder, und das kulturelle System ist ein Steuerungssystem für Sozialsysteme" (Parsons 1976, S. 171).

[62] "Wir sind der Meinung, " schreibt Parsons, "dass die Grenze zwischen jeweils zwei Handlungssystemen eine 'Zone' strukturierter Bestandteile oder Muster umfasst, die theoretisch als *zu beiden* Systemen *gehörig*, also nicht bloß dem einen oder anderen System zugeordnet, behandelt werden muss" (Parsons 1972, S. 14).

lichkeit besteht aus den verinnerlichten Elementen der in dem Sozialsystem institutionalisierten Kulturmuster. Diese wechselseitige Durchdringung der Subsysteme wird von Parsons auch als "Interpenetration" (Parsons 1976, S. 124) bezeichnet. Diese Zonen gegenseitiger Durchdringung machen nach Parsons „Austauschprozesse zwischen Systemen erst möglich" (Parsons 1972, S. 14). Institutionalisierung und Internalisierung sind verschiedene Formen der gegenseitigen Durchdringung oder Interpenetration.

2. Die Beziehungen der einzelnen Subsysteme untereinander und die Beziehungen des Handlungssystems zu seinen Umweltsystemen sind nach Parsons pluralistischer Art. Insbesondere meint Parsons, dass es zwischen den verschiedenen interpenetrierenden Systemen "keine Punkt-für-Punkt-Entsprechung" (Parsons 1976, S. 280) geben kann. Dies gilt, so Parsons weiter, "für die Beziehungen zwischen 'Anlage und Umwelt' sowie für die Beziehungen zwischen 'Ideal'- und 'Real'-Faktoren in Sozialsystemen" (Parsons 1976, S. 280). Dieser Aspekt der Steuerungshierarchie wird von Parsons u. a. anhand des Zusammenhanges zwischen Sozialsystem und Kultursystem illustriert. Das Ideensystem der westlichen Christenheit bildet nach Parsons im Wesentlichen die gemeinsame Kultur aller westlichen Gesellschaften. Dieses Kultursystem ist aber in den Sozialsystemen der einzelnen Gesellschaften in sehr unterschiedlichen Formen institutionalisiert.[63]

3. Die jeweils tieferliegenden Systeme der Steuerungshierarchie sind häufig sperrige Instrumente. Das gilt insbesondere auch für die Beziehung des Bewusstseins zum Verhaltensorganismus und für die Beziehung des Verhaltensorganismus zu den ausführenden physiologisch-anatomischen Aspekten des Organismus. Neue oder ungewohnte Verhaltensprogramme müssen erst aufgebaut und eingeübt werden. Verhalten ist letztlich immer nur ein Versuch, "ein bestimmtes, ideales Schema mehr oder weniger gut zu realisieren" (Jensen 1976, S. 30). Anderseits sind bereits ausgebildete Strukturelemente, d. h. Selektionen oder Programme, sagen wir z. B. des Bewusstseins, nur schwer modifizierbar. Parsons meint z. B., dass die Herausbildung einer besonderen erotischen Orientierung – welche auch immer – Ergebnis des Sozialisierungsprozesses[64] ist. Ist eine erotische Orientierung aber erst einmal

---

[63] "Man darf auf keinen Fall vergessen, dass kulturelle Systeme nicht genau mit sozialen Systemen, Gesellschaften eingeschlossen, übereinstimmen. Im Allgemeinen werden die wichtigeren kulturellen Systeme in einer Reihe von Gesellschaften in jeweils verschiedenen Formen institutionalisiert, obwohl es innerhalb von Gesellschaften auch Subkulturen gibt. Das kulturelle System, welches sich auf das westliche Christentum stützt, ist z. B., mit gewissen Einschränkungen und zahlreichen Variationen, dem gesamten europäischen System modernisierter Gesellschaften gemeinsam gewesen" (Parsons 1972, S. 18f.).

[64] Nach Parsons ist "jedes normale Kind potentiell in der Lage (ist), *jeden beliebigen Typ* der bekannten erotischen Orientierungen zu entwickeln: Homosexualität, Auto-Erotik und Perversionen genauso gut wie die von uns als normal betrachtete Heterosexualität.

entstanden, so ist das ein festes und nur schwer veränderbares Element der Persönlichkeitsstruktur.

Die Verwandtschaft der beiden Konzepte ist offensichtlich. Sowohl Popper als auch Parsons gehen davon aus, dass die Welt eine hierarchische Struktur aufweist. Bezüglich der Zahl der zu unterscheidenden Ebenen sind die beiden Autoren aber uneins. Popper unterscheidet drei, bzw. fünf, Parsons zunächst vier, bzw. nach Ausdifferenzierung des Handlungssystems insgesamt (d. h. einschließlich der beiden Umwelten des Handlungssystems) sechs Ebenen.

Lässt man sich von diesem Unterschied und von vielen anderen Differenzen nicht zu sehr beeindrucken, so erkennt man allerdings bald die strukturelle Ähnlichkeit der beiden Konzepte.

Geht man von der subjektiven Welt (Popper) bzw. vom Persönlichkeitssystem (Parsons) aus, so gibt es in beiden Konzepten unterhalb dieser Ebene 1. biologische und 2. physikalisch-chemische und oberhalb dieser Ebene 1. normative (Popper) bzw. soziale (Parsons) und 2. kognitive (Popper) bzw. kulturelle (Parsons) Phänomene. Einzig für Parsons "transzendente Wirklichkeit" fehlt bei Popper etwas Entsprechendes. Schließlich ist es aber so, dass die Fragen nach der Zahl der Ebenen und nach den Orten der zu legenden Schritte, nicht unabhängig von einer konkreten Fragestellung entschieden werden können (vgl. Popper 1973, S. 124).

Übereinstimmung zwischen den beiden Konzepten besteht darüber hinaus bezüglich folgender Punkte:
1. Die in der Hierarchie tiefer liegenden Ebenen bilden die materiell-energetische Grundlage oder die Basis für die Existenz der darüber liegenden Ebenen.
2. Die Steuerung des hierarchischen Systems geht von der jeweils höheren Ebene aus.
3. Nur die Phänomene zweier benachbarter Ebenen können unmittelbar aufeinander einwirken. Alle anderen Beziehungen innerhalb der Hierarchie sind durch die Phänomene der dazwischenliegenden Ebenen vermittelt.
4. Es handelt sich hier um eine besondere Steuerungsart. Sie wird als plastisch (Popper) oder als pluralistisch (Parsons) bezeichnet.
5. Weder in Poppers noch in Parsons' Hierarchien geht es um konkrete Einheiten, wie Menschen oder besondere Gruppen von Menschen. Beide Konzeptionen behandeln nur bestimmte Aspekte solcher konkreter Einheiten. Beide Entwürfe thematisieren empirische, jedoch nicht konkrete Phänomene.
6. Beide Konzeptionen sind betont antireduktionistisch. Sowohl Popper als auch Parsons gehen davon aus, dass man die menschliche Persönlichkeit und

---

Dies kann aber nur bedeuten, " schreibt er weiter, "dass die letztere in weitgehendem Maße ein Ergebnis des Sozialisierungsprozesses und nicht einfach der Ausdruck eines Instinktes ist" (Parsons 1968, S. 124).

menschliche Handlungen nicht auf Grundlage von psychischen oder organisch-materiellen Gesetzmäßigkeiten verstehen und erklären kann.

Betrachten wir nach den Gemeinsamkeiten die Unterschiede. Zunächst einmal differieren die beiden Konzepte hinsichtlich des gewählten Zuganges. Popper interessiert sich für die Fragen: Welche Typen von Phänomenen mit welchen Eigenschaften gibt es? Und wie hängen diese Phänomene zusammen? Inhaltlich geht es Popper um die Lösung des Leib-Seele-Problems. Parsons interessiert sich dagegen für Systembildungen im Allgemeinen und für Systeme des Handelns im Besonderen. Zudem betrachtet Parsons Systeme auf eine besondere Weise: vom Blickwinkel der strukturfunktionalistischen Systemtheorie.

Die beiden Zugangsweisen führen zu Antworten, die jeweils unterschiedliche Aspekte oder Qualitäten der Erscheinungen betonen. Betrachten wir, um das zu zeigen, zwei korrespondierende Ebenen, nämlich Poppers subjektive und normative Ebenen und Parsons' Persönlichkeits- und Sozialsysteme.

Poppers 2. Welt, die Welt der subjektiven Erfahrungen, besteht aus dem ewig fließenden Strom von Empfindungen, Gefühlen, Vorstellungen und Gedanken. Parsons' Persönlichkeitssystem besteht dagegen aus verinnerlichten, festen Bestandteilen der normativen Kultur. Was Parsons mit seinem Konzept zu erfassen sucht, sind die mehr oder weniger festen Koordinaten der Persönlichkeit, die den Einfluss der Gefühle und Gedanken strukturieren und den Handlungsentwürfen der Person ihren charakteristischen Stempel aufdrücken.

Poppers normative Ebene besteht aus den unzähligen normativen Vorschlägen und Entscheidungen der handelnden Individuen, sowohl aus den vielen flüchtigen und alltäglichen als auch aus den beharrenden festen Normen und Institutionen. Parsons' Sozialsystem besteht dagegen aus den festen, d. h. auf dieser Ebene, institutionalisierten, Mustern der normativen Kultur. Es besteht aus Handlungsmustern, aus Werten, Normen, Rollen und Kollektiven. Worauf Parsons' Begriff des Sozialsystems abzielt, sind wieder die festen oder strukturalen, d. h. hier auch, institutionalisierten normativen Handlungsmuster, die die unzähligen Handlungen der Individuen zu einem koordinierten Ganzen zusammenfügen.

Insgesamt können wir festhalten, dass hinsichtlich der zu unterscheidenden Ebenen zwischen Popper und Parsons keine grundlegenden Unterschiede bestehen. Auch der Charakter des Zusammenhanges zwischen den Ebenen wird von den beiden Autoren recht ähnlich beschrieben. Popper interessiert sich, wie wir bereits gesehen haben, für die verschiedenen Arten des Seins im Zusammenhang mit den Leib-Seele-Problemen. Seine Fragestellung ist eine sehr allgemeine. Die Antwort, die er vorlegt – seine Drei(Fünf)-Welten-Theorie – ist entsprechend eine sehr grundlegende und allgemeine Theorie.

Parsons' Fragestellung ist spezifischer. Er interessiert sich für Systembildungen, insbesondere aber für das Handlungssystem. Er betrachtet zudem das Handlungssystem aus einer spezifischen Perspektive, aus dem Blickwinkel der strukturfunktionalistischen Systemtheorie. Er interessiert sich einerseits für die strukturalen, d. h. festen Elemente des Handlungssystems, andererseits für die Leistung und Funktion dieser Systeme bzw. seiner Subsysteme. Seine Fragestellung ist eine recht komplexe. Entsprechend ist das von ihm vorgelegte theoretische System ein recht differenziertes.

Die Differenz der beiden theoretischen Systeme auf der Dimension "allgemein – spezifisch" kann leicht gezeigt werden.

Sowohl Popper als auch Parsons sind der Ansicht, dass man seelische Phänomene, d. h. Phänomene des Bewusstseins, einerseits von gesellschaftlich-kulturellen und andererseits von organischen und physikalisch-chemischen Phänomenen (Prozessen und Strukturen) unterscheiden muss.

Popper kommt bei seinen Analysen gewöhnlich mit diesen drei Ebenen, oder wie er sich ausdrückt, Welten, aus. Es gelingt ihm zu zeigen, dass die zweite, subjektive Welt, die Welt des spezifisch menschlichen Bewusstseins, ein Wechselwirkungsprodukt von organisch-materiellen (d. h. erstweltlichen) Strukturen und der von Menschen geschaffenen Phänomene der dritten Welt (Normen, Institutionen und "objektive Gedankeninhalte") ist.

Parsons muss dagegen bei der Konstruktion des Handlungssystems einerseits zwischen Sozialsystem und Kultursystem und andererseits zwischen Verhaltensorganismus und den nicht unmittelbar verhaltensrelevanten (d. h. physiologisch-anatomischen Aspekten des Organismus) Aspekten des Organismus unterscheiden. Zudem differenziert er noch zwischen den festen oder strukturalen Handlungsmustern oder Handlungsprogrammen und den mehr oder weniger zufälligen tatsächlichen Handlungen.

Bewertung, Diskussion und Vorschlag

Die Bewertung der von Popper und Parsons vorgeschlagenen hierarchischen Ordnungen sollte in diesem Aufsatz anhand dreier Kriterien erfolgen. Das erste dieser Kriterien lautet: Ist die betreffende hierarchische Ordnung durchgehend nach einem einheitlichen Prinzip konstruiert?

Ich gehe hier davon aus, dass es zwei grundlegend verschiedene Arten gibt, eine hierarchische Ordnung zu konzipieren. Diese zwei Arten sind 1. die Hierarchie 1. Art, konzipiert nach dem Prinzip "Teil und Ganzes" und 2. die Hierarchie 2. Art, konzipiert nach dem Prinzip der "Hierarchie emergenter Steuerungen".

Weder Poppers noch Parsons' Hierarchien sind nach dem Prinzip der Hierarchie 1. Art entworfen. Poppers 2. Welt (Welt der subjektiven Erfahrungen und Prozesse) ist nicht aus erstweltlichen (d. h. organischen und physikalisch-chemischen) Phänomenen zusammengesetzt oder gebildet und Poppers 3. Welt (Welt der objektiven

Gedankeninhalte sowie Normen und Institutionen) ist nicht aus zweitweltlichen, subjektiven Phänomenen zusammengesetzt oder gebildet. Dasselbe können wir auch von Parsons' Handlungssystem aussagen: Das Persönlichkeitssystem ist nicht aus Verhaltensorganismen zusammengesetzt oder gebildet, das Sozialsystem ist nicht aus Persönlichkeitssystemen zusammengesetzt oder gebildet und das Kultursystem ist nicht aus Sozialsystemen zusammengesetzt oder gebildet.

Beide hierarchische Ordnungen sind nach dem Prinzip der Hierarchie 2. Art (Hierarchie emergenter Steuerungen) konzipiert. Bei beiden hierarchischen Ordnungen handelt es sich um Steuerungshierarchien. Dieser Umstand wurde im letzten Abschnitt deutlich herausgearbeitet. Aber, und das ist hier die eigentlich interessante Frage, handelt es sich hier um reine Steuerungshierarchien?

Betrachten wir zunächst Poppers Welt 2. Diese Welt der subjektiven Erfahrungen und Prozesse, der Strom von Gefühlen, Gedanken und Entscheidungen, wird unmittelbar von den normativen Inhalten von Entscheidungen, zum Teil internalisierten Werten und Normen, zum Teil von aktuellen individuellen Entscheidungen, dieses oder jenes zu tun, gesteuert. Innerhalb des Handlungssystems von Parsons wird das Persönlichkeitssystem dagegen vom Sozialsystem gesteuert. Also wird die 2. subjektive Welt (Popper) oder das Persönlichkeitssystem (Parsons) hier durch normative Entscheidungen, dort durch das Sozialsystem gesteuert.

Das Sozialsystem, als ein Wechselwirkungszusammenhang individueller Handlungen, scheint aber innerhalb einer Steuerungshierarchie irgendwie ein Fremdkörper zu sein.

Auf den besonderen Charakter des Sozialsystems macht auch der exzellente Kenner der Parsonsschen Systemtheorie, Stefan Jensen, aufmerksam. Diese Besonderheit manifestiert sich zunächst auf der sprachlichen Ebene. Wir können bei drei der vier Subsysteme des Handlungssystems, nämlich beim Kultursystem, Persönlichkeitssystem und Organismussystem (Verhaltensorganismus) den Zusatz System weglassen und einfach von Kultur, Persönlichkeit und Organismus reden, beim vierten Subsystem, beim Sozialsystem, ist das nicht möglich.[65]

Hinter dieser sprachlichen Eigentümlichkeit vermutet Jensen einen tieferen Grund. Das Sozialsystem und die drei anderen Subsysteme liegen, seiner Auffassung nach, auf unterschiedlichen Ebenen der Abstraktion. Während das Kultursystem, das Persönlichkeitssystem und das Organismussystem sich unschwer verdinglichen lassen – man redet von Kultur, Persönlichkeit und Organismus und meint tat-

---

65 "Hier sei am Rande auf eine sprachliche Eigentümlichkeit der vier Systemkategorien hingewiesen: Es ist bei drei der vier Handlungssysteme möglich, den Begriff des 'Systems' fortzulassen und stattdessen von 'Organismus', 'Persönlichkeit' und 'Kultur' zu sprechen – im Deutschen so gut wie im Englischen. Über das vierte System lässt sich nur in Form des 'Sozialsystems' sprechen – die Verwendung des Ausdrucks 'System' ist unvermeidlich" (Jensen 1976b, S. 309).

sächlich konkrete Kulturen, Persönlichkeiten und Organismen –, ist das beim Sozialsystem nur schwer möglich. Das abstrakte Sozialsystem lässt sich eben nicht so leicht mit einem Haufen miteinander interagierender konkreter Menschen verwechseln. Aber Parsons' Subsysteme dürfen, und damit schließt Jensen sein Argument, in keinem Fall mit konkreten Dingen verwechselt werden. Sie sind hier wie dort durch Abstraktion gewonnene theoretische Konstruktionen.[66]

Mit dieser Argumentation trifft Jensen, meiner Meinung nach, nicht den zentralen Punkt. Tatsächlich besteht die Gefahr der Reifikation am ehesten beim Organismussystem und beim Sozialsystem. Diese beiden Systeme lassen sich mittels des Prinzips der Hierarchie 1. Art – Teil und Ganzes – konzipieren. Entsprechend dieser Vorstellung besteht ein biologischer Organismus aus Organen oder, wenn man weitergeht, aus Zellen, ein soziales System aus biologischen Organismen. Richtig ist dagegen Jensens Hinweis, dass Parsons' Organismus- und Sozialsysteme nicht mit solchen konkreten Erscheinungen der Hierarchie 1. Art verwechselt werden dürfen. Tatsächlich haben solche konkreten Erscheinungen, wie Organismus und Sozialsystem im Sinne Comtes sozialem Organismus, innerhalb seiner Steuerungshierarchie oder Hierarchie 2. Art nichts zu suchen. Es handelt sich hier, wie mir scheint, letztlich um ein sprachliches Problem, um ein Problem der Benennungen. Poppers normative Ebene besteht, wie wir gesehen haben, u. a. aus den Inhalten der das Verhalten der Individuen steuernden normativen Entscheidungen. Die festen oder strukturalen Elemente dieses Systems sind die von Parsons innerhalb des "Sozialsystems" thematisierten Komponenten: Werte, Normen, Rollen und Kollektive. Die Komponenten des Parsonsschen Sozialsystems sind, wie wir gesehen haben, sämtlich normativer Natur. Also könnten wir in diesem Zusammenhang statt von Sozialsystemen auch von Normensystemen sprechen. Die von Jensen diskutierte sprachliche Besonderheit wäre damit eliminiert. Wir könnten jetzt, genauso wie von Kulturen, Persönlichkeiten und Organismen, auch von Normen oder Institutionen reden. Damit wäre auch klargestellt, dass es sich auch bei Parsons' Hierarchie um eine

---

66 "Diese semantische Besonderheit deutet auf einen tieferen Grund: nämlich die ungleiche erkenntnismäßige Anschaulichkeit der einzelnen Systeme. Organismus, Persönlichkeit und Kultur lassen sich 'reifizieren' und bilden konkrete Gegenstände unserer Erfahrung. Für den als 'Sozialsystem' bezeichneten Gegenstand gilt dies nicht. Diese Beobachtung bliebe eine bloße Trivialität, führte sie nicht zu der Einsicht, dass Parsons' Handlungssysteme in *keinem Fall* reifiziert und als konkrete Gegenstände der Erfahrung genommen werden dürfen: Alle Handlungssysteme sind Abstraktionen, theoretische Systeme, von denen als 'Organismus', 'Persönlichkeit' oder 'Kultur' zu sprechen nur irreführen kann, weil diese Sprechweise zu sehr an unser konkrete Alltagserfahrung appelliert. Die Gefahr der Reifizierung (oder – in Parsons' Lieblingswendung – 'the fallacy of misplaced concretness', d. h. die Gefahr der falschen Konkretisierungen) ist am geringsten beim Sozialsystem, weil dies ohnehin am weitesten von jeder konkreten Alltagserfahrung entfernt ist" (Jensen 1976, S. 309f.).

reine Steuerungshierarchie handelt. Sowohl Poppers als auch Parsons' Hierarchien sind nach einem einheitlichen Prinzip, nach dem Prinzip der "Hierarchie emergenter Steuerungen", gebildet.

Das zweite Kriterium, das für die Bewertung der beiden Konzepte herangezogen werden soll, lautet: Lässt sich der eigene Gegenstandsbereich, in diesem Fall der Gegenstandsbereich der Soziologie, innerhalb der betreffenden Ordnung deutlich lokalisieren?

Popper geht davon aus, dass wir bei soziologischen Untersuchungen von der Existenz einer sozialen Welt ausgehen müssen. Diese soziale Welt ist ausgestattet einerseits mit Menschen, andererseits mit sozialen Institutionen.[67] Bestandteile der sozialen Welt sind nach Popper allerdings keine konkreten Menschen. Menschen als materiell-biologische Wesenheiten sind Bestandteile der 1. natürlichen Welt. Und auch die menschlichen Psychen sind, betrachtet aus dem Blickwinkel der sozialen Welt, externe (zweitweltliche) Phänomene. Bestandteile der sozialen Welt sind nur menschliche Handlungen, oder genauer, die normativen Entwürfe dieser Handlungen.

Nach Popper ist es die Aufgabe der Soziologie, die normativen Handlungsentwürfe der Individuen, sowie die beabsichtigten wie unbeabsichtigten institutionellen Folgen dieser Handlungen objektiv zu verstehen. Die dabei verwendete Methode wird von Popper als "Situationslogik" (Popper 1970, S. 120) bezeichnet. Das objektive Verstehen mittels der Situationslogik besteht darin, dass man die Situation der Handelnden möglichst genau rekonstruiert, mit dem Ziel, die Handlungen aus der Situation heraus zu erklären.[68] Die "Erklärungen der Situationslogik sind rationale, theoretische Rekonstruktionen" (Popper 1970, S. 121).

---

[67] "Darüber hinaus muss die Situationslogik auch eine soziale Welt annehmen, ausgestattet mit anderen Menschen, über deren Ziele wir etwas wissen (oft nicht sehr viel), und überdies mit *sozialen Institutionen*. Diese sozialen Institutionen bestimmen den eigentlichen sozialen Charakter unserer sozialen Umwelt. Sie bestehen aus allen jenen sozialen Wesenheiten der sozialen Welt, die den Dingen der physischen Welt entsprechen. Eine Gemüsehandlung oder ein Universitätsinstitut oder eine Polizeimacht oder ein Gesetz sind in diesem Sinn soziale Institutionen. Auch Kirche und Staat und Ehe sind soziale Institutionen, und gewisse zwingende Gebräuche, wie zum Beispiel in Japan Harakiri" (Popper 1970, S. 121).

[68] Popper schreibt in diesem Zusammenhang, "dass es eine rein *objektive Methode* in den Sozialwissenschaften gibt, die man wohl als die *objektiv*-verstehende Methode oder als Situationslogik bezeichnen kann. Eine *objektiv*-verstehende Sozialwissenschaft kann unabhängig von allen subjektiven oder psychologischen Ideen entwickelt werden. Sie besteht darin, dass sie die *Situation* des handelnden Menschen hinreichend analysiert, um die Handlung aus der Situation heraus ohne weitere psychologische Hilfe zu erklären. Das objektive 'Verstehen' besteht darin, dass wir sehen, dass die Handlung objektiv *situationsgerecht* war" (Popper 1970, S. 120).

Sämtliche Elemente Poppers sozialer Welt sind normativer Natur. Sie sind einerseits mehr oder weniger flüchtige individuelle normative Entscheidungen, andererseits sind sie gewichtige und feste normative Wesenheiten wie Institutionen und Traditionen.[69]

Der Gegenstandsbereich der Soziologie ist nach Popper die soziale Welt. Poppers soziale Welt ist, wie wir gesehen haben, normativer Natur. Sie besteht aus normativen Phänomenen. Der Gegenstandsbereich der Soziologie bildet innerhalb Poppers Hierarchie eine eindeutig identifizierbare und abgrenzbare Ebene.

Die Soziologie teilt diesen Gegenstandsbereich allerdings mit den anderen Sozialwissenschaften. Dabei sollte die Soziologie nach Popper als die grundlegende Sozialwissenschaft – etwa vergleichbar mit der Stellung der theoretischen Physik im Rahmen der Naturwissenschaften – konzipiert werden.

Es wäre naheliegend anzunehmen, dass nach Parsons Sozialsysteme den Gegenstandsbereich der Soziologie bilden würden. Das ist aber nur teilweise zutreffend. Mit diesem Gegenstandsbereich beschäftigen sich nach Parsons neben der Soziologie auch die anderen etablierten Sozialwissenschaften, darunter insbesondere die Wirtschaftswissenschaft und die Politikwissenschaft. Wie ist also das Verhältnis der Soziologie zu diesen beiden Wissenschaftszweigen zu denken? Die eine Möglichkeit wäre, die Zuständigkeit der Soziologie auf das gesamte Sozialsystem auszudehnen. Ökonomie und Politikwissenschaft wären dann, ähnlich wie bei Popper, spezialisierte Teilbereiche der Soziologie. Das ist aber nicht Parsons' Konzeption.[70] Soziologie bildet nach ihm aber auch keine Restkategorie, indem sie sich Fragen oder Problemen widmet, die von ihren spezialisierten Konkurrentinnen bisher vernachlässigt wurden.[71] Parsons ordnet den drei Sozialwissenschaften, Ökonomie, Politikwissenschaft und Soziologie, drei verschiedene, analytisch klar abgrenzbare Teilbereiche (Subsysteme) des Sozialsystems als Gegenstandsbereiche zu. Dazu wird das Sozialsystem mittels der Parsonsschen strukturfunktionalistischen Konzeption[72], d. h. wiederum funktional, auf vier Subsysteme aufgespalten. Die einzelnen

---

[69] "Als die Grundprobleme der reinen theoretischen Soziologie können vielleicht vorläufig die allgemeine Situationslogik und die Theorie der Institutionen und Traditionen angenommen werden" (Popper 1970, S. 122).

[70] "Für manche umschließt die Soziologie, in einem nahezu enzyklopädischen Sinne, alle Strukturen und Funktionen von Sozialsystemen. Kraft dieser Definition wären Ökonomie und politische Wissenschaft Zweige der Soziologie. Dies entspricht allerdings nicht unserer Konzeption" (Parsons 1976, S. 165).

[71] "Obwohl es historisch zutrifft, dass die ökonomische und politische Theorie vor der Soziologie bestand, so folgt daraus nicht, dass Soziologie eine Residualwissenschaft sein müsste" (Parsons 1976, S. 166).

[72] "Unserer Ansicht nach sollten Wirtschaft und Politik als funktionale Subsysteme innerhalb der Gesellschaft behandelt werden. Das primäre Interesse der Soziologie gilt nicht

Subsysteme des Sozialsystems sind zuständig für jeweils eine der vier Funktionen: Strukturerhaltung, Integration, Zielerreichung und Adaptation. Auf diese Weise können die Zuständigkeiten der drei zuvor genannten Sozialwissenschaften funktional bestimmt werden. Die Wirtschaftswissenschaft ist zuständig für diejenigen Strukturen, die die Funktion der Adaptation, die Politikwissenschaft für diejenigen Strukturen, die die Funktion der Zielerreichung, erfüllen. Das Interesse der Soziologie sollte sich nach Parsons dagegen auf diejenigen Strukturen konzentrieren, die innerhalb des Sozialsystems für die Erfüllung der Funktionen Strukturerhaltung und Integration zuständig sind. Damit wäre auch das Verhältnis der Gegenstandsbereiche der drei Sozialwissenschaften bestimmt. Die Ökonomie und die Politikwissenschaft beschäftigen sich, und zwar in dieser Reihenfolge, mit den im Sinne der materiell-energetischen Hierarchie dominanteren Strukturen, die Soziologie befasst sich dagegen mit den im Sinne der kybernetischen Steuerungshierarchie höher liegenden Strukturen.[73]

Der Gegenstandsbereich der Soziologie lässt sich innerhalb beider hierarchischer Ordnungen recht präzise lokalisieren, innerhalb Poppers Hierarchie als die normative Ebene, innerhalb Parsons' Hierarchie als ein klar umrissener Teilbereich des Sozialsystems. Weder Poppers soziale Welt noch Parsons' Sozialsysteme sind konkrete Phänomene, also konkrete Systeme miteinander interagierender Organismen oder anders ausgedrückt, soziale Organismen im Sinne Comtes. Beide Gegenstandsbereiche sind normativer Natur. Dabei ist Poppers Gegenstandsbereich weiter, er umfasst alle normativen Phänomene. Parsons' Gegenstandsbereich ist in zweifacher Hinsicht begrenzter. Er besteht 1. nur aus festen oder strukturalen Elementen und er umfasst 2. nur einen Teilbereich dieser strukturalen Elemente.[74]

---

dem Funktionieren dieser, sondern dem jener Subsysteme, die auf Funktionen der Integration und Strukturerhaltung basieren" (Parsons 1976, S. 166).

[73] "Zunächst gehen wir vom Problem der gesellschaftlichen Struktur und der Hierarchie der Kontrollbeziehungen in einem Sozialsystem aus; dabei werden wir argumentieren, dass die wirtschaftliche und politische Ebene zwei distinkte und relativ gut definierte Stufen – und zwar vom technischen Standpunkt der Analyse von Sozialsystemen aus die unteren Stufen – bilden" (Parsons 1976, S. 166).

[74] Jensen ist der Meinung, dass Parsons' Festlegung der Soziologie auf Institutionen mit strukturerhaltender und integrativer Funktion unbefriedigend, und selbst innerhalb Parsons' eigenem Argumentationszusammenhang nicht schlüssig sei (vgl. Jensen 1976, S. 66). Das Sozialsystem würde, seiner Meinung nach, für die Soziologie einen zu engen Rahmen abgeben. Sozialwissenschaft, aber auch Soziologie, lässt sich nach ihm nur als Handlungstheorie konzipieren: "Auf der Basis der Sozialsysteme allein lässt sich die Soziologie nicht ausreichend entfalten, sie bedarf des größeren Rahmens der Handlungstheorie" (Jensen 1976, S. 51).

Das dritte Kriterium, welches wir für die Bewertung der beiden Entwürfe heranziehen wollen, lautet: Nützt die betreffende hierarchische Ordnung der interdisziplinären Kommunikation oder behindert sie diese?

Sowohl Poppers als auch Parsons' Hierarchien sind nach dem Prinzip der Hierarchie 2. Art konzipiert. Beide Hierarchien sind Steuerungshierarchien. Beide Konzepte thematisieren gleichzeitig mehrere Steuerungsarten. Diese werden aber nicht einfach nebeneinandergestellt und bilden den Ausgangspunkt für voneinander unabhängige Ursachen- oder Faktortheorien, die für die Erklärung von Fragen oder Problemen beliebig herangezogen werden können. Innerhalb dieser Konzepte werden die verschiedenen Steuerungsarten systematisch miteinander verknüpft. Beide Theorien liefern auf diese Weise überzeugende Argumente gegen einseitige, reduktionistische Erklärungen, einerlei, ob es sich bei diesen Erklärungen um biologistische, psychologistische oder kulturalistische Erklärungen handelt. Beide Konzepte sind soziologische und/oder sozialwissenschaftliche Grundlagentheorien. Beide Konzepte ermöglichen das Zusammenführen und die Integration verschiedenster Faktortheorien. Solche Ansätze sind für die Diskussion innerhalb der Soziologie und innerhalb der Sozialwissenschaften durchaus nützlich.

Beide Autoren konzipieren Sozialsysteme als Handlungssysteme, d. h. als Wechselwirkungssysteme ideeller (drittweltlicher) Wesenheiten, von drittweltlichen normativen Handlungsentwürfen. Beide Konzeptionen sind, vom Standpunkt der Hierarchie 1. Art betrachtet, daher kopflastig oder idealistisch.

Dieses Urteil lässt sich anhand Parsons' eigenem Anspruch leicht begründen. Er beansprucht mit seinem Ansatz, ein Konzept für die Analyse des Verhaltens biologischer Organismen vorgelegt zu haben.[75] Das ist ein recht hoher Anspruch. Ein solcher Anspruch kann nur von einer sehr grundlegenden oder allgemeinen Theorie erfüllt werden. Parsons' Handlungstheorie ist aber nur für die Analyse menschlichen Sozialverhaltens geeignet. Sie ist auf die Analyse tierischen Sozialverhaltens nicht anwendbar. Tatsächlich ist die Handlungstheorie lediglich ein Instrument für die Analyse menschlichen Sozialverhaltens. Der Grund dafür ist folgender: Die strukturalen Komponenten des Sozialsystems sind, wie wir gesehen haben, sämtlich normativer Natur. Sie sind Werte, Normen, Rollen und Kollektive. Das ist aber nur bezogen auf menschliche Sozialsysteme richtig. Aber auch Tiere bilden Gruppen und Gesellschaften. Auch sie sind, worauf Comte deutlich hingewiesen hat, soziale Wesen. Dasselbe können wir auch bezüglich Poppers Konzeption der sozialen Welt

---

[75] Auf diesen Umstand hat bereits Jensen hingewiesen: "Der erste Satz in Abschnitt 1, Teil 2 von Toward A General Theory of Action (...) lautet: 'The Theory of Action is a conceptual scheme for the analysis of the behavior of living organism.' Man könnte daraus schließen, daß auch das Verhalten von Tieren eingeschlossen wäre; tatsächlich aber ist die Handlungstheorie auf 'human social behavior' beschränkt" (Jensen 1976, S. 58f.).

aussagen. Auch seine soziale Welt ist rein normativer Natur. Sie ist ein Wechselwirkungszusammenhang individueller normativer Entscheidungen und ebenfalls normativer gesellschaftlicher Institutionen.

Verständlicherweise können Biologen, welcher Art auch immer, mit solchen Vorstellungen nichts anfangen. Für sie ist es ja selbstverständlich, dass sie die sozialen Systeme von Organismen studieren, auf die Poppers und Parsons' normativistische Konzeptionen einfach nicht passen. Die Konzeption von Sozialsystemen als Handlungssysteme ist gegenüber dem Prinzip der Hierarchie 1. Art (sozialer Organismus) und für Biologen, Ethologen, Soziobiologen usw., die das soziale Leben nicht menschlicher Organismen untersuchen, eine unverständliche Einschränkung des Begriffs "soziales System". Konzeptionen, die diesen Sachverhalt außer Acht lassen, behindern die interdisziplinäre Kommunikation. Ein wirklich allgemeines Konzept sozialer Phänomene muss daher sowohl auf tierische als auch auf menschliche Sozialsysteme anwendbar sein. Es darf daher nicht von vornherein als Handlungssystem konzipiert werden.

Man müsste, meiner Meinung nach, bei der Konzeption eines wirklich allgemeinen und integrativen Entwurfs sozialer Systeme von dem Prinzip der Hierarchie 1. Art "Teil und Ganzes" ausgehen. Sozialsysteme wären, entsprechend dieses Prinzips konzipiert, Wechselwirkungssysteme individueller Organismen. Und zwar, damit das deutlich ausgesprochen wird, konkrete Wechselwirkungssysteme konkreter Organismen. Eine solche Vorstellung ist, wie wir gesehen haben, an und für sich weder irgendwie neu noch irgendwie originell: 1. ist diese Vorstellung innerhalb der Biologie allgemein akzeptiert und 2. war diese Vorstellung, wie wir gleichfalls gesehen haben, diejenige von Comte und seinen Schülern gewesen. Zudem kann man diese Vorstellung durchaus auch in der aktuellen Soziologie antreffen. Um Missverständnisse zu vermeiden, möchte ich an dieser Stelle darauf hinweisen, dass diese Vorstellung keineswegs die Behauptung inkludiert, ein soziales System (der soziale Organismus) sei wirklich ein lebendiger Organismus. Das haben übrigens weder Comte noch Herbert Spencer, dem das gerne angedichtet wird, wirklich jemals gemeint.

Bei einem solchen allgemeinen und integrativen Entwurf müsste natürlich auch das Prinzip der Hierarchie 2. Art, "Hierarchie emergenter Steuerungen" berücksichtigt werden.

Damit sollte dem Umstand Rechnung getragen werden, dass sich die sozialen Systeme der Pflanzen, primitiven tierischen Organismen, höheren Tiere und Menschen hinsichtlich ihrer Steuerung grundlegend voneinander unterscheiden. So erfolgt, um nur ein Beispiel zu erwähnen, die innerartliche Abstimmung und Koordination des Verhaltens der einzelnen Individuen bei sozialen Insekten durch chemische Botenstoffe, bei Menschen dagegen u. a. durch normative Vorschläge und Entscheidungen.

Eine solche Konzeption würde also durchaus berücksichtigen, dass die sozialen Systeme der Pflanzen, niederen und höheren Tiere und Menschen sich deutlich voneinander unterscheiden. Das würde aber gleichzeitig bedeuten, dass das Zusammenwirken von Individuen in Gruppen, Horden und Gesellschaften, das Bilden höherer, mehr oder weniger komplexer sozialer Einheiten, kein Spezifikum menschlicher Gesellschaften ist. Wir müssten auch einsehen, dass soziale Phänomene älter sind als die Menschen und auch als die höheren Tiere. Das würde gleichzeitig die Frage aufwerfen, ob die verschiedenen Sozialsysteme, trotz ihrer ersichtlichen Unterschiede, nicht vielleicht doch auch gemeinsame Prinzipien aufweisen? Damit wäre die forschungsleitende Grundidee eines integrativen allgemein soziologischen Forschungsprogramms formuliert.

Innerhalb einer solchen Konzeption wäre damit sowohl das Anliegen Comtes und seiner Schüler (der soziale Organismus) als auch das Anliegen Durkheims und seiner Nachfolger (die spezifische normative oder moralische Steuerung menschlichen Sozialverhaltens) berücksichtigt. Die beiden, zum Teil als widersprüchlich empfundenen Konzeptionen wären miteinander versöhnt.

Zusammenfassung

Ausgegangen wurde in diesem Aufsatz von der Beobachtung, dass bei den Versuchen, innerhalb der Welt der Erscheinungen eine Ordnung zu entdecken, zwei grundlegend verschiedene hierarchische Ordnungen unterschieden werden können. Bei der ersten Ordnung handelt es sich um eine Hierarchie, die nach dem Prinzip "Teil und Ganzes" konzipiert ist, bei der zweiten Ordnung handelt es sich dagegen um eine Hierarchie emergenter Steuerungen. Anschließend wurde gezeigt, dass diese beiden hierarchischen Ordnungen bereits bei der Entstehung der Soziologie im 19. Jahrhundert eine wichtige Rolle gespielt haben: Die Konzeption der Soziologie von Comte beruhte auf der Idee der Hierarchie 1. Art, die Konzeption der Soziologie von Durkheim auf der Idee der Hierarchie 2. Art. Danach wurden Poppers und Parsons' hierarchische Ordnungen dargestellt und vergleichend diskutiert. Die Untersuchung der beiden Entwürfe hat gezeigt, 1., dass es sich in beiden Fällen um reine Steuerungshierarchien handelt, 2., dass der Gegenstandsbereich der Soziologie innerhalb beider Konzeptionen sich deutlich lokalisieren lässt und 3., dass soziale Phänomene innerhalb beider Entwürfe als normative Phänomene konzipiert werden. Das entspricht, wie wir gesehen haben, Durkheims Konzeption. Auf dieser Grundlage gibt es aber nur menschlich-soziale Systeme. Eine solche Konzeption, so wurde anschließend argumentiert, beeinträchtigt die interdisziplinäre Kommunikation ganz entschieden.

Schließlich wurde vorgeschlagen, dass wir bei der Konzeption sozialer Systeme beide Hierarchien berücksichtigen sollten. Soziale Phänomene sollten innerhalb der Hierarchie 1. Art als Erscheinungen, die zwischen den Einheiten Individuum und Art zu lokalisieren sind, d. h. als Systeme miteinander interagierender Organismen einer Art, konzipiert werden. Ergänzt werden müsste diese Konzeption, so lautet der Vorschlag weiter, um die spezifischen Eigenheiten unterschiedlicher sozialer Systeme thematisieren zu können, durch die Hierarchie der Steuerungen. Auf diese Weise würde eine wirklich allgemeine und integrative Konzeption sozialer Systeme entstehen.

Literatur

Bailey, Kenneth D.: Sociology and the New Systems Theory. State University of New York: Albany, 1994.
Bertalanffy, Ludwig von: Das biologische Weltbild. Die Stellung des Lebens in Natur und Wissenschaft. Mit einem Vorwort von Felix D. Bertalanffy und einer Einleitung von Josef Schurz. Wien/Köln: Böhlau (Neudruck der 1. Auflage Bern 1949), 1990.
Bischof, Norbert: Das Rätsel Ödipus. München/Zürich: Piper, 3., überarbeitete Auflage (der Neuausgabe 1989), 1991.
Comte, Auguste: Die Soziologie. Die positive Philosophie im Auszug. Stuttgart: Kröner, 1974 (1830-1842).
Durkheim, Emile: Die Regeln der soziologischen Methode. Frankfurt am Main: Suhrkamp, 1961 (1895).
Durkheim, Emile: Die elementaren Formen des religiösen Lebens. Frankfurt am Main: Suhrkamp, 1984 (1968).
Elias, Norbert: Engagement und Distanzierung. Frankfurt am Main: Suhrkamp, 1983.
Engel, Gerhard: Zur Logik der Musiksoziologie. Tübingen: Mohr, 1990.
Fuchs-Heinritz, Werner: Auguste Comte. Einführung in Leben und Werk. Opladen/Wiesbaden: Westdeutscher Verlag, 1998.
Jensen, Stefan: Einleitung. In: Talcott Parsons: Zur Theorie sozialer Systeme. Hg. von Stefan Jensen, Opladen: Westdeutscher Verlag, 1976a, S. 9-67.
Jensen, Stefan: Anmerkungen des Herausgebers. In: Talcott Parsons: Zur Theorie sozialer Systeme. Hg. von Stefan Jensen, Opladen: Westdeutscher Verlag, 1976b, S. 307-318.
Lorenz, Konrad: Die Rückseite des Spiegels. Versuchs einer Naturgeschichte menschlichen Erkennens. München: (Piper, 1973) DTV, 1977.
Maturana, Humberto R./Varela, Francisco J.: Der Baum der Erkenntnis. Die biologischen Wurzeln des menschlichen Erkennens. Bern/München/Wien: Scherz, 1987.
Mauss, Marcel: Soziologie und Anthropologie 2. Gabentausch, Soziologie und Psychologie, Todesverantwortung, Körpertechniken, Begriff und Person. Frankfurt am Main: Fischer, 1989 (1950).
Miller, James Grier: Living systems. New York: McGraw-Hill, 1978.
Meleghy, Tamás: Karl Poppers Evolutionäre Erkenntnistheorie und die drei Gegenstandsbereiche soziologischen Denkens. In: Österreichische Zeitschrift für Soziologie, 18. Jg., Heft 1, 1993, S. 18-35.
Meleghy, Tamás: Soziologie als Sozial-, Moral- und Kulturwissenschaft. Untersuchungen zum Gegenstandsbereich, zur Aufgabe und zur Methode der Soziologie auf Grundlage Karl Poppers Evolutionärer Erkenntnistheorie. Habilitationsschrift: Innsbruck, 1997.

Meleghy, Tamás: Verhaltenstheorie und Handlungstheorie. Versuch einer Abgrenzung. In: Andreas Balog/Manfred Gabriel (Hg.): Soziologische Handlungstheorie. Einheit oder Vielfalt (Österreichische Zeitschrift für Soziologie, Sonderband 4). Opladen/Wiesbaden: Westdeutscher Verlag, 1998.
Parsons, Talcott: Soziologische Theorie (Beiträge zur soziologischen Theorie). Neuwied am Rhein/Berlin: Luchterhand, 2. Aufl., 1968.
Parsons, Talcott: Das System moderner Gesellschaften. München: Juventa, 1972.
Parsons, Talcott: Zur Theorie sozialer Systeme (Herausgegeben und eingeleitet von Stefan Jensen). Opladen: Westdeutscher Verlag, 1976.
Parsons, Talcott: Concrete Systems and "Abstracted Systems". In: Contemporary Sociology, Vol. 8, 1979, S. 696-705.
Popper, Karl: Die Logik der Sozialwissenschaften. In: Theodor Adorno u. a.: Der Positivismusstreit in der deutschen Soziologie. Neuwied/Berlin: Luchterhand, 1970, S. 103-123.
Popper, Karl: Objektive Erkenntnis. Ein evolutionärer Entwurf. Hamburg: Hoffmann und Campe, 1973.
Popper, Karl: Ausgangspunkte. Meine intellektuelle Entwicklung. Hamburg: Hoffmann und Campe, 1979.
Riedl, Rupert: Kultur. – Spätzündung der Evolution? Antworten auf Fragen an die Evolutions- und Erkenntnistheorie. München/Zürich: Piper, 1987.
Solms, Max Graf: Analytische Gesellungslehre. Tübingen: Mohr, 1956.
Sombart, Werner: Vom Menschen. Versuch einer geisteswissenschaftlichen Anthropologie. Berlin: Duncker & Humblot, 1956.
Spencer, Herbert: The Nature of Society. In: Talcott Parsons et al. (Hg.): Theories of Society. New York: The Free Press, 1961 (1898), S. 139-143.
Squillace, Fausto: Die Soziologischen Theorien. Leipzig: Klinkhardt, 1911.
Staubmann, Helmut: Handlungstheoretische Systemtheorie: Talcott Parsons. In: Julius Morel u. a.: Soziologische Theorie. Abriss der Ansätze ihrer Hauptvertreter. München/Wien: Oldenbourg, 1999, S. 147-170.
Vanberg, Viktor: Nachwort. Der verhaltenstheoretische Ansatz in der Soziologie – theoretische und wissenschaftsgeschichtliche Fragen. In: George C. Homans: Grundfragen soziologischer Theorie, Aufsätze. Herausgegeben und mit einem Nachwort versehen von Viktor Vanberg. Opladen: Westdeutscher Verlag, 1972.
Vanberg, Viktor: Die zwei Soziologien, Individualismus und Kollektivismus in der Sozialtheorie. Tübingen: Mohr, 1975.
Vollmer, Gerhard: Was können wir wissen? Band 2: Die Erkenntnis der Natur: Beitrag zur modernen Naturphilosophie. Mit einem Geleitwort von Hans Sachsse. Stuttgart: Hirzel, 2. durchgesehene Auflage, 1988.
Wiese, Leopold von: System der Allgemeinen Soziologie als Lehre von den sozialen Prozessen und den sozialen Gebilden der Menschen (Beziehungslehre). Berlin: Duncker & Humblot, 1955.
Wolf, Ulrich: Georg Lukács: Zur Ontologie des gesellschaftlichen Seins. Studie zum Verhältnis von Marxismus und Ontologie. Dissertation: Universität/Gesamthochschule Paderborn, 1986.

Talcott Parsons und die formale Soziologie
Gerald Mozetič

Steht ein soziologischer Autor, wie das bei Parsons der Fall war, über viele Jahre an der Spitze einer theoretischen Schule und damit im fachlichen Rampenlicht, nimmt die Sekundärliteratur Ausmaße an, dass sie nur für jene noch einigermaßen überschaubar ist, die ihr wissenschaftliches Leben der einschlägigen Rezeption verschrieben haben (so dass man hier in Fortsetzung von Wissenschaft als Beruf und Max Weber als Beruf nun Parsons als Beruf anführen könnte). Auch eine gute Portion Skepsis mag sich einstellen, ob denn – sein Werk stand schließlich sehr lange im Zentrum des Interesses und der Auseinandersetzung – heute noch irgend etwas Neues zu Parsons und seiner Soziologie gesagt werden könne. Freilich hat der Rückgang des Funktionalismus seit den 60er Jahren auch das Interesse am Werk von Parsons erheblich gedämpft, und die in den letzten Jahren zu konstatierenden Bemühungen um einen Neofunktionalismus blieben insgesamt doch marginal und vermochten der Soziologie keinen Stempel aufzudrücken. So tritt das Werk von Parsons in eine Phase der Rezeption ein, die vor allem soziologiegeschichtlich zentriert ist und nicht mehr von der Überzeugung getragen wird, mit einem Beitrag zu diesem Autor an einer aktuell-brisanten Debatte teilzunehmen.[1] Mithin dürfte es angebracht sein, einige Hinweise auf jene Perspektive zu geben, unter der hier das titelgebende Thema aufgegriffen wird. Dabei geht es um ein sehr spezielles Interesse, nämlich um die Frage, ob Parsons der formalen Soziologie Simmels gerecht geworden ist bzw. wie er mit dieser umgeht.

Als "äußerer" Kontext kommt in Betracht, dass die "formale" Soziologie Georg Simmels, der Parsons keinen zentralen Platz in seiner "Konstituierung" soziologischer Klassik zugestanden hatte, in den letzten Jahren eine mehr oder weniger erstaunliche, jedenfalls unbestreitbare Aufwertung erfahren hat, während der in der soziologischen Theorie so lange dominierende Parsons, von wenigen Ausnahmen abgesehen, nur mehr als ein Denkmal wahrgenommen wird, das von seinem Sockel gestürzt wurde und reichlich Patina angesetzt hat. Aber darum geht es hier *nicht*. Mein spezielles Thema nochmals einschränkend, möchte ich eine Konzentration auf den frühen Parsons vornehmen, und ich nehme als Ausgangspunkt für die folgenden

---

[1] Eine andere Frage ist es, wie viel funktionalistisches Gedankengut in der heutigen Soziologie enthalten und vielleicht auch dort anzutreffen ist, wo keinerlei explizite Bezugnahme auf den Funktionalismus erfolgt. So wie man vom Marxismus gesagt hat, sein wahrer Triumph liege darin, sich ohne Etikett in den sozialwissenschaftlichen Köpfen festgesetzt zu haben, so könnte der Erfolg des Funktionalismus größer sein, als seine gegenwärtige Reputation vermuten lässt.

Überlegungen daher neben einigen Aufsätzen aus den 30er Jahren das Werk *The Structure of Social Action* sowie jenes Kapitel über "Georg Simmel and Ferdinand Tönnies: Social Relationships and the Elements of Action", das Parsons 1936 für *The Structure of Social Action* geschrieben, dann aber in das Werk doch nicht aufgenommen hat, und das erst aus seinem Nachlass veröffentlicht wurde. Ganz kurz sei in Erinnerung gerufen, dass Parsons als Grund für die Nichtaufnahme noch 1968 in der Einleitung zur paperback-edition der *Structure* gemeint hatte, das sei "partly for reasons of space" geschehen, um dann zu ergänzen: "Simmel was more a micro- than a macrosociologist; moreover, he was not, in my opinion, a *theorist* on the same level as the others [Marshall, Pareto, Durkheim, Weber]" (Parsons 1968: xiv) 1979, kurz vor seinem Tode, bemerkte er dazu: "The decision not to include [the section on Simmel] had various motives [...] It is true that Simmel's program did not fit my convergence thesis" (zit. in Levine 1991). Es wird hier auf die wohlbekannte "Konvergenzthese" – derzufolge die vier bereits genannten Autoren die entscheidenden Beiträge in Richtung und zur Vorbereitung einer voluntaristischen Handlungstheorie leisteten, durch die die Verkürzungen und Unzulänglichkeiten des Utilitarismus (und auch des Behaviorismus) überwunden werden können – nur insoweit eingegangen werden, als sich die Frage stellt, warum Parsons im Werk von Simmel gleichsam zu wenig Voluntarismus gefunden hat.

Zum besseren Verständnis der frühen Schriften von Parsons hat Charles Camic (1987, 1989, 1990) in einer Reihe von Publikationen jene Situation zu rekonstruieren versucht, die Parsons vorfand, als sich für ihn in den 30er Jahren an der Harvard University die Frage nach einer akademischen Karriere stellte. Die Wissenschaftslandschaft, die Camic beschreibt, lässt sich im Hinblick auf die für Parsons besonders wichtigen Fächer wie folgt kurz charakterisieren: eine schwache Soziologie steht einer starken Ökonomik gegenüber, die vom neoklassischen Denken dominiert wird; daneben gibt es freilich auch eine an Veblen anschließende institutionalistische Schule, die für ihn durchaus von Bedeutung ist. Dass sich Parsons sicher stärker an der Neoklassik als dem Institutionalismus orientierte, hat nicht nur mit der Dominanz der ersteren zu tun; der Institutionalismus tendierte infolge seiner holistischen Ausrichtung zu einer "unified social science" in einem enzyklopädischen Sinne, in der all das eingebunden ist, was von der Ökonomik, der Anthropologie, der Soziologie, der Psychologie und der Geschichtswissenschaft als ihr jeweiliges Spezialgebiet beansprucht wird. Ist jedoch die "Ausdifferenzierung" einzelner Sozialwissenschaften im vollen Gange, so wird es für die Soziologie gleichsam zu einer "Überlebensfrage", ob sie einen autonomen Status gewinnen kann. "Entökonomisierung" und "Enthistorisierung" bieten sich als erfolgversprechende Strategien an (wie schon für Durkheim die "Entpsychologisierung" Bedingung für die Etablierung der Soziologie gewesen war). Für das Erreichen dieses Ziels – die Soziologie als eine der neoklassischen Ökonomie ebenbürtige Wissenschaft zu etablieren –

nimmt Parsons eine Reihe von Anleihen bei der vorbildhaften Disziplin, und im speziellen ist auch sein Wissenschaftsverständnis von ihr geprägt. Wenn er daher in *Structure* einen "analytischen Realismus" propagiert, befindet er sich in voller Übereinstimmung mit den wissenschaftstheoretischen Prämissen der erfolgreichen Neoklassik. Dass Parsons sich hier ganz in den Bahnen bewegt, die etwa ein Carl Menger vorgegeben hat, ist schon vor einiger Zeit von Thomas Burger (1977) konstatiert worden. Menger unterschied bekanntlich zwischen einem praktischen, einem historischen und einem theoretischen Zweig der Nationalökonomie, und im letzteren wiederum zwischen einer "realistisch-empirischen" und einer "exakten" Grundrichtung. In der exakten Theorie werden die "*einfachsten Elemente* alles Realen" isoliert, und zwar "ohne Rücksicht darauf, ob dieselben in der Wirklichkeit als *selbständige* Erscheinungen vorhanden" sind (Menger 1883, S. 41). Von den exakten Wissenschaften sagt Menger (1883, S. 42 f.), dass "keine einzelne uns die volle empirische Wirklichkeit, sondern nur besondere Seiten derselben verstehen lernt und desshalb auch vernünftigerweise nicht unter dem Gesichtspunkte des einseitigen empirischen Realismus beurtheilt werden darf, deren Gesammtheit uns indess ein ebenso eigenartiges als tiefes Verständniss der realen Welt vermittelt". Einschlägige Überlegungen zur Methode der Nationalökonomie hatten übrigens auch schon den alten Empiristen John Stuart Mill (1844/1976, S. 167f.) zum Schluss geführt, dass der pure Empirismus nicht möglich sei: "Die Folgerungen der politischen Ökonomie sind wie die der Geometrie daher nur in der Abstraktion wahr."[2] Zusammenfassend lässt sich sagen: Vieles von dem, was sich in *The Structure of Social Action* an Bemerkungen über "the line between the historical and the analytical sciences" (Parsons 1968, S. 760) findet, bewegt sich in den Bahnen von Denkmustern und Konzeptualisierungen, wie sie jedenfalls seit Carl Menger bereits geläufig geworden sind, der im Methodenstreit mit Gustav Schmoller die Position einer exakten Theorie verteidigt hatte. Dass Parsons bereits am Beginn seiner Tätigkeit an der Harvard University den österreichischen Ökonomen Joseph Schumpeter kennenlernte, der dort 1927/28 als Gastprofessor tätig war und schließlich 1932 eine dauernde Anstellung fand, sei nur am Rande vermerkt; jedenfalls war auch für Schumpeter die Position eines analytischen Realismus eine Selbstverständlichkeit.[3]

---

2   Dieses Zitat ist auch unter dem Gesichtspunkt bemerkenswert, dass Georg Simmel zur Charakterisierung seiner formalen Soziologie bekanntlich eine Analogie zur Geometrie herstellte. Genaueres dazu bietet Abschnitt (3) der vorliegenden Arbeit.
3   Als Schumpeter 1936 für das *Committee on Research in the Social Sciences* in Harvard über Parsons' Manuskript *Sociology and the Elements of Human Action*, das 1937 unter dem Titel *The Structure of Social Action* veröffentlicht werden sollte, ein Gutachten verfasste, kam er zu einer insgesamt eindeutig positiven Beurteilung, und vor allem schätzte Schumpeter die Weber-Analysen Parsons', die er freilich mit der ihm eigenen Ironie kommentierte: "Die wissenschaftliche Sorgfalt, mit der die Hauptelemente von Max We-

Was bedeutet nun aber der analytische Realismus für die Konstituierung eines autonomen Faches Soziologie? Gewiss wurde auch zur Zeit des frühen Parsons unter dem Etikett der Soziologie ganz Unterschiedliches verstanden, und auch Varianten eines kruden Empirizismus wird es sicherlich auch gegeben haben. Dennoch ist festzuhalten, dass alle anerkannten und bedeutenden Fachvertreter die simple Abbildtheorie der Erkenntnis als naiv und inadäquat ablehnten. Dass keine Wissenschaft die "Wirklichkeit" als solche gleichsam abbildhaft "verdoppelt", war beispielsweise für alle jene Soziologen, die unter dem Einfluss des Neukantianismus standen, eine unbezweifelbare Prämisse – also natürlich auch für Max Weber und Georg Simmel. Bei allen Differenzen im einzelnen besteht in dieser Hinsicht daher eine klare *Konvergenz* zwischen den bereits zitierten Ökonomen (wie Menger und Schumpeter) und den Soziologen Weber und Simmel. Für diese etwas andere "Konvergenzthese" gibt es eine Fülle von Belegen. Da es hier um das Verhältnis von Parsons zur formalen Soziologie geht, ist die Position Simmels von besonderem Interesse. Simmel hat immer wieder den standpunktspezifischen, fokussierenden, konstruktivistischen Charakter von Wissenschaft unterstrichen:

Wissenschaft ist eine Abstraktion "von der Wirklichkeit, die als solche überhaupt nicht Wissenschaft sein kann, sondern erst vermittels solcher Kategorien die Form der Erkenntnis annimmt" (Simmel 1917/1984, S. 11). "*Jede* Wissenschaft zieht aus der Totalität oder der erlebten Unmittelbarkeit der Erscheinungen *eine* Reihe oder *eine* Seite unter Führung je eines bestimmten Begriffes heraus" (S. 14) Die Gegenstände der soziologischen Analyse sind

> durch Abstraktionsprozesse zustande gekommen; aber damit unterscheiden sie sich nicht von den Wissenschaften wie Logik oder theoretische Nationalökonomie, die gleichfalls unter der Anleitung durch bestimmte Begriffe – dort des Erkennens, hier der Wirtschaft – zusammenhängende Gebilde aus der Wirklichkeit zustande bringen, und Gesetze und Evolutionen an ihnen entdecken, während diese Gebilde als isolierte Erfahrbarkeiten gar nicht bestehen (S. 15).

Da es sehr fraglich erscheint, ob Parsons die Argumentationen und Abstraktionsstufen, die Simmel zur Begründung seiner formalen Soziologie einführt, korrekt interpretiert, sei hier zunächst eine Rekonstruktion angeboten, in der Simmels Vorgehen genauer beschrieben wird.

---

bers Denken untersucht, auf ihre Ursprünge zurückverfolgt und in ihrer Bedeutung vorgeführt werden, kann nicht hoch genug gelobt werden. Der Autor ist derart tief in das deutsche Dickicht eingedrungen, daß er an einigen Stellen die Fähigkeit einbüßt, darüber in klarem Englisch zu schreiben, und einige Redewendungen werden erst dann voll verständlich, wenn man sie ins Deutsche übersetzt" (Schumpeters Gutachten ist abgedruckt in Swedberg 1994, S. 304f.).

Die erste Bedeutung von Soziologie, die Simmel erwähnt, leitet sich vom Standpunkt ab, dass alles menschliche Tun sich in der Gesellschaft vollzieht. Die Berücksichtigung der Gesellschaftlichkeit konstituiert jedoch keinen eigenen Gegenstandsbereich, sondern nur eine spezifische Betrachtungsweise dessen, was in den Wissenschaften vom Menschen behandelt wird.

> Die Soziologie also, in ihrer Beziehung zu den bestehenden Wissenschaften, ist eine neue *Methode*, ein Hilfsmittel der Forschung, um den Erscheinungen aller jener Gebiete auf einem neuen Wege beizukommen [...] Soweit sie sich darauf stützt, daß der Mensch als Gesellschaftswesen verstanden werden muss und daß die Gesellschaft der Träger alles historischen Geschehens ist, enthält sie kein *Objekt*, das nicht schon in einer der bestehenden Wissenschaften behandelt würde, sondern nur einen neuen Weg für alle diese, eine Methode der Wissenschaft, die gerade wegen ihrer Anwendbarkeit auf die Gesamtheit der Probleme nicht eine eigne Wissenschaft für sich ist (Simmel 1908/1983, S. 3).

Die Soziologie wird hier mit der Induktion als einer Methode verglichen, die in allen empirischen Wissenschaften verwendet werden kann. Die Möglichkeit einer neuen Wissenschaft beruht nicht auf der Entdeckung eines neuen Gegenstandes – dies anzunehmen, verkennt den abstrahierenden Charakter jeder Wissenschaft. (Soweit stimmt Parsons mit Simmel überein.)

> Jede Wissenschaft beruht auf einer Abstraktion, indem sie die Ganzheit irgendwelchen Dinges, die wir als einheitliche durch keine Wissenschaft erfassen können, nach je einer ihrer Seiten, von dem Gesichtspunkt je eines Begriffes aus, betrachtet. Die Totalität des Dinges und der Dinge gegenüber erwächst jede Wissenschaft durch arbeitsteilige Zerlegung jener in einzelne Qualitäten und Funktionen, nachdem ein Begriff aufgefunden ist, der diese letzteren herauszulösen und in all ihrem Vorkommen an den realen Dingen nach methodischen Zusammenhängen zu erfassen gestattet (S. 3).

Dies gilt natürlich auch für die Soziologie:

> Soll es nun eine Soziologie als besondere Wissenschaft geben, so muss demnach der Begriff der *Gesellschaft* als solcher [...] die gesellschaftlich-geschichtlichen Gegebenheiten einer neuen Abstraktion und Zusammenordnung unterwerfen, derart, daß gewisse, bisher nur in anderen und mannigfaltigen Verbindungen beachtete Bestimmungen derselben als zusammengehörig und deshalb als Objekte *einer* Wissenschaft erkannt werden (S. 4).

Genau dies – so Simmels zentrale Annahme – vermag die Trennung zwischen Form und Inhalt des Sozialen zu leisten:

> Daß dieses beide, in der Wirklichkeit untrennbar Vereinte, in der wissenschaftlichen Abstraktion getrennt werde, daß die Formen der Wechselwirkung oder Vergesellschaftung, in gedanklicher Ablösung von den Inhalten, die durch sie erst zu gesellschaftlichen werden, zusammengefaßt und einem einheitlichen wissenschaftlichen Gesichtspunkt methodisch unterstellt werden – dies scheint mir die einzige und die ganze Möglichkeit einer speziellen Wissenschaft von der Gesellschaft als solcher zu begründen (S. 6).

Simmel bemüht zur Charakterisierung der formalen Methode in der Soziologie die Analogien zur Geometrie und zur Grammatik:

> Soziologie als Lehre von dem Gesellschaft-Sein der Menschheit, die auch in unzähligen andern Hinsichten noch Wissenschaftsobjekt sein kann, verhält sich also zu den übrigen Spezialwissenschaften, wie sich zu den physikalisch-chemischen Wissenschaften von der Materie die Geometrie verhält: sie betrachtet die Form, durch die Materie überhaupt zu empirischen Körpern wird – die Form, welche freilich für sich allein nur in der Abstraktion existiert, grade wie die Formen der Vergesellschaftung. Sowohl Geometrie wie Soziologie überlassen die Erforschung der Inhalte, die sich in ihren Formen darstellen oder der Totalerscheinungen, deren bloße Form sie betrachten, andern Wissenschaften (S. 9f.).

Verweist diese Aussage auf eine Senkung des Abstraktionsniveaus auf jene Ebene, die eine Erfassung historischer Besonderheiten ermöglicht, merkt Simmel an anderer Stelle an, dass die von ihm beispielhaft bemühten historischen Fakten relativ willkürlich ausgewählt sind und es überdies auf ihren Wahrheitsgehalt im einzelnen gar nicht ankomme:

> Allein bei diesem Versuche, dem gesellschaftlichen Dasein die Möglichkeit einer neuen wissenschaftlichen Abstraktion abzugewinnen, kann das wesentliche Bemühen nur sein, diese Abstraktion an irgendwelchen Beispielen zu vollziehen und als sinnvoll zu erweisen. Darf ich es, um der methodischen Klarheit willen, etwas übertrieben ausdrücken, so kommt es nur darauf an, daß diese Beispiele *möglich*, aber weniger darauf, daß sie *wirklich* sind. Denn ihre Wahrheit soll nicht – oder nur in wenigen Fällen – die Wahrheit einer generellen Behauptung erweisen, sondern selbst, wo der Ausdruck es so erscheinen lassen könnte, sind sie doch nur der an sich irrelevante Gegenstand einer Analyse, und die richtige und fruchtbare Art, wie diese vollzogen wird, nicht die Wahrheit über die Realität ihres Objektes ist dasjenige, was hier entweder erreicht oder verfehlt ist. Prinzipiell wäre die Untersuchung auch an fingierten Schulbeispielen zu führen und für ihre Wirklichkeitsbedeutung auf das jeweilige Tatsachenwissen des Lesers zu verweisen gewesen (S. 33, Fn.).

Simmel selbst weist übrigens darauf hin, dass die Aufzählung der Formen des Sozialen niemals ausreichend sein kann:

> Wenn man also auch z. B. sagt, daß Über- und Unterordnung eine Formung ist, die sich fast in jeder menschlichen Vergesellschaftung findet, so ist mit dieser allgemeinen Erkenntnis wenig gewonnen. Es bedarf vielmehr des Eingehens auf die einzelnen Arten der Über- und Unterordnung, auf die speziellen Formen ihrer Verwirklichung, die nun in dem Maße ihrer Bestimmtheit natürlich an Umfang ihrer Gültigkeit verlieren (S. 10).

Vielleicht erweist es sich als zweckmäßig, die unterschiedlichen Abstraktionsschritte, die bei Simmel auftauchen, nochmals zu benennen und systematisch zu ordnen. Als *Abstraktion 1* kommt das in Betracht, wodurch aus der "vollen Fülle" dessen, was Realität genannt wird, die Gegenstände der einzelnen empirischen Wissenschaften separiert werden. Der "Blick auf den ersten prinzipiellen Problemkreis der Soziologie" (Simmel 1917/1984, S. 20) führt zur "Erkenntnis, dass neben dem gesellschaftlichen Leben als begründender Kraft und umfassender Formel des menschheitlichen Lebens auch noch Herleitung und Deutung des letzteren aus dem sachlichen Sinn seiner Inhalte und auch noch aus dem Wesen und der Produktivität der Individuen als solcher besteht" (S. 23). Soziologie in diesem Verständnis ist eine Wissenschaft neben vielen anderen. "Diese Zerlegungen und Konstruktionsarten unseres unmittelbaren, als Einheit von all diesem empfundenen Lebens und Schaffens liegen in der gleichen Schicht und haben das gleiche Recht" (Ebd.). Wo es um "Geschehnisse oder Zustände als Summierungen ununterscheidbarer Beiträge, als Ergebnisse der Wechselwirkung von Individuen, als Lebensstadien überindividueller Gruppeneinheiten" geht, ist eine besondere Wissenschaft zuständig, und "so mag man diese nach soziologischer Methode geführten Untersuchungen als Soziologie bezeichnen" (S. 24).

Durch eine weitere, eine *Abstraktion 2* ergibt sich erst "eine Problemgruppe von im engeren Sinne soziologischer Natur" (ebd.). Welche Gemeinsamkeiten weisen die Tatsächlichkeiten des Lebens dadurch auf, dass sie Resultate des Gruppenlebens sind, welche Gesetzmäßigkeiten sind etwa unter diesem Gesichtspunkt zu finden? Die Beispiele, die Simmel für diesen Typus einer "allgemeinen Soziologie" anführt, verweisen zunächst – ohne dass diese Autoren explizit genannt werden – auf Versuche von Comte, Spencer, Durkheim, Tönnies, so etwas wie Sukzessionsgesetze des Sozialen nachzuweisen (S. 24 f.). Auch Bedingungen der Machtausübung in Gruppen werden unter diese Rubrik einer allgemeinen Soziologie subsumiert, wobei aber "die Frage nicht auf das Zustandekommen der Vergesellschaftung als solcher, sondern auf die induktiv festzustellenden Schicksale von Gesellschaft, als eines schon zustande gekommenen Subjekts" zielt (S. 26).

Nun aber geht Simmel zu einer *3. Abstraktion* über, wodurch erst das benannt werden kann, was ihm in einem "ganz entscheidend erscheinenden Sinne 'soziologisch' ist" (S. 27). Hier erst formuliert er die Grundidee einer "reinen Soziologie", die sich ausschließlich mit den Formen des Sozialen befasst und die mit der Geometrie und der Grammatik hinsichtlich der spezifischen Abstraktionsweise in Analogie gesetzt wird.

Schließlich kann man noch eine *4. Abstraktion* ausfindig machen, durch die die in der sozialwissenschaftlichen Forschung benutzten Kategorien und Verfahren analysiert werden: "Hier also tritt die Soziologie als die Erkenntnistheorie der sozialen Sonderwissenschaften ein, als die Analyse und Systematik der Grundlagen, die in diesen formend und normierend wirken" (S. 30) Dies konstituiert das Gebiet der philosophischen Soziologie.

Simmel sieht sehr deutlich, dass es bei der Vielfalt und -zahl möglicher Abstraktionen, durch die jeweils spezifische Aspekte isoliert werden, irgendeine Legitimation für diejenigen unter ihnen geben muss, die Wissenschaften begründen – "denn nur in irgendeiner funktionellen Beziehung zur Tatsächlichkeit kann der Schutz gegen unfruchtbare Fragestellungen, gegen einen Zufallscharakter der wissenschaftlichen Begriffsbildung liegen" (Simmel 1908/1983, S. 6).

Dieser Gesichtspunkt ist in Bezug auf das System von Parsons von Interesse – denn wie kommt dieser dazu, "common-value integration" zu jenem analytischen Merkmal zu machen, das allein die Autonomie der Soziologie begründet?!

Zur Beantwortung dieser Frage ist es notwendig, die einzelnen Schritte zu rekonstruieren, durch die Parsons die Besonderheit der Soziologie begründen zu können meint. Die Abgrenzung der Soziologie als eigenständiges Fach unter den Prämissen eines analytischen Realismus kann nur gelingen, wenn eine "Lücke" vorhanden ist, genauer: wenn es Aspekte von Handlungen gibt, die zum einen von den anderen, bereits etablierten Sozialwissenschaften nicht berücksichtigt werden, und wenn zum andern diese Aspekte bedeutungsvoll genug, dass sie die Existenz einer eigens für sie zuständigen Wissenschaft rechtfertigen. Wie geht Parsons nun in *Structure* vor, um dies zu erreichen?

Innerhalb der "analytical sciences" unterscheidet er "three great classes of theoretical systems" (Parsons 1968, S. 762):

(1) system of nature
(2) system of action
(3) system of culture

Hier wird das "system of culture" als "nicht-empirisch" aufgefasst, denn darunter fallen Logik, Mathematik, Rechtswissenschaft, aber auch ganz allgemein Ideen. Methodisch läßt sich (1) durch Beobachtung erschließen, (3) durch Verstehen, und (2) nur durch beides, also Beobachtung und Verstehen. Die Merkmale von (2) bestehen in a. "irrelevance of the spatial frame of reference" und b. "the means-end schema", was Subjekte impliziert und daher die "method of Verstehen" nötig macht (S. 764 f.). Warum wird nun aber das "system of action" nicht bereits im Rahmen einer etablierten Wissenschaft behandelt? Die Antwort lautet: Weil es eine Reihe von emergenten Merkmalen aufweist, die nicht weiter reduzierbar sind – was unter der Voraussetzung, dass wissenschaftliche Disziplingrenzen entlang analytisch erschlossener Aspektstrukturen verlaufen, zu folgender Aufschlüsselung des Handlungssystems führt:

– Economics (Emergenzfaktor: "economic rationality")
– Political science (Emergenzfaktor: "problem of power solution and order"
– Sociology (Emergenzfaktor: "common-value integration")

Daneben werden noch als weitere sich mit Aspekten des Handlungssystems befassende Wissenschaften die Psychologie (Emergenz: Persönlichkeit) und die "technologies" (Emergenz: concrete content of ends, norms and knowledge) angeführt.

Es verdient Beachtung, dass Parsons in seiner Einteilung der Wissenschaften, wie er selbst anmerkt, durch Hans Freyer und dessen Werk *Soziologie als Wirklichkeitswissenschaft* beeinflusst war. Freyer unterscheidet zwischen Naturwissenschaften, Logoswissenschaften und Wirklichkeitswissenschaften. Diese für uns heute ungewohnte Terminologie macht einige klärende Bemerkungen nötig. In den Logoswissenschaften werden gegenständliche Sinnzusammenhänge allein nach ihrer sachlichen Bedeutung (und daher nicht in Bezug auf ihr konkretes Sein und Werden) zum Objekt gemacht. Die ausführlichen Verweise auf Dilthey (und Hegel) machen klar, dass es sich hier um die "Objektivationen des Geistes" handelt. Der "Terminus Wirklichkeitswissenschaft" – den ja bereits Max Weber verwendete – bezeichnet "die adäquate Erkenntnishaltung gegenüber einem sinnvollen Geschehen, dem der Erkennende selbst existenziell angehört" (Freyer 1964, S. 199). Freyer betont den "scharfen Gegensatz" zwischen Logos- und Wirklichkeitswissenschaft. Allerdings ist ein naheliegendes Missverständnis des Terminus "Wirklichkeitswissenschaft" zu vermeiden:

> Wirklichkeitswissenschaft heißt selbstverständlich nicht, daß ein wirkliches Geschehen so wie es ist abgespiegelt werden sollte. Alle Wissenschaft ist denkende Umformung des Wirklichen, Auswahl unter seinen Momenten, Herausarbeitung eines bestimmt gearteten Begriffs von ihm (S. 206).

Soziologie ist bei Freyer eine Wirklichkeitswissenschaft in diesem spezifischen Verständnis, wobei insbesondere der historische Charakter dieser Wirklichkeit essentiell ist, für den die Logoswissenschaften gleichsam keine Verwendung haben (können). Simmels Soziologie, die Freyer ausführlich bespricht (S. 46-57), trägt nun einen "rein logoswissenschaftliche[n] Charakter" (S. 50) – und das ist auch schon der Haupteinwand Freyers gegen diese, die als eine "konsequent morphologisch denkende Soziologie" ihre Gegenstände – die "Formgesetze der Konkurrenz, der Nachahmung, der Parteibildung, des Boykotts, der Vertretung" und wie die Formen des Sozialen bei Simmel lauten – "grundsätzlich genau so behandelt [...] wie eine formal denkende Kunstwissenschaft die Formprinzipien eines bestimmten Kunststils oder wie die Sprachwissenschaft die Grammatik einer bestimmten Sprache" (S. 51). Anders gesagt, besteht "der entscheidende Einwand gegen die nähere Fassung des Simmelschen Formbegriffs" (S. 54f.) darin, "daß sie die Wissenschaft der Soziologie auf das falsche Gleis leitet: anstatt sie logisch von den systematischen Geisteswissenschaften zu trennen, stellt sie sie ihnen gleich; sie macht die Soziologie zur typischen Logoswissenschaft" (S. 55). Die Analogie zur Geometrie ist schief und erweist sich "als verhängnisvoll" (ebd.), wenn man die Konsequenzen bedenkt:

> Wir erhalten als Objekt der Soziologie ein Reich reiner und unbewegter Sozialformen, die analysiert und systematisch geordnet werden können – unterhalb dieser klaren Geometrie der sozialen Formen aber bleibt die trübe Flut des gesellschaftlichen Lebens. Damit aber

sind die gesellschaftlichen Wirklichkeiten ihres Charakters als Wirklichkeiten völlig beraubt, sie sind ein Raub des an der Geometrie orientierten Formbegriffs geworden (Ebd.).

Geht man mit Freyer (S. 56) davon aus, "daß die Gegenstände der Soziologie wesentlich historischer Natur sind", stellt Simmels Formbegriff nicht bloß eine an sich durchaus berechtigte Abstraktion dar, sondern bewirkt eine "verhängnisvolle Veränderung am Objekt":

> Was geschichtliches Geschehen ist, wird zu ruhenden Strukturen fixiert. Der Nerv der Zeit, das heißt der Wirklichkeit, wird aus den sozialen Wirklichkeiten herausgerissen. Die Soziologie wird aus einer Wirklichkeitswissenschaft in eine Logoswissenschaft verwandelt (Ebd.).

An diesem Punkt lässt sich nun schon genauer bestimmen, inwiefern Parsons die von Freyer vorgenommene Einteilung aufgreift, und auch, was ihn so definitiv von Freyer trennt, dass dessen Kritik an Simmels Formen sich – mutatis mutandis – auch in eine Kritik an Parsons' Schemata verwandeln ließe.

Beziehen wir Freyers Einteilung auf Parsons' Klassifikation, so ergibt sich eine Zuordnung der formalen Soziologie zum System der Kultur, während Parsons seine eigene Soziologie als eine mit dem Handlungssystem befasste charakterisiert. Von Freyers Position aus könnte man an Parsons kritisieren, dass in dessen Analyse des Handlungssystems infolge des Bemühens, gleichsam zu den immer elementareren Schichten vorzustoßen und die Abstraktion erst bei den grundlegenden "Atomen" an ihr Ziel kommen zu lassen, sich die logoswissenschaftliche Denkweise einschleicht.

Hier wird die Hauptdifferenz also besonders deutlich sichtbar. Und die Unterscheidung zwischen deskriptiver und analytischer Abstraktion, die Parsons gegen Simmel wendet, ist interpretativ unterbestimmt. Sie dient vor allem dazu, nur jene Konstituierungen der Soziologie zuzulassen, die auf analytischer Abstraktion beruhen. Simmel verwende eben durchgehend deskriptive Abstraktionen, und daher sei sein Ansatz systematisch wenig ergiebig. Nebenbei sei bemerkt, dass Parsons (1994, S. 68) den Weberschen Idealtypus als geradezu paradigmatisches Beispiel für Simmels "Form" nennt: "this schema is, I think, in all essentials, formal sociology in Simmel's sense" – was ihn, Parsons, allerdings nicht davon abhält, die Handlungskonzeption Webers ausgiebig zu besprechen. Da er dies mit dem Hinweis auf den "bloß" formalen Charakter des Idealtypus hätte unterlassen können, muss der entscheidende Grund für die Berücksichtigung von Weber und die Ignorierung Simmels in *Structure of Social Action* ein anderer sein. Dass die Gleichsetzung von Idealtypus und Form korrekt ist, darf füglich bezweifelt werden; man nehme nur jene Stelle aus dem programmatischen Aufsatz *Das Problem der Soziologie*, wo Simmel (1894/1992, S. 55) über die Formen des Sozialen sagt: "Diese Formen entwickeln sich bei der Berührung der Individuen, relativ unabhängig von dem Grunde dieser Berührung, und ihre Summe macht dasjenige konkret aus, was man mit dem

Abstraktum Gesellschaft benennt". Von Webers Idealtypen kann genau das eben nicht behauptet werden.

Auf einen Punkt soll hier nur kurz verwiesen werden, aus dem die Besonderheit des Freyerschen Systems hervorgeht und der wohl noch nicht hinreichend daraufhin untersucht wurde, ob er nicht doch auch – trotz allem, was prima facie dagegen spricht – für Parsons erhebliche Bedeutung besitzt: Soziologie ist zwar "auf den Strukturgehalt der sozialen Welt gerichtet", doch sie muss nach Freyer (1964, S. 206) "die existenzielle Bedeutung der gesellschaftlichen Gegenwart, ihr Weiterdrängen durch die Gegenwart hindurch in die Zukunft" in sich aufnehmen. Wir lesen heute diese Worte natürlich im Wissen, dass sie drei Jahre vor der Machtergreifung des Nationalsozialismus veröffentlicht wurden und Freyer danach eine exponierte Rolle spielen wird. Darüber darf jedoch nicht übersehen werden, dass die Soziologie von Beginn an mit dem Anspruch auftritt, Gegenwart und Zukunft der Gesellschaft in den Blick nehmen zu können. Mögen auch die Vorstellungen darüber, in welche Zukunft die Gesellschaft sich entwickelt und entwickeln soll, erheblich differieren – dass auch die amerikanische Soziologie im Allgemeinen und auch der Funktionalismus mit ethisch-politischen Idealen und Programmen aufs engste verknüpft sind, dürfte kaum zu bestreiten sein.[4]

In systematisch-methodischer Hinsicht sollte noch besonders beachtet werden, dass Parsons zunächst das Verstehen als grundlegend zur Analyse des Kultursystems ansieht, das Handlungssystem hingegen durch Verstehen und Beobachtung analysiert werden muss. Schon in *The Social System* wird allerdings das Verstehen und insbesondere das Verstehen des subjektiv gemeinten Sinnes (M. Weber) in der Wertigkeit herabgestuft:

> Contrary to the view held by the author in the *Structure of Social Action* it now appears that this postulate ["the study of action 'from the point of view of the actor'] is not essential to the frame of reference of action in its most elementary form (Parsons 1951, S. 543).

In *The Social System* wird "social action" im Sinne von "interaction" in drei Systeme aufgegliedert: social system, personality system, cultural system – und letzteres deckt sich nicht mit dem "system of culture", wie es im Werk von 1937 definiert wird. Diese Verschiebung des Kulturbegriffs mündet schließlich in der Konzeptualisierung von Kultur als einem eigenen Subsystem – was J. Habermas (1981, S. 355) als "einen, wie immer stillschweigenden, Bruch mit der methodologischen Auffassung, die Parsons als 'analytischen Realismus' bezeichnet hatte" interpretiert: "Aussagen über die analytischen Beziehungen zwischen Werten, Normen, Zielen und

---

4 Als Stichworte genügen hier Sozialtechnik und demokratische Wertorientierung. Inwiefern nach 1945 eine "Amerikanisierung" der deutschen Soziologie stattfand, ist noch strittig und wird in einer der nächsten Editionen des "Jahrbuchs für Soziologiegeschichte" aus unterschiedlichen Perspektiven eingehend diskutiert werden.

Ressourcen verwandeln sich unter der Hand zu Aussagen über empirische Beziehungen zwischen Systembestandteilen" (Ebd., S. 356). In ähnliche Richtung zielt die Anmerkung von Klaus Müller (1996, S. 293), die Ausdifferenzierung des personalen, des kulturellen und des sozialen Subsystems sei "insofern aufschlußreich, als sie nochmals den problematischen Zug des *analytischen* Realismus hervorhebt: begrifflichen Unterscheidungen wird je nach Bedarf eine 'realistische', d. h. empirische Bedeutung unterschoben."[5]

Wie bereits erwähnt, erblickt Parsons in der "common-value integration" das entscheidende emergente Merkmal des Handlungssystems. Über dieses Merkmal definiert Parsons (1968, S. 768) bekanntlich das spezifisch soziologische Arbeitsfeld:

> This is a clearly marked emergent property readily distinguishable from both the economic and the political. If this property is designated the sociological, sociology may then be defined as ‚the science which attempts to develop an analytical theory of social action systems in so far as these systems can be understood in terms of the property of common-value integration'.

Einige Schwierigkeiten mit dieser Art der Begründung einer Wissenschaft seien wenigstens erwähnt. Parsons' Wissenschaftsklassifikation wird von der Emergenzidee geleitet. Demzufolge müsste es so viele Wissenschaften geben, wie es emergente Faktoren gibt. Was bedeutet aber in diesem Zusammenhang Emergenz? Zweierlei muss offenbar gegeben sein: Emergent sind nur jene Eigenschaften, die nicht "reduzierbar" sind; und diese Eigenschaften dürfen keine konkret-empirischen sein, sondern müssen durch spezifische Abstraktionen "gebildet" werden. Demnach darf "common-value integration" keinen empirischen Sachverhalt selber beschreiben, sondern muss einen spezifischen "Aspekt" ausdrücken. Aber wieso bildet dann etwa Konkurrenz nicht auch einen emergenten Faktor und warum gibt es keine Wissenschaft, die der Konkurrenz ihre Existenz "verdankt"? Man ersetze einmal probeweise im letzten angeführten Parsons-Zitat "common-value integration" durch "Konkurrenz", konstatiere dann, dass es bisher keine wissenschaftliche Disziplin gab, die sich mit dem Sozialen einzig unter dem Gesichtspunkt der Konkurrenz befasste – und schon haben wir eine neue, ganz andere Soziologie definiert. Die von Parsons gewählte Begründungsstrategie lässt sich so leicht konterkarieren, und es stellt sich

---

5   Dass Parsons' Theorie nur begriffliche Vorschläge und Systematisierungen enthält und sich gar nicht an die Erklärung empirischer Sachverhalte wagt, ist eine Einschätzung, die Kritiker des Funktionalismus wie George Caspar Homans schon früh ausgesprochen haben. Die problematische Beziehung zwischen dem Analytischen und dem Empirischen bei Parsons ist gleichsam zu einem fixen Bestandteil der Funktionalismus-Kritik geworden; sie wird etwa auch in einem unlängst erschienenen Buch von Max Haller (1999. S. 198ff.) über soziologische Theorien angesprochen.

dann die Frage, ob nicht Simmels formale Soziologie mindestens ebenso plausibel gemacht werden kann. Dazu sollen hier nur zwei Anmerkungen gemacht werden. Zum einen kommt Parsons (1968, S. 772) im Anschluss an jene Stelle in *The Structure of Social Action*, an der er stolz vermeldet, es sei ihm gelungen, die Soziologie als "a special analytical science on the same level as economic theory" zu begründen, auch auf Simmel zu sprechen:

> The procedure here is not, however, altogether without precedent. Simmel's was, perhaps, the first serious attempt to gain a basis for sociology as, in this sense, a special science. His formula is unacceptable for reasons that cannot be gone into here. But it was founded on sound insight and the view just stated may be regarded as a restatement of its sound elements in more acceptable terms. The main difficulty for Simmel was that the view he took of the other social sciences precluded relating his concept of sociology to other analytical social sciences on the same methodological level. To him sociology was the only abstract analytical science in the social field (Parsons 1968, S. 772 f.).

Zum anderen ist auf eine Konsequenz dieser Art von Soziologie zu verweisen, die Parsons in seiner Erwiderung auf die von Thomas Burger (1977) vorgetragene Kritik selbst explizit angesprochen hat:

> As *theorist* I have chosen the analytic path, the consequence of which is that, in dealing with many if not most empirical problem areas, it is necessary to invoke a *plurality* of analytical schemes [...] Thus Burger is essentially correct in his contention that, in the analytic conception of sociological theory which I have supported, a purely sociological explanation of the problem of social order cannot be attained (Parsons, in: Hamilton II, S. 315).

Das heißt aber nichts anderes, als dass für das so zentrale "problem of social order" nicht allein die Soziologie zuständig ist. Daraus folgt wiederum die Notwendigkeit einer Kooperation verschiedener Sozialwissenschaften, und zwar in Bezug auf "many if not most empirical problem areas". Der von Parsons eingeschlagene Weg nimmt daher seinen Ausgang bei einer strikt analytischen Trennung der Wissenschaften, welche aber dann zum Zwecke von Erklärungen wieder zusammengeführt werden müssen. Hier ist also keineswegs von einer gleichsam selbstbewusst-selbstgenügsamen Autonomie der Soziologie die Rede; vielmehr wäre der nächste konsequente Schritt die Ausarbeitung eines arbeitsteiligen Programms. Dass Parsons und der Funktionalismus diesen Schritt tatsächlich gesetzt haben, ist freilich eine nur schwer zu verteidigende Annahme. Will man – um das Problem bildhaft zu veranschaulichen – ein Fahrzeug erzeugen, das sich von der Stelle bewegt, kann man sich nicht mit der Produktion von Fahrgestellen und deren permanenter Verbesserung begnügen und darauf verweisen, anderswo würden ohnehin die Karosserien und die Motoren hergestellt. Passen all diese und weitere Teile zusammen und kann man sie so zusammensetzen, dass daraus ein *Automobil* entsteht? Wenn die faktische Entwicklung, die der Funktionalismus genommen hat, in eine andere Richtung ging, könnte das die Frage aktualisieren, wovon es abhängig ist, ob gewisse Optionen wahrgenommen werden. Im konkreten Fall müsste nicht nur die Geschichte der Soziologie, sondern auch die verwandter Disziplinen und möglicher Kooperationspartner berücksichtigt werden. Das heißt nun, dass eine derartige Rekonstruktion selber nur gelingen kann, wenn zumindest in Ansätzen jene Art von Zusammenarbeit verwirklicht wird, die den virtuellen Gegenstand der angestrebten Untersuchung bildet. Hier kann dies nur als ein Desideratum festgehalten werden.

Für die höchst unterschiedliche Interpretation, die Parsons' Beziehung zu Simmel gefunden hat, sei hier auf zwei Exponenten verwiesen: Während Donald N. Levine von einer gröblichen und sich auf die Theorie von Parsons sehr negativ auswirkenden Vernachlässigung Simmels und dessen formaler Soziologie spricht, hält Gary Dean Jaworski dem entgegen, Parsons sei nicht nur mit Simmels Werk vertraut gewesen, dieses spiele vielmehr in zentralen Passagen von *The Structure of Social Action* eine referentielle Rolle (ohne dass es explizit analysiert werde). Jaworski will also zeigen, dass die Auseinandersetzung, die Parsons im in *Structure* nicht aufgenommenen Kapitel über Simmel vorlegt, hinsichtlich des argumentativen Kerns sehr wohl publiziert wurde (wenn auch nicht explizit oder im gleichen Wortlaut). Allerdings spricht die Tatsache, dass der Tönnies-Abschnitt des unpublizierten Kapitels publiziert wurde (s. Parsons 1968, S. 686-694), der Simmel-Teil hingegen nicht, gegen die Deutung Jaworskis. Auch die Annahme, Parsons' frühe Arbeiten hätten dort, wo es nicht um den "unit act" und die Handlungen von Individuen, sondern um "the problem of building ethical communities" gegangen sei, auf die Hilfe der formalen Soziologie bauen können (Jaworski 1991, S. 96 f.), erscheint fragwürdig.

In einer anderen Hinsicht kann die "Verträglichkeit" der beiden Standpunkte argumentiert werden: Jaworski kann recht haben, insofern als Parsons mit Simmels formaler Soziologie durchaus vertraut war; Levine kann recht haben, weil er die formale Soziologie als für sein eigenes theoretisches Vorhaben als zu wenig "analytisch" in den Hintergrund treten ließ. Die perspektivischen Besonderheiten sind die folgenden: Jaworski sieht einen Parsons am Werk, der ohnehin alles von Simmel, was ihm für die Lösung seiner zentralen Anliegen (und diese seien nicht nur wissenschaftlich-theoretische, sondern auch kulturell-moralische) dienlich sein konnte, aufgegriffen habe. Levine geht von einer grundlegenden Insuffizienz des Ansatzes von Parsons aus, der von einer Berücksichtigung der Simmelschen Soziologie nur hätte profitieren können.

Eine letzte Reflexion zu diesem Thema: Obwohl Parsons in seinen frühen Schriften des öfteren auf die Bedeutung Simmels verweist, verbindet ihn mit diesem ersichtlich keine Affinität. Bezeichnend ist etwa, dass Parsons (1994, S. 66) in seinem "gestrichenen" Kapitel meint: "we may surmise that Simmel's insight was primarily into the importance of what we called the institutional aspect of social systems" (ob dieses Urteil Simmel gerecht wird, ist sehr zweifelhaft), und ebenso nennt er in den ebenfalls aus den 30er Jahren stammenden und erst nach seinem Tod veröffentlichten "Prolegomena to a Theory of Social Institutions" unter den für ihn besonders bedeutsamen Autoren neben Pareto, Durkheim, Max Weber und Tönnies auch Simmel (Parsons 1990, S. 23). Doch letztlich bleibt Parsons unbeeindruckt und ist nicht willens (fähig?), sich auf Simmels Denkstil ernsthaft einzulassen. Wäre es nicht reizvoll und aufschlußreich, eine detailliertere Auseinandersetzung Parsons' mit der formalen Soziologie hypothetisch-gedankenexperimentell in der Weise vorzunehmen, dass als Vorlage, gleichsam als script dafür der Briefwechsel zwischen Parsons und Alfred Schütz (s. Schütz/Parsons 1977) diente?! Dies soll nun nicht eine Nähe der Positionen von Simmel und Schütz suggerieren, sondern böte vielleicht die Grundlage für ein besseres Verständnis, wie Parsons mit ihm fremden Denkweisen, die er sich nicht zu assimilieren und für sein theoretisches Konzept nicht nutzbar zu machen weiß, umgeht. Ob diese Fremdheit und fehlende Sensibilität überhaupt erst das grandiose Werk Parsons' möglich gemacht hat und ob damit diese Bedingung der Möglichkeit vergebene Chancen impliziert, die eigene Theorie im Rahmen einer vollwertigen Soziologie zu situieren und fruchtbar zu machen – solche Fragen können hier nur mehr gestellt, aber nicht mehr behandelt werden.

Literatur

Burger, Thomas (1977): Talcott Parsons, the Problem of Order in Society, and the Program of an Analytical Sociology. In: American Journal of Sociology 83, S. 320-339. [Wiederabgedruckt in Hamilton 1992, II, S. 301-314.].
Camic, Charles (1987): The Making of a Method: A Historical Reinterpretation of the Early Parsons. In: American Sociological Review 52, S. 421-439. [Hamilton I, S. 269-298.].
Camic, Charles (1989): *Structure* after 50 Years: The Anatomy of a Charter. In: American Journal of Sociology 95, S. 38-107. [Hamilton I, S. 323-382.].
Camic, Charles (1990): An Historical Prologue to "Prolegomena to a Theory of Social Institutions" by Talcott Parsons. In: American Sociological Review 55, S. 313-319. [Hamilton II, S. 14-22.]
Freyer, Hans (1964): Soziologie als Wirklichkeitswissenschaft. Logische Grundlegung des Systems der Soziologie. Stuttgart: Teubner (unveränd. Nachdruck der 1. Aufl. 1930).
Habermas, Jürgen (1981): Theorie des kommunikativen Handelns. Bd. 2: Zur Kritik der funktionalistischen Vernunft. Frankfurt/M.: Suhrkamp.
Haller, Max (1999): Soziologische Theorie im systematisch-kritischen Vergleich. Opladen: Leske + Budrich (UTB. 2074.)
Hamilton, Peter (ed.) (1992): Talcott Parsons: Critical Assessments. Vol. I – IV. London/New York: Routledge.
Jaworski, Gary Dean (1991): Parsons, Simmel and the Eclipse of Religious Values. In: Simmel Newsletter 1, S. 90-102.
Levine, Donald N. (1980 [1957]): Simmel and Parsons: Two Approaches to the Study of Society. New York: Arno.
Levine, Donald N. (1984): Ambivalente Begegnungen: "Negationen" Simmels durch Durkheim, Weber, Lukács, Park und Parsons. In: H.-J. Dahme/O. Rammstedt (Hg.): Georg Simmel und die Moderne. Neue Interpretationen und Materialien. Frankfurt/M.: Suhrkamp (stw. 469.), S. 318-387.

Levine, Donald N. (1989): Parsons' *Structure* (and Simmel) Revisited. In: Sociological Theory 7, S. 129-136 [Hamilton II, S. 3-13].
Levine, Donald N. (1991): Simmel and Parsons Reconsidered. In: American Journal of Sociology 96, S. 1097-1116 [Hamilton II, S. 62-78].
Menger, Carl (1883): Untersuchungen über die Methode der Socialwissenschaften, und der Politischen Oekonomie insbesondere. Leipzig: Duncker & Humblot. [Reprint als Band II von Menger: Gesammelte Werke, Hg. F. A. Hayek. Tübingen: Mohr (Siebeck) 1969.]
Mill, John Stuart (1844/1976): Einige ungelöste Probleme der politischen Ökonomie. Hg. Hans G. Nutzinger. Frankfurt/M. - New York 1976. (Orig.: Essays on some Unsettled Questions of Political Economy. 1844).
Müller, Klaus (1996): Allgemeine Systemtheorie. Geschichte, Methodologie und sozialwissenschaftliche Heuristik eines Wissenschaftsprogramms. Opladen: Westdeutscher Verlag (Studien zur Sozialwissenschaft. 164.)
Parsons, Talcott (1951): The Social System. Glencoe, Ill.: The Free Press.
Parsons, Talcott (1968 [1937/1949]: The Structure of Social Action. A Study in Social Theory with Special Reference to a Group of Recent European Writers. New York: The Free Press/London: Collier-Macmillan.
Parsons, Talcott (1990): Prolegomena to a Theory of Social Institutions. In: American Sociological Review 55, S. 319-333. [Hamilton II, S. 23-42.].
Parsons, Talcott (1994): Georg Simmel and Ferdinand Tönnies: Social Relationships and the Elements of Action. In: Simmel Newsletter 4, S. 63-78.
Parsons, Talcott / Bales, Robert F. / Shils, Edward A. (1953): Working Papers in the Theory of Action. New York: The Free Press/London: Collier-Macmillan.
Schimank, Uwe (1996): Theorien gesellschaftlicher Differenzierung. Opladen: Leske + Budrich (UTB. 1886.)
Schmid, Michael (1998): Soziales Handeln und strukturelle Selektion. Beiträge zur Theorie sozialer Systeme. Opladen/Wiesbaden: Westdeutscher Verlag.
Schütz, Alfred/ Parsons, Talcott (1977): Zur Theorie sozialen Handelns. Ein Briefwechsel. Hg. u. eingeleitet von Walter M. Sprondel. Frankfurt/M.: Suhrkamp (stw. 202.)
Simmel, Georg (1894/1992): Das Problem der Sociologie. (Wiederabgedruckt) in: Georg Simmel: Aufsätze und Abhandlungen 1894 bis 1900 (= Gesamtausgabe, Band 5) Frankfurt/M.: Suhrkamp 1992 (stw. 805.), S. 52-61
Simmel, Georg (1908/1983): Soziologie. Untersuchungen über die Formen der Vergesellschaftung. Berlin: Duncker & Humblot (6. Aufl. 1983).
Simmel, Georg (1917/1984): Grundfragen der Soziologie (Individuum und Gesellschaft). Berlin/New York (4. Aufl. 1984).
Staubmann, Helmut Michael (1998): Overcoming Flawed Dichotomies: The Impact of Georg Simmel on American Sociology. In: International Journal of Politics, Culture and Society 11, S. 501-515. [Review essay of Gary D. Jaworski: Georg Simmel and the American Prospect. Albany, NY: State University of New York Press 1997.].
Swedberg, Richard (1994): Joseph A. Schumpeter. Eine Biographie. Stuttgart: Klett-Cotta.

Parsons Reads Durkheim
Dénes Némedi

It is a commonplace that Parsons was one of the greatest social theorists of the second half of our waning century. The book on him was "reopened" in the eighties (Sciulli, Gerstein 1985, 383), his importance for contemporary sociology is beyond doubt. He shaped sociology, as it emerged in the second half of the century, in a way as no one of his contemporaries did. At the same time, he was the last of the 'founding fathers'. He was as much concerned with the disciplinary status of sociology as the leading social theoreticians of the first half of the century, Durkheim, Toennies, Simmel or Weber were (Camic 1989). He tried, as they did, to establish that there has to be an independent and fully scientific research in society, a legitimate discipline besides other, no less legitimate and more firmly constituted disciplines. He did that not so much by his voluminous theories (they came later, in a period when sociology seemed to achieve the status Parsons longed for) but by integrating European social theorists of the turn of century in American sociology and by that way in the emerging new European sociology (and by deliberately excluding much of early American sociology from the sanctified tradition of the discipline) – in his famous *The Structure of Social Action*.

The early Parsons (as opposed to the later Parsons) was thus on the divide between two very different sociologies: he was on the one hand prolonging the quest for the true subject area of sociology (as Toennies, Simmel, Durkheim and Weber did before him) and on the other hand looking toward the emergence of a 'normal' discipline. It is this particular emplacement of *The Structure of Social Action* (Parsons 1937) which makes its investigation important and interesting. He summed up what he thought was the most important of the contributions of his predecessors and handed it down to the discipline which was about to enter the mature phase of real research (once the task of establishment completed – as Parsons believed). The impact of *The Structure* on the conception sociology created of his own past was incomparable (even if in the years following its first publication the influence it had was restrained – the real recognition arrived after ten years of latency). Parsons' contribution to the inauguration of Weber and Durkheim as the founding fathers of sociology was crucial, and therefore the process of inauguration is an interesting topic for research in itself. However, it is not alone curiosity in the transmission of ideas which should lead the research in the development of Parsons' thought. The way in which Parsons assimilated social theories and created the venerable tradition of sociology should be studied because it can shed light on basic characteristics of the discipline. First of all, it can help to understand the difference between the sociology of the turn of century and the relatively well developed academic sociology of the fifties and sixties.

To sum up, Parsons had and has a privileged position in the history of sociology. His 'invention of tradition' had an impact on the image sociology had and has of itself. Central to the 'invention of sociological tradition' was the creation of 'founding fathers' – Weber and Durkheim. In this paper, I will restrain the discussion to certain aspects of Durkheim's assimilation by Parsons.

Parsons did much to rescue Durkheim to sociology. In the interwar period the Durkheimian school was declining, its influence in France was waning (Heilbron 1985), its impact in American sociology was minimal (Besnard 1987, 157-169). Perhaps we would consider Durkheim as a somewhat strange speculative precursor to functional and structural anthropology, had not Parsons come and showed that he was really an important theorist of capitalism.[1] It was extremely important that he recognised changes in the Durkheimian thought and thereby encouraged much historical research. His characterisation of Durkheim's style of thought (Parsons 1937, 301-2) is accurate and to the point. Many of his analyses remain a source of inspiration. He called attention to the Durkheimian emphasis on the 'non-contractual' elements in the contract and the problems resulting from this insight (Parsons 1937, 310 ff., 318-19), perhaps to the detriment of the main argument of Durkheim's Division of Labour. His remarks on Durkheim's conception of moral individualism (e.g. Parsons 1937, 334, 338) were very much to the point and more pertinent than many of later interpretations.

However, was not the service Parsons rendered to Durkheimism of the kind the Germans call 'ein Bärendienst'? The correctness of the interpretation of Durkheim by Parsons was in the lifetime of Parsons (e.g. Pope 1973, 1975, Gerstein 1979) and after his death (e.g. Besnard 1987, 49-52, Némedi 1990) debated. The general result was that Parsons' interpretation of Durkheim was in many respects certainly flawed, if not misleading. My present paper follows this line of argument, but I would like

---

[1] Parsons' first encounter with Durkheim was before his departure for London at Amherst and then in London when he was studying with Hobhouse and Malinowski (Camic 1991, xvi, xxxix, Parsons 1977a, 25). Returning to the United States, he read, once again, Durkheim (Parsons 1977b, 77). Parsons recalled that after studying Marshall, Pareto and Weber he came back to Durkheim and discovered that his study of the division of labour was crucial to the understanding of capitalism. "Careful study of this book showed that its analysis could indeed be very directly articulated with Weber's analysis of capitalism, and that in turn with Marshall's conception of free enterprise. The theory as such then articulated with the sociological, rather than strictly economic, components of the work of Pareto and Weber and, more indirectly, Marshall." Actually, the first chapters of *The Structure of Social Action* committed to paper were some pages on Durkheim (Parsons 1977a, 25). "Durkheim is, in my opinion, the most important single theoretical father of the concept of social system" (Parsons 1977b, 79).

to suggest that the misinterpretations were necessary. In other words: if Parsons was to succeed in his efforts as the founder of a new kind of sociology, he had to deform the Durkheimian categories and arguments. Otherwise, it would have been impossible to introduce Durkheim as forerunner of the new science of sociology. Parsons' ambition[2] was to construct sociology as a science equal to and independent of, economics in two respects: as a basic science explaining social behaviour in terms of action (and in this sense functioning as an integrator to social sciences in general) and as a rigorous science. The goal set in this way, the accents had to be shifted. General theoretical statements became more important, elements related to the 'diagnosis of time' had to be pushed in the background. The result was often a positively misleading reading of the classics. However, I am not interested in misinterpretations or misreading per se. I am interested in them because they reveal procedures of theory construction and discipline creation.

As far as Parsons' interpretation of the Durkheimian concept of 'social fact' is concerned, the case is relatively simple. Basic to the efforts of Parsons was the well known 'convergence thesis' (Camic 1989). To prove this he had to construct a Durkheimian action theory and as Durkheim was in no way an action theoretician he had to suppress some statements and to interpret others in a dubious way (Némedi 1990). Due to his action theoretical viewpoint, he did not realise that the Durkheimian analysis of the impact of Protestantism on suicide rates was not the result of special value contents (Parsons 1937, 333). The Parsonian analysis of Durkheim's positivistic methodology was also distorted by his constant effort to understand him as an action theoretician. Thus, he interpreted the Durkheimian conception of the thinglike character of social facts in the action frame of reference (Parsons 1937, 349, 352) which led to the deformation of the basic structure of Durkheimian theory.

The same can be said of his treatment of anomie. He was instrumental in introducing the concept in modern sociology, but he did that by hiding the special Durkheimian theory of social integration and regulation (Besnard 1987). He understood regulation (the absence of which is anomie) as the type of collective control where control "enters into the formulation of the ends [of people's action] themselves" (Parsons 1937, 337, 376 ff.). Of course, Durkheim's idea was quite different.[3] Parsons forgot that "opposite to the state of anomie" was not 'perfect integration', but fatalism resulting from too much regulation (Parsons 1937, 377) – the only context where this statement makes sense is the action frame of reference.

---

[2] See in this respect Camic 1991.
[3] It is difficult to decide whether the very meagre attention paid to the Durkheimian analysis of the impact of familial status on suicide rates (Parsons 1937, 334, 336) was the result or the cause of the misinterpretation of Durkheim's theory.

He did not see the specificity of the Durkheimian concept of 'representation' and equated it with the 'idea' resulting from 'experience'. Then, he treated the Durkheimian concept of collective representation as 'beliefs concerning the collectivity' (instead of 'beliefs, ideas held in common') (Parsons 1937, 359-361, 365). It is difficult to understand the reasons for this construction of a straw man.[4]

The list of Parsons' faults can be prolonged. In this paper, I would like to concentrate on just one aspect, on the interpretation of the Durkheimian analysis of religious effervescent ritual. What I am interested in this case, is the Parsonian practice of 'reading Durkheim'.[5] I understand this practice as the constitutive element of the Parsonian enterprise. I think that some crucial aspects of the Parsonian enterprise can be understood if one poses the simple question: why did not read Parsons Durkheim more attentively? To be able to answer to this, we, on our part, we have to read Parsons very attentively.

Parsons began the analysis of *The Forms* by interpreting Durkheim's famous definition of religion (Parsons 1937, 411 ff.). Durkheim proceeded by eliminating possible alternative definitions (as he used to do) and arrived at a doubly formal definition. First of all he declared that there are two distinct elements in religion: the rites and the beliefs, and then he decided that it was the beliefs which differentiated between religious rituals and other human activities and not vice versa. Durkheim did not adduce any proofs for this statement (Durkheim 1912, 50). Then he declared (without further proof, once again) that all religious beliefs

> présentent un même caractère commun: elles supposent une classification des choses, réelles ou idéales ... en deux genres opposés, désignés généralement par deux termes distincts que traduisent assez bien les mots de profane et de sacré (Durkheim 1912, 50).

Discussing the difference of profane and sacred, Durkheim enumerated some examples (taken from Schultze and Frazer) demonstrating that practically any thing can be sacred and that people do not feel themselves being in an inferior or dependent position towards sacred things or beings.

> Mais, si une distinction purement hiérarchique est un critère à la fois trop général et trop imprécis, il ne reste plus pour définir le sacré par rapport au profane que leur hétérogénéité. Seulement, ce qui fait que cette hétérogénéité suffit à caratériser cette classification des choses et à la distinguer de toute autre, c'est qu'elle est très particulière: elle est absolue (Durkheim 1912, 53).[6]

---

[4] Perhaps they prepare the ground for the rejection of the late Durkheim's epistemology.
[5] As I had no access to archival materials, I had to restrict myself to printed sources and to the texts themselves.
[6] It remains an 'enigma' in what extent Durkheim's conception of religion was influenced by Jewish religiosity he learned in his childhood (Pickering 1994).

Parsons did not adhere to this highly formal definition of the sacred and of religion. It is important to remark that he inverted the two steps of the Durkheimian definition: he took as the first 'basic distinction' the one between sacred and profane and as the second one that between beliefs and rites (Parsons 1912, 411-2). The inversion of the procedure seems to be of minor interpretative importance, but it is not.

The Durkheimian definitional sequence implied that the emergence of the formal and absolute distinction between sacred and profane beliefs should be explained as the first step of religious theory, followed by the second step, the analysis of the religious rituals of Australians. This is the procedure Durkheim followed. Book I of *The Forms* defined totemism as the elementary religious belief complex, Book II described in detail the totemistic beliefs and then attempted to explain the origin of these beliefs. The crucial point was in Chapter VII of Book II where Durkheim came to the conclusion that the origin of the difference of sacred and profane was to be found in the effervescent ritual practices (Durkheim 1912, 293-342). It is obvious that Durkheim committed elementary mistakes in the procedure: he explained the specificity of sacred beliefs by specific rites, whereas he declared that rites are defined by the beliefs attached to them.

By inverting the two steps of the definition, Parsons escaped from committing Durkheim's mistake. He even avoided to mention it.[7] The definitional inversion had two consequences. On the one hand, it reinforced Parsons' inclination to give a substantial and not formal definition of the sacred,[8] on the other hand, it allowed Parsons not to follow through Durkheim's analysis of totemism.

1. The substantial definition of the sacred bears witness to Parsons' admitted efforts to transcribe the Durkheimian theory in an action theoretical frame. While it is true that Durkheim tended to identify the profane with the economical and utilitarian and in this sense it is not totally foreign to Durkheim the statement that "sacred things are distinguished by the fact that men do not treat them in a utilitarian manner..." (Parsons 1937, 412), it is already contrary to Durkheim's explicit assertions to propose as the Durkheimian definition of sacred the following sentences:

> Sacred things are things set apart by a peculiar attitude of respect which is expressed in various ways. They are thought of as imbued with peculiar virtues, as having special powers ... Above all man's relations to sacred things are not taken as an ordinary matter of course, but always as a matter of special attitudes, special respect, special precautions. (Parsons 1937, 411-12)

---

[7] In 1973, Parsons mentioned that Durkheim dealt first with beliefs and only then with rites, but he maintained that that was only a symptom of Durkheim's opposition to the 'sociology of knowledge' which would make beliefs dependent of other functions. Parsons confirmed that central to Durkheim's theory was the ritual (Parsons 1978, 226).

[8] That was – if one accepts that the extreme formalism of the Durkheimian definition of sacred was related to Durkheim's Jewishness – a disguised 'Christianisation' of the idea.

The "special precautions" is right; the definition of sacred by attitudes is obviously wrong: Durkheim explicitly stated that sacred things do not necessarily inspire the feeling of inferiority and respect in believers (Durkheim 1912, 52). Parsons' proposition about the Durkheimian definition prepared his prolonged analysis of the sacred. He agreed with Durkheim upon the symbolic character of the sacred and then came to the avowedly not-Durkheimian conclusion that the reference of the sacred symbols is "the ultimate value complex", "aspects of 'reality' significant to human life and experience, yet outside the range of scientific observation and analysis" (Parsons 1937, 421). That was an idea Parsons was fond of. He discarded Durkheim's explicit statement that the referent of the religious symbol must be the social element[9] as a kind of 'religious materialism' and proposed "that it is in terms of what we call religious ideas that men attempt a cognitive apprehension of the non-empirical aspects of reality to which they are actively related" (Parsons 1937, 425).[10] I am not particularly interested in the well-known theoretical ramifications of this idea. It was central to Parsons' own theory of action. What I want to stress is that it was linked to the inversion of the Durkheimian definition. Indeed, if one defined first the sacred and then interpreted the sacred as related to ultimate reality (the source of ultimate values making social integration possible) and sacred practices and beliefs were conceived in conformity with this definition, then it became impossible to search for the origins of sacred beliefs in those practices.

2. The second consequence of the inversion of the Durkheimian definition of the sacred was that Parsons proceeded without giving much attention to the discussions in Book II. That was that part of the book where Durkheim developed the social explanation of religion, discarded by Parsons. Parsons referred occasionally to pages in this part of the book (e.g. Parsons 1937, 416, 417, 435), but then went on to dis-

---

[9] "D'une manière générale, il n'est pas douteux qu'une société a tout ce qu'il faut pour éveiller dans les esprits, par la seule action qu'elle exerce sur eux, la sensation du divin; car elle est à ses memebres ce qu'un dieu est à ses fidèles" (Durkheim 1912, 295). "Puisque la force religieuse n'est autre chose que la force collective et anonyme du clan, et puisque celle-ci n'est représentable aux esprits que sous la forme de totem, l'emblème totémique est comme le corps visible du dieu" (Durkheim 1912, 316).

[10] It is positively misleading that Parsons considers his own definition as being "more acceptable than his [Durkheim's] own of the important scientific truth in Durkheim's view" (Parsons 1937, 426). Later Parsons himself wrote: "Durkheim arrives at the equation of religion and society by emphasising not the material aspect of religion, but rather the ideal aspect of society" (Parsons 1937, 427). That was correct and was obviously incompatible with Parsons' view "that to the actor *no* empirical reality in the scientific sense underlies religious ideas" (Parsons 1937, 427). Whereas for Durkheim it was the social experience which created religion, for Parsons it was the 'ultimate reality' which, mediated by religion, engendered the common value elements which, in turn, made society possible.

cuss religious rituals by taking as starting point certain discussions in Book III of *The Forms*.

Parsons accorded primary functional and expressive significance to ritual while Durkheim always stressed the necessary duality of ritual and belief.[11]

> For by the common ritual expression of their attitudes men not only manifest them but they, in turn, reinforce the attitudes. Ritual brings the attitudes into a heightened state of self-consciousness which greatly strengthens them, and through them strengthens, in turn, the moral community. ... As Durkheim sometimes puts it, it recreates the society itself (Parsons 1937, 435).

To demonstrate the primary recreative and expressive function of ritual, Parsons referred to Durkheim's treatment of the sacrifice (Book III, Chapter II), to funeral rites (Book III, Chapter V) and to the Conclusion (Parsons 1937, 435, 436, 437). On occasion of the great collective ceremonies described by Durkheim the state of 'effervescence' is produced – said Parsons (Parsons 1937, 437). In this context, he mentioned the Durkheimian theorem that the life in primitive Australian societies passed through two phases: the dispersed economical and the condensed religious ones (Parsons 1937, 436). However, the footnote referred not to the statement where Durkheim formulated the theorem of two phases,[12] but to a later, rather vague formulation (Parsons 1937, 436). The original formulation was in Book II, Chapter VII, containing the famous description of the festivity of the serpent Wollunqua (Durkheim 1912, 307), the chapter Parsons tended to avoid.[13]

---

[11] Parsons committed an elementary interpretative error in proving that rites are the primary element. He cited Durkheim in a footnote (Parsons 1937, 437) – truncated. Durkheim wrote: "Nous avons dit qu'*il y a dans la religion quelque chose d'éternel; c'est le culte*, la foi" (Durkheim 1937, 615). Parsons did not cite but the italicised part of the phrase. Why was it so important for Parsons to state that rites had primary importance? Obviously, the belief was related to something extra- (or super-)social: to the non-empirical ultimate reality. Beliefs concerning the ultimate reality were therefore not drawn into the social intercourse (in contradistinction to the common values recreated in the ritual). Durkheim on the contrary, stated that beliefs were central as his ambition was to create a 'sociological theory of knowledge', based on insights from his theory of religion.

[12] The theorem was originally formulated by members of the Durkheim group, not by Durkheim himself. See Mauss-Beuchat 1906.

[13] The same avoidance can be observed in his analysis of the Durkheimian religion more than thirty years later. After repeating the essential statements of *The Structure*, he stressed once again the dual characteristic of the ritual: the high emotional excitement, the effervescence and the meticulous ordering of the ritual. The only reference was to the chapters on mimetic and representative (commemorative) rites, Chapters III and IV of Book III. (Parsons 1978, 222-3). I do not see the opening toward the "active, creative potential in collective cognitive processes", Gerstein observed in the late Parsons (Gerstein 1979, 34).

In fact, he could not avoid it totally. The last part of the chapter on Durkheim's theory of religion dealt with Durkheim's social epistemology (about this some remarks later). Parsons' text concluded by a curious appendix. After criticising Durkheim's epistemological ideas, Parsons returned to the problem of social change[14] – a problem which obviously should have been dealt with in earlier parts of the text. Parsons stated that from Durkheim's thought was absent "any clear-cut theory of social change" (Parsons 1937, 448). Parsons developed in four paragraphs the totally unjustified blame and then, unexpectedly, admitted that there was indeed a rudimentary theory of social change: Durkheim described "the effervescence of great common rituals [where] not only are old values recreated, but new ones are born" – but it was "hardly more than a suggestion" (Parsons 1937, 450). Even here, Parsons could not persuade himself that the idea was central to Durkheim. He wrote that the idea occurred "at the very end of his work" which was not true: in the Conclusion Durkheim repeated statements he made earlier in Book II Chapter VII – in the chapter Parsons tended to avoid. What was in this chapter which repelled Parsons?[15]

Parsons had epistemological reasons to object to the ideas developed by Durkheim in this chapter. His criticism of the ambiguous character of the concept "society" in Durkheim's theory was partly justified. On the one hand, said Parsons, "society has become the thing the idealist philosophers are talking about" (Parsons 1937, 444). On the other hand, " 'society' is still held to be an observable reality, is still the object of positive science" (Parsons 1937, 444). In other words, Parsons objected that Durkheim was obscure because he conceived society, in the same context, as an empirical being and as a supra-empirical entity.

Indeed, Durkheim stated in the introductory chapter and in the conclusion that the universality and solidity of the categories (in a modified Kantian sense of the word) could not be explained if one did not suppose that they were of social (religious) origin (Durkheim 1912, 12-28, 616-638). This was the essence of the Durkheimian "sociological theory of cognition/knowledge". Accordingly, Durkheim asserted that his theory had a certain resemblance to the aprioristic (idealist) theory.[16]

---

[14] As if someone, after the conclusion of the manuscript, would have proposed to give more attention to the Durkheimian ideas on change.

[15] Gerstein believes that Parsons accorded equal significance to the regulating and creative functions of the ritual (Gerstein 1979, 33). As it can be seen in the above analysis, this is not true.

[16] The essential principle of apriorism which Durkheim wanted to preserve was the irreducibility of categories and empirical observation to each other. The difference between them is the same as that between the social and individual (Durkheim 1912, 21-2). To the unfoundedness of Parsons' criticism see Alexander 1983, 217.

Resemblance is not the same as identity. On the one hand, Durkheim stated that there must be a relatively *a priori* categorical frame for the human cognition to be able to order empirical observations. This categorical frame was, according to him, of social origin - which meant that it was not identical with social structure, so to say. On the other hand, he denied, of course, the ideality (in the strict sense of the word) of the categorical frame. If society would be identified by Durkheim "with the world of eternal objects" as Parsons suggested (Parsons 1937, 445), then indeed the theory would be absurd because it would mean that society was empirical and transcendental, in the same respect. Durkheim was all too eager to explain in which sense empirical observations and categories were different. At the same time, he explicitly argued against the conception, too, that categories were "eternal" and unchanging.[17] He argued against the apriorists because they were unable to explain the necessary character of categories[18] – he did not identify himself with them. However, there are many unclear points in Durkheim's epistemological theory and Parsons repulsion to accept it is fully understandable.

It is less understandable why he felt it necessary in this context to criticise Durkheim for the exclusion of the creative aspect of action from his theory.

> For the effect of identifying society with the world of eternal objects is to eliminate the creative element of action altogether. Their defining characteristic is that categories of neither time nor space apply to them. They 'exist' only in the 'mind'. Such entities cannot be the object of an explanatory science at all. For an explanatory science must be concerned with events, and events do not occur in the world of eternal objects (Parsons 1937, 445).

It is not the objection itself which is interesting, but the context in which it occurred. For it was specifically the Chapter VII of Book II (which was cited by Parsons on the previous page) and the Conclusion, both highly relevant from the epistemological point of view, where Durkheim was explicitly concerned with the creativity of (social) action.[19] Parsons' *lapsus* is symptomatic: he avoided to take into account the specific content of two crucial chapters of Durkheim's work.

---

[17] "De plus, les catégories de la pensée humaine ne sont jamais fixées sous une forme définie; elles se font, se défont, se refont sans cesse; elles changent suivant les lieux et les temps" (Durkheim 1912, 21).

[18] "... de ce pouvoir singulier, ils [les aprioristes] ne donnent ni explication ni justification. Car ce n'est pas l'expliquer que se borner à dire qu'il est inhérent à la nature de l'intelligence humain." (Durkheim 1912, 20) For a more detailed analysis of the Durkheimian sociological theory of knowledge see chapters 8., 9., 10. of Némedi 1996.

[19] Later, these aspects of the Durkheimian theory attracted some attention. See in this respect the group of surrealists around Georges Bataille and Roger Caillois (Hollier 1979, Caillois 1950), Habermas' theory of the sacral origins of moral (Habermas 1981, 2, 75-

The centrality of Chapter VII of Book II (and of the Conclusion) results from the theoretical significance of the explanation given there of the origin of conceptual thinking. The explanation was faulty, from a logical point of view because it was circular.[20] However, the impression remains that Durkheim said something important in this chapters. The most important thing, from our present point of view, is that there were, so to say, "political" elements in these parts of the book.[21]

Durkheim stressed the political aspects of effervescence in general. In the part of the text where the general theoretical statements are to be found, he spoke in general terms of the elevating and renovating impact of society – i.e. he did not reduce the discussion to the specific case of Australian totemism.[22] He gave examples from French political history: the night of the 4th August 1789, the period of the crusades, the Revolution (Durkheim 1912, 300-301).

> Il ne peut pas y avoir de société qui ne sente le besoin d'entretenir et de raffermir, à intervalles réguliers, les sentiments collectifs et les idées collectives qui font son unité et sa personnalité. Or, cette réfection morale ne peut être obtenue qu'au moyen de réunions, d'assemblées, de congrégations où les individus, étroitement rapprochés les uns des autres, réaffirment en commun leurs communs sentiments; de là, des cérémonies qui, par leur objet, par les résultats qu'elles produisent, par les procédés qui y sont employés, ne diffèrent pas en nature des cérémonies proprement religieuses (Durkheim 1912, 610).

What Durkheim had in mind, was not only integration and recreation of common sentiments. He spoke of the creation of new political ideas, too. Basic to his conception of "civil religion" was the conviction that modern political society was in a morally deplorable situation. He saw moral and political mediocrity, "moral frost" (*froid moral*). There was no common faith that could integrate society. That was a theme which reappeared again and again in Durkheim.

---

97) and Joas theory of creativity (Joas 1992, 76-99, 1997, 87-109). Cf. Alexander 1983, 482-3.

[20] For a more detailed analysis see Némedi 1998.

[21] Durkheim did not make a categorical difference between general notions, categories in the Kantian sense, and ideals, general values. Both, categories ordering experience and central to cognition, and ideals leading action were conceived by him as emerging in the same process of creative effervescence. Parsons thinking in the action frame of reference where goals, means and norms regulating the selection of means had to be differentiated, could not accept the Durkheimian indifference to fact/value division.

[22] "Au sein d'une assemblée qu'échauffe une passion commune, nous devenons susceptibles de sentiments et d'actes dont nous sommes incapables quand nous sommes reduits à nos seules forces; et quand l'assemblée est dissoute, quand, nous retrouvant seul avec nous-même, nous retombons à notre niveau ordinaire, nous pouvons mesurer alors toute la hauteur dont nous avions été soulevé au-dessus de nous-même" (Durkheim 1912, 299-300).

> Si nous avons peut-être quelque mal aujourd'hui à nous représenter en quoi pourront consister ces fêtes et ces cérémonies de l'avenir, c'est que nous traversons une phase de transition et de médiocrité morale. Les grandes choses du passé, celles qui enthousiasmaient nos pères, n'excitent plus chez nous la même ardeur ... et cependant, il n'est encore rien fait qui les remplace (Durkheim 1912, 610).

The periodic return of ceremonial occasions, rituals in the Parsonian sense, would not help if there were no common ideals. The social bonds had to be re-created and only critical periods, effervescent rituals (in the Durkheimian sense) could do that. In fact, Durkheim attributed two different functions to rituals: they had to reinforce, renovate existing beliefs, ideals *and* they were the necessary preconditions of the emergence of new beliefs, ideals. Parsons did not retain but the first function.

Durkheim did not exclude the possibility that creative rituals will be possible, in the future.

> Un jour viendra où nos sociétés connaitront à nouveau des heures d'effervescence créatrice au cours desquelles de nouveaux idéaux surgiront, de nouvelles formules se dégageront qui serviront, pendant un temps, de guide à l'humanité ... Il n'y a pas d'évangiles qui soient immortels et il n'y a pas de raison de croire que l'humanité soit désormais incapable d'en concevoir de nouveaux (Durkheim 1912, 611).

Taken together, Durkheim's discussion of "creative effervescence" contained important statements about the modern condition – statements which were consonant with Durkheim's earlier discussions of "problems of the time". Durkheim felt that modernity was in a critical phase. He believed that a general moral and social renovation was necessary to rescue modernity from decline. That was a feeling which was rather general among social scientists, philosophers and intellectuals around the turn of century.[23]

The case study of the Parsonian interpretation of effervescent ritual reveals that Parsons avoided to take notice of elements in the Durkheimian argument which were related to the feeling of "malaise". Parsons' neglect of "criticism of modernity" in the late Durkheim's religious theory, more generally his disinterest in the "political" aspects of this theory sheds light on a curious aspect of Parsons' interpretation of *The Division of Labour*. Parsons saw quite clearly the argumentative significance of the chapter on "contractual solidarity" (Book I, Chapter VII) (Durkheim 1893,

---

[23] Durkheim wrote to his nephew, Marcel Mauss, on the eve of the Dreyfus 'affaire': "Ce qui est grave c'est d'abord qu'une aussi mince affaire – car en elle-même elle n'est rien – ait pu produire un tel trouble. Comme il fallait qu'il y eût sous tout cela une désorganisation morale profonde pour qu'un incident aussi peu important ait pu déterminer de tels bouleversements... Tu vois que je ne suis pas optimiste. Mais ce n'est pas une raison pour se décourager de la lutte. Au contraire, c'est un des bons côtés de la situation, d'avoir réveillé le goût de combativité qui sommeillait depuis si longtemps" (Durkheim 1998, 110).

177 ff.; Parsons 1937, 310 ff.). He stressed the importance of this chapter from the point of view of anti-utilitarianism. According to Parsons, Durkheim proved that the contract presupposed rules which did not enter in the contract, but which were indispensable for the maintenance of contractual relationship. These rules were essentially moral rules (Parsons 1937, 311-2).[24] As far as the invalidation of utilitarian principles were concerned, Parsons could have found other and perhaps more compelling arguments in Book III of *The Division of Labour*. However, he scarcely mentioned (Parsons 1937, 333-334) the fact that Durkheim there developed an extensive criticism of the modern system of the division of labour.[25] Even if one sometimes has the impression that Book III of *The Division of Labour* was an appendix to the theory, it provided the necessary underpinning to the conclusion of the whole book. The conclusion was a characteristic example of the "sociological criticism of modernity". Durkheim began the last paragraph in the following way: "On a dit avec raison que la morale ... traversait une crise redoutable. Ce qui précède peut nous aider à comprendre la nature et les causes de cet état maladif" (Durkheim 1893, 404-5). Then he depicted the modern condition where the traditional moral was destroyed and nothing was there to replace it. He identified deep-seated social causes which led to the deplorable situation. He then concluded by the famous sentence: "En un mot, notre premier devoir actuellement est de nous faire une morale" (Durkheim 1893, 406). To create a moral was for Durkheim equivalent to radical social reform. In this respect, he was certainly opposed to the shallow optimism of the utilitarians. However, his opposition was motivated by the anxiety common to turn of century social theoreticians. Once again, Parsons accepted much of the theoretical content and neglected the "criticism of modernity" inherent in the argument.[26]

---

[24] "There are features of the existing 'individualistic' order which cannot be accounted for in terms of the elements formulated in utilitarian theory. The activities that the utilitarians, above all the economists, have in mind can take place only within a framework of order characterised by a system of regulatory rules" (Parsons 1937, 314).

[25] Durkheim differentiated between anomic (not regulated), forced (exploitative) and "dysfunctional" types of division of labour. (Durkheim 1893, 343-390) Contemporary writers have seen in these chapters the key to an understanding of Durkheim (Mülller 1983, 1994, Schmid 1989).

[26] In his later treatment of the problem, Parsons (1960) further reduced the elements related to the "criticism of modernity" in Durkheim's theory. While Durkheim conceived mechanic and organic solidarity as phases in a general evolutionary scheme, Parsons interpreted mechanic solidarity as related to the 'governmental organisation' of society and organic solidarity as related to the structure of (economic) roles (Parsons 1960, 127-8). Certainly, much was gained in theoretical complexity by this modification, but it erased the traces of the Durkheimian problematic which was related to phenomena appearing with the emergence of the modern division of labour.

The same can be said, as Habermas observed (Habermas 1981, 2, 421-2, 431-2, 447), of Parsons' treatment of Weber. Nowhere in the extremely interesting two-hundred pages on Weber did Parsons mention the famous characterisation of modern capitalism as a "stahlhartes Gehäuse" (Weber 1920, I, 203). Nowhere did he treat Weber's vision of a possible total bureaucratisation of the world (Weber 1922, 128, 825 ff), he did not take up Weber's view of the disenchantment of the world (Weber 1922, 308; Robertson 1991). While Parsons wrote extensively about the Weberian concept of charisma (Parsons 1937, 662 ff.), he avoided to talk of its political aspects. He mentioned the value pluralism of Weber, he even registered the tragic (Nietzschean) aspect of it (Parsons 1937, 644), but the effects of this pluralism/relativism were downplayed in the Weber chapters.[27] The notes on Tönnies' *Gemeinschaft* and *Gesellschaft* (Parsons 1937, 686) witness to the importance of this work for Parsons' theoretical development, but there, too, was no trace of Tönnies' highly ambivalent feelings about modern capitalist development.

Conclusion

Parsons straddled the divide separating early academic sociology from the "mature" discipline, the sociology of the years between 1945 and 1970. Parsons was, in a generational sense, very near to the generation of the "founding fathers". When he published *The Structure*, Durkheim's *Forms* was a not very old publication, and the first editions of Weber's most important works were in the bookshops when he arrived in Heidelberg. By summarising the works of the great men, he accomplished and closed the enterprise of early theoretical sociology. He did that, knowingly or by intuition, in a way that reduced or effaced the elements relating to the feeling of modernity's crisis.

The general impression to be gained from the lecture of *The Structure* is that Parsons, who was extraordinarily sensible to theoretical issues, systematically avoided problems and texts which were related to the problematical nature of modernity. This feature of Parsons has nothing to do with his supposed conservativism. Conservativism has something to learn from the classics: from Durkheim's anti-individualism or from Tönnies' nostalgic description of *Gemeinschaft* – these aspects of the classics were not treated by Parsons. Weber's political ideas contain some suspicious ideas about charismatic leadership – Parsons did not take notice of

---

[27] As Ghosh proved, Parsons' translation of Weber was systematically distorted, eliminating the psychologistic elements in Weber's arguments (Ghosh 1994).

them. Parsons was not a conservative for whom modernity would be suspect – he was (a little bit boring) liberal.

Neither have the omissions to do with Parsons being American. Early American sociology as represented by the Chicago school was as much critical of modern development as the Europeans were. Disorganisation, the central concern of Park, Thomas and several others, was the perspective unifying a broad spectrum of research. Parsons was uninterested in it.

The point is that sociology as Parsons conceived it changed its evaluation of modernity. The turn-of-century generation of sociologists, the real "founding fathers" of the discipline had a double objective: they wished to create a honourable science among other sciences and, at the same time, they had felt a growing concern with aspects of modernisation. Indeed, the three authors, whose Parsonian interpretation I have briefly mentioned, were interested in phenomena resulting from industrialisation and urbanisation in 19th century: the growing rationality of human relations, moral and political diversification of modern societies, consequences of democratic participation and the changing nature of politics, and – in a lesser extent – the social problems of industrialisation. They were critical of these developments. Some of their formulations suggest that they had a feeling of a coming crisis of modernity – which duly came with World War I.[28] The impression that the early sociologists contributed to the elucidation of these problems, explained their, very limited, success.

Sociology, as it emerged after the two great wars, was more sure of itself and of modernity. The predominant interest was not in the coming crisis of modernity, but in modernisation. (The last three decades of the century brought in this respect many changes.) Parsons was the central figure of this change of interest. Willingly or unconsciously, he purged classical sociology of ideas related to the turn-of-century 'malaise'. In this sense his work can be read as "a 'constructive' interpretation of modernity" (Lechner 1991, 177). The peculiar nature of his reading of Durkheim was a symptom of these interpretational tendencies.

While sociologists of the turn-of-century were deeply conscious of the historical situatedness of social problems, Parsons' really lasting contribution was to "dehistoricize the problem of order" (Camic 1989, 84). That was the way "mature" sociology emerged.

---

[28] While agreeing with Turner and Robertson that Parsons was a truly modernist theoretician, I do not think that, in contrast, turn-of-century sociologists were "nostalgic" or "backward-looking" thinkers, as they seem to suggest (Turner-Robertson 1991, 252-3). The difference between Parsons and the theorists whom he analyses is that they were more conscious of problems resulting from modernisation and less optimistic about possibilities of harmonious resolution of the tensions of modern societies than Parsons was.

Bibliography
(in brackets the date of publication of the edition actually used)
Alexander Jeffrey C. (1983): Theoretical Logic in Sociology. Vol. Four: The Modern Reconstruction of Classical Thought: Talcott Parsons, Berkeley – Los Angeles: University of California Press
Besnard,, Philippe (1987): L'anomie, ses usages et ses fonctions dans la discipline sociologique depuis Durkheim. Paris: Presses Universitaires de France.
Caillois, Roger 1950 [1988]: L'homme et le sacré. Partis: Gallimard.
Camic, Charles (1989): Structure after 50 Years: The Anatomy of a Charter. In: American Journal of Sociology, 95, 38-107.
Camic, Charles (1991): Introduction: Talcott Parsons before The Structure of Social Action. In: Talcott Parsons: The Early Essays, Chicago and London: The University of Chicago Press, 1991, ix-lxix.
Durkheim, Émile 1893 [1978]: De la division du travail social. Paris: Presses Universitaires de France.
Durkheim, Émile 1912 [1985]: Les formes élémentaires de la vie religieuse. Le système totémique en Australie. Paris: Presses Universitaires de France.
Durkheim, Émile (1998): Lettres à Marcel Mauss. Paris: Presses Universitaires de France.
Gerstein, Dean R. (1979): Durkheim and The Structure of Social Action. In: Sociological Inquiry, 49 (1) 27-39.
Ghosh, Peter (1994): Some problems with Talcott Parsons' version of 'The Protestant Ethic'. In: Archives européennes de sociologie, XXXV, 104-123.
Habermas, Jürgen (1981): Theorie des kommunikativen Handelns. 2 Bde, Frankfurt a.M.: Suhrkamp.
Heilbron, Johan 1985: Les métamorphoses du durkheimisme 1920-1940. In: Revue française de sociologie, XXVI-2, 203-237.
Hollier, Denis (1979): Le Collège de Sociologie (1937-1939). Paris: Gallimard.
Joas, Hans (1992): Die Kreativität des Handelns. Frankfurt a.M.: Suhrkamp.
Joas, Hans (1997): Die Entstehung der Werte. Frankfurt a.M.: Suhrkamp.
Lechner, Frank J. (1991): Parsons and Modernity: an Interpretation. In: Roland Robertson and Bryan S. Turner (eds): Talcott Parsons. Theorist of Modernity, London: Sage, 166-186.
Mauss, Marcel, Henri Beuchat (1906): Essai sur les variations saisonnières des sociétés eskimo. Etude de morphologie sociale. In: Années sociologique, 9, 39-132, republished: Marcel Mauss: Sociologie et anthropologie (8. edition), Paris: PUF, 1983, 389-477.
Müller, Hans-Peter (1983): Wertkrise und Gesellschaftsreform. Emile Durkheims Schriften zur Politik. Stuttgart: Enke.
Müller, Hans-Peter (1994): Social Differentiation and Organic Solidarity: The Division of Labor Revisited. In: Sociological Forum, 9, 73-86.
Némedi Dénes (1990): Durkheim and modern sociological action theory. In: Social Science Information, 29, 211-248.
Némedi Dénes (1996): Durkheim. Tudás és társadalom. Budapest: Áron.
Némedi Dénes (1998): Change, innovation, creation: Durkheim's ambivalence. In: N.J. Allen – W.S.F. Pickering – W. Watts Miller (eds): On Durkheim's Elementary Forms of Religious Life, London and New York: Routledge, 162-175
Parsons, Talcott 1937 [1949]: The Structure of Social Action. A Study in Social Theory with Special Reference to a Group of Recent European Writers. New York - London: The Free Press - Collier-Macmillan.

Parsons, Talcott (1960): Durkheim's Contribution to the Theory of Integration of Social Systems. In: K.H. Wolff (ed): E. Durkheim (1858-1917), Columbus: Ohio State University Press, 118-153.
Parsons, Talcott (1977a): On Building Social System Theory: A Personal History: In: Talcott Parsons: Social Systems and the Evolution of Action Theory, New York: The Free Press, 1977, 22-76.
Parsons, Talcott (1977b): Review of L.T. Hobhouse, Sociology and Philosophy: A Centenary Collection of Essays and Articles. In: Talcott Parsons: Social Systems and the Evolution of Action Theory, New York: The Free Press, 1977, 77-81.
Parsons, Talcott (1978): Durkheim on Religion Revisited: Another Look at The Elementary Forms of the Religious Life. In: Talcott Parsons: Action Theory and the Human Condition, New York - London: The Free Press, 213-232.
Pickering, W.S.F. (1994): The Enigma of Durkheim's Jewishness. In: W.S.F. Pickering - H. Martin (eds): Debating Durkheim, London - New York: Routledge, 10-39.
Pope, Whitney (1973): Classic on classic: Parsons' interpretation of Durkheim. In: American Sociological Review, 38,399-415.
Pope, Whitney (1975): Parsons on Durkheim revisited. In: American Sociological Review, 40,111-115.
Robertson, Roland (1991): The Central Significance of 'Religion' in Social Theory: Parsons as an Epical Theorist. In: Roland Robertson and Bryan S. Turner (eds): Talcott Parsons. Theorist of Modernity, London: Sage, 137-165.
Schmid, Michael (1989): Arbeitsteilung und Solidarität. Eine Untersuchung zu Emile Durkheims Theorie der sozialen Arbeitsteilung. In: Kölner Zeitschrift für Soziologie und Sozialpsychologie, 41, 619-643.
Sciulli, David, Dean Gerstein (1985): Social Theory and Talcott Parsons in the 1980s. In: Annual Review of Sociology, 11, 369-387.
Turner, Bryan S. and Roland Robertson (1991): How to Read Parsons In: Roland Robertson and Bryan S. Turner (eds): Talcott Parsons. Theorist of Modernity, London: Sage, 252-259.
Weber Max 1920 [1988]: Gesammelte Aufsätze zur Religionssoziologie. Tübingen: J.C.B. Mohr.
Weber, Max 1922 [1972]: Wirtschaft und Gesellschaft. Grundriss der verstehenden Soziologie. Tübingen: J.C.B. Mohr.

Bausteine der Theorie des Handelns

Theorie als "theoretisches System"
Parsons' Beitrag zur soziologischen Theorie[1]
Andreas Balog

In diesem Aufsatz versuche ich die Frage zu beantworten, worin der andauernde Einfluss des Werkes von Parsons besteht. Ich möchte nachweisen, dass die Entstehung von "soziologischer Theorie" als einer eigenen Subdisziplin der Soziologie untrennbar mit Parsons und vor allem mit *The Structure of Social Action* verbunden ist. Bis heute prägt das in diesem Buch artikulierte Verständnis von Theorie die Diskussionen, wobei gerade Autoren, die Parsons gegenüber eine kritische Haltung einnehmen, seinem Theorieverständnis häufig zutiefst verpflichtet sind. Daher werde ich nach einer kurzen Schilderung der Rolle von "Theorie" bei Weber und Durkheim das Vorgehen von Parsons bei der Konstruktion der "voluntaristischen Handlungstheorie" nachvollziehen und ihre Konsequenzen für die Analyse sozialer Sachverhalte aufzeigen.

Die Bezugnahme auf Durkheim und Weber ist umso wichtiger als das Spezifische des Parsonsschen Theorie-Modells auf einer Synthese ihrer programmatischen Arbeiten beruht. Ich werde dabei die These vertreten, dass die Theorie von Parsons auf einem grundlegenden Kategorienfehler beruht, womit weitreichende Konsequenzen verbunden sind. Mein Interesse richtet sich dabei ausschließlich auf die ersten Phasen der Arbeit von Parsons, da die kategorialen Brüche hier offen zutage treten. In den späteren Arbeiten werden ähnlich grundlegende Fragen nicht mehr diskutiert, sondern ihre Lösungen vorausgesetzt. Im dritten Abschnitt gehe ich auf die weitere Entwicklung nach Parsons ein und versuche die Fortwirkung des Theorie-Verständnisses von Parsons an repräsentativen Beispielen aufzuzeigen. Dabei wird deutlich, welche problematischen Auswirkungen die Übernahme seines Theorie-Modells hatte und wie sich neuere Theoretiker davon zu befreien versuchen. Im abschließenden Teil ziehe ich daraus allgemeine Konsequenzen für den Aufbau und die Beurteilung von soziologischen Theorien.

Weber und Durkheim als "Theoretiker"

Bei Weber wie bei Durkheim sind die im engeren Sinn "theoretischen" Arbeiten untrennbar mit ihren inhaltlichen Interessen verbunden. Weber wie Durkheim ging

---

[1] Teile dieses Aufsatzes sind Auszüge aus einer größeren, noch nicht erschienenen Arbeit über Entwicklung der soziologischen Theorie.

es dabei um die Lösung methodischer Fragen nach der Konzeptualisierung und Erklärung von Phänomenen. Die Schwerpunkte sind auf Grund ihrer theoretischen Ausgangspunkte völlig unterschiedlich gesetzt und sie führen zu differierenden Antworten, worin der Gegenstandsbereich der Soziologie besteht, wie er identifiziert und erklärt werden kann.

Webers methodische Arbeiten sind durch seine neukantianische Sichtweise bestimmt. Das Material der Wahrnehmung, die Art und Weise, wie uns die Beschaffenheit der "Welt" präsentiert wird, sind aus dieser Sicht strukturlos und unerkennbar. Zwischen der "Welt" und den Begriffen, die auf ihre Erfassung gerichtet sind, besteht ein "hiatus irrationalis", eine unüberwindliche Schranke, die Begriffe erfassen stets nur spezifische Aspekte eines unausschöpflichen Kosmos. Das Primärmaterial, auf dessen Erfassung und Erklärung Alltagsdenken wie Wissenschaft gerichtet sind, ist daher im Prinzip unendlich auslegungsfähig. Die erste Aufgabe jeder Wissenschaft besteht zunächst darin, die Prinzipien ihrer Begriffsbildung klarzulegen, um die Phänomene in einer nachvollziehbaren Weise zu definieren, auf deren Erklärung sie gerichtet ist.[2] Die Objektivität und Nachvollziehbarkeit ihres Vorgehens und der Ergebnisse sind erst auf dieser Grundlage möglich. Nach Weber bieten "Werte" die Voraussetzung dafür, dass identifizierbare Phänomene aus der "Sinnlosigkeit der endlosen Flucht unendlicher Mannigfaltigkeit" herausgehoben werden können.[3] Der Bezug auf Werte ermögliche erst das Fällen von Urteilen über eindeutig umrissene Phänomene, also auch über deren faktische Existenz. Der Umstand, dass Weber zwar einige Beispiele für Werte genannt hat (wie wissenschaftliche Wahrheit, die sich zeitlich ändernden forschungsleitenden Interessen), sie aber letztlich nur funktional in ihrer Rolle für die Erzeugung von bestimmten Inhalten definiert sind, hat Anlass für eine Reihe von, wie es mir scheint, berechtigten Kritiken geboten, die darauf hinzielen, dass es keine Kriterien gibt, nach denen Werte bestimmt werden können, was als "Wert" bezeichnet wird daher beliebig ist (Oakes 1980). Ich möchte mich mit diesem Problem nicht auf der allgemeinen Ebene befassen, sondern zeigen, wie Weber die theoretische Wertbeziehung für die soziologische Begriffsbildung konkretisiert hat.

Angesichts der "ungeschiedenen Mannigfaltigkeit" der Daten müssen Kriterien gefunden werden, um die Objekte abzugrenzen und sinnvolle Fragestellungen zu

---

[2] Als Ziel der Wissenschaft ist dabei die Kausalerklärung vorausgesetzt. (Weber 1968, S. 83, S. 270, S. 437).

[3] "Denn im Gegensatz zum bloßen 'Gefühlsinhalt' bezeichnen wir als 'Wert' ja eben gerade das und nur das, was fähig ist Inhalt einer Stellungnahme eines artikuliert – bewußten, positiven und negativen Urteils zu werden, etwas, was 'Geltung heischend' an uns herantritt, und dessen 'Geltung als 'Wert' 'für' uns demgemäß nur 'von' uns anerkannt, abgelehnt oder in den mannigfachsten Verschlingungen 'wertend beurteilt' wird" (Weber 1968, S. 123).

entwickeln. Was ist nun das eigentlich sozialwissenschaftliche Interesse an Phänomenen, wie etwa der Schwarzen Pest? Weber bestimmt als die für die Sozialwissenschaft relevante Wertbeziehung, die ihre Besonderheit gegenüber den Naturwissenschaften ausmacht, als "Kulturbedeutung". Nur jene Aspekte der Welt sind von Interesse, denen "wir eine allgemeine Kulturbedeutung beimessen (...) sie allein sind Gegenstand der kausalen Erklärung" (1968, S. 178). Die Frage, was das Spezifische der Sozialwissenschaften ausmacht, wird auf die "Kultur" verschoben, diese ihrerseits als "ein vom Standpunkt des Menschen aus mit Sinn und Bedeutung bedachter, endlicher Ausschnitt aus der sinnlosen Unendlichkeit des Weltgeschehens" (180) bestimmt. "Kulturbedeutung" heißt, dass Ereignisse und Phänomene für bestimmte Menschen Bedeutung besitzen und sie daher ihnen gegenüber Stellung beziehen.

Die Sozialwissenschaft ist demnach eine Wissenschaft, die auf einer Begriffsbildung zweiter Ordnung beruht. Um "kulturbedeutende" Phänomene zu identifizieren, müssen zunächst die Sichtweisen der Gesellschaftsangehörigen verstanden und rekonstruiert werden. Die "unendliche Mannigfaltigkeit" wird nicht erst von der Sozialwissenschaft, sondern von den Gesellschaftsangehörigen selber in einer für sie sinnvollen Weise strukturiert.[4] "Die Sozialwissenschaft, die wir treiben wollen, ist eine Wirklichkeitswissenschaft. Wir wollen die uns umgebende Wirklichkeit des Lebens, in welches wir hineingestellt sind, in ihrer Eigenart verstehen – den Zusammenhang und die Kulturbedeutung ihrer einzelnen Erscheinungen in ihrer heutigen Gestaltung einerseits, die Gründe ihres geschichtlichen So-und nicht anders-Gewordenseins andererseits" (Weber 1968, S. 170).

Im Ausdruck "Wirklichkeitswissenschaft" sind die beiden Elemente enthalten, die für Webers Vorstellung von Sozialwissenschaft charakteristisch sind. *Erstens* besteht das Material, auf dessen Erkenntnis sie gerichtet ist, bereits in Deutungen und Interpretationen, die sie voraussetzen muss, da gerade diese den Gegenstand ihres Interesses bilden und *zweitens* ist sie auf die Erfassung dieses Materials auf Grund eigener Selektionsprinzipien ("Wertideen") gerichtet. Diese Prinzipien weisen ihrerseits zwei Aspekte auf: Nach der inhaltlichen Seite sind sie durch die vorherrschenden Ideen der Zeit bestimmt, sie sind veränderbar je nach der historischer Situation.[5] Wenn das "Licht der großen Kulturprobleme" weitergezogen ist, "rüstet sich auch die Wissenschaft, ihren Standort und ihren Begriffsapparat zu wechseln und aus der Höhe des Gedankens auf den Strom des Geschehens zu blicken" (1968,

---

[4] Genauer gesagt: Das relevante Phänomen ist durch die Sichtweisen und Deutungen der Gesellschaftsangehörigen konstituiert.
[5] Die idealtypische Begriffsbildung schafft eine Flexibilität bei der Konstitution wissenschaftlich relevanter Phänomene, da sie ermöglicht Einzelphänomene nach unterschiedlichen Gesichtspunkten zusammenzufassen.

S. 214). Der zweite Aspekt bezieht sich auf grundsätzliche Prinzipien der Wissenschaft, wie auf ihre Verpflichtung zur intellektuellen Rechtschaffenheit, sowie auf ihre für Weber selbstverständlichen Orientierung am Kausalitätsprinzip.

Wie lässt sich nun der primäre "subjektive" Sinn und die Strukturierung der Welt für die Gesellschaftsangehörigen selber in einer intersubjektiv nachvollziehbaren Weise erfassen? Die Intuition, die von Weber im einzelnen ausgearbeitet und begründet wird, besteht darin, dass Stellungnahme zur und die Deutung der Welt, also jene kognitiven Voraussetzungen, die eine nachvollziehbare Abgrenzung identifizierbarer Objekte gewährleisten, in Handlungen realisiert werden, d. h. konstitutive Aspekte von Handlungen bilden. Diese Aspekte von Handlungen verweisen ihrerseits auf intersubjektive Regelungen. Die Handlungen sind keine "privaten", prä- oder asozialen Phänomene, beruhen nicht auf "bloß" subjektiven Willensakten, sondern in ihnen werden Regelungen und Strukturen erkennbar, die ihnen überhaupt einen Sinn verleihen und vor deren Hintergrund sie hervorgebracht werden können. Sinngebung und Deutung der Welt werden in den Zweck-Mittel-Relationen, den nach Weber konstitutiven Elementen der Handlung, vorausgesetzt. Der Handlungszweck, definiert als "die Vorstellung eines Erfolges, welche Ursache einer Handlung wird" (Weber 1968, S. 183), bildet für die handelnde Person jene übergreifende Perspektive, die es ihm erlaubt die Unendlichkeit des Mannigfaltigen zu ordnen. Für die Sozialwissenschaft übernimmt daher auf der primären Ebene sozialer Abläufe der Handlungszweck die konstitutive Rolle der "Wertbeziehung". Bei der Strukturierung des für den Akteur relevanten Ausschnitts der sozialen Welt durch den Handlungszweck werden die intersubjektiven, der Handlung vorgegebenen Regelungen sichtbar, auf die sich die Person beziehen muss, falls sie erfolgreich handeln möchte. Die Durchsetzung von Zwecken ist nur unter bestimmten Bedingungen und der Anwendung bestimmter Mittel möglich. Die Anwendung der Kategorien "Zweck" und "Mittel" setzt daher den rationalen, also nachvollziehbaren Umgang mit der empirischen Wirklichkeit voraus (1968, S. 131, S. 545).[6] Die Kohärenz zwischen Zwecken und Mitteln bildet die Voraussetzung einer verstehbaren Handlung.

Die Grundbegriffe der Soziologie beziehen sich auf Handlungen, die auf Grund ihrer Zwecke bzw. Aspekte der Zweckverfolgung unterschieden werden. Das "Gemeinschaftshandeln", der einfachste Begriff der Explikation der Grundbegriffe, wie sie im "Kategorienaufsatz" niedergelegt ist, ist "subjektiv sinnhaft auf das Verhalten anderer Menschen bezogen" (Weber 1968, S. 441), etwa im Fall einer Schlägerei oder einer Verhandlung. Die beiden anderen Grundbegriffe bezeichnen jeweils komplexere Ebenen, nämlich Gemeinschaftshandlungen, die sich auf Regelungen

---

[6] Webers Definition der Handlung auf Grund der Zweck-Mittel Beziehung ist nicht unproblematisch. Vgl. dazu Balog (1989).

beziehen ("Einverständnis") bzw. durch diese erst ermöglicht werden und Handlungen, die auf Grund der Aktivitäten einer besonderen Kategorie von Akteuren (dem "Erzwingungsstab") einer Ganzheit (dem "Verband") zugerechnet werden. Die durch "Einverständnis" und "Verband" bezeichneten Sachverhalte verweisen in der Regel auf Bedingungen, unter denen "Gemeinschaftshandeln" (das in den "Grundbegriffen" "soziales Handeln" heißt) ausgeführt wird. Dies entspricht auch Webers Vorstellung, wonach diese komplexeren Formen Abwandlungen von "Gemeinschaftshandeln" sind.

Während für Weber die eigene Identität der Soziologie als Disziplin durch eine spezifische Form der Konzeptualisierung von Phänomenen als aufeinander bezogene Handlungen begründet ist, die nachvollziehbare Erklärungen ermöglicht, verfolgt Durkheim das gleiche Ziel auf einem völlig unterschiedlichen Weg. Es geht ihm um den Beweis, dass der Objektbereich der Soziologie eine eigene Ebene der Realität bildet, die eine autonome kausal wirksame Kraft entwickelt. Durch diese Zielrichtung bestimmt, gewinnt die Theorie einen völlig anderen Charakter. Ihm geht es *erstens* um den Nachweis der Nicht-Reduzierbarkeit des Sozialen auf Verhaltensweisen einzelner Menschen. *Zweitens* identifiziert er "Gesellschaft" als eine kausal wirkende Kraft, die den Zusammenhalt von Handlungen gewährleistet, also von vornherein als Lösung des Koordinationsproblems. Damit ist auch die Vorstellung einer funktionalen Einheit der Gesellschaft verbunden. Eine weitere Konsequenz besteht darin, dass die relevanten sozialen Kausalfaktoren, die für Durkheim die Grundlage soziologischer Erklärungen bilden, von vornherein durch die konstitutiven Merkmale von Gesellschaft bestimmt sind (wie vor allem ihre "moralische Dichte").

Auf der Ebene des Gegenstandsbereichs geht es Durkheim zunächst um die Irreduzibilität sozialer und kollektiver Phänomene, um den Nachweis ihrer Autonomie. Die Argumentation hat dabei einen stark analogen Charakter: So wie Bewusstseinsinhalte nicht aus dem physiologischen Substrat ableitbar sind, gilt dies auch für das Verhältnis kollektiver Phänomene zu den Verhaltensweisen und Einstellungen der Individuen, in denen sie realisiert werden. Solche Phänomene weisen eine Eigendynamik und Eigengesetzlichkeit auf (1967, S. 45, S. 56, S. 71), sie bilden ein "kontinuierliches Ganzes" (1967, S. 63), das eigenen kausalen Gesetzen unterliegt, eigene kausale Wirksamkeit entfaltet und nicht aus den Bewegungen ihrer einzelnen Teile erklärt werden kann, aus denen sie zusammengesetzt ist.

Die Metapher, mit denen Durkheim die Autonomie des Sozialen illustriert, entstammen der Naturwissenschaft. "Chemische Synthese" (1967, S. 73), und "Synthese sui generis" (1981, S. 567), charakterisieren die Emergenz neuartiger Phänomene aus einzelnen Bestandteilen. So spricht er auch vom "Eigenleben" der Kollektivströmungen, die als "Kräfte genauso wirklich (sind) wie kosmische Kräfte, wenn auch von anderer Art" (1973a, S. 359). Die Assoziation einzelner Teile, seien es physiologische Prozesse, seien es Individuen führt zum Entstehen von "besonderen

Kräften", die ihrerseits die konstitutiven Bestandteile verändern: "aufgrund dieser Vereinigung und der daraus entstehenden wechselseitigen Veränderung *werden sie etwas anderes*"(1967, S. 73). Es handelt sich um eine Transformation, deren einzelne Schritte von Durkheim nicht rekonstruiert, sondern in ihrer Gesamtheit vorausgesetzt werden.[7] Die Gesellschaft oder die sozialen Prozesse, die er analysiert, sind bereits fertig konstituiert und stehen – in unterschiedlichen Graden der Verfestigung – den Gesellschaftsangehörigen gegenüber.

Wie äußert sich nun diese Kraft, wie lässt sich ihre Realität nachweisen? Im Grunde läuft Durkheims Beweis auf die Gleichsetzung sozialer Kräfte mit vorgegebenen Handlungsmustern hinaus, die den Charakter von Verpflichtungen und Obligationen annehmen können, aber nicht müssen (Durkheim 1967, S. 72; 1973, S. 107). Damit sind nicht nur explizite Normen und Pflichten gemeint, sondern all jene, den einzelnen vorgegebene "Arten des Handelns, Denkens und Fühlens, die außerhalb der einzelnen stehen und mit zwingender Gewalt ausgestattet sind, kraft derer sie sich ihnen aufdrängen" (ebd.), sie bilden nach einem eingängigen Bild "Gussformen" für Handlungen (Durkheim 1970, S. 126). Also die Tatsache, dass "jedes soziale Phänomen eine Kraft darstellt, welche die unsere beherrscht und eine eigene Natur hat" (Durkheim 1970, S. 177) ist das konstitutive Merkmal des Sozialen, nicht der Umstand, dass sich diese Kraft als normative Vorschrift äußern muss. Am ausführlichsten hat sich Durkheim mit solchen Strömungen bei der Analyse der Selbstmordraten befasst. Es gibt keine Norm, die vorschreiben würde, wie viele Leute sich in einer Population oder der Subgruppe einer Population umbringen sollten und keine Organisation, die die Einhaltung dieses Gebots überwachen würde, gleichwohl sind diese Raten nicht zufälligen Schwankungen unterworfen und ihre Regelhaftigkeiten können in statistische Maßzahlen sichtbar gemacht werden.

Durkheim begründet diese Auffassung vom Gegenstandsbereich durch eine Reihe von Argumenten, die auf die kausale Bedeutung von Gesellschaft für die Konstitution von Personen, für soziale Interaktionen generell verweisen. In ihrer Gesamtheit zielt Durkheim auf den Nachweis, dass ohne die Voraussetzung einer eigenen Ebene von Gesellschaft weder das Zusammenleben der Menschen, noch geregelte Interaktionen und sinnvolle Handlungen oder auch nur Personen mit einer Identität möglich wären. Die mehr oder minder erfolgreiche Koordination des Zusammenlebens ist der letzte Beweis für die Ebene der Gesellschaft und der Wirksamkeit ihrer kausalen Kräfte.

---

[7] "Eine lebende Zelle besteht aus nichtlebendigen Mineralmolekülen. Durch ihre Verbindung weisen sie Eigenschaften auf, die für das Leben charakteristisch sind: die Fähigkeit sich zu ernähren und fortzupflanzen, die das Mineral nicht einmal im Zustand der wahrnehmbaren Entstehung besitzt. Es handelt sich also um eine feste Tatsache, daß ein Ganzes etwas anderes ist, als die Summe seiner Teile" (Durkheim 1973, S. 113).

Am genauesten hat Durkheim die kausale Kraft der Gesellschaft in ihrem Verhältnis zu den Individuen begründet, wohl auch in der Absicht, der Soziologie einen eigenen Objektbereich gegenüber der Psychologie zu sichern. Die Gesellschaft "nistet sich uns ein" (Durkheim 1981, S. 357), indem sie den Eindrücken und Bildern, "die von allen Punkten des Organismus stammen" eine weitere Ebene von "Ideen und Gefühlen, die von der Gesellschaft stammen und diese ausdrücken" hinzufügt (ebd., S. 368). Vermittels dieser Ideen und Gefühle vermögen wir uns auch von Determinationen der individuellen, letztlich der physiologischen Ebene frei zu machen. Der "Anschluss" an die Gesellschaft ermöglicht es demnach erst, dass das Individuum "wahrhaft es selbst" sein kann (Durkheim 1973, S. 118) und nur als einem sozialen Objekt kommen den Menschen die Gefühle der Würde, Individualität und Freiheit zu (Durkheim 1981, S. 357), die auf Grund der physiologischen Faktoren, die sein Handeln beeinflussen, nicht erklärbar wären.

Webers Theorie zielt auf die Erarbeitung von Kriterien für soziale Sachverhalte, die in Handlungen erkannt werden. Durkheim identifiziert dagegen als Gegenstand der Soziologie *ein* Phänomen, das außerhalb der Akteure existiert und kausal auf ihre Äußerungen wirkt. Das konforme, aufeinander abgestimmte, an gemeinsamen Symbolen und Ritualen orientierte Verhalten von Personen und Gruppen, die einzelnen "sozialen Tatsachen" bilden den Ausdruck der Existenz von "Gesellschaft". Die Kraft der Gesellschaft, die ihr Bestehen gewährleistet, ist in ihrer Bindungskraft gegenüber den einzelnen Bestandteilen erkennbar und Durkheims Arbeiten bilden Versuche, diese in ihren unterschiedlichen Aspekten (als Wissen, Religion und Ritual, Sozialisation, Moral, Formen der Arbeitsteilung) zu erfassen.[8]

"Analytischer Realismus" und "Voluntaristische Handlungstheorie"

Parsons' Bemühen ist in den frühen Arbeiten darauf gerichtet die Legitimität einer eigenen Wissenschaft "Soziologie" nachzuweisen (Camic 1989). Dies geschieht – wie ich zeigen werde – indem er die Möglichkeit von "objektiver" also nachvollziehbarer Begriffsbildung in der Soziologie beweist und dieser Wissenschaft zugleich einen eigenen Forschungsbereich, nämlich jenen der sozialen Integration zuweist. Beide Zielsetzungen werden von ihm in einen engen Zusammenhang gebracht. Schon von der Programmatik her wird auf Weber wie Durkheim Bezug genommen.

---

[8] Aus den beiden Konzeptionen folgen auch völlig heterogene Vorstellungen über die der Soziologie angemessene Form der Erklärung.

Nach Parsons bildet das Bestehen einer Sichtweise, die einen spezifischen Ausschnitt von Phänomenen sichtbar macht und die in eigenen Grundbegriffen formuliert, die Voraussetzung dafür, die Tatsachen der Welt aus einer eigenständigen Perspektive zu erfassen und zu erklären. Der Ausgangspunkt ist durch Webers Neukantianismus bestimmt, die Ausformulierung der Perspektive ist Webers Vorstellungen vollkommen fremd. Jede Wissenschaft beruht auf einer selektiven Perspektive, die darüber bestimmt, wie die Tatsachen aus der Fülle des prinzipiell unendlichen Materials zusammengefasst werden und auf Grund derer sich ihre Bedeutung erst erschließt. Das, was bei Weber als "Wertbeziehung" beschrieben wurde, heißt bei Parsons "theoretisches System". Der Unterschied zu Weber besteht vor allem darin, dass für Parsons die für die wissenschaftliche Praxis konstitutive Perspektive nicht nur deskriptive Begriffe umfasst, sondern ihr eine systematische und kohärente Theorie zu Grunde liegen soll (Parsons 1968, S. 10). Unter systematischer Theorie versteht nun Parsons eine Reihe von "logischen", also gesetzesförmigen Verknüpfungen zwischen Variablen nach dem Muster der klassischen Mechanik. Die Variablen beziehen sich auf "analytische Elemente", als jenen elementaren Komponenten, die im Rahmen des theoretischen Systems unterschiedliche Werte annehmen können und deren Zusammenwirken das Bestehen von Zuständen erklärt, die im Rahmen der Wissenschaft von Interesse sind.[9]

Die Theorie von Parsons stellt in allen Phasen den Versuch dar, das verbindliche theoretische System der Sozialwissenschaften im Allgemeinen und der Soziologie im Besonderen zu entwickeln, also die relevanten Grundbegriffe zu bestimmen und in ihrem gegenseitigen Zusammenhang zu beschreiben. Dieses Verständnis von Theorie, das er in Auseinandersetzung mit dem "Empirismus" dargelegt hat, ist für ihn bis zuletzt bestimmend gewesen.[10] Empirismus heißt für Parsons die Gleichsetzung eines theoretischen Rahmens mit einem Wirklichkeitsbereich (1968, S. 69 ff., S. 730 ff, S. 757) und ist mit der Annahme verbunden, dass es für spezifische Objekte daher nur eine angemessene Form der Beschreibung geben könne. Die Idee, wonach eine jede Wissenschaft ein theoretisches System zugrunde liegt, besagt, dass sich das Interesse von Disziplinen auf spezifische Aspekte realer Phänomene richtet, die als solche auch im Kontext anderer Wissenschaften analysiert werden können. So ist ein physikalisches Objekt im sozialwissenschaftlichen Bezugsrahmen ein anderes Phänomen als im naturwissenschaftlichen: Im ersten Fall ein Objekt, das im Rahmen von Handlungen erkannt wird, im zweiten Fall eine durch "natürliche Kräfte" bestimmte Anhäufung von Elementen der Materie.

---

9   Im theoretischen System der Physik ist Geschwindigkeit ein solches analytisches Element (Parsons 1968, S. 29).
10 Vgl. dazu die Replik Parsons' gegenüber der Kritik von Burger (Parsons 1977).

Die Konsequenz der Ablehnung des "Empirismus" besteht darin, dass der Bezugsrahmen nicht einfach durch die Übereinstimmung mit vorgegebenen Tatsachen gerechtfertigt werden kann. Für die von ihm postulierte Verbindung zwischen Theorie und den sozialen Sachverhalten prägt Parsons den Begriff "analytic realism" (1968, S. 730). Die Grundbegriffe der Wissenschaft entsprechen bestimmten Aspekten der beobachteten empirischen Phänomene, ohne diese vollständig, d. h. aus allen möglichen Gesichtspunkten erschöpfend zu beschreiben. Die theoretisch entwickelten Begriffe beziehen sich auf *eine* faktische Organisation der Welt und die Tatsache, dass die Begriffe der Theorie auf Phänomene angewendet werden können, stellt nach Parsons den relevanten Beweis für das Bestehen *dieser* Ordnung der Phänomene dar und schließt damit ihre bloß zufällig-chaotische Verknüpfung miteinander aus. Die faktischen Ordnungen, die Korrelate anderer theoretischer Systeme sind, rücken bei der Anwendung eines Bezugsrahmens in den Hintergrund und werden als Konstante behandelt, die nicht aktuell analysiert, aber vorausgesetzt werden müssen (1968, S. 736). Dies trifft etwa auf Individuen zu, die für die Soziologie stets als handelnde Personen, nicht aber als bloße Organismen wahrnehmbar sind. Die Tatsache, dass sie immer zugleich auch Organismen sind, bildet einen Hintergrund, der nicht weiter problematisiert, sondern vorausgesetzt wird.

Bevor ich auf das theoretische System, wie es in *The Structure of Social Action* entwickelt wurde, eingehe, möchte ich auf das Problem hinweisen, das bei diesem Verständnis der Theorie deutlich wird und das den im folgenden diskutierten Kategorienfehler verständlich macht. Es wird eine konstitutive Verbindung zwischen zwei Ebenen oder Fragestellungen hergestellt. *Erstens* ist es wohl unbestreitbar, dass man über Begriffe verfügen muss, sofern man einzelne Phänomene oder einen umfassenden Objektbereich beschreiben möchte. Ein "theoretisches System" in diesem Sinn muss auf einen "deskriptiven Bezugsrahmen" (Parsons 1968, S. 28) verweisen, der die Begriffe enthält, mit derer Hilfe der Objektbereich erfasst wird. *Zweitens* besagt die Voraussetzung, wonach konstitutive Begriffe notwendig sind, um Phänomene erfassen zu können, noch nichts darüber, dass diese Begriffe zugleich erklärende *Variablen* sind, die auf kausale Faktoren verweisen und miteinander auf Grund von "logischen" Beziehungen verbunden sind. Welche Rechtfertigung besteht dafür, Beziehungen zwischen Begriffen zugleich als Kausalbeziehungen zu interpretieren? Dieser Frage liegt das Problem zugrunde, dass deskriptive Begriffe in anderer Weise bestimmt werden müssen als Beziehungen zwischen Variablen. Die Verwendung deskriptiver Begriffe ist dadurch zu rechtfertigen, dass sie imstande sind spezifische Phänomene in konsistenter und nachvollziehbarer Weise zu identifizieren, Beziehungen zwischen Variablen verweisen auf empirisch zu erfassende Kausalbeziehungen, die der Bestätigung durch empirische Analysen bedürfen.

Der Ausgangspunkt für die Entwicklung des sozialwissenschaftlichen Bezugsrahmens ist für Parsons das Phänomen der Handlung, das, wie er zeigen kann, bei allen sozialwissenschaftlichen Bemühungen immer schon im Mittelpunkt gestanden ist (Parsons 1968, S. 39). Erst durch die Betrachtung von Phänomenen als Handlungen wird die Autonomie einer soziologischen Analyse sozialer Phänomene deutlich. Soziale Phänomene bzw. die sozialen Aspekte natürlicher Phänomene können erst Objekte der Sozialwissenschaft werden, insofern sie im Bezugsrahmen der Handlung beschrieben werden, also Ereignisse sind, auf die die Kriterien zutreffen, mit denen Handlungen beschrieben werden. Die "Voluntaristische Handlungstheorie" ist nach Parsons nicht ein beliebiger Bezugsrahmen zur Analyse sozialer Phänomene, sondern der auf Grund des verfügbaren Wissens einzig angemessene (1968, S. 762), da sie imstande ist, soziale Phänomene sichtbar zu machen, die von den kritisierten "positivistischen" bzw. "utilitaristischen" Ansätzen gar nicht gesehen werden konnten, sie vermag gleichzeitig die logischen Widersprüche aufzulösen, in die sich diese verstricken.[11]

Der elementare Handlungsbezugsrahmen, der "unit act" besteht bekanntlich aus vier analytischen Elementen, nämlich der handelnden Person (1), die einen Zweck verfolgt (2) im Kontext einer Situation, die unveränderliche, der Handlung vorgegebene Bedingungen enthält wie auch Mittel zur Realisierung der Handlung (3) und schließlich Beziehungen zwischen diesen Elementen, die bestimmte Zuordnungen von Mitteln zu Zielen erlaubt, eine "normative" Orientierung (4) (1968, S. 44).

Diese inhaltliche Formulierung des Bezugsrahmens ist eng mit Parsons' Kritik am Utilitarismus verbunden, die an der Unvereinbarkeit zweier Hintergrundsannahmen hinsichtlich des Unit Act anknüpft. Diese beziehen sich *erstens* auf die "subjektive Perspektive", die für die Handlung konstitutiv ist: Das was jeweils Zwecke, Mittel, Bedingungen oder Normen sind, ist aus der Sicht der handelnden Person definiert. *Zweitens* kennt der Utilitarismus nur ein Wissen analog dem wissenschaftlichen Wissen, das sich in einer deskripten Weise auf die Tatsachen der Welt bezieht. Dies ist für das Verständnis der Handlung jedoch unzureichend. Wird das Handlungswissen ausschließlich nach diesem Muster vorgestellt, so – darin besteht Parsons' Kritik – erübrigt sich die subjektive Perspektive der handelnden Person für das Verstehen der Handlung. Dann sind Handlungen nichts anderes als automatisch ablaufende Anpassungsprozesse und die Person ist letztlich nur eine, wenn auch rationale, Registriermaschine, die entsprechend den Kriterien der Wissenschaft und der technischen Effizienz sich für die anstehenden Handlungen in einer gleichsam unpersönlichen Weise entscheidet und sie dann vollzieht. Die Handlungsziele verlieren ihre Selbständigkeit, da sie eine Funktion des objektiv – unpersönlichen Wissens werden. Entsprechend diesem Verständnis gibt es keine alternativen Orientierungsmöglichkeiten, außer Irrtum und Unwissen (Parsons 1968, S. 66/7). Ein Spielraum für die Freiheit des Handelns ist in beiden Fällen nicht vorhanden, da es letztlich nur

---

[11] Die Frage nach der historischen Richtigkeit von Parsons' Interpretationen des Utilitarismus ist hier irrelevant.

um die Realisierung der vorgegebenen Verbindung von Zielen und Mitteln an Bedingungen besteht, die auf Grund eines unpersönlichen Wissens ausgewählt werden. "Action becomes a process of rational adaptation to these conditions. The active role of the actor is reduced to one oft the understanding of his situation and forecasting of its future course of development" (1968, S. 64).

Diese restriktive Sicht der Handlung und ihrer Determiniertheit auf Grund eines rein deskriptiven und effizienzorientierten Wissens verletzt nicht nur die Hintergrundannahmen der utilitaristischen Theorie, sie wird auch der Rolle der normativen Orientierung des Akteurs nicht gerecht. Diese ermöglicht Handlungsorientierungen, die über die Anpassung an externe Bedingungen hinausgehen. Die normative Orientierung von Akteuren definiert Parsons als Konformität gegenüber "patterns which are by the actors and other members of the collectivity, deemed desirable". Dies gewährleiste erst die Freiheit menschlichen Handelns gegenüber bloß stimulusbedingten Reaktionen (1968, S. 76).

In dieser Definition von normativer Orientierung wird eine Verbindung zweier Elemente hergestellt, die den Kern von Parsons' Theorie ausmacht. *Erstens* kann man von eigenständigen Zielen einer Handlung und letztlich von einer Handlung überhaupt erst dann sprechen, wenn die Person sich für sie entscheiden kann. Parsons weist nach, dass im Utilitarismus eine Kategorie für die aktive Entscheidung der Person für eine Handlung fehlt, die unabhängig von rationaler Einsicht in ihren Nutzen wäre. Die normative Orientierung trägt der Tatsache Rechnung, dass sich Ziele nicht "von selbst" aufdrängen und sich ohne Zutun der Person durchsetzen, sondern Handlungsoptionen immer aktiv von der Person bewertet und realisiert werden. Es gibt ein performativ-voluntaristisches Handlungswissen, das den Spielraum für die handelnde Person erst gewährleistet und das die Hervorbringung von Handlungen erst möglich macht.[12] Die Stimmigkeit des Arguments, demnach die utilitaristische Theorie falsch ist, beruht darauf, dass sie Handlungen nicht in angemessener Weise erfasst, da sie ihre konstitutiven Elemente nicht zureichend berücksichtigt. Denn auf der begrifflichen Ebene liegt ein eindeutiges Kriterium vor, das aus der notwendigen Übereinstimmung mit dem intuitiven Alltagswissen resultiert.

Zweitens identifiziert Parsons das performativ-voluntaristische Handlungswissen mit der Orientierung der Person an Handlungsmustern, die zugleich immer schon von den anderen Gesellschaftsangehörigen als erwünscht angesehen und erstrebt werden. Dies ist aber eine Aussage über mögliche empirische Vorkommnisse, nicht über begriffliche Zusammenhänge. Der intuitive Handlungsbegriff ist mit der möglichen empirischen Tatsache vereinbar, dass eine Person idiosynkratische oder abweichende Ziele verfolgt. Die Aussage, dass jemand aus spezifischen Gründen han-

---

[12] Performatives Wissen in dem von mir verwendeten Sinn ist der Ausdruck einer Absicht, ist also nicht eine deskriptive Aussage über eine Absicht.

delt, bezieht sich daher auf eine andere Ebene, die, je nachdem, empirisch verifiziert werden kann, während eine Person, in deren Tun sich keine eigene Absicht manifestiert, nicht handelt. Ob die Handlung aus Eigennutz oder Altruismus, Normkonformität oder emotionaler Bewegtheit gesetzt wird: Alle diese Motive (und viele andere mehr) sind mit dem Handlungsbegriff verträglich.

Die Tatsache, dass es sich um zwei Ebenen handelt, lässt sich daran erkennen, dass die Kriterien für die Richtigkeit begrifflicher Argumente andere sind als für das Zutreffen kausaler Verknüpfungen. Ein Begriff von Handlung, der die konstitutive Rolle des voluntaristisch-performativen Wissens missachtet, entspricht nicht den Kriterien einer Handlung. Die Frage nach den empirischen Motiven bezieht sich dagegen auf die jeweiligen Gründe, die Akteure zu spezifischen Handlungen veranlassen. Aus den Begriffen, die den Handlungsbeschreibungen zugrunde liegen, können keine Aussagen über spezifische Gründe für die Hervorbringung von Handlungen abgeleitet werden. Die begriffliche Untersuchung kann nur ergeben, daß Normkonformität als mögliches Motiv des Handelns in Frage kommt. Ob dies tatsächlich zutrifft, kann nur auf Grund empirischer Analysen erfasst werden. Eine Ableitung von spezifischen Motiven aufgrund begrifflicher Argumente ist unzulässig.

Parsons' Utilitarismus-Kritik besteht daher in einer Vermengung begrifflicher Argumente über Handeln mit Annahmen über empirische Vorgänge. Parsons engt das voluntaristisch-performative inhaltlich auf soziale Normen ein, denen er zugleich eine kausal determinierende Bedeutung für den Ablauf des Handelns zuweist.[13] Diese Lösung, die die Grundlage für die "voluntaristische Handlungstheorie" bildet, läuft auf eine Neudefinition der Handlung hinaus, in der die kausale Wirksamkeit der Norm in die Definition der Handlung aufgenommen ist. "As process, action is, in fact, the process of alteration of the conditional elements in the direction of conformity with norms" (1968, S. 732).[14]

Das Element der Norm gewinnt auf diese Weise eine wesentlich neue Bedeutung, die nicht aus der Kritik am Utilitarismus abgeleitet werden kann. Die normative Orientierung, genauer die Absicht, sich gegenüber geteilten sozialen Wertmustern konform zu verhalten, wird von Parsons als kausale Determinante der Handlung

---

[13] Die Kritik von Warner (1978) drückt das Unbehagen über die normative Einengung des performativen Wissens aus. Es ist allerdings fraglich, ob Warner dem voluntaristisch-performativen Aspekt des Handlungswissens durch die Betonung der kognitiven Dimensionen gerecht wird. Vgl. die Replik Parsons' dazu (Parsons 1978).

[14] Diese Vermengung von Ebenen kommt auch im folgenden Zitat zum Ausdruck: "A normative orientation is fundamental to the scheme of action in the same sense that space is fundamental to classical mechanics; in terms of the given conceptual scheme there is no such thing as action except as effort to conform with norms just as there is no such thing as motion except as change of location in space" (Parsons 1968, S: 76/7).

bestimmt, die deren Hervorbringung und deren Ablauf steuert. Die "normative orientation" wird mit "conformity with norms" identifiziert und als determinierende Motivation jeder Handlung bestimmt.

Die Vermengung der Ebenen hat zwei Konsequenzen. *Erstens* gerät Parsons in Widerspruch zu seinem eigenen Programm, die in unserem intuitiven Begriff der Handlung enthaltene Tatsache der Handlungsfreiheit zu berücksichtigen. Indem die normative Orientierung als kausal wirksame Motivationsvariable bestimmt wird, nimmt Parsons den Spielraum des Handelns, den er selbst aus der Kritik am Utilitarismus entwickelt, durch eine definitorische Setzung zurück. Jede Handlung dient dazu, bestimmten Normen gegenüber Konformität zu erweisen. Die Norm wird dadurch genauso zu einer externen Determinante des Handelns, die letztlich Anpassung an äußere Umstände nach sich zieht, wie die "rationale" wissenschaftlich-technische Orientierung. Verbunden mit dieser Neufassung des Handlungsbegriffs ist eine selektive Wahrnehmung der Motive: Kennt der Utilitarismus (in der Darstellung von Parsons) überall nur vorteilsorientierte, rational kalkulierende Subjekte, so erscheinen aus der Sicht von Parsons alle Personen als durch Normkonformität motiviert und in ihrem Handeln dadurch erklärbar. In beiden Fällen ist die Motivation der Handlung durch den theoretischen Bezugsrahmen festgelegt.

Zweitens wird die Frage nach den Ursachen der sozialen Integration auf Grund von theoretischen und begrifflichen Argumenten über die Funktion von Normen beantwortet. Der utilitaristische Bezugsrahmen macht keine Aussagen über die Verknüpfungen der Handlungsziele eines Akteurs bzw. von mehreren Akteuren. Daraus folgt für Parsons, dass die Integration eines Handlungszusammenhanges mit seinen Begriffen nicht angemessen analysiert werden kann. Diese Konstellation mache jedoch der utilitaristischen Theorie Probleme, da sie letztlich die Tatsache der sozialen Integration erklären möchte. Wenn die Ziele im Belieben der Einzelnen und durch deren Eigeninteressen bestimmt sind und damit Rationalität nur auf die Durchsetzung von gegebenen Zielen (im Eigeninteresse isolierter und rational orientierter Individuen) beschränkt ist, so ist das Bestehen einer geordneten Gesellschaft nach Parsons unverständlich. Eine auf Interessen beruhende Konformität ist nach Parsons notwendigerweise problematisch: "A purely utilitarian society is chaotic and unstable" (1968, S. 94).[15] Der Utilitarismus kompensiere daher diesen Mangel durch die "metaphysische" Unterstellung, wonach sich die einzelnen Handlungen gleichsam aus der "natürlichen Identität der Interessen" in ihren Ergebnissen ergänzen und ein integriertes Ganzes produzieren (1968, S. 701).

---

15 Dieses Zitat zeigt deutlich, dass es Parsons um die Angabe von empirischen Stabilitätsbedingungen von Gesellschaften geht, nicht aber um eine "transzendentale" Reflexion darüber, wie wir uns Gesellschaft vorzustellen haben.

Sind dagegen die Zwecke durch vorgegebene Normen einer Gesellschaft geordnet oder repräsentieren sie solche Normen, so sind beide Probleme von vornherein gelöst: Die Wahl der Handlung ist dann nicht zufällig und durch Eigeninteresse bestimmt, sondern Entscheidungen für die Realisierung von Zwecken werden nur gemäß übergeordneter Normen getroffen, die auf das Bestehen und die Aufrechterhaltung der vorgegebenen Ordnung gerichtet sind. Durch die definitorische Festlegung, wonach dem voluntaristisch-performativen Wissen zugleich immer gemeinsame Werthaltungen zugrunde liegen, werden das Bestehen einer geordneten Gesellschaft und das Hervorbringen von Handlungen untrennbar verknüpft. Die einzelnen Normen sind demnach nicht voneinander isoliert, sondern bilden von vornherein schon Präzisierungen eines "letzten" Wertsystems. Aus der Sicht der Akteure definieren sie zulässige Verknüpfungen von Zielen mit den Bedingungen der Handlung, aus der Perspektive der Sozialwissenschaftler wird die Bedingtheit der normkonformen Handlungen durch die "letzten" Werte sichtbar, sowie die Rolle dieser Werte für die Integration der Handlungen und damit für die Stabilität des gesamten Handlungssystems. Die letzten Werte stellen einen vorgegebenen Rahmen dar, der mittels akzeptierter Normen die Auswahl möglicher Handlungen einschränkt (vgl. Parsons 1968, S. 668).

Bemerkenswert an dieser Lösung des "Ordnungsproblems" ist der Umstand, dass es auf Grund von Definitionen und theoretischen Postulaten nicht aber auf Grund einer Analyse tatsächlicher Ordnungsleistungen gewonnen wurde. In diesem Zusammenhang sieht Parsons als die wichtigste Leistung der von ihm angeführten Klassiker der Soziologie, das (von Durkheim und vor allem von Weber in der Religionssoziologie herausgearbeitete) wirksame "ultimate value system" (1968, S. 718), das zugleich in den Handlungen als Motivation enthalten ist, wie auch deren Zusammenhalt verbürgt.[16]

Parsons behauptet damit nicht mehr oder weniger, als dass alle Formen der sozialen Integration durch die vorausgesetzte Geltung eines solchen Wertsystems geleistet werden. Dies ist eine Aussage, die sich auf reale Prozesse in der sozialen Welt bezieht und daher nicht auf Grund der Analyse von Begriffen, der Kritik an Theorien und des Aufzeigens ihrer Schwächen, sondern nur auf Grund der empirischen Analyse solcher Prozesse und ihrer Ursachen Gültigkeit erlangen kann. Diese Annahme wird aber bei Parsons zu einem konstitutiven Bestandteil der Theorie. Die Folge ist, dass die ihm zugrunde liegende Frage nach den Ursachen der sozialen Integration sich gar nicht mehr als empirische Frage stellen lässt, sie ist durch die Anwendung des theoretischen Systems bereits beantwortet: Jede geordnete Gesell-

---

[16] Die Durkheim- und Weber-Interpretationen Parsons' sind (meiner Ansicht nach zu Recht) in Frage gestellt worden. Vgl. Cohen/Hazelrigg/Pope (1975) und Whitney/Cohen/ Hazelrigg (1975).

schaft gründet demnach auf der Geltung eines solchen Wertsystems und Nicht-Ordnung oder Chaos sind durch den Mangel an geteilten Werten bedingt. Die Frage nach Ursachen der sozialen Integration wird auf diese Weise durch den Theoretiker auf Grund einer theoretischen Behauptung (die durch schlüssige Argumente nicht gedeckt ist) gelöst, nicht auf Grund der Analyse von Aktivitäten der beteiligten Personen.

Die zentrale Idee beruht auf der kategorialen Transformation des voluntaristisch-performativen Wissens in eine spezifische Motivation, die in der Konformität gegenüber allgemein anerkannten Normen besteht.. Parsons verwendet das Phänomen der Norm in einer doppelten Bedeutung, einmal als unabdingbares Element jeder Handlung (als performativ-voluntaristisches Wissen), einmal als kausal wirksames Motiv (das zudem die soziale Integration erst gewährleistet). Die Grundlage dafür ergibt sich aus der Gleichsetzung des performativ-voluntaristischen Wissens mit sozial erwünschten Normvorstellungen.

Diese Vermengung von Ebenen ist nur vor dem Hintergrund von Parsons' Vorstellungen über den Stellenwert und die Funktion der Theorie möglich, die eine solche Umdeutung von Begriffen zu Variablen (also zur Bezeichnung kausal wirksamer Kräfte) zulässt. Deskriptive Begriffe werden von vornherein mit kausal wirksamen Variablen identifiziert. Die Kritik am Utilitarismus beruht auf begrifflichen Argumenten und der Kritik an miteinander unverträglichen theoretischen Annahmen und führt zum Ergebnis, dass die konstitutive Subjektivität der Handlung mit einer Reduktion des voluntaristisch-performativen Handlungswissens auf "wissenschaftliches" Wissen unvereinbar ist. Damit ist über die Motivation der Akteure noch nichts ausgesagt.

Diese fehlerhafte theoretische Ableitung von Motiven und der auf sie gegründeten sozialen Ordnung ist das Ergebnis *von The Structure of Social Action* und sie liegt auch Parsons' Verständnis von Soziologie zugrunde. Gegenstand der Soziologie ist demnach die soziale Integration vermittels eines "common value system". Parsons' Definition der Soziologie lautet dementsprechend "the science which attempts to develop an analytical theory of social action systems in so far as these systems can be understood in terms of the property of common value integration" (Parsons 1968, S. 768). Damit ist der Kreis geschlossen: Aus dem übergreifenden theoretischen System wird die Erklärung für das Bestehen geordneter sozialer Zustände abgeleitet, indem die Elemente des Handelns als kausale Faktoren interpretiert werden. Das Bestehen des gemeinsamen Wertsystems erscheint als die theoretische Erklärung für die Abstimmung der auf die Realisierung von Normen gerichteten Handlungen. Der Bezugsrahmen definiert nicht nur den Objektbereich, sondern in ihm sind auch schon die kausalen Verknüpfungen festgelegt, deren Analyse den Gegenstand der Soziologie bildet.

Dieser Aufbau des theoretischen Systems ändert sich auch in der nächsten-funktionalistischen Phase der Soziologie von Parsons nicht. Statt der Simultangleichungen bilden allerdings Beziehungen, die auf die Bestandsbedingungen eines vorausgesetzten und integrierten Gesamtsystems (Parsons 1964, S. 38) bezogen werden, die Grundlage für die Entwicklung der Theorie. Ich möchte diese Form der Theorie-Konstruktion nur in ganz allgemeinen Grundzügen rekonstruieren.

Erstens wird Handeln der einzelnen durch institutionalisierte und in sich konsistente normative Handlungsmuster bestimmt. Die Prozesse in der Person, die nach Parsons der Hervorbringung von Handlungen vorgeschaltet sind (die Handlungsorientierungen), haben äußere, das heißt normative Korrelate, die in der Form von Standards die konkreten Entscheidungen determinieren und zugleich aufeinander abgestimmt und institutionalisiert sind.[17] Parsons gewinnt die Kategorien für den Aufbau der Theorie aus der Externalisierung von Prozessen, die in der Person lokalisiert und dann als Ausdruck der integrierten Wertstandards interpretiert werden, die in sozialen Institutionen verkörpert sind. *Zweitens* gibt der Funktionsbegriff das methodische Instrumentarium zur Hand, die einzelnen Handlungen in ihrem Beitrag zur Integration eines geschlossenen Ganzen zu bestimmen. Der *dritte* Baustein wird durch die weitere Eingrenzung des Objektbereichs gewonnen: Nicht Personen sind es, auf deren Handlungen sich die Regelungen und Standards richten, sondern die unpersönlichen Aspekte ihres Handelns, die Rollen, die von ihnen verinnerlicht und zugleich durch normative Regelungen institutionalisiert und durch die Erwartungen anderer abgesichert sind. Der Rollenbegriff wird als konstitutives Element des sozialen Systems bestimmt. Konkrete Handlungen bzw. Handlungsorientierungen lassen sich daher sowohl der Person selbst zurechnen, wie auch dem sozialen System, dessen konstitutive Elemente sie zugleich bilden. Rollen bilden die einzelnen elementaren Bestandteile des sozialen Systems, die es ermöglichen, dass seine funktionalen Bedürfnisse befriedigt werden. "The allocative foci of social systems are roles and role expectations. The social system is in a sense composed of a variety of roles or role expectations; each of these assures that some need of the social system will be met" (Parsons/Shils 1951, S. 92).

Die funktionalistische Sicht von Rolle verweist auf jenen Prozess, in dem die aneinander gerichtete Handlungen zweier Individuen durch die Bezugnahme auf übergreifende Wertmuster abgestimmt werden. Jede Person weiß, welche Verhaltensweisen sie unter den gegebenen Bedingungen von der interagierenden Person zu erwarten und zugleich wie sie den Erwartungen des Interaktionspartners zu entsprechen hat. Indem komplementäre Rollenerwartungen erfüllt werden, die Elemente

---

[17] Es sind dies die kognitive, die kathektische und die evaluative Orientierung. (Parsons/Shils 1951, S. 59). Den einzelnen Orientierungsmodi liegen normative Standards zugrunde, die von den jeweiligen Handlungen abgelöst sind und ein integriertes Wertsystem ergeben. Black (1961) zeigt in plausibler Weise, dass die empirische Realität der einzelnen Orientierungen und die Beziehungen zwischen ihnen unklar sind.

des gleichen Wertmusters zum Ausdruck bringen, wird die soziale Ordnung auf der Ebene elementarer Interaktionen hergestellt und aufrechterhalten. Abgestützt werden diese Erwartungen durch Sanktionen von außen wie durch internalisierte Wertvorstellungen. "A role then is a sector of the total orientation system of an individual actor which is organized about expectations in relation to a particular interaction context, that is integrated with a particular set of value standards which govern interaction with one or more alters in the appropriate complementary roles" (1951, S. 38/9).

Der Konstruktion eines "sozialen Systems" liegt die gleiche kategoriale Umdeutung zugrunde wie bei der Transformation des performativ-voluntaristischen Wissens in ein allgemein wirksames Motiv des Handelns. Es ist eine Sache, die Aufmerksamkeit auf die unpersönlichen, normativ fixierten Aspekte des Handelns zu lenken. "Rolle" bezieht sich auf ein vertrautes Phänomen des Alltagslebens: Viele Handlungen werden hervorgebracht, um unpersönlichen Erwartungen zu entsprechen und verweisen auf überpersönliche Regelungen und Standards. Auf diese Weise kann ein soziales System als aus Rollen bestehend bestimmt werden. Diese Definition von Rolle bzw. des sozialen Systems hat allerdings nichts mit kausalen oder funktionalen Beziehungen zu tun. Ganz eine andere Frage ist es daher, dem Bestehen der für Rollen konstitutiven normativen Erwartungen die Ursache für das Gelingen von Interaktionen zuzuschreiben und Handlungen im Rollenkontext die Funktion der Erfüllung von "Systembedürfnissen" zuzuweisen. Das sind keine Definitionen oder begriffliche Umformulierungen, sondern vielmehr Behauptungen über den Ablauf sozialer Interaktionen und deren Integration zu einem geschlossenen Ganzen. Ihnen kommt der Status von Hypothesen zu, die nur durch die Berücksichtigung unabhängiger empirischer Fakten bestätigt oder widerlegt werden können.

Parsons' Aussagen über normativ integrierte "soziale Systeme" setzen diese theoretisch-definitorischen Annahmen über Handlungen, Motive und normative Muster voraus, die den Status von selbstverständlichen Hintergrundannahmen gewinnen. Die weiteren Arbeiten von Parsons zielen darauf, den Aufbau von "sozialen Systemen" und die für ihre Stabilität und Veränderung relevanten Systemprozesse zu identifizieren. Von den Grundbegriffen her kommt den Werten bzw. dem Wertsystem von vornherein die kausale Priorität zu, die Parsons später als "kybernetische" Steuerungshierarchie bezeichnet. Es sind die Werte, die die Identität der sozialen Systeme bestimmen und die zu ihrer Aufrechterhaltung erforderlichen konformen Handlungen definieren. Die Umsetzung der Werte in konforme und aufeinander abgestimmte Handlungen von Rollenträgern, die den Fortbestand eines stabilen Interaktionszusammenhanges gewährleisten, ist die definitorisch festgelegte Aufgabe des sozialen Systems. "The leading element in the real interindividual or systemic integration is the major value-orientation pattern dominant in the system (ethos)" (Parsons/Shils 1951, S. 177).

Parsons hat durch diese Umformulierungen eine eigene Diskursebene geschaffen, die in dieser Form Durkheim wie Weber unbekannt war. Es geht um den Nachweis von kausal-funktionalen Zusammenhängen auf Grund von begrifflichen Untersuchungen wie von theoretischen Zuschreibungen und deren Projektion in die soziale Welt. Die Parsonssche Soziologie konstituiert eine selektive, durch die Theorie vorgegebene Perspektive.[18] Aussagen über die Struktur der sozialen Welt, über statische Vorgänge, wie dynamische Prozesse, haben nur dem Anspruch nach einen deskriptiven Bezug, faktisch sind sie ein Produkt theoretischer Ableitungen und Umformulierungen und ihre Plausibilität beruht *ausschließlich* auf dem vorausgesetzten theoretischen System. Aussagen, die erst auf Grund empirischer Analysen getroffen werden könnten (über Motive von Akteuren, über die Bestandsbedingungen stabiler Handlungszusammenhänge) werden als theoretische Einsichten einfach vorausgesetzt. Die sozialen Zustände und Prozesse auf die Parsons zur Exemplifikation der Theorie verweist, ergeben sich aus einer selbstbezüglichen Theorie, die soziale Sachverhalte nur in Zusammenhang mit kausalen und funktionalen Prozessen wahrnehmen kann, mit denen sie auf Grund theoretischer Zuschreibungen untrennbar verbunden sind. Wenn in der Tradition von Parsons häufig von "Theorieentscheidungen", "Theoriestrategie" oder "Theoriearchitektur" die Rede ist, so wird damit dieser selbstbezügliche Aspekt gut zum Ausdruck gebracht. Es geht immer um die Ausarbeitung eines Bezugsrahmens, der die relevanten sozialen Prozesse theoretisch ableitet und der empirischen Forschung ein Kategorisierungs- und Klassifikationsschema zur Verfügung stellt, in dem zugleich auch die kausalen und funktionalen Verbindungen festgeschrieben sind.[19] Der Gegenstandsbereich wird gleichsam aus der Theorie heraus konstruiert, deren Entwicklung weitgehend ein Selbstzweck ist.

Die Herstellung einer theoretisch konzipierten sozialen Realität durch Parsons hat große Ähnlichkeiten mit dem Marxismus, der als soziologische Theorie zu ähnlich allgemeinen Aussagen auf der gleichen Abstraktionsstufe führt. Aus der hier interessierenden Sicht geht es dabei nicht um die Inhalte: Ob die Stabilität des Handlungssystems oder der Wandel von Gesellschaftsformationen im Mittelpunkt steht, ob normative Integration oder die Desintegration durch divergierende Klasseninteressen als zentrale Mechanismen der sozialen Dynamik definiert werden, ob

---

[18] Ein Beispiel ist Parsons' Analyse von politischer Macht. Es wird dabei ein spezifischer Aspekt verallgemeinert, andere Formen politischer Macht werden definitorisch ausgeblendet (Parsons 1967).

[19] Gouldner macht auf die im Bezugsrahmen des interdependenten und nach Gleichgewicht strebenden sozialen Systems enthaltene substanzielle Annahme aufmerksam: "Es macht einen erheblichen Unterschied aus, ob Interdependenz und Gleichgewicht als Dimensionen analysiert werden, die eine eindeutige Variabilität zulassen oder – wie von Parsons – begrifflich als substanzielle Entitäten gefaßt werden"(Gouldner 1974, S. 265).

schließlich materielle Interessen an Ausbeutung und deren Abwehr oder verinnerlichte Rollenmuster als primäre Motive der Akteure bestimmt werden, spielt aus der hier vorgetragenen methodischen Perspektive keine Rolle. In beiden Fällen wird auf Grund unterschiedlicher theoretischer Annahmen ein konzeptuelles Instrumentarium entwickelt, das es erlaubt, bestehende Phänomene in die Theorie einzufügen, indem sie als Indizien für die von der Theorie postulierten Prozesse identifiziert werden. Die Richtigkeit der jeweils zugrunde liegenden Theorie über den sozialen Zusammenhang wird aus theoretischen und philosophischen Vorannahmen abgeleitet. Bei Parsons, wie bei den unterschiedlichen Formen des Marxismus, hat die Theorie ein derartiges Übergewicht gegenüber den Phänomenen der sozialen Welt erlangt – die aber dem Anspruch nach den Gegenstand der Analyse bilden – dass sie erst dann zur Kenntnis genommen werden können, sofern sie in die Kategorien der Theorie eingepasst werden, die ihren kausal-funktionalen Stellenwert bestimmt. In beiden Fällen – im orthodoxen Marxismus wie im normativen Funktionalismus – sind die begrifflichen Grundlagen so konzipiert, dass im Rahmen der Theorie die soziale Realität nur so wahrgenommen werden kann, wie sie auf Grund von definitorischen Setzungen vorgegeben wird. Da der "Eigensinn" sozialer Sachverhalte gar nicht zur Geltung kommen kann, spielen sie für die Bestätigung oder Widerlegung der Theorie praktisch keine Rolle.

In Parsons' Theorie lässt sich eine spezifische Synthese zentraler Elemente der Arbeiten von Durkheim und Weber erkennen. Inhaltlich ist die Soziologie Parsons' eine Weiterführung von Durkheims Ideen.[20] Die kausal wirkende Kraft, als die Durkheim die Gesellschaft summarisch bestimmt, wird von Parsons mit Hilfe seines theoretischen Systems in den normativen Orientierungen und den mit ihnen korrelierten Wertmustern identifiziert und in weiterer Folge, auf die ich hier nicht eingehen kann, in einzelne, funktional differenzierte Subsysteme zerlegt. Gesellschaft erscheint als ein komplexer Zusammenhang von Abhängigkeiten und kausal/funktionalen Beziehungen zwischen Subsystemen, deren Grundlage das integrierte Wertsystem bildet.

Mit Weber verbindet Parsons die Überzeugung, dass der Objektbereich der Soziologie letztlich aus Handlungen besteht. Auch das Handlungsmodell, das als Kriterium für die Bestimmung der sozialen Phänomene verwendet wird, ist weitgehend identisch.[21] Der Handlungsbegriff bildet die Grundlage für ein theoretisches System, der – primär aus der Geschichte der Theorie legitimiert – zum Ausgangspunkt begrifflicher Analysen und funktionaler Ableitungen auf der theoretischen Ebene

---

[20] Diese enge Verknüpfung der zentralen Fragestellungen wird in einem späteren Aufsatz von Parsons (1967) explizit herausgearbeitet.
[21] Nicht umsonst bildet Webers Aussage, wonach Zwecke und Mittel die letzten Elemente der Handlung bilden, das Motto von *The Structure of Social Action*.

wird. Die Gliederung der Handlung in Elemente (der "unit act"), wie auch die Analyse der Orientierungsprozesse, die dem Handeln vorgeschaltet sind, bilden begriffliche Instrumente, um zu den Prozessen zu gelangen, in denen die Wirksamkeit der "Kraft" zum Ausdruck gelangen soll, die von Durkheim als Gesellschaft bestimmt wird. Durkheim hat diese Kraft primär mit Hilfe von Analogien und Bildern aus der Naturwissenschaft ("Kraft", "Dichte", "Volumen") erfasst, von Parsons wird sie in einen engen Zusammenhang mit den Handlungen der Akteure gebracht. Während "Gesellschaft" als Objekt immer erläuterungsbedürftig ist, sind Handlungen immer direkt erfassbar. Dies wirkt sich auch auf die kausalen und funktionalen Beziehungen zwischen den Phänomenen aus, die aus Handlungszusammenhängen gebildet sind. Daher sind auch die Metaphern überflüssig geworden, die Durkheim zur Beschreibung des Objektbereichs und der integrativen Prozesse verwendet hat.

Theorie nach Parsons

Meine Kritik geht dahin, dass die Theorie, wie sie von Parsons konzipiert wurde, auf Grund theoretischer Annahmen Aussagen über kausale und funktionale Zusammenhänge macht, die legitimerweise erst auf Grund der Analyse empirischer Ereignisse gemacht werden könnten. Parsons' Methode bestand darin, Annahmen über soziale Vorgänge bereits in den Begriffen zu verankern, mit derer Hilfe soziale Sachverhalte erst erfasst werden können. Damit ist im Prinzip der Beliebigkeit Tür und Tor geöffnet und jeder Theoretiker und jede Theoretikerin kann – unter Hinweis auf spezifische Aspekte sozialer Phänomene, die er oder sie als besonders wichtig empfindet – andere Behauptungen über Motive des Handelns, über Formen der sozialen Integration oder auch über ganz andere Abläufe aufstellen. Die soziologische Theorie als eine eigenständige Diskursebene in der Nachfolge Parsons' ist genau durch diese Situation geprägt, die auch die Grundlage für das Bestehen einer Pluralität von "theoretischen Ansätzen" bildet. Im folgenden möchte ich an repräsentativen Beispielen zeigen, wieweit auch andere Theorien das Parsonssche Verständis von Theorie übernommen haben bzw. dieses zunehmend in Zweifel ziehen.

    1. Gegenstand einer möglichen Kritik an Parsons ist die inhaltliche Beschränkung auf Prozesse der sozialen Integration vermittels normativer Elemente. Daher kritisiert Lockwood (1956, 1969) die Missachtung des "sozialen Substrats", der materiellen Lebensbedingungen, auf deren Regelung die Normen bezogen sind. Lockwood meint damit die materiellen Interessen relevanter Gruppen, die sich systematisch auf ihre Position im Rahmen des Produktionsprozesses beziehen. Soziale Prozesse der Integration und Desintegration sind nach Lockwood das Ergebnis des Zusammenwirkens von sozialer Integration (vermittels Motive, die durch die Orientierung an Werten bestimmt sind) und Systemintegration (autonome Strukturen des

ökonomischen Systems). Es gelte nach Lockwood zu erkennen, dass beide Theorien partikulär und ergänzungsbedürftig sind und dass weder die normative noch die faktische Ordnung allein erklärt werden können, falls sich die Theorie nur auf eine der beiden Formen von Integration beschränkt.

Es ist sicher ein berechtigter Einwand, dass die Differenzierung des sozialen Systems, wie sie Parsons analysiert "keinen Platz für Widersprüche" zulässt, "wie sie Marx ins Auge faßte" (Lockwood 1969, S. 129). Diese Kritik besteht in der Ergänzung der Parsonsschen Theorie, die aber in ihrem Kern unproblematisiert übernommen, allerdings in ihrem Geltungsbereich auf spezifische Fragestellungen eingeschränkt und durch weitergehende Faktoren und Variable erweitert wird. Argumente für die Notwendigkeit, das Parsonssche Modell einzugrenzen, werden genauso wenig vorgebracht wie eine Begründung für die Angemessenheit der marxistischen Tradition. Eine kritische Diskussion des Gesamtentwurfs von Parsons, der theoretische Konstruktion der sozialen Phänomene und ihres systematischen Zusammenhanges stand dabei gar nicht zur Debatte.

Bei Dahrendorf wird der Konflikt zur anthropologischen Grundlage des sozialen Lebens verklärt: Die Bezugnahme auf Konflikte – und eben nicht auf Integration – verbürge erst, dass soziale Phänomene erklärt werden können. Der methodisch relevante Unterschied zu Parsons besteht darin, dass Dahrendorf die zentrale Kategorie des Konflikts nicht auf Grund begrifflicher Analysen und theoretischer Annahmen über das Gelingen von Interaktionen, sondern auf Grund anthropologischer Setzungen begründet. Es gibt Konflikt "wo immer wir soziales Leben finden: er ist nichtsdestoweniger unumgänglich für unser Verständnis sozialer Probleme" (Dahrendorf 1965, S. 109). Werte sind nach Dahrendorf nicht notwendigerweise Ausdruck eines sozialen Konsenses, sondern sie werden von bestimmten Gruppen anderen aufgezwungen. Die geltenden Werte sind daher "herrschende, nicht gemeinsame, erzwungene, nicht akzeptierte Werte zu einem gegebenen Zeitpunkt. (...) Wir setzen voraus, daß Konflikt allgegenwärtig ist, wo immer Menschen sich soziale Verbände schaffen" (Dahrendorf 1965, S. 110). Er führt dann zu "strukturell erzeugten Gegensatzbeziehungen von Normen und Erwartungen, Institutionen und Gruppen" (S. 125), an denen divergierende Interessen anknüpfen, die ihrerseits das Handeln der Menschen zu einem großen Teil bestimmen. Im Gegensatz zu diesen umfassenden Behauptungen, deren Geltungsgründe völlig unklar sind, erhebt Dahrendorf keinen "Anspruch auf umfassende und ausschließliche Geltung" (S. 111), sondern versteht sich als eine Erweiterung des Modells der normativen Integration, die Phänomene und Prozesse zu erklären vermag, die diesem unzugänglich sind. Es bleibt auch für Dahrendorf eine offene Frage, ob bestimmte Prozesse oder soziale Vorgänge eher durch Orientierung am Konsens oder am Konflikt bestimmt sind.

2. Eine umfassendere Alternative zur Theorie von Parsons findet sich in der Ethnomethodologie, wie sie von Garfinkel (1967) konzipiert wurde. Ich sehe dabei von immanenten Aspekten und der spezifischen Terminologie möglichst ab und

konzentriere mich auf das analoge Verständnis über die Aufgaben der Theorie. Garfinkels Ansatz beruht auf einer Annahme über die ontologische Beschaffenheit der sozialen Welt, die keine inhärente Stabilität aufweise, sondern deren Phänomene grundlegend situationsspezifisch ("indexikalisch") seien. Die typisierende Kategorisierung durch die Gesellschaftsangehörigen ist aus dieser Sicht erst die Voraussetzung dafür, dass Standardphänomene erkennbar werden – dies ist eine Leistung, die ständig mitproduziert wird. Die "Ethnomethodologie" ist die Analyse jener kognitiven Prozesse, mit derer Hilfe die diffuse Vielfalt der Phänomene erst eine kommunizierbare Gestalt bekommt. Es sind dies Leistungen, die kontinuierlich und unbemerkt vollzogen würden. "Those ordered properties are ongoing achievements of the concerted commonplace activities of investigators" (Garfinkel 1967, S. 11). Mit "investigator" ist zugleich das "Laienmitglied" der Gesellschaft gemeint wie auch professionelle Sozialwissenschaftler und Wissenschaftlerinnen.

Diese theoretischen Voraussetzungen, deren rationalen Gehalt ich hier nicht diskutieren möchte, bilden die Voraussetzung für die Lösung des Ordnungsproblems.[22] Die Ordnung beruht demnach nicht auf einem stabilen Wertmuster, das den Akteuren vorgegeben ist, sondern diese sind mit der permanenten Hervorbringung dieser Ordnung beschäftigt, indem sie ihre Handlungen und Wahrnehmungen an selbstverständlichen Vorgaben ausrichten und prinzipiell instabile Vorkommnisse als Indizien für geordnete Strukturen auffassen ("dokumentarische Methode") und damit erst schaffen. Die gegenseitige Abstimmung von Handlungen beruht auf Unterstellungen und Projektionen, die sich im Verlauf der Handlungen verifizieren. Die Störanfälligkeit dieser Konstruktionen wird durch ihren routinehaften Vollzug in der Regel unsichtbar gemacht.

Obwohl sich die Ethnomethodologie bewusst von kausalen Fragen distanziert, hat sie Konsequenzen für die Beantwortung der Frage nach den Ursachen der sozialen Ordnung. Die Rolle der konzeptuellen Überlegungen bei Parsons übernehmen Annahmen über den ontologischen Status sozialer Phänomene, aus denen auf die relevanten Ordnungsleistungen geschlossen wird. Eine etwas abweichende Version dieser Theorie liegt im Symbolischen Interaktionismus vor, dem zufolge sich die Stabilität und Integration der Gesellschaft nicht externen Vorgaben verdanken (also Werten oder Normen), sondern dem Prozess der kollektiven Interpretation (Blumer 1969). Die Abstimmung zwischen Akteuren ergibt sich aus dieser Perspektive auf

---

22 Meiner Ansicht nach ist die Annahme der "indexikalischen" Beschaffenheit von Phänomenen nicht gerechtfertigt. Garfinkels Theorie beruht auf einer zu weitreichenden Interpretation der Tatsache, dass beim Erkennen von Gegenständen immer kognitive Prozesse im Spiel sind. Daraus zieht er die Schlussfolgerung, dass die Objekte, auf die sich diese Prozesse beziehen, ein Produkt dieser Prozesse sind. Auch die von Garfinkel herangezogenen empirischen Beispiele (wie seine Experimente) bilden keine Bestätigung seiner theoretischer Annahmen.

Grund gemeinsamer Bedeutungen, die ihrerseits in Interaktionen zwischen Akteuren geschaffen werden. Es sind auch in dieser Theorie die gemeinsamen Bedeutungen, die erst einen koordinierten Handlungszusammenhang ("joint action") schaffen. Grundlage dafür ist ein Postulat, demnach "action on the part of a human being consists of taking account of various things that he notes and forging a line of conduct on the basis of how he interprets them" (1969, S. 15).[23] Wie bei Parsons auch werden durch begriffliche Setzungen und durch theoretische Annahmen, deren Voraussetzungen und Implikationen nicht diskutiert werden, Behauptungen über die Funktionsweise sozialer Prozesse abgeleitet, die nur auf Grund empirischer Evidenz belegbar wären.

Diese Beispiele könnten um eine Reihe weiterer ergänzt werden. Der Rational-choice Ansatz beruht auf der Annahme von nutzenorientierter und vorteilsmaximierender Handlungsorientierung. Die Argumente dafür sind dürftig: Coleman (1991, S. I 23) räumt ein, dass "die Vorstellung der Nutzenmaximierung weder in der qualitativen Darlegung der Theorie (...) noch in der Anwendung dieser Theorie in der Forschung explizit eingeführt", also nicht argumentativ begründet wird. Dennoch baut Colemans Theorie auf nutzenmaximierenden Handlungen auf, weil damit quantitative Gesichtspunkte in die Handlungsbeschreibungen integriert werden können, was dazu führt, dass ein "größeres Maß an Erklärungskraft" erreicht werde (ebd.). Bei Lindenberg wird schlicht auf Adam Smith Vorschlag verwiesen "der besagt, daß alle Menschen mindestens zwei Dinge maximieren wollen: soziale Wertschätzung und physisches Wohlbefinden" (Lindenberg 1990, S. 271). Auf dieser Grundlage wird ein Modell menschlichen Handelns entwickelt, das so gut wie alle Phänomene in ihrem Bestehen oder in ihren Veränderungen erklären soll.[24] Die Erklärung besteht aber nicht in der Überprüfung von Annahmen anhand sozialer Prozesse, sondern ist bereits konzeptuell vorausgesetzt. Man kann, wenn man diese Theorie akzeptiert, die Handlungen gar nicht anders wahrnehmen als durch Nutzenmotive angetrieben.

3. Damit ist das letzte Wort über die Theorie allerdings noch nicht gesprochen. In Opposition zu Parsons wie auch zu jenen "Ansätzen", die aus theoretischen Überlegungen heraus in ähnlich dogmatischer Weise alternative Lösungen vorschlagen, haben sich neuere Theorien herausgebildet, die bereit sind den sozialen Sachverhal-

---

[23] Dem empirischen Anspruch der Theorie gemäß handelt es sich dabei um offenkundige Wahrheiten. "The principles of symbolic interactionism (...) can be readily tested and validated merely by observing what goes on in social life under one's nose" (Blumer 1969, S. 50). Es geht hier um die Bezugnahme auf das alltägliche Verständnis darüber, was Handlungen sind.

[24] Diese Voraussetzungen können nicht einfach als unbefragte Prämissen akzeptiert werden, die sich in der Forschung zu "bewähren" haben, da sie von vornherein schon konzeptuelle Fehler enthalten (Balog 1997).

ten selbst ein größeres Gewicht bei der Beantwortung von Fragen über soziale Prozesse einzuräumen. Es geht dann nicht um die übergreifende Erklärung *des* Integrations- oder Koordinationsproblems, sondern um die Erklärung der Entstehung, des Bestehens oder der Veränderung unterschiedlicher sozialer Sachverhalte. Eine wichtige Rolle kommt bei diesem veränderten Verständnis über die Aufgaben der Theorie den Arbeiten von Giddens (1988; 1979) zu.[25]

Diese Ansätze, zu denen etwa die Arbeiten von Archer (1995), Alexander (1987) und J. Elster (1989) zu rechnen sind, differieren voneinander auf Grund ihrer Verankerung in unterschiedlichen Traditionen. Sie weisen trotz Ambivalenzen und Unklarheiten dennoch soweit Gemeinsamkeiten auf, dass man von einem neuen Verständnis der Theorie sprechen kann. Im Rahmen dieses Aufsatzes kann ich auf die einzelnen Autoren nicht eingehen, daher fasse ich die sich abzeichnende neue Sichtweise in drei Punkten zusammen. Auf Grund von Gegentendenzen auch in den genannten Ansätzen handelt es sich dabei eher um eine idealtypische Skizze, der sich die einzelnen Theorien in ihren unterschiedlichen Problemstellungen graduell mehr oder minder annähern.

(1) Direkt gegen Parsons gerichtet ist die Kritik an der theoretischen Festschreibung sozialer Prozesse und sozialer Entwicklungen. Giddens' Bestimmung sozialer Systeme als Formen der "Bindung" von Raum und Zeit ist der Versuch, das Bestehen geordnete Interaktionen unabhängig von Mechanismen der Integration zu identifizieren und ist zugleich eine Stellungnahme gegen die theoretische Gleichsetzung von sozialer und normativer Integration und damit für die Trennung deskriptiver und kausal-funktionaler Fragestellungen. In ähnlicher Weise ist die Ablehnung einer theoretisch konzipierten Evolutionstheorie mit der Zurückweisung der Vorstellung verbunden, dass auf theoretischer Grundlage soziale Entwicklungstendenzen konstruiert werden könnten. Die Aufgabe der Theorie nach Giddens besteht vielmehr in der Konstruktion von Begriffen, um Veränderungen zu erfassen, ohne Erklärungen oder Entwicklungen vorwegzunehmen.

(2) In Zusammenhang mit der theoretischen Definition sozialer Prozesse steht die Kritik am Determinismus der struktur-funktionalistischen Soziologie. Determinismus in der Soziologie ist zugleich Antwort auf die Frage nach der angemessenen Erklärung und nach den Kausalfaktoren, auf die man dabei zurückgreifen muss. Auf Grund der expliziten oder impliziten handlungsbegrifflichen Konzeptualisierung in der Soziologie nimmt er zumeist die Form einer theoretischen Festlegung oder Ableitung der Motive an. Von Giddens über Archer zu den Neo-Funktionalisten und Elster herrscht Übereinstimmung darüber, dass man die Motive des Handelns nicht auf Grund theoretischer Überlegungen zuschreiben könne, vielmehr eine Pluralität

---

[25] Die theoretisch innovativen Aspekte der Arbeiten von Giddens werden besonders von Cohen (1987) herausgearbeitet.

von Motiven existiert und es nicht vorhersehbar ist, aus welchen Gründen Personen in unterschiedlichen Zusammenhängen zu ihren Handlungen motiviert werden.

(3) In der Parsonsschen Tradition war die Soziologie von vornherein auf die Frage nach der sozialen Integration zugeschnitten. Eine Folge davon ist die konzeptuelle Privilegierung integrierter Gesamtheiten als Gegenstände des soziologischen Interesses. Es ist dies eine Verengung möglicher Problemstellungen und eine Privilegierung bestimmter Forschungsobjekte, die zunehmend in Frage gestellt wird. Der Titel von Giddens' Buch ist zum Beispiel irreführend: Es geht nicht um die "Konstitution der Gesellschaft", sondern um die Reproduktionsprozesse einer Vielfalt unterschiedlicher "sozialer Systeme", die allerdings auch von vornherein als integrierte Gesamtheiten bestimmt werden. Noch deutlicher wird die Abkehr von der Integrationsproblematik bei Elster, sofern es um die Erklärung des Zustandekommens, des Bestehens oder der Veränderung unterschiedlicher sozialer Phänomene geht. Zwar steht die Dokumentation unterschiedlicher Formen der Kooperation im Mittelpunkt der Arbeit Elsters (1989), diese hat jedoch einen anderen Stellenwert als in der Parsons-Tradition. Nicht nur wird kein Anspruch erhoben, "das Problem der Integration" zu lösen, Kooperation wird nur als ein Phänomen unter anderen gesehen und der Ansatz Elsters nicht an integrierte Ganzheiten (wie "Systeme") gebunden. Ähnliches gilt für Alexander: Weder können ihm zufolge die Bedingungen der sozialen Integration auf Grund theoretischer Erörterungen geklärt werden noch gibt es gute Gründe dafür, in soziologischen Fragestellungen immer integrierte Gesamtheiten vorauszusetzen.

Mit diesen drei Schwerpunkten der Kritik sind veränderte Vorstellungen darüber verbunden, worin die Aufgaben der Theorie besteht und was sie leisten kann. Es geht nicht mehr darum, eine spezifische inhaltliche Theorie, die sich als *die* Lösung *der* zentralen Frage versteht, zurückzuweisen, zu ergänzen oder eine Alternative vorzuschlagen (wie dies etwa die Rational-choice Theorie tut), sondern diese Art von Theorie durch ein anderes Verständnis zu ersetzen. Theorie ist aus dieser Sicht ein Instrument, um zu Erklärungen unterschiedlicher Sachverhalte zu gelangen, nicht aber um inhaltliche Ergebnisse vorwegzunehmen und übergreifende Erklärungen zu entwerfen. Sie wird in dieser Perspektive zu einem mehr oder minder offenen Bezugsrahmen, der für die Konzeptualisierung und Erklärung unterschiedlicher sozialer Zusammenhänge notwendig ist. Es werden keine Modelle kausaler oder funktionaler Zusammenhänge aufgestellt, vielmehr wird auf die Voraussetzungen von Erklärungen hingewiesen. Das Ziel ist, unterschiedliche soziale Phänomene zu analysieren, ohne theoretische Annahmen festzuschreiben oder sich auf eine dogmatische "Wissenschaftstheorie" zu stützen.

Schlussfolgerungen

Was kann man aus der Konzeption von Theorie bei Parsons und den Kritiken daran lernen? Drei Punkte scheinen mir zentral zu sein.

(1) Die theoretischen Aussagen sind auf die Beantwortung unterschiedlicher Fragestellungen gerichtet. Es ist daher zu berücksichtigen, welche Antworten darauf jeweils angemessen sind. Das, was soziale Sachverhalte sind, ist nicht selbstverständlich und muss auf Grund rekonstruierbarer Kriterien bestimmt werden. Aus diesen Kriterien sind keine Erklärungen abzuleiten, warum es diese Phänomene gibt und wie sie entstanden sind. Solche Fragestellungen können nur mit Hilfe zusätzlicher Analysen beantwortet werden. Die Vermengung konzeptueller mit kausalen und funktionalen Fragestellungen führt automatisch zu einer Projektion von theoretisch "abgeleiteten" Sachverhalten in die soziale Realität. Man kann an der Theorie von Parsons studieren, welche problematischen Konsequenzen mit einer kausalfunktionalen Umdeutung von Antworten auf begriffliche Fragestellungen verbunden sind.

(2) Betrachtet man nur die konzeptuelle Ebene und sieht man von den kausal/funktionalen Aspekten der einzelnen Theorien ab, hat sich bei Parsons selbst und allen seinen Kritikern und Kritikerinnen ein Konsens darüber gebildet, worauf sich soziologische Begriffe beziehen. Soziale Phänomene werden durchgehend als Handlungszusammenhänge zum Thema soziologischer Analysen gemacht. Die gemeinsamen Werte verweisen ebenso auf Handlungszusammenhänge, für die sie gelten und in denen sie realisiert werden wie auch die gemeinsamen Bedeutungen, die in kollektiven Interpretationen übernommen oder geschaffen werden. Auch die nutzenorientierten Handlungen sind, sofern mit ihnen soziale Sachverhalte erklärt werden, keine isolierten Entitäten, sondern sie sind auf die Durchsetzung von komplexen Interessen und auf den Erwerb von sozial definierten Gratifikationen hin gerichtet. Handlungszusammenhänge weisen auch jene Einheit von "subjektiven" und "objektiven" Aspekten auf, die in den neueren Theorien für die Konzeptualisierung der Phänomene (Giddens, Archer, Alexander) eingefordert wird. Diese sind "subjektiv" in dem Sinn, dass sie in den Handlungen von Akteuren realisiert werden, zugleich "objektiv", weil sie den Akteuren als externe Objekte gegenüberstehen.

(3) Sachverhalte als Handlungszusammenhänge zu erfassen bedeutet, die Handlungen zu identifizieren, aus denen sie bestehen, und ihre konstitutiven Beziehungen zueinander aufzuzeigen. Die Identifikation von Handlungen ist nicht beliebig, da sie auf die Handlungsbeschreibungen der Akteure Bezug nehmen muss. Damit ergibt sich ein Theorie-externes Korrektiv, an dem sich Konzeptualisierung und Erklärung zu bewähren haben. Handlungen und Handlungszusammenhänge haben ein soziales Eigengewicht und man kann nicht einfach auf Grund einer selbstgenügsamen Theorie den Sachverhalten Eigenschaften zuschreiben oder ihnen Ursachen und Funktio-

nen zuordnen. Aus der Tatsache, dass manchmal eine Mehrzahl sinnvoller Beschreibungen von Sachverhalten möglich ist, folgt nicht, dass Beschreibungen oder Erklärungen willkürlich wären.

Diese hier nur kursorisch angedeuteten Tendenzen weisen darauf hin, dass hinter der Zersplitterung der soziologischen Theorie in einzelne "Ansätze" durchaus gemeinsame Tendenzen bestehen. Diese sind Ausdruck des Unbehagens an der Vermengung von Phänomenen mit der Theorie, die Parsons im Rahmen seines "theoretischen Systems" als selbstverständlich vorausgesetzt hat und die dazu führt, dass man nicht mehr weiß, wo die Grenzen zwischen Theorie und Realität verlaufen. Die Bezugnahme auf Handlungszusammenhänge zeigt auch, dass mit der Differenzierung von Ebenen und Fragestellungen keine relativistischen Konsequenzen verbunden sind. Die Beschreibung wie die Erklärung von Handlungen und Handlungszusammenhängen ist durch intersubjektiv nachvollziehbare Kriterien bestimmt und es gibt gute Gründe, bestimmte Beschreibungen und Erklärungen anderen vorzuziehen. Die Erkenntnis der gemeinsamen Fragestellungen könnte daher zur Abschwächung von Unterschieden zwischen Ansätzen, zum Abbau einseitiger Sichtweisen und theoretischer Dogmen, sowie zur Zurücknahme nicht einlösbarer Ansprüche nach Gesamterklärungen führen. Da damit generell die Zunahme rationaler Argumente verbunden ist, lässt sich diese Tendenz wohl als "Fortschritt" bewerten.

Literatur

Alexander, Jeffrey C. (1987): Action and ist Environments. In: Jeffrey C. Alexander et al.(eds.), The Micro-Macro Link. Berkeley: University of California Press. S. 289-318.
Archer, Margaret (1995): Realist social theory: the morphogenetic approach. Cambridge: Cambridge University Press.
Balog, Andreas (1997): Handlungsrationalität und Nutzenkalkül. In: Tamás Meleghy et al. (Hg.): Soziologie im Konzert der Wissenschaften. Zur Identität einer Disziplin. Opladen: Westdeutscher Verlag. S. 1-110.
Black, Max (1961): Some Questions about Parsons' Theories. In: Max Black (ed.), The Social Theories of Talcott Parsons. New York: The Free Press. S. 268-288.
Blumer, Herbert (1969): Symbolic Interactionism, Perspective and Method. Englewood Cliffs: Prentice Hall.
Camic, Charles (1989): *Structure* after 50 Years: The Anatomy of a Charter. American Journal of Sociology, 95, S. 38-107.
Cohen, Ira J. (1987): Structuration Theory and Social *Praxis*. In: Anthony Giddens/Jonathan Turner (eds.), Social Theory Today. Cambridge: Polity Press. S. 273-308.
Cohen, Jere / E. Hazelrigg, Lawrence / Pope, Whitney (1975): De-Parsonizing Weber: A Critique of Parsons'Interpretation of Weber's Sociology. American Sociological Review, 40, S. 29-241.
Coleman, James (1991): Grundlagen der Sozialtheorie. Band 1, München: Oldenbourg.
Dahrendorf, Ralf (1965): Gesellschaft und Freiheit. München: Piper.
Durkheim, Emile (1967): Soziologie und Philosophie. Frankfurt/M.: Suhrkamp.
Durkheim, Emile (1970): Die Regeln der soziologischen Methode. 3. Auflage. Neuwied und Berlin: Luchterhand.

Durkheim, Emile (1973): Erziehung, Moral und Gesellschaft. Vorlesungen an der Sorbonne 1902/1903. Neuwied am Rhein und Darmstadt: Luchterhand.
Durkheim, Emile (1973a): Der Selbstmord. Neuwied und Berlin: Luchterhand.
Durkheim, Emile (1981): Die elementaren Formen des religiösen Lebens. Frankfurt/M.: Suhrkamp.
Elster, Jon (1989): The cement of society. A study of social order. Cambridge: Cambridge University Press.
Garfinkel, Herold (1967): Studies in Ethnomethodology. Englewood Cliffs: Prentice Hall.
Giddens, Anthony (1979): Central Problems in Social Theory: Action, Structure and Contradiction in Social Analysis. London: Methuen.
Giddens, Anthony (1988): Die Konstitution der Gesellschaft. Grundzüge einer Theorie der Strukturierung. Frankfurt/M. und New York: Campus.
Gouldner, Alvin W. (1974): Die westliche Soziologie in der Krise. Reinbek b. Hamburg: Rowohlt.
Lindenberg, Siegwart (1990): Rationalität und Kultur. Die verhaltenstheoretische Basis des Einflusses von Kultur auf Transaktionen. In: Hans Haferkamp (Hg.), Sozialstruktur und Kultur. Frankfurt/M.: Suhrkamp. S. 249-287
Lockwood, David (1956): Some Remarks on the 'Social System'. British Journal of Sociology, 7, S. 134-146.
Lockwood, David (1969): Soziale Integration und Systemintegration. In: W. Zapf (Hg.), Theorien sozialen Wandels. Köln: Kiepenheuer & Witsch. S. 124-137.
Oakes, Guy (1980): Die Grenzen kulturwissenschaftlicher Begriffsbildung. Frankfurt/M.: Suhrkamp.
Parsons, Talcott (1951): The Social System. London: Routledge.
Parsons, Talcott (1964/1945): Systematische Theorie in der Soziologie. Gegenwärtiger Stand und Ausblick. In: Talcott Parsons, Soziologische Theorie. Darmstadt/Neuwied a. Rh.: Luchterhand. S. 31-64.
Parsons, Talcott (1967): On the Concept of Political Power. In: Talcott Parsons, Sociological Theory and Modern Society. New York/London: The Free Press. S. 297-354.
Parsons, Talcott (1967a): Durkheim's Contribution to the Theory of Integration of Social Systems. In: Talcott. Parsons, Sociological Theory and Modern Society. New York: The Free Press. S. 3-34.
Parsons, Talcott (1968/1937): The Structure of Social Action. A Study in Social Theory with Special Reference to a Group of Recent European Writers. New York/London: The Free Press.
Parsons, Talcott (1978): Comment on R. Stephen Warner's "Toward a Redefinition of Action Theory: Paying the Cognitive Element Its Due". American Journal of Sociology, 83, S. 1350-1358.
Parsons, Talcott (1977): Comment on Burger's Critique. American Journal of Sociology, 83, S. 335-339.
Parsons, Talcott / Shils, E.A. (1951): Values, Motives and Systems of Action. In: dies., Toward a General Theory of Action, Harvard: Harvard University Press. S. 47-243.
Pope, Whitney / Jere, Cohen, / Hazelrigg, Lawrence E. (1975): On the Divergence of Weber and Durkheim: A Critique of Parsons' Convergence Thesis. American Sociological Review, 40, S. 417-427.
Warner, R. Stephen (1978): Toward a Redefinition of Action Theory: Paying the Cognitive Element Its Due. American Journal of Sociology, 83, S. 1317-1349.
Weber, Max (1968): Gesammelte Aufsätze zur Wissenschaftslehre: 3. Aufl. Tübingen: J.C.B. Mohr (Paul Siebeck).

The Critique of Utilitarianism in *Structure* and *Gorgias*
Keith Doubt

> But we will never have peace in the world until men everywhere recognize that ends are not cut off from means, because the means represent the ideal in the making, and the end in process, and ultimately you can't reach good ends through evil means, because the means represent the seed and the end represents the tree. (King 1967, p. 71)

> A social order is always a factual order in so far as it is susceptible of scientific analysis but, as will be later maintained, it is one which cannot have stability without the effective functioning of certain normative elements. (Parsons 1968, p. 92)

In 1942 in his masters thesis written for the Department of Sociology at the University of North Carolina, Harold Garfinkel comments on the significance of Talcott Parsons' *The Structure of Social Action*:

> It seems to this writer that too little recognition is made of the fundamental services that Parsons has performed ... If sociologists are looking today for indication of maturity of thought and synthesis in their discipline, they will be fruitfully repaid for any trouble it might cause them to examine ... the writings of Talcott Parsons (1942, p. 37).[1]

Forty-six years later, Garfinkel repeats the encomium in *Theoretical Sociology*.

> "[*Structure*] gave to professional sociology a way to find and exhibit the real production and accountability of immortal, ordinary society ... [*Structure*] set an example for formal analytic sociology and of the world-wide social science movement" (1988, p. 104).

Structure starts as a detective story – "Spencer is dead. But who killed him and how? This is the problem" (Parsons 1968, p. 3). Parsons' role is comparable to a detective; his responsibility is to discover not simply who killed Spencer, but also why and how Spencer was killed.

---

[1] Garfinkel wrote his masters thesis, "Inter-racial and Intra-racial Homicide in Ten Counties in North Carolina, 1930-1940," in the Department of Sociology at the University of North Carolina at Chapel Hill under the supervision of Professors Guy B. Johnson and Howard Odum (See Johnson & Johnson 1980, p. 141). The striking feature of Garfinkel's masters thesis is that, while its methodological approach is influenced by Johnson and Odum, its theoretical perspective is determined by Talcott Parsons and the very recent publication of *Structure*.

There may well be particular reasons why Spencer rather than others is dead, as there were also particular reasons why he rather than others made such a stir. With these this study is not concerned. But in the 'crime', the solution of which is here sought (Parsons 1968, p. 3).

The issue, of course, is not Spencer himself, but what Spencer stood for. "Spencer was ... a typical representative of a system of thought about man and society ... the positivistic-utilitarian tradition. What has happened to it? Why has it died?" (Parsons 1968, p. 3). To find the reason for the death of the positivistic-utilitarian tradition is, Parsons indicates, the most pressing issue in contemporary sociological theory today. Why and how was utilitarianism killed? *Structure* investigates the affair.

There is, of course, a significant problem here. The positivistic-utilitarianism tradition is anything but dead; it is very much alive and well. It is hard to imagine how the positivistic-utilitarian tradition could possibly be stronger. Sjoberg and Vaughan (1993, p. 125) observe:

> Utilitarianism is perhaps the dominant ethical commitment of contemporary American sociologists. Although Parsons, in his *The Structure of Social Action* (1937) challenged the foundations of utilitarian thought, and although both Durkheim and Weber reacted, from differing perspectives, against the utilitarian doctrine, the ethics of utilitarianism appear more widely accepted in the latter part of the twentieth century than the classical sociological theorists might ever have imagined.

Is the reconsideration of Parsons' critique of utilitarianism an untimely reconsideration? Did Parsons incorrectly assume that utilitarianism has been killed by an important development in contemporary social theory, namely, the voluntaristic theory of action? If so, is *Structure* then a meaningless work in that it investigates a murder that never even took place? Wherein lies what Garfinkel calls the "maturity of thought" in *Structure*? What principle governs *Structure's* capacity for theoretical synthesis and formal analysis? What makes *Structure*, to the mind of many contemporary social theorists, a monumental work in twentieth century sociology?[2]

Let us assume, for the sake of argument, that Parsons correctly assumed that utilitarianism had been killed by an important development in contemporary social theory. The question then becomes what has brought utilitarianism back from the dead? How is it that utilitarianism has resurrected itself and resurrected itself with a vengeance? How has utilitarianism covered up the investigation of its own death and murdered the detective? "Parsons is dead. But who killed him and how. This is the problem."

---

[2] Camic writes, "*The Structure of Social Action* has established itself as one the great "watershed[s] in the development of American sociology in general and sociological theory in particular" and as the virtual baseline for "the modern period in sociology" (1989, p. 39).

To address these questions, this study juxtaposes Parsons' modern and empirical resistance to utilitarianism with ancient philosophy's resistance. This approach may seem unorthodox, but, as will be seen, the juxtaposition is fruitful in that it identifies the character and limit of *Structure's* critique of utilitarianism.

Plato's *Gorgias* dramatizes the tension between sophism and philosophy much as Parsons' *Structure* dramatizes the tension between utilitarianism and the voluntaristic theory of action. The dynamic is the same in both works. The three interlocutors in Plato's dialogue – Gorgias, Polus, and Callicles – articulate strong commitments to utilitarianism, whether in the realm of everyday life, culture, or politics. Sophism, for the purposes of this study, is formulated as the ancient's commitment to utilitarianism. Charles Taylor (1989, pp. 31-32) writes, "The utilitarian lives within a moral horizon which cannot be explicated by his own moral theory. This is one of the great weaknesses of utilitarianism."

In *Structure*, four classical social theorists – Alfred Marshall, Vilfredo Pareto, Emile Durkheim, and Max Weber – articulate ambivalent relations to utilitarianism as an adequate theory of action. Much as Socrates questions and transforms Gorgias, Polus, and Callicles's commitment to sophism, Parsons questions and transforms Marshall, Pareto, Durkheim, and Weber's work on the theory of action.

Parsons' theorizing is constructive, that is, it is inherently positive and, in this sense, Platonic. Much as Parsons depicts Marshall, Pareto, Durkheim, and Weber striving for a better theory of action than utilitarianism, Plato portrays Gorgias, Polus, and Callicles desirous of a better philosophy than sophism.

The first section of this study is disruptive in that it reviews Parsons' account of utilitarianism through the unconventional example of ancient sophism. The second establishes conceptual linkages between Parsons and Plato's critique of utilitarianism. The third contrasts Parsons' empirical resistance to utilitarianism with Plato's so as to formulate the epistemological foundation of analytical realism. The third section is the most crucial in that it shows how Parsons is not always as empirical as he claims to be and why this characteristic is Parsons' strength rather than his weakness. The problem of order is "an immortal one" (Garfinkel 1988, p. 104), and sociology waxes and wanes in proportion to its capacity to construct an adequate account of this matter.

Sophism as Ancient Utilitarianism

Structure addresses the theory of action in sociology and how the theory of action changes in modern social thought from a utilitarian one to a voluntaristic one. The change involves the theoretical recognition of certain flaws in the utilitarian's theory of action, especially in regard to accounting for the phenomenon of order. It is important to keep in mind that utilitarianism, the object of *Structure's* attack, is to begin with a compelling and persuasive theory of action. It is also important to keep in mind that, throughout, utilitarianism is the object of *Structure's* attack – "*All of the versions of positivistic social thought constitute untenable positions*, for both empirical and methodological reasons" (Parsons 1968, p. 125).

A similar dialectic holds for the careful reading of *Gorgias*. *Gorgias* dramatizes the difference between sophism and philosophy. The three interlocutors – Gorgias, Polus, and Callicles – speak of sophism as the ideal and most rational commitment. Socrates, in turn, defends philosophy's desire to understand truth and justice rather than seek power and victory as the ideal commitment. Sophism and philosophy are both theories of what constitutes the good life, and *Gorgias* dramatizes the tension between the two commitments.

On the defining features of utilitarianism, Parsons (1968, p. 60) writes:

> The theoretical action system characterized by these four features, atomism, rationality, empiricism and randomness of ends will be called in the present study the utilitarian system of social theory.

These four features – atomism, rationality, empiricism, and randomness of ends – characterize as well the logic and argumentation of Gorgias, Polus, and Callicles, logic and argumentation that Socrates, much like Parsons, attacks as inadequate versions of what constitutes the good life and the ideal actor.[3]

Speaking of atomism as a leading characteristic of utilitarianism, Parsons (1968, p. 54) writes:

> ... in so far as there was intensive concern with the ends of human action, particularly the ultimate ends, it was in terms which emphasized their diversity, especially as between one individual and another. This preoccupation contains the germs of what will be called the 'utilitarian' mode of thinking.

A preoccupation with atomism is evident as well in the argumentation of the sophists. Socrates asks Polus, a student of Gorgias, "Do you suppose that you could answer better than Gorgias?" Polus answers, "What difference does it make, provided that my answer satisfies you?" (Plato 1960, p. 20). The reasoning behind Polus's thinking is critical. For Polus, whether or not his answer is better is not the point. The point is whether or not his answer satisfies his listener. Success, for Polus, is

---

[3] While the secondary literature on *Structure* takes issue with Parsons' conceptual as well as historical presentation of utilitarianism (Alexander 1978; Camic 1979 & 1989; Mayhew 1984), this study accepts Parsons' formulation as true to the Weberian tradition of sociological inquiry. Parsons' presentation of utilitarianism is not a description; it employs an ideal type for adequately explaining the meaningfulness of utilitarianism as a theory of action (Weber 1964, pp. 87-115).

measured not according to the standard of knowledge or excellence, but according to the satisfaction and approval of his audience. Ronald Dworkin provides a good example of how to resist Polus's assumption in his lively exchange with the postmodern theorist, Stanley Fish, "No one who has a new interpretation to offer believes his interpretation better because it will convince others, though he may believe that it will convince others because it is better" (Dworkin 1982, p. 297).

Gorgias's reasoning with Socrates also exemplifies a preoccupation with atomism. Socrates asks Gorgias what is the greatest blessing of oratory. What standard, what measure, portrays oratory as a good practice? Gorgias replies, "I mean ... what is in actual truth the greatest blessing, which confers on every one who possesses it not only freedom for himself but also the power of ruling his fellow-countrymen." Although the answer which Gorgias gives is self-evident, Socrates asks, "What do you mean by that?" Gorgias responds – "By the exercise of this ability you will have the doctor and the trainer as your slaves, and your man of business will turn out to be making money not for himself but for another; for you, in fact, who have the ability to speak and to convince the masses" (Plato 1960, p. 28). According to Gorgias, the greatest blessing of oratory is that it secures for you power over others, what exchange theorists speak of as "credit" (Blau 1964).

The second distinguishing feature of the utilitarian theory of action is rationality. Parsons (1968, p. 19) writes:

> The utilitarian branch of positivistic thought has, by virtue of the structure of its theoretical system, been focused upon a given range of definite empirical insights and related theoretical problems. The central fact – a fact beyond all question – is that in certain aspects and to certain degrees, under certain conditions, human action is rational.

To demonstrate this point, we again employ *Gorgias*. Socrates asks Polus, "When a man performs an act as a means to an end, he wills not his act, but the object of his act." Polus answers yes. "Take, for example, patients who drink medicine by doctor's orders. Do you think that they will the act of drinking the medicine with its attendant disagreeableness or the object of the act, that is, health?" Polus answers, the object of the act, health. For Polus, an unquestionable feature of human action is that it is rational (Plato 1960, pp. 50-51).[4]

Careful readers of *Gorgias* witness that Gorgias, Polus, and Callicles are all rational with respect to what Parsons speaks of as the "rational norm of efficiency." If

---

[4] At this point it helps to mention the quotation from Max Weber that Parsons cites in German as the epigram for *Structure*, a passage which Garfinkel, while a graduate student at University of North Carolina, Chapel Hill, took the time and trouble to translate in his masters thesis – "Every thoughtful contemplation of the final elements of meaningful human actions is closely tied to the categories of ends and means" (Garfinkel 1942, pp. 36-37).

Gorgias, Polus, and Callicles were not, Socrates would be unable to refute them. For Gorgias and his followers, sophism is the most efficient method of satisfying self-interest and political ambition, and to them this point seems irrefutable. Polus even expresses frustration with Socrates for his unwillingness to accede this point, "In your heart you think as I do" (Plato 1960, p. 57).

Empiricism is the third distinguishing characteristic of the utilitarian theory of action. For the utilitarian position, "The rational unit act ... is a concrete unit of concrete systems of action" (Parsons 1968, p. 59). The persuasive feature of utilitarianism as a theory of action is its rhetorical use of empiricism as the exclusive arbitrator of truth. For instance, for Callicles the problem with Socrates' reasoning in favor of justice over injustice and in favor of the good over pleasure is not that it is unintelligent, but that it does not correlate with the real world. For Callicles, the real world is analogous to a Hobbesian jungle, where force and fraud are the only cardinal virtues. If Socrates were rational, that is, if Socrates would just admit to what all man are interested in, namely, his interest in survival and self-satisfaction, Socrates could not deny the empirical foundation of the utilitarian argument. To Callicles, Socrates's thinking is unreal, unafraid of force and fraud, when in fact Socrates should be. "You seem to me, Socrates, as confident that none of these things will happen to you as if you were living in another world and were not liable to be dragged into court, possibly by some scoundrel of the vilest character" (Plato 1960, p. 139).

Empiricism – the third characteristic of utilitarianism – leads to Parsons' formulation of the fourth and most problematic characteristic of utilitarian's theory of action – randomness of ends. Throughout *Structure*, Parsons (1969, p. 59) laments the naivete of the utilitarian theory of action.

> ... there is nothing in the theory dealing with relations of ends to each other, but only the character of the means-end relationship.... For the failure to state anything positive about the relations of ends to each other can then have only one meaning – that there is no significant relations, that is, that ends are random in the statistical sense.

To state the point in another way, Parsons writes, "there has been [in the positivistic-utilitarianism tradition] ... a common standard of rationality and, equally important, the absence of any other *positive* conception of a normative element governing the means-end relationship" (Parsons 1968, p. 56).

To demonstrate the significance of this crucial point, we employ *Gorgias*. Socrates asks Gorgias what if a pupil ignorant of right and wrong were to come to him to learn oratory? Would Gorgias teach the pupil oratory without giving the pupil moral instruction, or would Gorgias teach the pupil knowledge of right and wrong before teaching the pupil oratory? Gorgias answers "I suppose, Socrates, that I shall have to teach a pupil those things as well, if he happens not to know them." Socrates replies, "Stop there; that is an excellent answer" (Plato 1960, p. 39). Notice that

Socrates did not coerce Gorgias's answer. It is likely that Socrates did not even expect Gorgias's answer. Gorgias gave his answer of his own volition, and this feature of the exchange models what Jurgen Habermas's speaks of as the ideal speech situation for demonstrating truth.[5]

The irony of Gorgias's admission is that Socrates' subsequent refutation of Gorgias's position is based not on how Gorgias is different from Socrates, but on how Gorgias is similar to Socrates. The insightful Callicles observes later in the dialogue (and here is Plato's way of reinforcing this turning point in the text):

> Gorgias said in answer to a question from you that if a would-be oratorical pupil came to him ignorant of the nature of right he would teach it to him, and Polus declared that this answer was dictated by false shame, because a refusal would outrage the conventional notions of society, and it was this admission which involved Gorgias in self-contradictioon, which was just the thing that you loved (Plato 1960, p. 77).

Whether based on false shame or not, Gorgias's admission illustrates what Parsons means when he says that randomness of ends becomes an untenable position for the utilitarian theory of social action. When Gorgias acknowledges the need to teach pupils ignorant of right and wrong knowledge of right and wrong before teaching them oratory, he acknowledges the weight of "the conventional notions of society" and the significance of his own relation to these notions. There are ultimate ends which superceed his own personal aspirations. It makes no sense even to Gorgias to teach the power of oratory ("the ability to speak and to convince the masses") to a pupil ignorant of right and wrong. The consequences would be dreadful. Gorgias is rational in that he recognizes the necessity of limits for the preservation of social order. In *Preface to Plato* Havelock writes, "As for the Sophists, it is not usually remarked, as it ought to be, that Plato's argument ... counts them not as his enemies but as his allies in the educational battle" (1963, p. 8).

Gorgias, we see, is unsatisfied with the limits of the utilitarian commitment much as Marshall, Pareto, Durkheim, and Weber, Parsons shows, are unsatisfied with the utilitarian account of social order. When Gorgias's rationality is limited to the utilitarian theory of action, Gorgias's rationality is at odds with itself. In contrast to Callicles, Parsons would say that Gorgias's admission is grounded in a sense of moral responsibility rather than false shame. "That men have this attitude of respect

---

[5] Habermas reasons in a Platonic vein in the following quotation, although Habermas himself would not agree with such a characterization of his work (See Doubt 1990). "... only in an emancipated society, whose members' autonomy and responsibility had been realized, would communication have developed into the non-authoritarian and universally practiced dialogue from which both our model of reciprocally constituted ego identity and our idea of true consensus are always implicitly derived. To this extent the truth of statements is based on anticipating the realization of the good life" (Habermas 1971, p. 314).

toward normative rules, rather than the calculating attitude, is, if true, an explanation of the existence of order" (Parsons 1968, p. 386). Socrates refutes Gorgias not because Gorgias is a "deviant" who rejects the normative orientation of society but because Gorgias is a "member" who shares with Socrates the normative orientation of society toward justice.

Thus Socratic refutation is not based on esoteric knowledge or complex logic; Socratic refutation is based on exoteric, that is, social knowledge. In "Shame and Truth in Plato's *Gorgias*," the classicist Richard McKim (1988, p. 48) affirms this point when he writes:

> If we demand a logical proof that shameful acts are harmful to their agents instead of acknowledging, as Polus must in the end, that we feel them to be shameful because we already believe this, we lower ourselves in Plato's view to the level of sophistic debaters, refusing to admit what we really believe in order to 'win' the argument regardless of the truth ... but can you honestly contend that you *need* logical demonstrations for Socrates' beliefs? Can you honestly deny that, like his answerers, you already share them so deeply that they beggar the power of logic?

The Platonic and Parsonian Critique of Utilitarianism

What do Plato and Parsons know such that they resist utilitarianism? Both show a pedagogical relation toward utilitarianism. Both theorize so as to influence readers to resist what utilitarian theorists assume to be fact and to recognize what utilitarian theorists, as rational actors, cannot themselves deny.

To repeat, Parsons (1968, p. 56) writes:

> ... there has been [in the positivistic-utilitarianism tradition] ... a common standard of rationality and, equally important, the absence of any other *positive* conception of a normative element governing the means-end relationship.

What is this other, more viable conception of the normative element governing the means-end relation? Can this other, more viable conception be be even more compelling than the utilitarian's standard of rationality? *Gorgias* and *Structure* share an interest in answering this question.

With an analysis of how the work of the economist Alfred Marshall verges from the hedonistic assumptions of his classical predecessors, Parsons addresses how the voluntaristic theory of action surpasses utilitarianism.

> [Marshall] makes a sharp distinction between what he calls the 'standard of life' and that of 'comfort'. The former means 'the standard of activities adjusted to wants'. A rise in it implies 'an increase of intelligence and energy and self-respect; leading to more care and judgment in expenditure, and to an avoidance of food and drink that gratify the appetite but afford no strength and of ways of living that are unwholesome physically and morally.' A rise in the standard of comfort, on the other hand, 'may suggest a mere increase of

artificial wants among which perhaps the grosser wants may predominate' (Parsons 1968, p. 139).

There is a similar dichotomy in *Gorgias*. Callicles says to Socrates, "I tell you frankly that natural good and right consist in this, that the man who is going to live as a man ought should encourage his appetites to be as strong as possible instead of repressing them, and be able by means of his courage and intelligence to satisfy them in all their intensity by providing them with whatever they happen to desire" (Plato 1960, p. 90). For Callicles power and self-gratification are the ultimate ends of human action. To make sure that he understands Callicles correctly, Socrates asks, "You maintain, do you not, that if a man is to be what he ought he should not repress his appetites but let them grow as strong as possible and satisfy them by any means in his power, and that such behavior is virtue?" "Yes, I do", Callicles replies (Plato 1960, p. 91).[6]

For the sociological explanation of order, what is the problem when wants, and wants alone, rule action? Parsons (1968, p. 145) writes, "Where men are ruled by animal wants, such as the instinct of reproduction, or by a *fixed* standard of living, a "standard of comfort," the iron law holds." Parsons adds, "They escape it only through a rising "standard of life" the essential element of which is the activities to which wants are adjusted."

How does "the standard of life," which is exemplified in activities, temper wants? Parsons (1968, p. 138) answers:

> The consideration of the economic order strictly as a mechanism of want satisfaction reduces the activities involved in the process to means to an end, and the human qualities expressed in those activities to the same status. But Marshall is quite unwilling to accept such implications even for limited methodological purposes; for him the development of character is the main issue of human life.

How is the main issue for modern social theory the development of character? Parsons' critique of hedonism, like Plato's, speaks of discipline as a value element. Parsons' critique of hedonism, like Plato's, portrays discipline as something that is both rational and good. Parsons states:

> ... why is the reaction to unusual prosperity not increased satisfaction all around, as any utilitarian point of view would take for granted as obvious? Because, Durkheim says, a sense of security, of progress toward ends depends not only on adequate command over means, but on clear definition of the ends themselves. When large numbers are the recipients of windfalls, having attained what had seemed impossible, they tend no longer to believe anything is impossible. This is, in turn, because human appetites and interests are

---

[6] *Michel Foucault (1973, p. xi) admires Callicles' argument and resents Socrates' "reassuring" refutation of Callicles.

inherently unlimited. For there to be satisfaction they must be limited, disciplined (Parsons 1968, p. 335).

Along the very same line, Plato writes:

> We can win happiness only by bending all our efforts and those of the state to the realization of uprightness and self-discipline, not by allowing our appetites to go unchecked, and, in an attempt to satisfy their endless importunity, leading the life of a brigand (Plato 1960, p. 117).

Happiness, Plato and Parsons argue, is won not through the endless gratification of wants but through disciplined actions in the service of "activities." Hedonism, Plato and Parsons argue, falls short of its own measure. Maximum satisfaction of wants fails to generate genuine satisfaction because maximum satisfaction of wants is an irrational way to achieve the ultimate ends of action.

The notion of "activities" in Marshall's work shows a divergence from the utilitarian conception of action, especially with respect to the explanation of order. "Activities" is a notion through which Parsons sees the voluntaristic theory of action emerge out of the utilitarian system of thought. Parsons identifies the significance of this break-through for sociology with the statement:

> The fact is that his 'activities' have no place there at all [in the positivistic repertoire]. They constitute rather a 'value' factor (Parsons 1968, p. 167).

To repeat the point, "There can be no serious doubt that the main supplement to the utilitarian element of his thought lies on the non-positivistic side of utilitarianism – it is a 'value elemen'" (Parsons 1968, p. 168).

Parsons next turns to Vilfredo Pareto to develop the significance of this "value element" for the explanation of social order. "What may be called value ideas," Parsons (1968, p. 277) writes, "are ... of the greatest importance to the understanding of social equilibrium." Pareto makes an important distinction for explaining action, namely, "Pareto's very frequently reiterated distinction between the 'truth' and the 'social utility' of a doctrine" (Parsons 1968, p. 275). Parsons writes:

> To confuse the two is, he says, a typical error of those who can see only the logical elements of action. The standard of truth which he continually employs is that of logico-experimental science. An untrue doctrine is, then, one which departs from this standard. But in this sense the view that only true doctrines should be useful would mean that society should be 'based upon reason'. This, however, as has been show, Pareto considered impossible since essential data were lacking. Hence society, so long as the value element plays a part, will always be characterized by the currency of untrue, *i.e.*, nonscientific doctrines. These doctrines moreover partly manifest, partly constitute, elements essential to the maintenance of social equilibrium. Hence their suppression could not be but harmful to the society (1968, pp. 275-6).

We employ *Gorgias* for purposes of demonstration where by demonstration we adhere to what Garfinkel means when he writes, "My studies are not properly speaking experimental. They are demonstrations, designed, in Herbert Spiegelberg's phrase, as 'aids to a sluggish imagination'" (1967, p. 38). Socrates asks Gorgias, "You would agree that there is such a thing as 'knowing'?" Gorgias answers, "Certainly." "And such a thing as 'believing'?" "Yes." "Well, do you think that knowing and believing are the same, or is there a difference between knowledge and belief?" "I should say that there is a difference." "Quite right," Socrates answers (Plato 1960, p. 31).

Notice that Gorgias's answer satisfies Socrates. Socrates proceeds to extend the significance of the distinction. "If you were asked whether there are such things as true or false beliefs, you would say that there are, no doubt." "Yes," Gorgias answers. "But are there such things as true or false knowledge?" "Certainly not," Gorgias answers (Plato 1960, p. 31).

It is important to note the significance of Gorgias's answer. If Gorgias were to say, as we ourselves might be tempted to say, that there is such a thing as true and false knowledge, belief and knowledge would be indistinguishable. Gorgias, however, reasons that there can be no such thing as false knowledge because if knowledge were false, it would not be knowledge. To be knowledge, knowledge has to be true, and Gorgias, the philosopher, knows this.

To account for order, social theorists, however, must, as Pareto says, account for how beliefs maintain order as much as, if not more than, knowledge. Insofar as this point depicts the reality of social order, social theorists can neither ignore nor neglect the point when objectively addressing the character of social action. When they do, "essential data are lacking." These beliefs that undergird social action are animated by nonlogical reasoning, beliefs that may or may not be true from a scientific standpoint. These subjective forces, however, that undergird social action are not random, and, in so far as they are not random, they are subject to scientific explanation. To insist that sociology not depart from the positivistic-utilitarian tradition unfairly thrusts sociology into a speculative realm.

In defense of this appreciation of *Structure*, consider Parsons' comments on the nature of analytical realism. Analytical realism, Parsons (1968, pp. 727-30) argues, represents the best epistemology for sociology in that it surpasses any of the four contrasting types of empiricism – positivistic empiricism, particularistic empiricism, intuitionist empiricism, and the idealistic use of "useful fictions" for empirical analysis as presented in Weber's methodological writing.

> As opposed to the fiction view it is maintained that at least some of the general concepts of science are not fictional but adequately 'grasp' aspects of the objective elements. Hence the position taken is, in an epistemological sense, realistic. These concepts correspond, not to concrete phenomena, but to elements in them which are analytically separable from other elements (1968, p. 730).

It is important to discuss this crucial passage carefully. What is often interpreted as an idealist strain in Parsons' theorizing is yet an essential component of analytical realism; in other words, this idealist strain in Parsons' work is not idealistic at all. Parsons says that "at least some of the general concepts of science" do not correspond to concrete phenomena, but "to elments in them which are analytically separable from other elements." Thus "at least some of the general concepts of science" are autonomous. Parsons insists that the value of these general concepts of science is not based on their being "completely descriptive of any particular concrete thing or event." Their value instead is their independence of the concrete phenomena.

Jeffrey C. Alexander finds it problematic that "The synthetic approach that Parsons so carefully develops is crosscut by a significant idealist strain" (1978, p. 192). The argument of this study is that what Alexander speaks of as "a significant idealist strain", far from crosscutting Parsons' synthetic approach, is the very cord which holds it all together. Moreover, when this cord is cut, as most secondary works on Parsonian sociology do, Parsons' theorizing begins to unravel.

What is analytical realism? Analytical realism is Parsons' understanding and affirmation of Plato's Divided Line as a categorical principle of inquiry. The Divided Line as an epistemological statement explicated in "Book Six" of Plato's *Republic*. What is below the line (concrete phenomena) – visible things and images of visible things – can be adequately grasped only with what is above the line – mathematical objects (hypothesis) and the Forms (laws). The lesson of analytical realism is that what is above the line and what is below the line are analytically distinct and analytically interdependent. The Divided Line teaches an epistemology that recommends the thoughtful and disciplined mediation of the distinction which the Divided Line makes. Notice that the Divided Line is itself a descriptive account; that is, the Divided Line is composed of both what is below the line [visible things and images of visible things (an actual line is drawn in the sand)] and what is above the line [a hypothesis and a law (the lesson is taught)].

The following passage provides textual evidence for Parsons' commitment to the principle of the Divided Line.

> This ... has been in large part a matter of the reciprocal interaction of new factual insights and knowledge on the one hand with changes in the theoretical system on the other. Neither is the „cause" of the other. Both are in a state of close mutual interdependence (1968, p. 11).

With this statement, Parsons confirms the Divided Line as the guiding epistemology of analytical realism. Factual insights do not cause changes in the theoretical system any more than the theoretical system causes changes in factual insights. "Both," Parsons says, "are in a state of close mutual interdependence."

Parsons uses Durkheim's work to preserve the significance of this principle in social inquiry.

> Now he [Durkheim] makes the far-reaching empirical observation that since individual wants are in principle unlimited, it is an essential condition of both social stability and individual happiness that they should be regulated in terms of norms. But here the norms thought of do not, as do the rules of contract, merely regulate 'externally', *e.g.*, as the conditions of entering into relations of contract – they enter directly into the constitution of the actors' ends themselves (Parsons 1968, p. 382).

Again, *Gorgias* helps demonstrate the significance of this point. Socrates asks Polus, "Which do you think the greater evil, Polus, doing wrong or suffering wrong?" Polus answers, "Suffering wrong." Polus thinks that a person who suffers wrong experiences the greater evil. For instance, a victim of rape experiences greater evil than does the rapist. A murdered child in Sarajevo experiences a greater evil than does the drunk sniper. Socrates next asks, "And which do you think the baser thing, doing wrong or suffering wrong. Answer." Polus replies, "Doing wrong" (Plato 1960, p. 62). Polus believes that the rapist is baser, that is, more offensive, than the victim of rape and that the drunk sniper is baser, that is, more offensive, than the murdered child.

If Polus, however, is to be consistent with respect to his empirical position that justice serves the interest of the stronger, that is, that might is right, Polus ought to answer that suffering wrong is baser than doing wrong. Given the principle of natural right, Polus ought to say that the victim of rape and the murdered child are more base than the rapist and the drunk sniper. Such, afterall, is the self-justifying logic of the rapist and the drunk sniper. Why then does Polus answer contrary to utilitarian logic? What prevents Polus from asserting that suffering wrong is more base than doing wrong when natural right dictates that, to be consistent, Polus should make exactly that claim? Order, Pareto teaches us, is not "based on reason" but on "nonscientific doctrines," and Polus demonstrates the point.

Parsons helps place the significance of Polus's admission. Parsons states, "The element of ends as it appears in the means-end schema is no longer by definition 'individual' but contains a 'social' element" (Parsons 1968, p. 382), and, later, "The normal concrete individual is a morally disciplined personality" (Parsons 1968, p. 385). Polus finds the wrong doer more offensive than the one who suffers wrong. Polus finds the rapist to be more offensive than the rape victim, and this is good. Polus is subject to a muse other than natural right (a muse which Richard Hilbert (1992, p. 37), in his discussion of Durkheim, wants to dismiss as "this moral something").

To use Freudian terminology, Polus has a superego, and, as Parsons argues, Polus's superego is involved in his choice of means and the determination of ends.

> Within the area of control of the actor, the means employed cannot, in general, be conceived either as chosen at random or as dependent exclusively on the conditions of action, but must in some sense be subject to the influence of an independent, determinate selective factor, a knowledge of which is necessary to the understanding of the concrete course of action. What is essential to the concept of action is that there should be a normative orientation ... (Parsons 1968, pp. 44-45).

It is important to stress this point. According to Polus, tyrants are the most powerful people in a community because tyrants can do with immunity whatever they please. Tyrants (for example, feudal lords) have omnipotent means. Socrates, however, asks if, by power, Polus means something that is a benefit to its possessor? Polus replies, "That is what I do mean" (Plato 1960, p. 48). Socrates then replies that tyrants are the least powerful people in a community because "They do practically nothing that they will, only what they think best" (Plato 1960, p. 49).

Polus is confused and asks Socrates to explain. Socrates says that, insofar as tyrants are ignorant of what is to their advantage (insofar as tyrants lack knowledge of their ends as social actors), they are the least powerful people in the community. That is, even if tyrants have the most powerful means imaginable for attaining whatever they wish, if they have no knowledge of what is in their interest with respect to "activities" rather than wants, their means are of no point in that their ends (wants) are randomly (that is, conditionally) determined. "They do nothing that they will, only what they think best" (Plato 1960, p. 49).

This point is not at all esoteric; for instance, it is comically portrayed in a recent popular film titled "Groundhog Day," where the leading character (played by Bill Murray) finds happiness and satisfaction only when his actions change from a utilitarian and hedonistic calculus to a morally principled one. That is, the leading character attains genuine satisfaction only after his actions become collectivity-oriented rather than self-oriented. The popularity of the film is based on the film's comedic depiction of a collective sentiment shared by members of society.

Plato's Science and Parsons' Philosophy

What must ground the critique of utilitarianism for Plato and Parsons respectively? As discussed earlier, analytical realism is Parsons' understanding and affirmation of Plato's Divided Line as a necessary principle for analysis in scientific inquiry. What is below the line (what is real) – visible things and images of visible things – can be adequately grasped only with what is above the line – mathematical objects and Forms, what Parsons means by "some of the general concepts of science" (1968, p. 730). Parsons (1968, p. 9) affirms this notion when he writes, "Theory not only formulates what we know but also tells us what we want to know, that is, the questions to which an answer is needed."

One irony of *Structure* is that, with respect to sociological inquiry, the positivistic-utilitarian tradition turns out to be neither realistic nor analytical. The tradition neglects what is above the line even though, as a course of action, the tradition is dependent upon what is above the line.

As noted in the beginning of the paper, the positivistic-utilitarian tradition is anything but dead; it is alive and well. If *Structure* successfully finds a solution to the murder which it investigates, if Parsons adequately explains why and how Spencer was killed, how is it that utilitarianism has resurrected itself and resurrected itself with a vengeance? It appears that all evidence of a crime has been erased. No investigation is called for. What happened? Has the detective been murdered?

Plato helps us solve the case. Socrates asks Gorgias, "We may assume, I suppose, the existence of body and soul?" Gorgias answers, "Of course" (Plato 1960, p. 45). No many theorists today would reply as Gorgias does. Many would reject any argument that grants a nonempirical reality for the meaningful understanding of action. Parsons, however, is not always one of these theorists. Parsons writes:

> When biologist or a behavioristic psychologist studies a human being it is as an organism, a partially distinguishable separate unit in the world. The unit of reference which we are considering as the actor is not this organism but an 'ego' or 'self' (1968, pp. 46-7).

The terms "ego" and "self" refer to an aspect of the actor that is distinct from the actor's existence as an organism; the terms "ego" and "self" refer to an aspect of the actor that is distinct from the actor's body as "a spatially distinguishable separate unit in the world." What is not clear is whether "ego" and "self" (terms for the part of the actor which is distinct from his or her being an organism in the world) are interchangeable with "soul".

Modernity balks at making this connection, and Leon Mayhew (1984) argues that Parsons is "a defender of modernity". For example, Mayhew argues that „Parsons did not in the last analysis reject either the utilitarian order of exchange or utilitarian approaches to the analysis of social solidarity (1984, p. 1301). Mayhew's statement is antithetical to the position of this study. This study argues that Parsons writing has strong affinities with Platonic philosophy. To reconcile this tension, it is suggested that the suppression of Parson's philosophical nature by not only leading Parsonian scholars but also Parsons himself provides for the eventual return of utilitarianism to not only contemporary sociology but Parsons' later work as the hegemonic position from which to understand the social.

For example, as a modern theorist, Parsons argues against equating the terms "self" and "ego" with "soul" because "soul" suggests an entity that is eternal. Consider Parsons (1968, p. 445) reasoning:

> For the effect of identifying society with the world of eternal objects is to eliminate the creative element of action altogether. Their defining characteristic is that the categories of neither time nor space apply to them. They 'exist' only 'in the mind'. Such entities cannot

be the object of an explanatory science at all. For an explanatory science must be concerned with events, and events do not occur in the world of eternal objects.

The problem of idealism, whether sociological or religious, is its conviction in the world of eternal objects, that is, the absolute which is independent of space and time. Idealism, Parsons reasons, eliminates the creative element of action.

Plato differs in the following way: Plato sees the Good as absolute and independent of space and time. Does Plato's eliminate or preserve the creative element of action? Action, as Parsons says, occurs in space and time. But if action is understood exclusively in terms of space and time, that is, from the viewpoint of what is below the line, "All things would be indistinguishably mixed together."

Consider how Plato and Parsons make the same points in different ways. Plato writes:

> The same confusion would occur with cookery and medicine if the body were left to its own devices instead of being controlled by the soul, which distinguishes the two from its superior viewpoint; if the body had to draw this distinction with no criterion but its own sensations of pleasure, the saying of Anxagoras – with which you are so well acquainted, Polus – would have more than one application. 'All things would be indistinguishably mixed together,' and there would be no boundaries between the provinces of medicine and cookery (Plato 1960, p. 47).

And Parsons says:

> It goes without saying that a theory to be sound must fit the facts but it does not follow that the facts alone, discovered independently of theory, determine what the theory is to be, nor that theory is not a factor in determining what facts will be discovered, what is to be the direction of interest of scientific investigation.

Plato and Parsons both assert that it is necessary to understand action from the viewpoint of what is above the line rather than from the viewpoint of what is below the line, although action is never understood independently of what is below the line.

Parsons sometimes slips as an empiricist and suggests that equating "self" and "ego" with "soul" may be inevitable. Parsons sometimes slips by indicating that it may be necessary to understand action in terms of "soul" rather than "body".

> For 'society,' to be the object of an explanatory science, must participate in empirical reality. But such participation does not preclude significant relations outside it (Parsons 1968, 448).

Society participates in relations outside of empirical reality; society's participation in these relations are a fact. Parsons may not directly examine these relationships, but Parsons thinks that it is imperative to acknowledge their existence. "Action is not only 'meaningfully oriented' as the positivist inevitably concludes, to reality as rationally understood by science but to the nonempirical as well" (Parsons 1968,

p. 424). For Plato the distinction between empirical reality and "relations outside it" is always an ironic one. For Parsons, it is a paradoxical one. Parsons' greatness, however, is that his wisdom is not confined to the parameters of modernity. As Martin Buber (1958, p. 34) says (and this study reads *Structure* as making the same point):

> And in all the seriousness of truth, hear this: without *It* man cannot live. But he who lives with *It* alone is not a man.

Literature

Alexander, Jeffrey C. (1978): Formal and Substantive Voluntarism in the Work of Talcott Parsons: A Theoretical and Ideological Reinterpretation. In: American Sociological Review 43:177-198.
Blau, Peter (1964): Exchange and Power in Social Life. New York: John Wiley.
Camic, Charles (1979).The Utilitarians Revisited. In: American Journal of Sociology. 85:516-550.
Camic, Charles (1989): Structure after 50 Years: The Anatomy of a Charter. In: American Journal of Sociology. 95:38-107.
Clough, Patricia Ticineto (1992): The End(s) of Ethnography: From Realism to Social Criticism. Newbury Park: Sage.
Dworkin, Ronald (1982): My Reply to Stanley Fish (and Walter Benn Michaels): Please Don't Talk about Objectivity Any More. Pp. 285-313 in The Politics of Interpretation. Edited by J. T. Mitchell. Chicago: University of Chicago Press.
Foucault, Michel (1973): Madness and Civilization: A History of Insanity in the Age of Reason. New York: Vintage Books.
Garfinkel, Harold (1988): Evidence for Locally Produced Naturally Accountable Phenomena of Order, Logic, Reason, Meaning, Method, etc., in and as of the Essential Quiddity of Immortal Ordinary Society (I of IV): An Announcement of Studies. Sociological Theory 6:103-106.
Garfinkel, Harold (1942): Inter-racial and Intra-racial Homicide in Ten Counties in North Carolina, 1930-1940. Masters Thesis. Department of Sociology. University of North Carolina, Chapel Hill.
Habermas, Jurgen (1971): Knowledge and Human Interests. Translated by Jeremy J. Shaprio. Boston: Beacon Press.
Heritage, John (1984): Garfinkel and Ethnomethodology. Cambridge: Polity.
Hilbert, Richard A. (1992): The Classical Roots of Ethnomethodology. Chapel Hill: University of North Carolina Press.
Johnson, Guy B. & Johnson, Guion Griffis (1980): Research and Service to Society: The First Fifty Years of the Institute for Research and Social Science at the University of North Carolina. Chapel Hill: University of North Carolina Press.
King, Martin Luther Jr. (1967): A Christmas Sermon On Peace. Pp. 67-78. In: The Trumpet of Conscience by Martin Luther King, Jr. New York: Harper and Row.
Mayhew Leon (1984): In Defense of Modernity: Talcott Parsons and the Utilitarian Tradition. In: American Journal of Sociology. 89:1273-1305.
McKim, Richard (1988): Shame and Truth in Plato's Gorgias. Pp. 34-48 in Platonic Writings, Platonic Readings, edited by Charles L. Griswold, Jr. New York: Routledge.
Parsons, Talcott (1964): The Social System. Glencoe: Free Press.

Parsons, Talcott (1968): The Structure of Social Action. New York: Free Press.
Plato (1960): Gorgias. Translated by Walter Hamilton. Middlesex, England: Penguin.
Sjoberg, Gideon & Vaughan, Ted R. (1993): The Ethical Foundations of Sociology and the Necessity for a Human Rights Perspective. Pp. 114-159 in A Critique of Contemporary American Sociology. Edited by Ted R. Vaughan, Gideon Sjoberg, and Larry T. Reynolds. Dix Hills, New York: General Hall.
Taylor, Charles (1989): Sources of the Self: The Making of the Modern Identity. Cambridge, Mass.: Harvard University Press.
Max, Weber (1946): Science as a Vocation. Pp. 129-156 in Max Weber: Essays in Sociology. Edited and translated by H. H. Gerth and C. Wright Mills. New York: Oxford Press.
Weber, Max (1964): The Theory of Social and Economic Organization. Edited with an Introduction by Talcott Parsons. New York: Free Press.

Zum Verhältnis von funktionaler, kausaler und historischer Erklärung bei Parsons
Eine kritische Betrachtung[1]
Max Haller

Die strukturell-funktionale Theorie Talcott Parsons' stellte von den 40er bis in die 70er Jahre hinein die soziologische Theorie schlechthin dar. Dies galt sowohl von ihrem umfassenden Anspruch her – Parsons verstand seine Theorie bekanntlich als die große, "definitive" Synthese der bedeutendsten Einsichten von Pareto, Durkheim und Weber – wie auch von ihrer Breitenwirkung. Nach vielfach heftigen Angriffen ist es inzwischen um sie eher still geworden. Es wäre aus diesen Gründen vielleicht gar nicht mehr angebracht, den Ansatz von Parsons als eine zeitgenössische Theorie zu behandeln; man könnte ihn bereits zu den "Klassikern" zählen (Hartfiel/Hillmann 1982, S. 571 f.) oder auch zu den (vielleicht nicht mit Unrecht) eher vergessenen Autoren der Vergangenheit. Als aktuell wichtig erscheint mir dieser Ansatz aber aus zwei Gründen.

Zum ersten, weil es heute in verschiedenen Ländern (wieder) bedeutende Theoretiker gibt, die den Ansatz von Parsons weiterhin vertreten bzw. direkt auf ihm aufbauen. Zu nennen sind hier – neben dem frühen Luhmann – vor allem Jeffrey Alexander in den USA, Richard Münch in Deutschland und Pier-Paolo Donati in Italien. Darüber hinaus gibt es nicht wenige Forscher, die in wichtigen Aspekten ihrer eigenen Ansätze auf Parsons Bezug nehmen (z. B. Habermas 1981/II, S. 295 ff.) oder den Parsonsschen Bezugsrahmen für ihre inhaltlichen Arbeiten anregend und nützlich finden (vgl. z. B. Jensen 1984; Turner 1994; Staubmann 1995; Gerhardt 1996).

Eine Beschäftigung mit Parsons ist zum zweiten auch deshalb wichtig, weil seine Art des evolutionistisch-funktionalistischen Denkens in der Geschichte der Sozialtheorie seit dem 18./19. Jahrhundert bis heute eine sehr bedeutende Rolle spielt. Man denke hier an so einflussreiche Autoren wie Herbert Spencer, die Sozialdarwinisten des späten 19. Jahrhunderts, die Funktionalisten in der Anthropologie (Malinowski, Radcliffe-Brown), die Verwendung des Begriffs in der Soziologie (Durkheim, Merton), bis hin zum modernen Neoevolutionismus und -funktionalismus in Biologie und Humanwissenschaften. Ich möchte behaupten, dass auch zeitgenössi-

---

[1] Dieser Beitrag stellt einen überarbeiteten und ergänzten Abschnitt aus dem Parsons-Kapitel in meinem Buch *Soziologische Theorie im systematisch-kritischen Vergleich* (1999, S. 197-260) dar.

sche Denker, wie Niklas Luhmann, dieser Tradition viel stärker verpflichtet sind, als sie es selber zuzugeben bereit sind.

In diesem Beitrag möchte ich diskutieren, in welcher Weise Parsons in seinem Ansatz historisch-beschreibende, funktionale und kausale Erklärungen verwendet. Meine These lautet, dass sich die Stärke vieler seiner Arbeiten daraus ergibt, dass er alle diese drei Grundformen wissenschaftlicher Darstellung und Erklärung einsetzt. Allerdings, so meine These, tendiert er dabei immer wieder zu einer unzulässigen Vermengung dieser unterschiedlichen Prinzipien. Daraus ergeben sich auch eine Vielzahl berechtigter Einwände gegen seine Schriften.

Bevor ich auf die Analyse der drei genannten Erklärungsmuster bei Parsons eingehe, scheint es angebracht zu sein, sich mit der generellen Intention seiner Theorie, einer "Kodifikation des bestehenden Wissens" bzw. einer "Vermessung der noch bestehenden Wissenslücken" zu befassen.

Kodifikation des bestehenden Wissens in der Soziologie: Die Grundintention und der "konstruktivistische" Charakter der Parsonsschen Theorie

Ich möchte hier die These aufstellen, dass die Grundintention von Parsons' Theoriebildung – die "Kodifikation" des (bestehenden) Wissens – von ihm selber nie klar expliziert, ja oft missverständlich interpretiert und daher von seinen Kritikern (verständlicherweise) vielfach missverstanden worden ist.

Betrachten wir diese Intention, wie sie im programmatischen, einleitenden Statement des grundlegenden Werkes *Toward a General Theory of Action*, verfasst von Parsons gemeinsam mit Edward Shils und sieben weiteren namhaften zeitgenössischen Soziologen, Psychologen und Anthropologen, zum Ausdruck kommt. Parsons und Shils schreiben hier, in den Sozialwissenschaften habe Theorie drei Funktionen:

> Sie sollte erstens bei der Kodifikation des bestehenden, konkreten Wissens helfen. Sie kann dies, indem sie allgemeine Hypothesen für die systematische Reformulierung bestehender Fakten und Einsichten bereitstellt, indem sie die Reichweite spezifischer Hypothesen erweitert, und indem sie es ermöglicht, unterschiedliche Beobachtungen unter einheitliche Begriffe zusammenzufassen. Durch Kodifikation fördert die allgemeine Theorie in den Sozialwissenschaften den Prozess des kumulativen Wissensfortschritts...

Allgemeine Theorie in den Sozialwissenschaften sollte zweitens eine Anleitung zur Forschung geben. Durch Kodifikation ermöglicht sie es, die Grenzen unseres Wissens und Nichtwissens genauer zu bestimmen und zu definieren. Kodifikation hilft bei der Auswahl von Problemen... Darüber hinaus sollte die allgemeine Theorie Hypothesen bereitstellen, die bei der Erforschung dieser Probleme angewandt und geprüft werden können...

Allgemeine Theorie sollte drittens, als Ausgangspunkt für spezialisierte Forschung in den Sozialwissenschaften, die Kontrolle von Lücken der Forschung und Interpretation erleichtern, die derzeit durch die Zersplitterung von Lehre und Forschung in den Sozialwissenschaften bestehen" (Parsons/Shils 1951, S. 3; Übersetzung dieses und folgender Zitate M.H. und Hervorhebungen M.H.).

Der zentrale Begriff ist hier *"Kodifikation des Wissens"*. Was heißt dies wirklich? Meiner Meinung nach wurde diese zentrale Absicht vielfach missverstanden und in Parsons' Theorie mehr hineininterpretiert, als sie wirklich zu leisten beabsichtigte. Allerdings bleibt auch Parsons selber hinsichtlich der Bedeutung und Leistung dieser Aufgabe vielfach unklar und überzieht sie immer wieder (vor allem durch die Vermengung von beschreibender, funktionaler und kausaler Analyse, wie ich unten zeigen werde).[2] Ich bin in dieser Hinsicht also durchaus der Meinung eines (sympathetischen) Parsons-Interpreten wie Stefan Jensen, der schreibt, Hauptziel von Parsons sei es gewesen, *Aussagen zu systematisieren*:

> Ein erheblicher Teil der Arbeiten Parsons' sind explizit als Versuch zu verstehen, eine systematische Ordnung, die auf ein axiomatisches System abzielt, aufzubauen. Die Aufgabe dieser Theorie ist es, eine *Rekonstruktion der empirischen Erfahrungswelt* zu liefern. Dabei wird nicht die ganze Welt rekonstruiert, sondern lediglich ihr sozialwissenschaftlich thematisierbarer Aspekt. Es handelt sich also um einen Versuch einer *Rekonstruktion der 'Lebenswelt'* (Jensen 1976, S. 13; Hervorhebungen M.H.).

Auf Grund dieser zentralen Intention von Parsons, so Jensen, könne sein Ansatz als *konstruktivistisch* bezeichnet werden. Wir werden in der Tat sehen, dass diese konstruktivistische Vorgangsweise bei allen Parsons-Schülern, auch bei Niklas Luhmann, eine zentrale Rolle spielt; sich über ihren Sinn und ihre Reichweite klar zu werden, ist daher von größter Bedeutung.

"Konstruktivismus" als Entwicklung von Begriffen und Begriffssystemen

"Konstruktivistisch" bezieht sich zunächst auf eine grundlegende philosophisch-wissenschaftstheoretische Position hinsichtlich des Verhältnisses zwischen Realität und Erkenntnis. Eine *realistische Position* nimmt an, dass die äußere Welt ein objektives Faktum darstellt, das durch wissenschaftliche Beobachtungen mehr oder weniger genau erfasst bzw. durch wissenschaftliche Theorien erklärt werden kann.

---

[2] Insofern ist es vielleicht kein Zufall, dass sich Parsons nie systematisch mit wissenschaftstheoretisch-methodologischen Fragen befasste (Mikl-Horke 1989, S. 211). Hätte er es getan (wie etwa Max Weber), wäre er vielleicht auf manche Mängel seiner Theorie in dieser Hinsicht aufmerksam geworden.

Dem widerspricht die zumindest seit Kant unbestreitbare Tatsache, dass Wahrnehmungen immer nur über allgemeine Begriffe möglich sind, dass nie die gesamte Welt erfassbar und erkennbar ist, und dass zahlreiche Begriffe zeit- und kulturspezifisch sind. Angesichts dieser Fakten nimmt die *idealistische Position* an, die Erkenntnis der Welt sei eine reine Funktion unseres Bewusstseins und Handelns; hier wird letztlich die Existenz einer äußeren Welt überhaupt geleugnet.

Beide Positionen sind aus der Sicht einer empirisch orientierten (Sozial-) Wissenschaft unhaltbar. Die *"konstruktivistische" Lösung* von Parsons besteht nun darin, dass die Begriffe "jeweils durch eine methodologische Regel oder eben per Konstruktion" eingeführt werden, wie Jensen (1976, S. 14) schreibt. Dahinter steht die durchaus plausible Idee, dass der menschliche Verstand auch von sich aus eine aktive Leistung, eben die Erfindung neuer Begriffe, erbringen muss, damit er die äußere Welt erkennen kann.

Meine These lautet: die Grenzen dieses konstruktivistischen Ansatzes – und der strukturell-funktionalen Systemtheorie insgesamt – liegen zunächst schon darin, dass es hier nicht primär um wissenschaftliche *Probleme* geht, sondern nur um *Begriffe* und *Begriffssysteme*. Damit begibt sie sich von Beginn an auf einen Weg, der nicht sehr produktiv sein kann, ja, der aus der Sicht einer wissenschaftstheoretischen Auffassung, die die moderne Sozialwissenschaft mit Popper als *Erfahrungswissenschaft* versteht, als Sackgasse bezeichnet werden muss. Popper schreibt zu diesem Sachverhalt im Anschluss an eine Übersicht, in der er auf der linken Seite Begriffe anführt, auf der rechten Seite Aussagen oder Theorien:

> Meine These ist: Die *linke Seite der Tabelle ist uninteressant* im Vergleich zur rechten. Uns sollten Theorien interessieren: die Wahrheit, das Argument. Wenn so viele Philosophen und Wissenschaftler immer noch glauben, Begriffe und Begriffssysteme (und Probleme ihrer Bedeutung oder der Bedeutung von Wörtern) seien ähnlich wichtig wie Theorien und theoretische Systeme (und Probleme ihrer Wahrheit oder der Wahrheit von Aussagen), dann leiden sie noch unter Platons Hauptfehler. Denn Begriffe sind teils Mittel zur Formulierung von Theorien, teils Mittel, sie zusammenzufassen. Auf jeden Fall haben sie hauptsächlich eine instrumentelle Bedeutung; und man kann sie immer durch andere Begriffe ersetzen (Popper 1973, S. 127 f.).

Dass es Parsons in allererster Linie um die Entwicklung eines Begriffssystems geht und nicht um *Probleme*, lässt sich an einer Vielzahl von Zitaten belegen. Betrachten wir etwa die folgenden Ausführungen aus *Toward a General Theory of Action*:

> Die vollständige Analyse eines Handlungssystems würde eine Beschreibung sowohl des Zustands eines Systems zu einem bestimmten Moment wie auch der Veränderungen im System über die Zeit beinhalten, einschließlich von Veränderungen in den Beziehungen der konstituierenden Variablen. Diese dynamische Analyse würde die Prozesse des Handelns betreffen und sie ist das angemessene Ziel der Begriffs- und Theoriebildung. Wir glauben aber, daß es unökonomisch ist, Veränderungen in einem System von Variablen zu beschreiben, bevor die Variablen selber isoliert und beschrieben worden sind; wir haben uns daher dafür entschieden, mit der Untersuchung bestimmter Kombinationen von

Variablen zu beginnen und erst dann zu einer Beschreibung dessen fortzuschreiten, wie sich diese Kombinationen wandeln, sobald eine feste Begründung für diese Analyse geliefert wurde (Parsons/Shils 1951, S. 6; Hervorhebungen M.H.).

Die Art dieser Aussage ist typisch für Parsons und sie kehrt an vielen Stellen wieder: "an sich" wäre es das Ziel der Theoriebildung, Erklärungen für dynamische Prozesse zu leisten; derzeit aber oder – im ersten Schritt – ist dies jedoch (leider noch) nicht möglich... Selbst bei der Betrachtung von Veränderungen geht es zunächst nur um die *Beschreibung* von "Strukturmustern" – ein Begriff, der in Parsons' Schriften immer wiederkehrt. Ein bezeichnender Hinweis auf Parsons' Ambivalenz in dieser Frage ist der Wechsel vom Konjunktiv in den Indikativ im letzten Satz des obigen Zitats: eine dynamische Analyse "würde" Prozesse betreffen, sie "ist" aber das eigentliche Ziel der Theoriebildung...

Ich behaupte, dass es prinzipiell unmöglich ist, von diesem vielbeschworenen "ersten Schritt" der *Beschreibung* irgendwann später weiterzugehen zu einer dynamischen Analyse. Durch die Festlegung auf das Ziel einer Identifizierung der relevanten Variablen und ihrer Beziehungen zueinander quasi im "Ruhezustand" eines sozialen Systems gibt Parsons die Möglichkeit auf, wirkliche *Erklärungen* für soziale Prozesse, d. h. für Veränderungen, entwickeln zu können. Um zu kausalen Hypothesen und Erklärungen (d. h., Aussagen über *Ursachen* bestimmter Ereignisse) zu gelangen, muss man sofort mit Problemstellungen beginnen, die Zusammenhänge zwischen Variablen und Veränderungen in diesen Variablen ("Variable" = veränderliche Größe!), also dynamische Phänomene, d. h. Prozesse betreffen. Es erscheint geradezu als logisch unmöglich, eine Theorie eines statischen Zustands zu entwickeln!

Dass es sich hier um eine wissenschaftstheoretische Ausgangsposition handelt, die aus der Sicht einer an *Erklärungen* orientierten Wissenschaftsauffassung in eine Sackgasse führen *muss*, wurde meiner Meinung nach in der Parsons-Kritik weithin übersehen. Der häufig gemachte Vorwurf an Parsons, er konzentriere sich nur auf *Systeme im Gleichgewicht*, behandle sozialen Wandel nicht oder sei überhaupt ein Verteidiger des status quo ist – als inhaltlicher Vorwurf – in der Tat falsch. Es lassen sich nicht nur zahllose Einzelbelege in Parsons' Werk finden, in denen er auf die Bedeutung des Wandels hinweist und sich mit ihm beschäftigt, sondern er widmet diesem Thema auch ganze Abschnitte in wichtigen Werken.[3] Stefan Jensen (1976, S. 38) stellt hier – gegen viele unzutreffende Kritiken gerichtet – richtig fest, dass es in Parsons' Systemtheorie um reine Strukturzusammenhänge geht, um eine *strukturalistische Betrachtung*, die nicht mit einer *statischen* (im Gegensatz zu einer *dynamischen*) *Analyse* verwechselt werden darf (ähnlich auch Alexander 1984).

---

3 Vgl. z. B. Parsons 1951, S. 480-535; 1972; 1975 und 1976.

Ich bin allerdings durchaus der Meinung vieler Kritiker, dass Parsons sozialen Wandel nicht adäquat erfassen könne (Kellermann 1967; Dahrendorf 1974, S. 213 ff.; Gouldner 1974/1). Zuwenig scheint mir jedoch in diesen früheren Kritiken von Parsons der wahre Grund dafür erkannt worden zu sein, nämlich die Tatsache, dass sein Denkansatz sich von vornherein auf die Entwicklung von Begriffen und Taxonomien konzentriert und darin verhaftet bleibt. Mit diesen Begriffen kann er zwar durchaus auch Wandel "erfassen", aber eben nur "abbilden" oder "rekonstruieren", aber nicht wirklich erklären.[4] Was Parsons dabei macht, ist im Grunde nichts anderes als eine statische Betrachtung oder Darstellung von Entwicklungs- und Wandlungsprozessen, indem der Wandlungsprozess selber in eine Kette von Stadien zerlegt und der Reihe nach beschrieben wird. So geht es Parsons auch bei Prozessen des Wandels nicht wirklich darum, dessen Dynamik oder Kräfte zu erfassen, sondern nur darum, die Strukturmuster des Wandels selber zu *beschreiben*. So heißt es z. B., im Rahmen der strukturell-funktionalen Theorie könne man den Begriff des Systems gebrauchen, "auch ohne ein vollständiges Wissen der Gesetze zu besitzen, die die Prozesse innerhalb des Systems bestimmen" (Parsons 1951, S. 483).

Diesem Mangel könne man aber, heißt es weiter, dadurch abhelfen, dass man *Strukturkategorien* verwendet. Durch ihre Hilfe sei es möglich, "eine systematische und präzise Beschreibung der Zustände des Systems, der Variationen des Zustandes von Systemen über die Zeit und der Ähnlichkeiten und Differenzen zwischen verschiedenen Systemen zu leisten" (ebenda). Zentral ist in diesem Zusammenhang die folgende Feststellung:

> Es ist außerordentlich wichtig sich klar darüber zu sein, daß das, was wir in diesen zwei Kapiteln präsentiert haben, ein *Paradigma* darstellt und nicht eine Theorie, im üblichen Sinne dieses Begriffes als einem System von Gesetzen. Dies ist fast nur eine andere Art und Weise zu sagen, dass wir die Gesetze der Motivation als Mechanismen, nicht als Gesetze formulieren mussten (Parsons 1951, S. 485).

Ein *Paradigma*, so Parsons weiter, hat durchaus einen Bezug zu Gesetzen im üblichen Sinne; diese Gesetze sind aber, bezogen auf die Komplexität der empirischen Welt, fragmentarisch und unvollständig. Das Paradigma hilft, relevante Gesetze ausfindig zu machen und es stellt Regeln (canons) bereit, um Forschungsprobleme zu formulieren:

---

4   So sah z. B. Dahrendorf (1974, S. 242) das Hauptdefizit von Parsons' Theorie offenkundig nur in der mangelnden Erfassbarkeit des Wandels, da er einen Aufsatz über ihn mit folgendem Urteil abschließt: "Dass er (d. h. Parsons) in wesentlichen Punkte ergänzt werden wird, tut weder seiner inhaltlichen Formulierung noch vor allem seiner Intention Abbruch. Seit Parsons ist die Soziologie dem Status einer reifen Wissenschaft näher als je zuvor".

> Insoweit als ein Paradigma nicht direkt Wissen über Gesetze beinhaltet, stellt es einen Satz von Regeln für die Formulierung von Problemen dar und zwar derart, daß sichergestellt wird, daß die Antworten Fragen von allgemeinerer Bedeutung betreffen, weil sie sich auf Beziehungen zwischen den fundamentalen Variablen des Systems beziehen (Parsons 1951, S. 485f.).

Dieser Aussage könnte man im Prinzip wohl zustimmen; es kann durchaus als sinnvoll erscheinen, ein allgemeines Begriffsschema zu besitzen, das einem hilft, die Vielfalt der empirischen Realität bzw. unserer Beobachtungen von ihr zu ordnen. Ganz ähnlich wie Weber argumentiert auch Parsons, dass es problematisch wäre, irgendwelche allgemeinen Aussagen über die Zusammenhänge zwischen materiellen, ökonomischen und Interessenfaktoren auf der einen Seite und ideellen und kulturellen Faktoren auf der anderen Seite zu machen:

> Eine allgemeine Theorie über die Priorität bestimmter Faktoren im sozialen Wandel würde, beim derzeitigen Stand des Wissens, die Frage der empirischen Interdependenz, die erst aufzuweisen ist, präjudizieren" (Parsons 1951, S. 494).[5]

Parsons vertritt mit seiner oben dargestellten "konstruktivistischen" Position – Kodifikation des Wissens als Hauptziel der Theoriebildung – eine Haltung, die kausale Erklärungen überhaupt nicht als (zentrale) Aufgabe der "allgemeinen Theorie" definiert. Meine These lautet, dass er sich damit auf ein Terrain begibt, das empirisch unfruchtbar und wissenschaftstheoretisch unbefriedigend bleiben muss. Tatsächlich hält er sich in seinen eigenen inhaltlichen Studien keineswegs an diese Beschränkung. Was diese Arbeiten charakterisiert, ist nicht eine systematische Verbindung, sondern eine kontinuierliche *Vermischung* von historischer und empirischer Beschreibung, funktional-evolutionistischer Deutung und kausaler Erklärung sozialer Sachverhalte. Bevor wir auf eine nähere Analyse von Parsons' eigenen Schriften eingehen, sollen diese unterschiedlichen Erklärungstypen kurz dargestellt werden.

Kurzcharakterisierung der kausalen, funktionalen und historisch-beschreibenden Erklärung

Vergegenwärtigen wir uns hier zunächst, was mit diesen drei Typen von Erklärung gemeint ist. Im Anschluss an Stinchcombe (1986) und andere möchte ich sie folgendermaßen definieren:

---

5 Viele dieser Kritikpunkte an Parsons – die unilineare Evolutionstheorie, der Mangel an eigener Forschung usw. – sind schon sehr klar in der scharfen Kritik des Kulturanthropologen Franz Boas an den amerikanischen Evolutionstheoretikern seiner Zeit formuliert worden (vgl. dazu die umfassende Grazer Diplomarbeit von Bernd Weiler 1997).

(1) Eine *kausale Erklärung* oder ein *kausales Gesetz* besteht in einer Aussage, die behauptet, dass es Kontexte gibt, in denen der Wandel im Wert einer Variable mit dem Wandel des Wertes in einer anderen Variable zusammenhängt, wobei die Veränderung des Wertes der einen Variable die Veränderung in der anderen Variable verursacht, ohne dass sich irgendeine andere Variable in diesem Kontext verändert (Stinchcombe 1986, S. 31).

(2) Eine *funktionale Erklärung* kann man in zweierlei Weise interpretieren.

a) Die grundlegende Bedeutung einer "Funktion", wie der Begriff auch in der Mathematik verwendet wird, besteht darin, dass es eine *Beziehung* zwischen zwei Variablen gibt, wie es die Basisformel y=f(x) zum Ausdruck bringt. Es wird nichts darüber ausgesagt, warum die Beziehung zustande kommt. In der quantitativen Sozialforschung unterscheidet man hier seit Lazarsfeld zwischen Scheinkorrelation und "echten" Korrelationen, wie Regressions- oder Pfadkoeffizienten, die eine kausale Beziehung darstellen. Dass in kleinen Orten mehr Kinder zur Welt kommen, dort aber auch mehr Störche zu finden sind, kann zwar statistisch signifikant zusammenhängen, stellt aber keine kausale Beziehung dar. Eine kausale Beziehung könnte bestehen zwischen Ortsgröße und familienbezogenen Werthaltungen einerseits, Kinderzahl andererseits; ebenso zwischen Ortsgröße und Vorkommen von Störchen.

Nun scheint mir, dass Parsons und andere Funktionalisten häufig schon auf dieser Ebene einen Fehlschuss begehen, indem vom bloßen Existieren eines Zusammenhangs zwischen zwei Phänomenen auf eine kausale Beziehung zwischen ihnen geschlossen wird. (Beispiele für Parsons werde ich im folgenden geben.) Diese Vermischung haben schon Durkheim und Weber in aller Schärfe kritisiert. So betont Durkheim in seiner Studie über die *Arbeitsteilung*, dass die Funktion der organischen Arbeitsteilung – Verstärkung der Interdependenz und Solidarität zwischen den Menschen auf einer höheren Stufenleiter – keineswegs zu verwechseln sei mit den Ursachen ihrer Entstehung. Die Entstehungsursache sei vielmehr der Kampf um Erwerbschancen, der – bei steigender Bevölkerungsdichte – zu einem Druck dahingehend führt, sich beruflich zu spezialisieren, neue Nischen für Erwerbsmöglichkeiten ausfindig zu machen.

Die Feststellung von funktionalen Zusammenhängen dieser Art mag auch sozialwissenschaftlich durchaus relevant sein, sie kann jedoch allenfalls als Ansatzpunkt für weitergehende Forschungen dienen.

b) Eine zweite, komplexere Interpretation einer funktionalen Erklärung gibt Stinchcombe (1968, S. 88ff.). Demnach kann man sagen, eine funktionale Erklärung bestehe in folgenden Schritten: (1) es gibt einen homöostatischen Prozess H, einen gewissen Zustand einer Variable, der zu einer gewissen Stabilität tendiert, obwohl es Kräfte gibt, die dazu tendieren, ihn zu verändern; (2) es gibt eine gewisse Struktur oder Verhaltensweisen S mit einer kausalen Wirkung auf H; S tendiert dazu, H aufrechtzuerhalten; (3) es gibt des weiteren noch andere kausale Faktoren, Prozesse oder Spannungen, die dazu tendieren, H zu unterminieren; würde H von selber bestehen bleiben, wäre keine Struktur S notwendig, H aufrechtzuerhalten (so gibt es kaum grüne Bewegungen auf dem Lande); (4) es gibt kausale Prozesse (wie Evolution, Wettbewerb, Belohnungen durch andere), die S darin bestärken, H aufrechtzuerhalten. Zusammenfassend: der homöostatische Prozess H wird tendenziell gestört durch die intervenierenden Faktoren T; als Ausgleich dazu wirken die Faktoren oder Prozesse S daraufhin, H aufrechtzuerhalten. Die folgende Grafik stellt diesen Zusammenhang anschaulich dar:

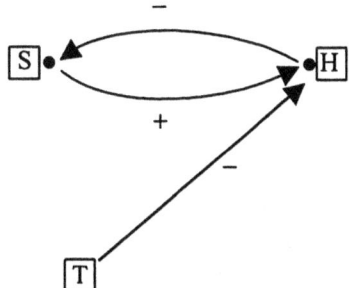

Aus diesem Modell kann man z. B. folgende Aussagen ableiten:
- Wenn T (Störungen oder Spannungen des Gleichgewichtszustands) zunimmt, führt die Gefahr einer Veränderung in H dazu, dass die Kausalfaktoren S eine stärkere Wirksamkeit entfalten. Wenn die objektive Unsicherheit in einer Gesellschaft steigt (T), steigt die kollektive Angst der Gesellschaftsmitglieder (H); um diese wieder zu reduzieren, nehmen magische Praktiken (S) zu.
- Ist T hoch oder variiert es, bleibt H jedoch konstant, so ist anzunehmen, dass eine kompensierende Kraft S wirksam ist, die H auf dem gleichen Niveau hält.
- Wird eine Struktur durch einen unbekannten Selektionsprozess, der von H ausgeht, erhalten, so ist zu erwarten, dass die Struktur stabil bleiben wird, auch wenn Spannungen bestehen. Die Menschen können oft Erklärungen dafür geben, die weder mit H noch T zusammenhängen.
- Umgekehrt kann man sagen: Besteht eine selektive Kausalbeziehung zwischen H und S, sodass bestimmte S's selegiert oder verstärkt werden, um H zu erhalten, so werden jene S eher funktional sein, die zur Erhaltung von H beitragen.

All diese Aussagen scheinen sozialwissenschaftlich durchaus sinnvoll zu sein. Der entscheidende Punkt liegt jedoch darin, dass die funktionale Erklärung hier letztlich auf kausale Erklärungen rekurriert. Die funktionale Perspektive gibt eine hilfreiche Anleitung dazu, wo man nach kausalen Prinzipien suchen muss. Entscheidend ist jedoch: auch hier muss man die kausalen Zusammenhänge dann eigens und getrennt von der funktionalen Erklärung empirisch untersuchen und überprüfen. So ist z. B. auch die marxistische Theorie voll von funktionalistischen Erklärungen, die kausale Elemente zwar implizieren, diese jedoch nicht wirklich spezifizieren und empirisch überprüfen. Dies gilt für alle Aussagen die behaupten, bestimmte Institutionen seien funktional für das Überleben des Kapitalismus, wie etwa das höhere Bildungswesen, die hohen Rüstungsausgaben usw. Es kann durchaus sein, dass die modernen Universitäten durch ihre Forcierung von technischem Fortschritt, systembejahenden Ideologien usw. "im Interesse" der Mächtigen, des Kapitals usw. wirken. Ob dies tatsächlich der Fall ist, wäre aber jeweils erst nachzuweisen, z. B. durch die Analyse ihrer Gründer, ihrer Ziele und Organisationsformen, der Absichten und des Einflusses ihrer Träger usw.

(3) Bei einer *historisch-beschreibenden Erklärung* würde ich hier ebenfalls zwei Varianten unterscheiden.[6]

(a) Wieder Stinchcombe (1968, S. 103ff.) folgend, kann man eine *historisierende Erklärung* durch die Annahme charakterisieren, dass ein Faktor, der in einer früheren Epoche einen Effekt anderer Ursachen darstellte, in einer späteren Epoche selber zur Ursache für andere Effekte wird. Ein trivialer Fall wäre der Familienstand: ein Mann ist in einem bestimmten Jahr deshalb mit seiner Frau verheiratet, weil er es bereits im vorhergegangenen Jahr war. In der Demographie gibt es viele weniger triviale Beispiele: die Anzahl der Heiraten in einem Jahr hängt ab von der Geburtenzahl ca. 25 Jahre vorher; die Zahl der Scheidungen in einem Jahr von der Zahl der Heiraten vor wenigen Jahren. Effekte ähnlicher Art sind wohl meist gemeint, wenn man in soziologischen Untersuchungen liest, dass bestimmte Aspekte einer Gesellschaft nur durch historische Charakteristika dieser Gesellschaft erklärt werden könnten. Erklärungen – oder besser: Verweise – dieser Art sind durchaus sinnvoll; sie erfordern jedoch selber noch eine systematisch-soziologische Erklärung.[7]

(b) Eine andere Form könnte man als *historisch-narrative Erklärung* bezeichnen. Diese findet sich vor allem bei den Historikern, vielleicht in ähnlicher Form auch bei qualitativ arbeitenden Sozialforschern, Anthropologen usw. Hier wird

---

[6] Vgl. dazu die umfassende und sehr klare Arbeit von Chris Lorenz (1997), die mir erst nach Abschluss dieses Manuskripts bekannt wurde.

[7] Ich habe diese Problematik auch kurz diskutiert am Beispiel der Erklärung der Unterschiede der Organisationsstrukturen deutscher und französischer Betriebe und die "Erklärung" von Maurice et al. (1980) als unzureichend kritisiert, die diesen Unterschied mit dem inhaltsleeren Begriff eines "gesellschaftlich-kulturellen Effekts" zu erfassen versuchten.

ein bestimmtes historisches Ereignis oder ein Ablauf sehr detailliert, faktenreich und anschaulich beschrieben und damit quasi "plausibel" gemacht. In der Anthropologie hat Clifford Geertz mit dem Konzept der *"dichten Beschreibung"* eine ähnliche Strategie vorgeschlagen. Die Absicht von Ansätzen dieser Art liegt weniger darin, spezifische kausale Beziehungen zwischen ganz bestimmten Variablen herauszuarbeiten, als die Fülle möglicher Ursachen und Effekte möglichst umfassend, plastisch und nachvollziehbar darzustellen. Bestimmte mögliche Ursachen werden dabei vielleicht auch dramatisierend hervorgehoben, ohne dass sie damit notwendig verabsolutiert würden. Diese Form der Analyse erscheint durchaus sinnvoll; jedoch kann auch sie nur als ein erster Schritt oder als Ergänzung zu einer strengen soziologisch-kausalen Betrachtung gesehen werden.

Wir können damit zurückkommen auf die These, dass Parsons in seinen Arbeiten diese drei Formen von Erklärung nicht ausreichend auseinanderhält.

Die Vermischung von historisch-beschreibender Erklärung, funktionaler Deutung und kausaler Erklärung bei Parsons

Die fortlaufende Verwischung zwischen historisch-soziologischer Beschreibung, funktionaler Deutung und kausaler Analyse lässt sich als das typische Denk- und Argumentationsmuster von Parsons schlechthin bezeichnen.[8] Diese Argumentationsfigur sieht meist so aus, dass ein sehr umfassender, komplexer historisch-kultureller Zusammenhang zunächst beschreibend dargestellt wird, dann aber zugleich als "funktional notwendig" interpretiert und, gewissermaßen unter der Hand, schließlich auch als kausal erklärt suggeriert wird. Auf allen drei Stufen der Argumentation werden sehr vage Begriffe hinsichtlich der Aspekte der Beschreibung, der funktionalen Deutung und der kausalen Erklärung des jeweiligen Sachverhaltes verwendet, sodass es schwerfällt bzw. nachgerade unmöglich ist, dem Autor wirkliche "Fehler" nachzuweisen.[9] Sehr treffend hat der Schweizer Soziologe (heute Journalist) Victor Willi in seiner umfassenden Studie über *Grundlagen einer*

---

8 Dass die zentrale Aufgabe der empirischen Forschung darin besteht, die Bedeutung ganz spezifischer Zusammenhänge zu erfassen und von allen anderen möglichen Effekten zu isolieren, scheint Parsons gar nicht erkannt zu haben (vgl. dazu schon Gruppe 1914, S. 47 ff. gegen die Parsons in manchem verwandte Denkweise von Hegel).

9 Man könnte auch behaupten, dass auch viele zentrale wissenschaftstheoretische Begriffe bei Parsons (wie "Konstruktivismus", "analytische Perspektive" usw.) schon rein sprachlich gesehen unklar sind; für ihn gilt aus dieser Sicht genau die gleiche Kritik, die Gruppe (1914, S. 45 ff.) gegen Hegel gerichtet hat.

empirischen Soziologie der Werte und Wertsysteme auf diese Schwäche von Parsons hingewiesen:

> Weil er weder nur von der Theorie noch nur von der Wirklichkeit verschiedenartiger Wertsysteme ausgeht und nicht zur wirklich vorhandenen weitgehenden Sinn-Notwendigkeit tieferliegender Kulturelemente vorstößt, scheint Parsons, der bewußt die Kluft zwischen Wirklichkeit und Spekulation überbrücken möchte, bei seiner Typologie unbewußt gleichsam zwischen zwei Stühle zu fallen. Sie dient als *Basis weder für eine theoretisch saubere Modelltypologie noch für einen faktisch sauberen Überblick der Wirklichkeit.* Sie will zu viel und erreicht deshalb wenig (Willi 1966, S. 247).

Alexander (1984, S. 8ff.) hat also, ebenso wie Lidz (1986), den ich bereits oben zitiert habe, durchaus zu Recht argumentiert, Parsons habe sehr wohl großes Interesse an empirischer Forschung gehabt und es stimmt auch, dass seine theoretischen Arbeiten häufig Bezüge zu empirischen Befunden aufweisen und manche seiner meist diskutierten Arbeiten direkt empirische Fragen betrafen (so etwa seine medizinsoziologischen Aufsätze). Was Parsons aber definitiv von Durkheim und Weber – wie von *jedem* anderen großen Theoretiker, so würde ich behaupten – unterscheidet, ist die Tatsache, dass er selber nie eine eigene gründliche empirische Arbeit durchführte.[10] Alexander, der dies zugibt, sieht in dieser "postpositivistischen" Haltung aber sogar eine Stärke: sie habe es Parsons ermöglicht, sich dafür umso systematischer mit der spezifischen und anspruchsvollen Arbeit der Theoriebildung zu befassen.

Wenn man diese These auch nicht grundsätzlich ablehnen kann, muss man im Falle einer sozialwissenschaftlichen Theorie im Allgemeinen und der Arbeiten von Parsons im Besonderen doch ein großes Fragezeichen dahinter setzen. Ganz allgemein schreibt der Wissenschaftstheoretiker Mario Bunge (1996, S. Xii) in seinem neuen Werk *Finding Philosophy in Social Science*, ein Philosoph der Sozialwissenschaften müsse sehr gut mit der neuesten sozialwissenschaftlichen Literatur vertraut sein, ja er sollte idealerweise selber Forschungen durchgeführt haben. Er selber habe dies gemacht – und er teile im übrigen auch Einsteins Verachtung für alle Formen "intellektueller Akrobatik", die nur nützlich sei für akademische Karrieren.

Im konkreten Falle von Parsons erscheint mir die Abstinenz von empirischer Forschung deshalb als besonders problematisch, weil sie bei ihm – wie im folgenden detailliert belegt werden wird – vielfach einhergeht mit einer wissenschaftlich untragbaren Sorglosigkeit im Umgang mit empirischen Befunden. Die These von Ale-

---

[10] Lidz (1986) schreibt dazu, dass Parsons drei Anläufe nahm, selber an empirischen Projekten mitzuarbeiten (das erste betraf die Arzt-Patient-Beziehung, das zweite soziale Mobilität, das dritte die amerikanische Universität). Das Resultat war in allen Fällen dasselbe: es entstanden innovative theoretische Essays und Interpretationen, die empirischen Befunde wurden jedoch nie so detailliert ausgearbeitet, wie es geplant gewesen war; Parsons zog sich meist bald aus dieser Arbeit zurück (Lidz 1986, S. 168ff.).

xander (1984, S. 10), Parsons sei dem Ideal wissenschaftlicher Objektivität und Wertfreiheit auch bei seiner Verwendung empirischer Befunde stets treu geblieben, kann ich daher nicht zustimmen.

Das Beispiel der "Saatbett"-Gesellschaften Israel und Griechenland

Als Beleg für meine These, dass Parsons immer wieder Beschreibung, Analyse und Bewertung vermengt, ein Beispiel aus dem Büchlein *Gesellschaften. Evolutionäre und komparative Perspektiven*, in dem Parsons die Rolle der beiden "Saatbett"[11]-Gesellschaften Israel und Griechenland für die soziokulturelle Evolution der Menschheit beschreibt. Er geht hier aus von der folgenden allgemeinen These: "Je niedriger die sozio-kulturelle Evolution eines Systems, desto koextensiver und weniger unabhängig sind seine gesellschaftlichen und kulturellen Systeme in empirischer Hinsicht" (Parsons 1975, S. 149). Schon dieser Satz ist typisch für die Vermengung von theoretisch-analytischen Aussagen und empirischen Behauptungen. Als "analytische" Aussage (im diffusen Sinne, wie Parsons selbst diesen Begriff gebraucht) ist dieser Satz nichts als eine Wiederholung seiner generellen These über den Prozess der soziokulturellen Evolution, den er im gleichen Band als Fortschreiten von "niedrigeren" zu "höheren" Formen der sozialen Differenzierung definiert hat:

> Wenn die Differenzierung ein ausgeglichenes, höher entwickeltes System erreichen soll, dann muss jede sich neu differenzierende Substruktur (...) eine verbesserte Anpassungsfähigkeit zur Erfüllung ihrer *primären* Funktion im Vergleich zur Erfüllung *dieser* Funktion innerhalb der vorhergehenden, diffuseren Struktur aufweisen (Parsons 1975, S. 40; Hervorhebungen im Original).

So stellt die Ausdifferenzierung von eigenen Produktionsstätten – Fabriken, Büros usw. – eine evolutionäre Höherentwicklung dar, weil das Produzieren dadurch effizienter erfolgen kann als vorher im Haushalt, wo es mit privat-familiären Funktionen vermischt war. Es ist dies der klassische funktionalistische Topos, wie wir ihn schon seit Herbert Spencer kennen. Die begriffliche Schlampigkeit von Parsons kommt deutlich zum Ausdruck im letzten Teil des weiter oben zitierten Satzes "... desto unabhängiger sind seine gesellschaftlichen und kulturellen Systeme *in empirischer Hinsicht*": Hier wird suggeriert, dass die *analytische* Bestimmung der Bezie-

---

[11] Im Deutschen wäre auch der Begriff "Saatbeetgesellschaften" anwendbar; ich halte mich hier an den in der deutschen Parsons-Übersetzung verwendeten Begriff.

hung zwischen Evolutionsniveau und Differenzierungsgrad einer Gesellschaft eben nicht nur "analytischen" Charakter hat, sondern auch empirisch vorfindlich ist!

Kommen wir zurück zur Darstellung und Interpretation der Rolle der Saatbett-Gesellschaften Israel und Griechenland. Zunächst wird festgestellt, dass von den großen Religionen der Erde zwar der Buddhismus die "tiefgreifendsten Wirkungen" außerhalb seiner eigenen Entstehungsgesellschaft zeigte; da er jedoch "nicht zur Modernität führte, und da er für die westliche Gesellschaft kaum fundamentale Bedeutung gewann, haben wir ihn nicht ausführlich diskutiert" (Parsons 1975, S. 149). Auch diese Entscheidung ist charakteristisch: Parsons entschließt sich deshalb, ein religiöses System nicht weiter zu behandeln, weil es historisch-empirisch nicht so folgenreich war wie andere. Also, nicht sein theoretisch-analytisches Kriterium ist entscheidend dafür, ob eine "Variable" – wie Religion – relevant ist oder nicht, sondern allein das empirische Faktum, ob sie historisch für den Westen folgenreich wurde oder nicht. Dies ist ein klassisches Beispiel für eine post-hoc "Erklärung", die jedoch in Wirklichkeit diese Bezeichnung nicht verdient. Diese Form der "Erklärung" steht offenkundig auch im eindeutigen Widerspruch zu dem ansonsten – zumindest verbal immer wieder betonten - Prinzip Parsons', soziologische Analyse streng nach "analytischen" Gesichtspunkten durchzuführen.

Das Faktum, dass gerade die Kultur der beiden kleinen, politisch bedeutungslosen Gesellschaften Israel und Griechenland historisch so folgenreich wurde, wirft laut Parsons zwei Probleme auf: Zum einen das Problem der *Bedingungen für die Entstehung* dieser kulturellen Neuerungen, zum anderen das Problem ihrer *Diffusion* (d. h. ihrer Verbreitung in Gebiete und Gesellschaften, die weit entfernt von ihrem Ursprung liegen) und ihrer tiefgreifenden Folgewirkungen für diese Gesellschaften. Dazu stellt er fest:

> Hinsichtlich des ersteren Problems halten wir diese kulturellen Neuerungen für so radikal, daß deren Träger sie unmöglich auf dem weiten Territorium und gegen die verschiedenen begründeten Interessen der großen 'Imperien' jener Zeit hätten durchsetzen können. Diese Prozesse mussten in kleinen Gesellschaften mit einem ungewöhnlichen Maß an Unabhängigkeit stattfinden. Außerdem bedingten diese Neuerungen in beiden Fällen notwendig, daß jeweils unter der Führung der wichtigsten Schichten eine Differenzierung der *Gesellschaft als ganzer* von den übrigen, ihnen nahe stehenden Gesellschaften eintrat. Damit entstand ein neuer *Gesellschaftstypus*, nicht bloß ein neues Subsystem innerhalb eines bereits existenten Typus (Parsons 1975, S. 150; Hervorhebung im Original).

Die erste terminologische Schlampigkeit in dieser Passage: Parsons spricht davon, man müsse die gesellschaftlichen Bedingungen definieren, die diese kulturellen Neuerungen in Israel und Griechenland ermöglichten. Was er damit meint, ist aber offensichtlich nicht eine *Definition*, sondern die Bestimmung "unabhängiger Variablen", also eine Spezifikation eines *kausalen Zusammenhangs*, eine Hypothese!

Er gibt dann auch unter der Hand eine kausale Erklärung in diesem Sinne, wenn er argumentiert, radikale Neuerungen wären nicht durchsetzbar auf einem "weiten

Territorium" und gegen die "herrschenden Interessen" in einer Großmacht – welche Interessen dies sein könnten, wird nicht gesagt. Genau genommen hat er damit aber nur vage angedeutet, warum diese Neuerungen in den Großstaaten *nicht* erfolgt sind, aber noch lange nicht gesagt, warum sie in Israel und Griechenland *schon* erfolgt sind! Der Hinweis auf die Notwendigkeit der "Kleinheit" eines Territoriums als Voraussetzung für die Durchsetzung radikaler religiöser Neuerungen erscheint mir eher als trivial: eine radikale Neuerung, die von einem Religionsstifter und seinen Anhängern ausgeht, kann zunächst ja nicht anders erfolgen als in einem kleinen Territorium – wie sollte sie je zugleich auf mehreren Orten eines riesigen Reiches stattfinden oder wie könnte sie sofort in alle Regionen eines solchen Reiches diffundieren?

Schließlich ist zu fragen, ob die historische Evidenz der These von Parsons tatsächlich entspricht. Wenn man auch den Buddhismus und den Konfuzianismus als revolutionäre kulturelle Neuerungen betrachtet, konnten solche sehr wohl in großen Reichen entstehen. Ein anderes Beispiel ist das *Recht*: von diesem gilt allgemein, dass es im Römischen Reich seine entscheidende erste Ausgestaltung erfuhr; die Tatsache, dass dieses Reich sich immer mehr ausdehnte und immer neue Völker unter römische Herrschaft gebracht wurden, machte es notwendig, für diese auch neue staatsrechtliche Kategorien zu entwickeln. Ein erstrangiger Kenner des Römischen Rechts (Stein 1996, S. 11f.) spricht hier von einer tausendjährigen ungebrochenen Tradition einer Rechtsentwicklung, in deren Verlauf das Recht bestimmte Züge annahm, die seinen Charakter für die Zukunft prägten: "Während dieser 1000 Jahre... entwickelte sich Rom von einem kleinen Stadtstaat zum Weltreich. Seine Verfassung wandelte sich von der Monarchie zur Republik und dann ... zum Kaiserreich. Parallel dazu wurde das Recht den Erfordernissen der sich stets wandelnden sozialen Lage angepaßt". Auch die von Anfang an bestehenden, spezifischen Verfahren der Rechtsfindung und -sprechung und die Entwicklung professionalisierter Rechtsberufe hatten einen wesentlichen Anteil daran, dass das Römische Recht bis zum Ende des Altertums und dann wieder ab dem späten Mittelalter die Rechtsentwicklung in ganz Europa (für Deutschland vgl. dazu Hattenauer 1980, S. 1ff.) und darüber hinaus entscheidend prägen konnte (und heute wieder als Modell für Rechtsinterpretation in der EU gelten kann). Trotzdem kann man sagen, dass die Entwicklung der Großmacht Rom eine ausschlaggebende Ursache zu seiner Ausdifferenzierung war. Für wertvolle Hinweise zu dieser Problematik danke ich Peter Koller (Graz).

In typisch Parsonsscher Diffusität verbleibt auch der zweite Teil der oben zitierten "Erklärung", wenn es heißt, diese Neuerungen "bedingten notwendig", dass diese Gesellschaften als ganze ungewöhnlich unabhängig sein mussten.

Betrachtet man die faktisch-historische Evidenz, so erweisen sich fast alle diese Behauptungen als fragwürdig. Durch wie viele Perioden seiner Geschichte war der Staat oder das Volk Israel wirklich "außerordentlich unabhängig"? Warum konnte sich das Christentum, nach jahrhundertlangen Verfolgungen, letztlich doch (im Jahre 380) als Staatsreligion im riesigen Römischen Reich durchsetzen? Hatten sich "die Interessen" in dieser Großmacht nun wesentlich verändert? Wurde dieses Reich bzw. diese Gesellschaft nun selber ein "anderer Gesellschaftstyp", ähnlich dem alten Israel oder Griechenland?

Man kann die Strategie Parsons' hier wie an vielen anderen Stellen auf einen recht einfachen Nenner bringen. Sie besteht in nichts anderem als einem recht leicht durchschaubaren *Induktivismus*: zuerst wird die faktisch abgelaufene, historisch-kulturelle Entwicklung betrachtet, und sodann werden die scheinbar "wesentlichen" Kausalfaktoren herausgehoben, die zu dieser Entwicklung geführt haben. Fast wörtlich spricht Parsons dieses Prinzip in der Folge der oben zitierten Passage aus:

> Eingedenk dieser Erwägungen wollen wir uns nun einen gewissen Überblick über die entscheidenden Tatsachen verschaffen und dann versuchen, *jene Faktoren* zu formulieren, die beiden Beispielen dieses Typus der Evolution gemeinsam waren. Es geht uns dabei nicht primär um den besonderen kulturellen Beitrag jeder dieser Gesellschaften und dessen spezifische Bedeutung für die folgende Evolution ... Hier geht es uns in erster Linie *um das Wesen jenes Prozesses*, durch den so radikale Neuerungen entstehen ... (Parsons 1975, S. 150f.; Hervorhebung M.H.).

Es legen sich noch zwei weitere Bemerkungen zu diesem Zitat nahe. Die erste Bemerkung: durch die Ausklammerung der *inhaltlichen Bedeutung* des Judentums bzw. Christentums und der hellenischen Zivilisation vergibt sich Parsons die zentrale, soziologisch interessante Frage, die bekanntlich Max Weber zu seiner bahnbrechenden Studie über den Protestantismus und den Geist des Kapitalismus inspiriert hat. Auch die asketischen, protestantischen Sekten, der Calvinismus, Puritanismus usw. entwickelten sich zuerst in kleinen Gemeinschaften und Stadtstaaten. Aber nicht dies war nach Weber der entscheidende Faktor für ihre kulturelle Breitenwirkung, sondern der *Inhalt ihrer Lehren* mit seiner völlig neuartigen Betonung der individuellen Verantwortlichkeit eines Gläubigen für sein Seelenheil (Weber 1905, 1988a).

Die zweite Bemerkung: mit dem Hinweis auf "das Wesen jenes Prozesses" begibt sich Parsons auf ein philosophisch-ontologisches Territorium, auf dem sich vielleicht trefflich diskutieren und streiten lässt[12], von dem jedoch schwerlich zu sehen ist, dass es für eine Soziologie als Wirklichkeitswissenschaft irgendwelche Bedeutung besitzt.

---

12 "Wesensnotwendig ist", etwa nach Nicolai Hartmann, "das, was einer Sache auf Grund ihrer idealen Struktur zukommt" (Stegmüller 1960, S. 1259). Eine große Bedeutung spielt die Vorstellung der "Wesenschau" in der Husserlschen Phänomenologie, an die wiederum Luhmann anknüpft. Auch hier zeigt sich wieder die sehr enge geistige Verwandtschaft zwischen Parsons und Luhmann (die letzterer eher relativiert wissen möchte).

Resümee

Ziel meines Beitrags war es, die Verwendung dreier unterschiedlicher Typen von Erklärung bei Parsons darzustellen. Ich versuchte die These zu belegen, dass bei Parsons alle drei grundlegenden Erklärungstypen – historisch-beschreibende, funktionale und kausale Erklärung – vorliegen, dass er diese jedoch in einer oft undurchschaubaren und unhaltbaren Weise vermischt. Daraus ergibt sich die Stärke, aber auch die Schwäche vieler seiner Arbeiten: ihre Stärke liegt darin, dass sehr viel empirisches Wissen verarbeitet und synthesisiert wird; ihre Schwäche liegt darin, dass durch die Vermischung der unterschiedlichen Erklärungsebenen Zusammenhänge vielfach suggeriert werden, die in Wirklichkeit so nicht existieren.

Um Parsons' Theorie produktiv aufzunehmen und weiterzuführen, wäre meiner Meinung nach unabdingbar notwendig:

a) Klar hervorzuheben, dass die strukturell-funktionale Systemtheorie eben nur funktionale Erklärungen liefern kann, welche nicht mehr als hypothetisch-forschungsleitenden Charakter haben können.

b) Diese morphologisch-statistische Betrachtungsweise immer und gleichzeitig zu ergänzen durch die kausal-erklärende, dynamisch-historische Perspektive.

Erklärungen in Parsons' Bezugsrahmen würden damit meiner Meinung nach weniger umfassend, aber wissenschaftstheoretisch einwandfreier und soziologisch gehaltvoller.

Literatur

Alexander, Jeffrey (1984): Theoretical Logic in Sociology, vol. 4: The Modern Reconstruction of Classical Thought: Talcott Parsons. London/Melbourne/Henley: Routledge & Kegan Paul.

Bunge, Mario (1996): Finding Philosophy in Social Science. New Haven/London: Yale University Press.

Dahrendorf, Ralf (1974): Pfade aus Utopia. Arbeiten zur Theorie und Methode der Soziologie. Gesammelte Abhandlungen I. München: Piper.

Gerhardt, Uta (1996): "Talcott Parsons and the Transformation of German Society at the End of World War II". European Sociological Review 12, S. 303-325.

Gouldner, Alwin W. (1974): Die westliche Soziologie in der Krise. 2 Bde. Reinbek: Rowohlt.

Gruppe, O.F. (1914): Philosophische Werke. I. Antäus. München: Georg Müller.

Habermas, Jürgen (1981): Theorie des kommunikativen Handelns. Band I: Handlungsrationalität und gesellschaftliche Rationalisierung, Band II: Zur Kritik der funktionalistischen Vernunft. Frankfurt a.M.: Suhrkamp.

Haller, Max (1999): Soziologische Theorie in systematisch-kritischen Vergleich. Leverkusen: Leske + Budrich (UTB 2074).

Hartfiel, Günter / Hillmann, Karl-Heinz (1982): Wörterbuch der Soziologie. Stuttgart: Krämer.

Hattenauer, Hans (1980²): Die geistesgeschichtlichen Grundlagen des deutschen Rechts. Zwischen Hierarchie und Demokratie – Eine Einführung. Heidelberg/Karlsruhe: C.F. Müller Juristischer Verlag.
Jensen, Stefan (1976): "Einleitung". In: Talcott Parsons, Zur Theorie sozialer Systeme. S. 9-67.
Jensen, Stefan (1984): "Aspekte der Medien-Theorie: Welche Funktion haben Medien in Handlungssystemen". Zeitschrift für Soziologie 13, S. 145-164.
Kellermann, Paul (1967): Kritik einer Soziologie der Ordnung. Organismus und System bei Comte, Spencer und Parsons. Freiburg/Br.: Rombach.
Lidz, Victor M. (1986): "Parsons and Empirical Sociology". In: Samuel Z. Klausner / Victor M. Lidz (eds.), The Nationalization of the Social Sciences. Philadelphia: University of Pennsylvania Press, S. 141-182.
Lorenz, Chris (1997): Konstruktion der Vergangenheit. Eine Einführung in die Geschichtstheorie. Köln/Weimar/Wien: Böhlau.
Maurice, Marc et al. (1980): "Societal differences in organizing manufacturing units: A comparison of France, West Germany and Great Britain". Organization Studies 1, S. 59-86.
Mikl-Horke, Gertraude (1989): Soziologie, Historischer Kontext und soziologische Theorie-Entwürfe. München/Wien: Oldenbourg.
Parsons, Talcott (1951): The Social System. London: Routledge & Kegan Paul.
Parsons, Talcott (1972): Das System moderner Gesellschaften. München: Juventa (amerik. 1971).
Parsons, Talcott (1975): Gesellschaften. Evolutionäre und komparative Perspektiven. Frankfurt a.M.: Suhrkamp (amerik. 1966).
Parsons, Talcott (1976): Zur Theorie sozialer Systeme. Hrsg. von S. Jensen. Opladen: Westdeutscher Verlag.
Parsons, Talcott / Shils, Eduard (eds.) (1951): Toward a General Theory of Action. Cambridge, Mass.: Harward University Press.
Popper, Karl R. (1973): Objektive Erkenntnis. Ein evolutionärer Entwurf. Hamburg: Hoffmann und Campe.
Staubmann, Helmut (1995): Die Kommunikation von Gefühlen. Ein Beitrag zur Soziologie der Ästhetik auf der Grundlage von Parsons' Allgemeiner Theorie des Handelns. Berlin: Duncker & Humblot.
Stegmüller, Wolfgang (1960): Hauptströmungen der Gegenwartsphilosophie. Eine kritische Einführung. Stuttgart: Kröner.
Stein, Peter G. (1996): Römisches Recht und Europa. Die Geschichte einer Rechtskultur. Frankfurt a.M.: Fischer Taschenbuch.
Stinchcombe, Arthur (1968): Constructing Social Theories. New York etc.: Harcourt, Brace & World.
Turner, Jonathan H. (1994): "A General Theory of Motivation and Emotion in Human Interaction". Österreichische Zeitschrift für Soziologie 19, S. 20-35.
Weber, Max (1905): "Die protestantische Ethik und der 'Geist' des Kapitalismus". Teil I und II, Archiv für Sozialwissenschaft. 20. Band, S. 1-54, 21. Band, S. 1-110.
Weber, Max (1988a): Gesammelte Aufsätze zur Religionssoziologie. 2 Bde. Tübingen: Mohr.
Weiler, Bernd (1997): Die Kulturanthropologie von Franz Boas im ideengeschichtlichen und wissenssoziologischen Kontext. Diplomarbeit am Institut für Soziologie der Karl-Franzens-Universität Graz.
Willi, Victor J. (1966): Grundlagen einer empirischen Soziologie der Werte und Wertsysteme. Zürich: Orell Füssli.

Scarcity of Means and Solidarity of Values
The Theory of Social Action in Talcott Parsons' General Sociology
Bryan S. Turner

Introduction

Although the notion that social existence is characterised by scarcity of adequate means to satisfy wants was shared by writers as different as Malthus and Marshall, the role of scarcity in the social sciences has been somewhat neglected, partly because it has been taken for granted. The assumption about scarcity was fundamental to economics as a dismal science, but the continuity of the concept from Hobbes to Darwin has not been fully recognised. The contrast between the concepts of scarcity and solidarity is useful in understanding the development of sociology as a debate with economics. We can regard classical sociology as an extended critical debate with economics with respect to the rationality of economic action in a context of scarcity. While the analytical relationship between economics and sociology was fundamental to the development of classical sociology, particularly in the work of Marx, Weber and Simmel, it was also crucial to the evolution of the sociological theories of Talcott Parsons (Holton and Turner 1986). In this paper, in order to develop an interpretation of *The Structure of Social Action* (Parsons, 1937) one can propose, following Parsons' definition of "the economic element", a fundamental distinction between economics as a science of scarcity, based on a presumed conflict of the real interests of possessive individuals and sociology as a science of social solidarity, based on a presumed common-value integration. The etymology of the concept of "sociology" itself is constituted by the stem: *socius* or "friendship", namely the study of the conditions that make friendship possible. We can argue that sociology is the study of the social relations that constitute companionship through the emotional ties that are created by rituals. The word "companionship" is derived from *pan*, indicating the social bonds that flow from the sharing of bread in a common meal. In the development of European sociology, William Robertson Smith's studies of the role of sacrificial meals and religious feasts in his *Lectures on the Religion of the Semites* (Smith 1997) in 1889 played a formative role in the emergence of Emile Durkheim's analysis of social solidarity in *The Elementary Forms of the Religious Life* (Durkheim 1954). We can understand Parsons' sociology as an attempt to interpret the implications of Durkheim's sociology of religion for classical economics.

Economics is a dismal science. With respect to eating as a metaphor of sociality, economics has been concerned with the impact of famine and hardship on social relations, for example the necessity for queues. By contrast, sociology and anthropology have also been interested in the ritualistic structures of festivals, and in such phenomena as violence, excess and abundance. For sociology, any discussion of scarcity must also include an anthropology of abundance, namely the question of luxury. While economics explores the conditions of calculating exchange, sociology examines the solidarities that arise from and make possible social reciprocity in everyday life.

In Parsons' early treatment of the means-ends paradigm, sociology was understood to be concerned with the ends of action which are determined by values, and economics was classified as a science of means to the efficient achievement of ends for the satisfaction of wants. These disciplinary issues emerged early in the Amherst essays, in Parsons' articles on German sociology (Parsons 1929) and of course in *Structure* (Turner 1996). Parsons regarded economics as obviously the most advanced of the social sciences in its conceptual parsimony, its relevance to policy formation, its quantification of variables and its institutional power within the academy. Nevertheless, classical economics was flawed as a general theory of action in terms of what Parsons called "the utilitarian dilemma". In Parsons' treatment of the social sciences, sociology was identified as a critical commentary on the limitations of marginal utility theory as an explanation of voluntary action. The aim of *Structure* was to criticise various positivistic forms of utilitarianism and secondly to establish the claims of sociology to be a separate and authentic discipline within general action-systems theory.

There were in fact several stages in this intellectual development. In *Structure*, there was the notion of "the economic element" in which economising behaviour is concerned with rational choice, namely the selection of scarce means to satisfy needs, where the goals of action are multiple. In the Marshall Lectures at Cambridge (Swedberg1986), Parsons attempted a more systematic integration of the instrumental features of economic action and the normative elements of choice. He sought to establish in the Marshall Lectures the argument that economics is a special case of a more comprehensive social theory which is concerned to develop a general analytical approach to social systems – a theory which will be genuinely interdisciplinary, inclusive and general. In *Structure* Parsons criticised classical economics in terms of the utilitarian dilemma where the ends of action are random and an explanation of order is impossible, or ends are reduced to the environment in which case the sovereignty of the autonomous actor is compromised. In *The Social System* (Parsons 1951), Parsons had moved on from classical economics to develop an action-systems paradigm that was based on the famous AGIL combination. Whereas *Structure* was based on Alfred Marshall, his later economic sociology embraced Keynes's *General Theory*, which encouraged Parsons to believe that micro and macro economic theory could be integrated with sociology (Parsons and Smelser, 1956). Despite these intellectual changes, Parsons aim was to produce a general, integrated and coherent theory of action that would embrace all the social sciences as sciences of action.

To be more precise, the AGIL system does not embrace the full range of action sciences in the humanities and social sciences. We might note immediately that this schema appears to elide sociology and anthropology, to marginalise social psychology and to leave some unresolved questions about history. In addition, Parsons' sociology does not concern itself, generally speaking, with spatial questions and hence geography as a discipline does not find a place in AGIL. While spatial issues do not become theorized, time (as a scarce resource) is central to the unit act where there is some "delay" between need and its resolution. Action which economizes on time is a crucial feature of the "economic element" in general theories of the social system.

In retrospect, it appears to be clear that Parsons' attempt to produce a general theory based primarily on a reconciliation of economics and sociology was probably a failure (Holton 1991). Economics as a discipline is in many respects indifferent to the perspective and findings of sociology. Economics is in terms of institutional power far more successful than sociology and it is typically housed in university faculties separately from sociology. Sociologists have retained an interest in some aspects of rational choice theory, but continue to believe that, generally speaking, economics offers few solutions to mainstream sociological problems and issues. The emphasis on rational action and the neglect of nonrational elements in the unit act continues to separate and differentiate economics and sociology (Swedberg 1998).

Despite these difficulties, the contrast between scarcity and solidarity provides a useful overview of action-systems theory. If social existence is characterised by an irreducible scarcity, then there are profound problems around economic allocation of resources and the political management of conflicting interests in terms of decisions about distribution and re-distribution. Economics and politics are thus fundamental social sciences. For Weber, economics was the peaceful management of scarcity and politics involved the violent management of scarcity. However, the conflicts around scarce resources have to be resolved or at least managed, if Marxian class war, Malthusian famine and Darwinian struggles for survival are to be contained. For Parsons, common or shared values are crucial to the creation of social solidarity, and at the same time individuals have to be motivated to co-operate with each other in a social environment which they regard as legitimate. Parsons' sociology was directed towards an empirical understanding of how contemporary American society could avoid the class struggles of Europe through the successful development of values of regulated or institutionalised individualism. In this sense, America had successfully incorporated the ideals of citizenship, despite the enduring problems of the inclusion of the black community in civil society (Turner 1999a).

Value integration was not of course a sufficient explanation. As the AGIL system indicates, the integrative problems of society also require commitment and loyalty from social actors for the performance of collective tasks. In his mature work, Parsons came to integrate psychological studies of human commitment and loyalty into his earlier studies of economics, politics and sociology as an expression of the relationship between individual and society (Parsons et al 1955). The allocative/integrative and scarcity/solidarity themes remained fundamental to his view of the social sciences and the empirical problems of social systems. The AGIL subsystem analysis provides in principle a general framework for the analysis of the requirements of social systems.

The Parsonian Critique of Utilitarianism

Parsons' sociology closely followed the legacy of classical sociology and a critique of utilitarianism, specifically the assumptions relating to possessive individualism. *Structure* was overtly a systematic critique of utilitarian theories of economic action, and an attempt to lay the foundation for an autonomous discipline of sociology, interconnected closely with economics and politics. For Parsons, classical economic theory had to assume the random nature of the goals of action, because it remains largely silent about values. Furthermore, the notion of instrumental rationality cannot preclude the use of force and fraud in human societies as rational solutions to scarcity, and thus the instrumental assumptions about action cannot provide a satisfactory account of social order. Rational actors would turn reasonably to violence to achieve their goals in a context of scarcity. Generally speaking, economic science rarely considers the black economy as a contribution to gross domestic product.

Given the inability of economics to address the randomness of ends, there was therefore a permanent theoretical crisis in classical utilitarianism which was resolved by an appeal to a set of assumptions which were not explicable within the original rationalist assumptions. Classical economics could only solve its theoretical dilemmas by ad hoc assumptions. This analysis provides a clear illustration of Parsons' use of the "residual category" as a critical or deconstructive device. In economics, the residual devices included Marshall's questioning of the hedonistic assumptions of the notion of need in his discussion of real and artificial wants, Pareto's difficulties in managing "non-rational" action in the distinction between residues and ideology, Durkheim's difficulties with the theory of happiness with respect to the division of labour and the problem associated with values as social facts, and the inherent problems of defining rational and irrational action in Weber in relation to behaviour versus action (Sica 1988). In general, classical economics solved the problem of order by ad hoc and random theoretical solutions which involved appeals to the "hidden hand of history", shared "sentiments" and common wants. The evolution of sociology can be measured in terms of its ability to grasp and to describe such non-rational elements of action.

In the history of social science, the theoretical crisis in utilitarianism was resolved by various forms of radical positivism which either explained action by reference to environmental features or hereditary. In fact utilitarianism had great difficulty in explaining rationality at all. If rational men[1] are driven by hedonistic desires to satisfy their wants in an environment of scarcity, how and why do they act irrationally? Given inadequate means, why will men allocate scarce resources to luxuries? Some aspects of these problems of irrationality are outlined in the section on "taste" towards the conclusion of *Structure* where Parsons provides a discussion of the problem of habitual action. Irrationality within a paradigm of radical positivism has to be explained either in terms of faulty psychology, or lack of sovereignty, or inadequate information about the market. Some set of circumstances has to inhibit the "natural" exercise of egoistic reason to explain why interest does not rationally determine the selection of means. There is a parallel problem in Marxism where the working class, following its own collective interests, should overthrow the ruling class and embrace socialism. Proletarian irrationality has to be explained by faulty knowledge which is produced by the existence of false consciousness or hegemony or a dominant ideology (Abercrombie, Hill and Turner 1982).

Structure has a remarkable coherence that is produced by this systematic reflection on the Hobbesian problem of order. In *Leviathan* rational actors are driven to agree to a social contract to end the state of nature in order to bring about stability and order, but fraud and force still remain viable and indeed rational options. A social contract is in the collective interest of society as a whole, but individuals or social groups may well turn to criminal behaviour to achieve personal advantage which erodes wider social benefits. Parsons' use of the fraud/force couple is a powerful criticism of radical positivistic utilitarianism in the 1930s but also raises important problems for contemporary economic rationalism, because Mafia-type organisations are effective means of social redistribution in societies where state organisations are corrupt and ineffectual. Mafia-type organisations are, in some sense, voluntary and local, and they are organised around principles of subsidiarity and solidarity. In Parsons' terms, they present a traditional pattern of exchange where values of loyalty and honour are dominant. But we also know that Mafia-type organizations represent what the American republic debates referred to as a "mischief of faction". They ultimately destroy society, because violent means are necessary to

---

[1] Throughout this paper I use the terms "men" and "man" deliberately to recognise the gendered nature of classical sociology and political economy. Furthermore political economy was literally about men engaging in economic conflict in the public sphere.

guarantee their operations, They rule out voluntary patterns of entry and membership .

The Hobbesian problem of order has to be resolved, in Parsons' systems theory, by reference to shared values which provide some solution to the problem of fraud and force by regulating contracts in a normative fashion. Thus in *Structure* one of the critical tests for sociology was the explanation of religious values. In fact the sociology of religion, as a special field of sociology, remained an ongoing preoccupation of Parsons throughout his academic career. The complex place of religion in the process of modernisation could not be resolved by some simple theory of secularisation. Parsons embraced neither a naive notion of disenchantment nor a nostalgic view of value-harmony in traditional societies (Robertson and Turner 1991). Parsons' rejection of nostalgia allowed him to see the United States as a society within which Protestantism had shaped the values of individualism and activism in a manner which made secular, liberal capitalism the fulfillment not the denial of the Reformation. America was the realization not the negation of the history of Protestantism.

The ability of a social theory to explain the importance of religion without recourse to reductionism was a major test of theoretical sophistication. Questions about the validity of sociological or economic explanations about religion play a dominant role in *Structure*. These aspects of Parsons' account of the failure of classical sociology to provide an understanding of religion, that was not individualistic, reductionist, positivist or rationalist, are well known (Turner 1999b). There is the famous commentary in *Structure* on Durkheim's attempt to treat religion as a social fact within the positivistic paradigm and the alleged idealism of Durkheim. Parsons believed of course that eventually Durkheim's sociology of religion lurched towards idealism in the notion that it is not society that produces religion, but religion which produces society. Durkheim looked for an elementary form of religion in the Arunta tribes, where ritualistic festivals brought these hunter-gatherer aboriginals together to celebrate god/society. We know that the question of religion was central to the historicism problem in Weber and that his work can be interpreted through his studies of the economic ethics of the world religions. Both Durkheim and Weber turned, for very different reasons, away from the reductionist tradition of Feuerbach, Marx and Engels to establish a deeper analysis of religion in relation to human values. Religious rituals were, as Durkheim noted, crucial in creating the effervescence necessary to make values appear vital.

There have been, therefore, two components to my argument. Firstly the emerging AGIL scheme in *Structure* provides a map of the interdisciplinary nature of the social sciences. Secondly, it was a justification of sociology as a critique of the limitations of the utilitarian dilemma. The social science disciplines are structured around the dialectic of scarcity and solidarity, or in more technical terms the allocative (political-economy) question and the integrative (psycho-sociological) problem.

The Hobbesian problem of scarcity can, for Parsons, not be resolved by marginal utility theory, but only by a deeper understanding of the role of values in human society. This interpretation of Parsons' sociology now deals with two questions – what produces scarcity and what produces solidarity? An answer to this question will also explain how economics relates to sociology.

Understanding Scarcity

By adopting Parsons' notion of the residual category, we can argue that "scarcity" itself is an absent category in *Structure*, or that it is at least a taken for granted assumption of classical utilitarianism. Scarcity can in classical political and economic theory be located in "nature". In the pessimistic version of utilitarianism, scarcity exists because nature is niggardly. While utilitarianism and liberalism are often presented as the optimistic ideologies of bourgeois capitalism, they often obscured a profound uncertainty about the social world. In Hobbes, the state of nature is not one of abundance, and thus rational men struggle over limited resources to satisfy their bodily needs. The Hobbesian problem of a war of all against all requires the state to regulate men through the political legitimation made possible by the social contract.

In the population theory of Malthus, the unrestrained sexual drives of men produce scarcity through over-crowding and the demographic equilibrium is restored either by periods of famine and pestulence, or because men are willing to restrain their sexual drives. The Malthusian population problem requires sexual restrain to avoid plague and war. Because Malthus did not offer men the possibility of contraception, he confined them to a life of sexual denial. In Durkheim, again we have the classical psychological model of *homo duplex*. Men are rational in terms their grasp of "interests", but their irrational and egoistic drives (especially their "sexual" drives) leads to excessive individualism and unhappiness – the result of which is suicide and social anomie. The Durkheimian problem of order requires religious restraint or parallel mechanisms such as nationalism, or professional ethics and civic morals, or intermediary institutions. In any event, hedonism was for Durkheim a particularly destructive feature of modern society.

Weber as we know was especially influenced by Nietzsche who gave the Darwinian theory of struggle an interesting reformulation in the notion of the Overman (Pearson 1997). In his Freiburg lecture, Weber embraced a Nietzschean view of the political and economic needs of the German state for "elbow-room" in eastern Europe. The scarcity which faces the nation requires a strong bureaucracy, a plebiscitary democracy and an imperialist strategy. Nietzsche's notions of resentment and the will to power played a significant role in shaping Weber's views on politics, and Weber's view of culture probably followed Nietzsche's distinction between Apollo and Dionysus, in which the erotic forces have to be reconciled with the rational powers if society is to achieve a "healthy" condition. This notion of scarcity is related to the struggle over the limited resource of power.

Apart from these Darwinian struggles, we can detect a second form of scarcity in Weber, namely a scarcity of religious meaning. With the disenchantment of the world, secularisation brings about a crisis of meaningfulness, as Weber argued in the lectures on science and politics as vocations. The old gods are dead, and the new ones are yet to be born. This we might call the second Nietzschean problem of values – God is dead, and the revaluation of values has yet to be achieved. This secularism is the famous issue of German historicism that runs through Dilthey, Troeltsch, and Weber. The principal solution for Weber is a stern and realistic commitment to authenticity in a vocation in politics or in science.

In Freudian psychoanalysis, about which Parsons was eventually to write much in the publications on socialisation and the family, scarcity is expressed in the struggle between the id and the superego. The ego is trapped between the endless play of libidinous desire and the needs of civilised society – a struggle that often leads to neurosis. Society has to impose limits on sexuality in the interests of the social order. Human beings experience desire in the form of a lack. Thus in Freudianism, scarcity manifests itself in the imbalance between sexuality and civilization.

Parsons' Account of Scarcity

Following Weber, scarcity is seen to be fundamental to what Parsons called "the economic element" (Parsons 1937: 89). Scarcity in Hobbes' theory of the state of nature is related to the fact that men are guided by "a plurality of passions", but these cannot be fully satisfied, because passions are infinite and nature is niggardly (Parsons 1937: 93). In Hobbes the precarious state of order rests on the scarcity of means: "on the existence of classes of things which are scarce, relative to the demand for them, which as Hobbes says 'two or more men desire' but 'which nevertheless they cannot both enjoy'" (ibid). The scarcity rests in the shortage of means to satisfy commonly held ends and as a result scarcity opens up the ever present threat of war.

Presenting a consistent view of economics as an activity of economizing on means, Parsons went on to observe that "This problem is that of the allocation of scarce means as between their various potential uses. This is what may most usefully be referred to as the specifically economic element of logical action" (Parsons 1937: 233). These regulations of resources are achieved by pricing, which "is society's principal instrument of economizing, of insuring that scarce resources will not be applied wholesale to the least important uses" (Parsons 1937: 234). In conclusion and with reference to Weber Parsons argued that "the fundamental economic facts are scarcity, adaptation of means to alternative ends and cost. The economic element involves the weighing of the relative urgency of different uses of a given scarce means, which the technology does not" (Parsons 1937: 655). In summary, Parsons identified two crucial elements of the theory of action in Pareto, Marshall, Durkheim and Weber. First, the economic element involves economizing – the selection of scarce means to ends. Secondly, there is the need for decision-making and "the element of coercive power may be called the 'political'" (Parsons 1937: 240). The sphere of economics and politics as disciplines are defined by these two features of action, one peaceful and the other potentially violent.

Parsons' theory of voluntaristic action recognised that the political-economy of action in utilitarianism could not solve the problem of order without recognizing the existence of an independent and autonomous realm of values without which ends would be random and action would be deterministic. Hence, a voluntaristic theory of action requires a social component and we might reasonably argue that "the social element" involves the creation and maintenance of the cultural system wherein lie ultimate values which in turn provide norms for the selection of means. Parsons' persistent emphasis on religion in human society can be seen as part of a larger question about social action as a whole.

Parsons' Understanding of Sociology

The status of sociology within the general theory of action remained a prominent element of Parsons' professional commitments. Towards the end of *Structure* (Parsons, 1937:768) Parsons offered a definition of sociology (or the social element) as a solution to the power question – a solution which was both anticipated by his earlier interest in "institutional economics" and which came to pre-occupy him in his later work on "action-systems theory" especially in the collaborative work with Smelser. The solution to the power problem (Hobbesian rationalist in an environment of scarcity) "involves a common reference to the fact of integration of individuals with reference to a common value system, manifested in the legitimacy of institutional norms, in the common ultimate ends of action, in ritual and in various modes of expression" (Parsons 1937: 768). This social element which he calls "common value integration" is an emergent property of action. He thus defined sociology unambiguously as "the science which attempts to develop an analytical theory of social action systems in so far as these systems can be understood in terms of the property of common value integration" (Parsons 1937: 768). He thus identified social, political and economic disciplines of the social sciences of action, and then recognized that the actor is not wholly explained by these three elements. At best they account for what he calls the "social component of personality" (Parsons 1937: 769). He then suggested that psychology, which deals with "the hereditary basis" of personality and psychology could enter the voluntaristic theory of action as "the analytical science concerned with the variable properties of action systems derived from their reference to the hereditary basis of personality" (Parsons 1937: 770)

This specific discussion of sociology therefore begins to outline systematically the more general AGIL scheme of later works. Economics (the supply and demand schema) are concerned with the adaptation of social systems to scarce resources; politics (power relationships between individual and group) are about decision making with respect to setting goals; sociology deals with the integration questions around common values; and psychology (the hereditary element of personality) comprehends the actor's motivational relations with the group (latency). In short, action-social systems have to resolve both allocative and integrative problems in solving both scarcity and solidarity issues. In this respect, the task of *Structure* was analytically to secure the place of sociology in the social sciences along side economics, politics and psychology. Parsons also had some important comments to make about the role of history in helping us to understand economic history, political and social history, and biography, but he does not want to place history within the core of the analytical theory of action-systems research. This issue may be indirectly related to later conflicts with historical sociology such as the work of Norbert Elias and with the criticism that Parsonian functionalism could not explain social change (Turner 1999a).

Action and the Emotions

Structure is a sustained critique of positivism in economic science, because a positivistic theory cannot solve basic issues about social order and the authority of a hierarchy of values. In this respect, we have seen that the notion of the "residual category" helped Parsons to identify certain recurrent analytical problems in utilitarianism and on the basis of a critique of positivism to construct his own voluntaristic theory of action (as a solution to the determinism and reductionism of the Benthamite view of the actor in terms of the calculus of happiness), the analysis of the emergent property of values (as a solution to the randomness of ends in economic theory) and the idea of common values as a solution to the Hobbesian war of all against all.

In my conclusion to this analysis of *Structure*, I wish to argue that we should use the notion of "residual category" to probe some under-theorized aspects of *Structure*. Parsons' main concern in *Structure* was first to establish the notion of common values as an emergent property of action and secondly to establish sociology, the science of "the social element" in voluntaristic action, as an independent discipline in the social science academy. He could therefore take "scarcity" (the core of "the economic element") and power (the core of "the political element") for granted, because his main concern was for common values (the core of "the social element"). Parsons' sociology theory after 1937 was largely devoted to the content of common values, their place in the social system and how they are internalised by social actors.

As we have seen, he defined scarcity in the context of delineating "the economic element" as arising because of the plurality of goals which force human beings to chose between alternative causes of action. I nevertheless find the minimalistic discussion of scarcity in the economic sciences as outlined in *Structure* somewhat unsatisfactory. We can identify three logical possibilities. Firstly, scarcity exists because nature is niggardly; it is not strictly speaking a sociological problem, because it exists in nature. But this is not convincing, because "nature" can only be scarce in relation to human wants. What is "natural" cannot be taken merely for granted.

Secondly, scarcity exists because human desire is infinite, elastic and rapacious. Scarcity exists at the level of the individual in the theory of the hedonistic actor. This fact was recognized in Parsons' discussion of Durkheim's theory of anomie, where he wrote that "since individual wants are in principle unlimited, it is an essential condition of both social stability and individual happiness that they should be regulated in terms of norms" (Parsons 1937: 382). Now these norms can only achieve this end not if they merely act externally but if "they enter directly into the constitution of the actors' ends themselves" (Parsons 1937: 382), that is if they become constitutive of the social nature of the actors. Parsons provided some time to the discussion of Marshall's classification of wants in terms of the biological needs which humans share with animals (food and sleep). Then there are wants "adjusted to activities" (Marshall) and the satisfaction of which "affords strength" that is increases the efficiency of labour, and finally there are "artificial wants" in relation to the "standard of comfort". Parsons argued that Marshall did not dwell on the problems of wants because he sought to define economics as a science of activities. Therefore the nature of wants and consumption remained somewhat outside the view of economics as developed by Alfred Marshall.

Finally, scarcity thus exists at the cultural level, because it is produced by the social construction of wants, especially so-called artificial wants. Modern theories of scarcity have tended to follow Marshall Sahlins in suggesting that scarcity is relative and historical, depending on the cultural production of the desire to consume. To provide an example, critical theorists of the Frankfurt School assumed that it was capitalism through the advertising industry that created a high level of individual needs to consume, but these needs are artificial.

This overview of the problem thus suggests that the notion of scarcity floats around nature or the hedonistic individual or artificially induced consumer needs. One can suggest that in the authors whom Parsons had studied in *Structure* (Hobbes, Locke, Malthus, Marshall, Pareto ,Weber, and Durkheim) and those who entered his later work such as Freud, it is the hedonistic nature of man which causes scarcity rather than the plurality of ends. Hobbesian man is driven by hedonistic wants that are infinite, elastic and evolving. Man is an emotional animal whose wants can never be fully satisfied; there is no possibility that human need can be finally satiated. Man is dangerous, reckless, and anti-social - hence the need for social contracts, states, religion and the accoutrements of civilization. Men are pushed along by the blind force of emotions which as a causal element acts against rationality (Barbalet 1998).

This view of the hedonistic man results in the famous *homo duplex* notion characteristic of Hobbes, Durkheim and Freud. Human beings have an animal side (hedonism) and a rational side (a capacity to calculate interests and to work cooperatively to satisfy wants through collective action). Man is an irrational animal combined with a rational mind. *Homo duplex* is thus Cartesian Man – divided neatly between a body as a desiring machine and a mind which is robustly rational. Desire can never be subordinated or finally controlled, but the rational mind also realises that individual interests can be satisfied through fraud and force. Society is thus an unstable mixture of contradictory forces which Parsons wanted to stabilize around emergent common value patterns, as the glue which holds or promises to hold the social contract together.

What, however, is the real essence of the hedonistic character of desiring man? I want to argue that sexual appetite is the underlying reality of the notion of hedonism. It is human sexuality that is infinite, unsatisfied, excessive, vicious and uncontrolled. Because human sexuality is "plastic" in the sense of having no particular target, it is not easily regulated. In the language of Arnold Gehlen, human sexuality is world-open and not instinctually specific and it is hedonistic sexuality which produces wants in the form of an absence or lack with the result than man appears as a perpetually unsatisfied animal. In the language of Nietzsche, man is a not-yet-finished animal, who is yet to be formed (Gehlen 1988).

Male sexuality in the state of nature brings men into conflict with other men over the ownership of women. Human sexuality is violent, producing the subordination of women to male desires and fantasies, and producing violent confrontations between men over the possession of women. In Malthus, human sexuality threatens to create a situation where population growth (as a consequence of uncontrolled sexuality) destroys men through famine and pestulence. Men will not only use force and fraud, but their sexual desires are driven by fantasies – the equivalent of the notion of "artificial wants". The social contract attempts to solve this problem in two ways: either the Hobbesian tradition of individualistic contracts to regulate interests through a contractual state or the patriarchal tradition of Sir Robert Filmer who sought a paternalistic theory of the state in which the King is God's representative and where in the family men must have patriarchal authority.

This theme of sexuality and power runs throughout the western tradition of social and political philosophy. The *humo duplex* theory was not only characteristic of Durkheim but we have already seen it outlined clearly in Nietzsche's contrast between the two gods Apollo and Dionysus where Apollo is the rational force and Dionysus the ecstatic and violent principle. For Nietzsche these forces have to be resolved in a recreation of culture if human society is to be restored to health. This Dionysus-Apollo theme runs throughout Weber, Freud, Klages, Adorno and Marcuse (Stauth and Turner 1988). The core of the tradition is the contrast between the sexual violence which men share with animals versus the prospect of civilization, or in Parsonian sociology the Hobbesian war versus shared values.

Conclusion

The tradition of dismal science has concentrated on the negative and destructive features of human sexuality and emotionality, or what we can call, following Nietzsche, the negative theory of the will to power. The Pauline theological tradition, upon which this vision of animal sexuality is based, also identified love (as charity and caring) as the antidote to sexuality, producing a theology of social relationships whereby the sexuality of men could be resolved through a collection of institutions (primarily celibacy, monasticism, dietary management and the family) that recognised sex as a necessary evil, if procreation was to take place at all. However, the Church also elaborated a view of human nature which distinguished between eros (the violent, negative and egoistic drive) and agape (the caring, forgiving and sharing principle of divine love). In *Structure* Parsons argued (often rather by implication than directly) that utilitarianism could not provide a satisfactory account of religious values because, for example, charity could not be understood within the paradigm of individualistic hedonism. The notion that charity is ultimately self-serving negates the essence of charity; it is no longer charity. Similarly, religion cannot be reduced to the environment or to biology; it is an emergent principle of action, that falls outside the paradigm of the rational and the irrational.

Love has the same theoretical "place" so to speak to charity in the action schema. If love is reduced to biology, then love is equated with sex, but love is by definition not an egoistic, individualistic or necessarily individualistic drive. Love is not about scarcity but about abundance. Furthermore, true love is not economizing but giving. It cannot be explained or understood within the utilitarian paradigm, unless that love is reduced to the hedonistic/animalistic schema of drives and wants. The whole point of the Parsonian account of religion is that we cannot understand religion in a reductionist framework that treats it as merely a function of biology.

The Cartesian option was not the only possibility for science in the seventeenth century. The Cartesian assumptions about individualistic rationality and the mind/body split as the basis of seventeenth century social contract theories was challenged profoundly by Spinoza, who provided an alternative to the transcendentalist assumptions of Christianity with its opposition between man and nature, and to the mind/body dichotomy of Descartes. For Spinoza, body is not merely an extension of mind but mind and body are related in a dialogic parallelism, and hedonistic man is not separated from nature in a relationship of competition. Spinoza had a vision of human beings as co-operatively and necessarily part of nature. Spinoza's philosophy of connectedness was close to the spirit of John Donne's humanistic vision (Send not to know for whom the bell tolls, it tolls for thee). Spinoza's theological-political treatise on the social contract provided an alternative framework for the Hobbesian action-system schema with its vision of endless violence by presenting an affirmative will to power.

Unfortunately, Parsons' unit act analysis in the 1930s looks profoundly cartesian. Now there is no reference to Spinoza in *Structure* and at least in the 1930s Parsons appears to adhere to a Cartesian view of the relationship between mind and body, because biology is merely a condition of action, and hereditary is not part of the unit act. The biological sciences stand outside the voluntaristic theory of action. Parsons' social actor in *Structure* is not an embodied actor as such, because Parsons adopted a view of action that emphasised the biological character of actors as an environmental condition or hereditary as the "natural" element of personality. Parsons' view of body and mind – biology and sociology – became more complicated and more sophisticated as he absorbed more of Freudianism into the analytics of the action-system schema but it is fair to argue that in Parsonian sociology the status of the body in relation to action and the possibility of a non-Cartesian understanding of embodiment were not adequately resolved (Turner 1992).

In the contemporary period, over half a century after the publication of *Structure,* we are all much more aware of the environmental crisis, the centrality of risk to human existence and the importance of a "social contract" with other species, if our world is to survive. As a result the problem of biology in relation to the action-system schema is much more pressing than when Parsons was a young man in Heidelberg. The Spinozian ethic of responsibility and inter-relatedness presents a more persuasive vision of man-in-nature than the Hobbesian waste-land and hence the politics of interdisciplinarity is somewhat different than when Parsons framed the problem in 1937. However, the idea of emergent common-value integration is still relevant to modern social science and to the green politics of the late twentieth century, and the relation of shared values to both communication and solidarity remains crucial. Parsons' critique of utilitarianism provided a valid basis for his criticism of economic models of rationalism, but it did not go far enough as an analysis of the relationship between society and environment.

References

Abell, P. (1996): Rational Choice Theory. In: B. S. Turner (ed), The Blackwell Companion to Social Theory Oxford: Blackwell, pp. 252-273.

Abercrombie, N., Hill, S. and Turner, B. S. (1982): The Dominant Ideology Thesis. London: Allen & Unwin.

Barbalet, J. M. (1998): Emotion, Social Theory and Social Structure. A Macrosociological Approach. Cambridge: Cambridge University Press.

Durkheim, E. (1954): The Elementary Forms of the Religious Life. London: Allen & Unwin.

Gehlen, A. (1988): Man. His Nature and Place in the World. New York: Columbia University Press.

Holton, R. J. (1991): Talcott Parsons and the Integration of Economic and Sociological Theory. In: Sociological Inquiry volume 61(1): 102-114.

Holton, R. J. and Turner, B. S (1986): Talcott Parsons on Economy and Society. London: Routledge.

Parsons, T. (1929): 'Capitalism' in recent German literature. In: Sombart and Weber' Journal of Political Economy, volume 36:641-61 and 37:31-51.

Parsons, T. (1937): The Structure of Social Action. New York : McGraw-Hill.

Parsons, T. (1951): The Social System. London: Routledge and Kegan Paul.

Parsons, T , Bales, R., Olds, J., Zelditch, M., and Slater, P. E. (1955):Family, Socialization and Interaction Process. Chicago: The Free Press.

Parsons, T. and Smelser, N. (1956): Economy and Society. London: Routledge.

Pearson, K. A. (1997): Viroid Life. Perspectives on Nietzsche and the Transhuman Condition. London: Routledge.

Robertson, R. and Turner, B. S. (eds.) (1991): Talcott Parsons: theorist of modernity. London: Sage.

Sica, A. (1988): Weber, Irrationality and Social Order. Berkeley: University of California Press.

Stauth, G. and Turner, B. S. (1988): Nietzsche's Dance. Oxford: Blackwell Publishers.

Smith. W. R. (1889):Lectures on the Religion of the Semites. Edinburgh: Adam and Charles Black.

Swedberg, R. (1986): 'Introduction' in Talcott Parsons. The Marshall Lectures. Uppsala: Uppsala University Department of Sociology Research Reports volume 4: i-xxxiv.

Swedberg, R. (1998): Max Weber and the Idea of Economic Sociology. Princeton, New Jersey: Princeton University Press.

Turner, B. S. (1992): Regulating Bodies: essays in medical sociology. London: Routledge.

Turner, B. S. (1996): Talcott Parsons on Economic and Social Theory: the relevance of the Amherst term papers. In: The American Sociologist volume 27(4): 41-47.

Turner, B. S. (1999a): The contribution of Talcott Parsons to the study of modernity. In: The Talcott Parsons Reader. Oxford:Blackwell,pp.1-20.

Turner, B. S. (1999b): Classical Sociology. London: Sage.

Anwendungen der Theorie des Handelns

Talcott Parsons' Kulturkonzept
Ein Zugang zum besseren Verständnis der Transformationsprozesse in Europa?
Josef Langer

Ende des zwanzigsten Jahrhunderts ist Europa wieder ins historische Rampenlicht gerückt. Wo sonst hat sich in letzter Zeit gesellschaftlich und geopolitisch so viel verändert? Grund für die Sozialwissenschaften bzw. die Soziologie, ihre Theorien und Ansätze zu überprüfen. Welche Potentiale beinhalten sie, diese epochemachenden Veränderungen auch interpretieren und verstehen zu können? Gerade die Neubewertung eines Theorieprogramms wird diese Frage nicht umgehen können, will sie nicht dem Verdacht der Mumifizierung oder des "Über den Wolken Schwebens" in die Hand spielen. Wenn das allgemein gilt, dann umso mehr für Talcott Parsons, der von manchen schon zu seinen Lebzeiten als "Klassiker" der Soziologie eingestuft wurde. Das Risiko im Auge, das auf Grund des komplexen und widersprüchlichen Charakters seiner Theorie mit dem Versuch einer empirisch-praktischen Applikation verbunden ist, möchte ich sie trotzdem am Beispiel der kulturellen Fragen, die heute in Europa an allen Ecken und Enden sichtbar werden, zur Diskussion stellen. Kann uns hier Parsons etwas bieten, das bei Problemlösungen in entscheidender Weise handlungsorientierend sein könnte oder die blinden Flecken anderer Theorien auszuleuchten in der Lage ist?

Dies anzugehen, ist leichter gesagt als getan. Schon Parsons selbst könnte einen hier entmutigen, wenn man an sein widersprüchliches Theorie-Praxis-Verständnis denkt. Eine Seite davon hat Niklas Luhmann, der bis zu seinem Tod vermutlich einer der besten Parsonskenner im deutschsprachigen Raum war, schon vor zwanzig Jahren bei einem ähnlichen Unterfangen – "Talcott Parsons – Zur Zukunft eines Theorieprogramms" – herausgestrichen. Luhmann war damals mit der Auffassung Parsons' *d'accord*, nach der die konkrete Handlung weder erkennbar noch systemfähig sei. Erst in ihren Aspekten würde sie zur (analytischen) Realität und kann dann Systemen oder Subsystemen zugeordnet werden. Kriterien hingegen, die eine solche Zuordnung ermöglichten, sieht er in dieser Theorie nicht. "Wie weit es darüber hinaus gelingt, konkrete Handlungen primär einem und nur einem Teilsystem zuzuordnen und in diesem Sinn systemspezifisch auszudifferenzieren, bleibt eine offene Frage. Der Theorie fehlen Instrumente, diese Frage zu beantworten" (Luhmann 1980, S. 8).

Da empirische Analysen in der Regel *konkrete Handlungen* und *Systeme* zum Gegenstand haben, ist damit zumindest ein Problem aufgeworfen: Wie kann Kultur überhaupt als Kultur identifiziert werden? Auf der anderen Seite trifft man in Parsons' Werk immer wieder empirisch-praktische Beispiele, an denen er seine Theorie exemplifiziert bzw. ist erkennbar, dass er mit ihr nicht nur die Abstraktionen der soziologischen Klassiker auf einen Punkt zu bringen versucht, sondern auch ganz konkrete gesellschaftliche Probleme reflektieren möchte. Allerdings hat Parsons selbst in seiner Reflexion konkreter Handlungssysteme (z. B. Familie, Beruf, moderne Gesellschaften) immer beträchtliche Abstriche von den eigenen analytisch-theoretischen Ansprüchen machen müssen.

Aber auch wenn man Parsons' Theorie eine gewisse Empiriefähigkeit zugesteht, bleibt die von Luhmann im zitierten Beitrag aufgeworfene Frage, warum man sie im sozialwissenschaftlichen Diskurs halten soll. Gibt es heute nicht bessere Theorien? Welche? Kann Parsons dazu eine Alternative bieten? Generell kann gesagt werden, dass die Sozialwissenschaften seit den siebziger Jahren einen Prozess der "Ethnologisierung" durchgemacht haben, der eine Verschiebung der Aufmerksamkeit vom Gesellschafts- auf den Kulturbegriff impliziert. In diesem Prozess drücken sich sowohl neue Problemlagen als auch innerwissenschaftliche Bewegungen aus. Zu den veränderten Problemlagen zählt, dass aus dem zu Parsons' Zeiten existierenden Systemgegensatz *Kommunismus* versus *Kapitalismus* der Kapitalismus 1989 als Sieger übrigblieb. In Europa haben sich dadurch die politischen Vorzeichen von Konfrontation zu Kooperation gewendet. Auf der Ebene der Problemperzeption gewinnen damit Wert- vor Strukturfragen an Bedeutung. Oder anders: Die Strukturfragen werden der Ökonomie und damit der wirtschaftswissenschaftlichen Perspektive überlassen. Was man dort nicht bearbeiten kann oder will, übernimmt das breite Feld der *cultural studies* (Alexander/Smith 1993), die weitgehend ohne expliziten Gesellschaftsbegriff auszukommen meinen. Wichtiger Hintergrund dieser Entwicklung ist einerseits der neue Status der Nationalstaaten (Stichwort: Europäische Union) und andererseits eine Transformation von Staats- zu Privateigentum. Letzteres betrifft vor allem die Gesellschaften der früheren Sowjetunion und ihrer ostmitteleuropäischen Satelliten. Eine andere, nicht nur Europa berührende Entwicklung, die offenbar überwiegend auch als Kulturproblem interpretiert wird, betrifft die Informationstechnologien, die innerhalb einer Dekade globale und zeitunabhängige Kommunikation prinzipiell für jeden möglich gemacht haben.

Die Verschiebung des Erkenntnisinteresses von der gesellschafts- zur kulturwissenschaftlichen Perspektive bzw. innerhalb der Soziologie vom sozialen zum kulturellen Wandel hat in den siebziger Jahren eingesetzt. Unter den ersten, die diesen Prozess im deutschsprachigen Raum artikulierten, war Karl-Siegbert Rehberg, der in einem Sonderheft (1986) der *Kölner Zeitschrift für Soziologie und Sozialpsychologie* im Titel seines Beitrags die Frage "Kultur versus Gesellschaft?" stellte. Wie einige andere (z. B. Tenbruck) beunruhigte ihn offenbar die "strukturelle" Schlagseite der Soziologie seiner Zeit. Demgegenüber wird von ihm die Bedeutung von Sinn- und Wertfragen herausgestrichen. Rehberg entwickelt seine Argumentation, indem er die Rolle des Kulturbegriffs in den Theorien von Dilthey, Weber, Scheler, Freyer und Habermas Revue passieren lässt. Er plädiert für ein Gleichgewicht von *Struktur* und *Semantik* in der soziologischen Analyse. Allerdings war zwischenzeitlich die Kulturperspektive bereits soweit akzeptiert, dass er mit seinem Appell weitgehend offene Türen einrannte.[1] Ausreichend Belege für den Perspektivenwechsel von "Gesellschaft" zu "Kultur" finden sich zum Beispiel im Tagungsband des Deutsch-Österreichisch-Schweizerischen Soziologiekongresses von 1988 in Zürich (Haller/Hoffmann-Nowotny/Zapf 1989; Münch 1989). Selbst die Wortfolge im Titel – Kultur und Gesellschaft – indiziert die Veränderungen: Kultur steht an erster Stelle. Dieser Wandel im Erkenntnisinteresse war offensichtlich nicht auf den deutschsprachigen Raum bzw. Kontinentaleuropa beschränkt. Alexander/Seidman (1990, S. vii) bestätigen ihn auch für Nordamerika: "In the past few years there has emerged a new and powerful interest in the study of culture ..."

Heute, mehr als eine Dekade später, scheint dieser Prozess der Perspektivenverschiebung noch immer in Gang zu sein. Nicht nur, dass die einstige Forderung nach Gleichwertigkeit des Kulturbegiffs innerhalb der Soziologie längst eingelöst, wenn nicht übererfüllt zu sein scheint, haben sich nach und nach auch andere Disziplinen (Psychologie, Wirtschaftswissenschaften, Ökologie etc.) dem Thema zugewendet. Der Kuluransatz nimmt heute sowohl in den Sozial- wie auch in den Geisteswissenschaften einen prominenten Platz ein. Wenn neben den alles dominierenden wirtschaftsliberalen Paradigmen überhaupt noch ein Rahmen für die Interpretation von menschlichem Verhalten in der informierten Öffentlichkeit akzeptiert wird, dann ist es die Kulturperspektive. Das gilt für Erkenntnis und Praxis gleichermaßen. Ob es um Fragen der Globalisierung, des internationalen Handels, des Tourismus oder um *Foreign Direct Investments* (FDI) geht – Themen, die noch mehr mit der europäischen Integration zusammenhängen, will ich erst gar nicht erwähnen –, immer wird heute so etwas wie *kulturelle Kompetenz* erwartet (Hall/Hall 1990; Hofstede 1984; Thomas 1996). Das gilt auch für soziale Mikrostrukturen wie Organisationen (Organisationskultur), Konsumverhalten, Nachbarschaft, Arbeitsgruppen, Schulen etc. Obwohl die These von der Dominanz der Kulturperspektive nicht immer gleich evident ist, wenn zum Beispiel nur die Inhalte der sozialwissenschaftlichen Zeitschriften als Beleg herangezogen werden, im Raum der medialen und öffentlichen Diskurse gilt sie ohne Einschränkung. Ich gehe noch etwas weiter: Welche Universität würde heute in Europa noch eine "Fakultät für Gesellschaftswissenschaften" einrichten? Wenn überhaupt ein Ausbau in diesem Bereich legitimiert werden kann, dann unter dem Titel "Kulturwissenschaften".

---

1 Im Hintergrund dieser Intervention stand offensichtlich die Gründung der Sektion "Kultursoziologie" in der Deutschen Gesellschaft für Soziologie 1984.

Dennoch, die Konzeption von Kultur ist auf diesem semantischen Eroberungsfeldzug umstritten geblieben. Das betrifft nicht nur die Versuche ihrer praktischen Umsetzung, die rapide zugenommen haben, sondern auch die Theorie. Was heißt schon Kultur? Kaum hatte die Umorientierung von Gesellschaft auf Kultur im deutschen Sprachraum voll eingesetzt, schrieb der renommierte amerikanische Historiker und Soziologe Immanuel Wallerstein (1990, S. 33) "... 'culture' is the term in our scientific vocabulary which has the broadest and most confusing usage ...". Ähnlich die englische Soziologin Margaret Archer, wenn sie Kultur als "the weakest analytical development of any key concept in sociology" bezeichnet, eine Entwicklung, die paradoxerweise "the most widely vacillating role within sociological theory" (Archer 1985, S. 333) gespielt hat. Ihre Kritik bezog sich sowohl auf die deskriptive als auch auf die explanatorische Ebene. Zum einen vermisst sie klare und elaborierte Definitionen, zum anderen Gewissheit über den Status von Kultur als Faktor sozialer Entwicklung. Und Niklas Luhmann schrieb noch 1995 (Luhmann 1995a, S. 31), als die Hinwendung zur Kulturperspektive kaum mehr zu übersehen war, folgendes: "Warum ist es den Sozialwissenschaften so schwer gefallen, sich auf einen theoretischen Begriff der Kultur zu verständigen? An Versuchen hat es nicht gefehlt ... Letztlich hat sich aber die Spannweite, die der Begriff ausfüllen sollte, als zu groß erwiesen". Im Vorgriff auf die Konzeption von Parsons ist interessant, dass dieses Dilemma schon in *The Social System* (1951/1967, S. 15) für die Anthropologie als sein damaliges Vorbild gesehen hat: "In anthropological theory there is not what could be called close agreement on the definition of the concept of culture".

Neben einer kurzen Replik auf Texte, in denen sich Parsons selbst diesem Definitionsproblem gestellt hat, möchte ich in der Folge versuchen, die Potentiale seines Konzepts von Kultur für die Analyse der gegenwärtigen Entwicklungen in Europa auszuloten. Dass dem Thema Kultur beim Aufbau der Europäischen Union mehr Aufmerksamkeit gebührt, wird immer wieder von allen möglichen Seiten herausgestrichen. Häufig wird sogar als Voraussetzung für die nachhaltige Integration Europas eine "gemeinsame Kultur" beschworen. Aktuell ist folgender Argumentationsstrang: Europa hat eine gemeinsame Währung (den Euro) geschafft, weiß aber nicht, wie es zur politischen Union fortschreiten soll. Dieser Prozess erfordert eine *europäische Öffentlichkeit*, die ihrerseits nur aus einer *gemeinsamen Kultur* entstehen kann.[2] Das Thema Kultur ist allerdings schon länger dabei, europapolitisches Profil zu gewinnen. Mindestens seit Mitte der achtziger Jahre. Im Maastricht Vertrag von

---

2 "Wir haben den Euro, aber wir wissen nicht, wie es mit dem politischen Einigungswerk weitergeht. Immer wieder höre ich, daß ein politisch geeintes, demokratisches Europa gar nicht möglich sei ohne eine europäische Öffentlichkeit, eine europäische Öffentlichkeit aber nicht ohne eine gemeinsame europäische Kultur. Die Frage der Zukunft Europas stellt sich deshalb als die Frage: Gibt es eine europäische Kultur" (Herzog 1999a, S. 117).

1992 (Art. 128) wurde das schließlich auch offiziell dokumentiert. Roman Herzog, bis vor kurzem noch deutscher Bundespräsident, sprach sogar von Kultur als zunehmend zentralem Fokus der (europäischen?) Außenpolitik (Herzog 1999b). Während also die Thematik grundsätzlich akzeptiert wird, ist es nach wie vor umstritten, ob die Union kulturelle Einheit, Vielfalt oder beides anstreben soll. Im Vertrag von Amsterdam (Fassung vom 2.10.1997) scheint das Pendel eher wieder in Richtung kulturelle Vielfalt auszuschlagen, auch wenn gleichzeitig, wie zitiert, prominente Stimmen die gemeinsamen Momente der europäischen Kultur unterstreichen. Ohne die Position der Europäischen Union unterschätzen zu wollen, werden wir noch sehen, dass diese selbstverständlich nur einen Teil der kulturellen Aspekte anspricht, die heute in Europa Aufmerksamkeit verdienen. Abgesehen von den begrifflichen Unklarheiten, die dem Kulturbegriff auch in diesem Zusammenhang eigen sind.

Die faszinierenden Entwicklungen kurz vor und nach der "Wende" 1989 hat Parsons nicht mehr erlebt. Wir können aus diesem Grund aus seinen Texten dazu keine unmittelbaren Aufschlüsse erwarten. Mit dem Kulturbegriff indes hat er sich lange und ausführlich beschäftigt. Es lohnt sich daher zu prüfen, wieweit die zitierten Vorwürfe auch auf seine Konzeption zutreffen. Außerdem kann gefragt werden, in welcher Weise sie die neuen Entwicklungen interpretieren und verstehen hilft. Wenden wir uns zuerst dem Ausgangspunkt zu. Das zentrale theoretische Anliegen von Talcott Parsons ist die Klassifizierung von *Handlungen* und *Handlungssystemen*. In diesem Sinne ist er genuin soziologisch und wer daher auf die Suche nach dem Kulturthema geht, wird bei ihm nicht gleich auf entsprechende Buchtitel stoßen. Trotzdem zeigt schon ein flüchtiges Einlesen in das Werk von Parsons, dass Kultur ein integraler Bestandteil seines Argumentierens ist, ja von ihm immer wieder zu Definitionen angesetzt wird. Eine solche *Tour d'horizon* kann zu folgenden ersten Begriffsaspekten führen: Kultur ist der Sinn hinter dem sozialen Handeln. Als symbolisch organisierte Form ist sie allen lebenden Arten eigen. In Bezug auf die Menschenart werden die Möglichkeiten der Sprache hervorgehoben. Auch wenn der einzelne Kultur schaffen und sich aneignen kann, ist sie nur kollektiv realisierbar. Was nicht von mehreren geteilt wird, kann nicht als Kultur bezeichnet werden. Dazu kommen Analogien zu den Genen des Organismus. Aber Kultur wird nicht nur als symbolische Form definiert, sondern auch als System und schließlich sogar als Handlungssystem. In dieser Funktion stützt sie spezifische Formen des Handelns. Die Umwelt des Handlungssystems Kultur sind andere Handlungssysteme – Persönlichkeit, Organismus und Sozialsystem. Mit diesen steht Kultur in Interrelation ("interpenetration"). In der Kontrollhierarchie der Systeme hat Kultur nach Parsons den höchsten informativen Status. Die Existenz von Gruppen ist von der Homogenisierung der kulturellen Orientierungen (Werte, Normen und Regulierungen) ihrer Mitglieder abhängig. Im Prozess der Evolution wird Kultur zunehmend von anderen Systemen unabhängiger.

Parsons' Verständnis von Kultur systematischer zu fassen, fällt nicht leicht, weil er seine Theorie immer wieder umgebaut und erweitert hat. Ich meine aber, dass man vereinfachend von zwei *Definitionsbrennpunkten* sprechen kann. Im einen wird Kultur objekthaft, als der Handlung äußerlich, wenn auch auf sie bezogen, verstanden, im anderen als eigenes Handlungssystem mit Umweltrelationen sowie als immanenter Aspekt von Handlungen. In seinem bekanntesten Spätwerk *The American University* (Parsons/Platt 1973) werden diese Brennpunkte in verschiedenen Zusammenhängen sichtbar. Zum Beispiel definiert er dort, wo es ihm um eine soziologische Charakterisierung von Wissen geht, zuerst einen Unterschied zwischen "Cultural Objects" und "Cultural System" als Handlungssystem: "A body of knowledge, though a cultural object, is more specifically a complex of meanings symbolized within a code. A cultural system as a system of action, however, consists not only of cultural objects but, as a system, of *all* the components of action insofar as they are oriented in terms of cultural objects" (Parsons/Platt 1973, S. 17). Kultur im ersten Sinn ist also eine die Bedeutung von Objekten (physischen und sozialen) ausdrückende Symbolisierung, zum Zwecke der Kommunikation, würde ich hinzufügen. Diese Symbole bzw. Codierungen können, wenn sie in einer bestimmten logischen Relation zueinander stehen, ein System bilden (Sprache, Habitus etc.), das allerdings noch nicht als Handlungssystem gelten kann. Indes bedeutet Kultur als Handlungssystem, dass Handlungen hauptsächlich auf kulturelle Objekte ausgerichtet sind. Nach Parsons ist das eine heuristische Abstraktion, da konkrete Handlungen nur von Personen gesetzt werden können, allerdings auch in ihrer Funktion als Repräsentanten von konkreten sozialen Systemen (Organisationen, Gruppen). In diesem Sinn sind auch Kollektive handlungsfähig. Parsons' Quintessenz an dieser Stelle ist, dass zwar jedes Interaktionssystem (soziales System) Kultur impliziert, aber allein deshalb noch nicht ein kulturelles Handlungssystem ist.

Ausgangspunkt von Parsons' Kulturbegriff ist seine frühe Handlungstheorie, in der der Handelnde sich an einer *Situation* orientiert, die sich ihrerseits über a) *soziale* und b) *nicht-soziale Objekte* definiert (Parsons/Shils 1951).[3] Kultur zählt er zu den nicht-sozialen Objekten. Zusammen mit den anderen Akteuren (sozial) und physischen Objekten bildet sie die Konstellation der Situation (siehe auch Parsons/Smelser 1956/1972, S. 11). Als symbolische Realität kann Kultur anders als soziale und physische Objekte vom Handelnden internalisiert und damit Teil seiner *Handlungsorientierung* werden. Der Objektbegriff liegt daher bei Parsons nicht auf der Dimension materiell-ideell, sondern ist im Sinn von Subjekt-Objekt (innen/außen) zu verstehen. Deshalb passt auch eine Unterscheidung zwischen mate-

---

3 Ohne großes Aufheben übernommen wird die Position der Kulturanthropologie, nach der Kultur übertragbar und lernbar ist, aber als solche auch von mehreren Personen geteilt werden muss (vgl. Parsons 1951/1967, S. 15).

rieller und immaterieller Kultur, wie sie etwa Alfred Weber getroffen hat, nicht in dieses Konzept. Parsons lässt bei dem, was als "materielle Kultur" bezeichnet wird, nur die symbolische Komponente als Kultur gelten. Sie kann prinzipiell von jedem internalisiert werden, während die physische Komponente nur als Besitzanspruch übertragbar ist[4] (Parsons/Shils 1951, S. 66). Übrigens streicht Parsons in dieser Phase der Begriffsentwicklung noch ausdrücklich hervor, dass anders als das Persönlichkeits- und Sozialsystem Kultur für sich *kein* Handlungssystem sein kann. "Apart from embodiment in the orientation systems of concrete actors, culture, though existing as a body (siehe auch Parsons/Platt 1973, S. 16) of artefacts and a system of symbols, is not in itself organized as a system of action" (Parsons/Shils 1951, S. 7). Hingegen spricht er von *cultural traditions* und *cultural elements*, die er a) nach den damit verbundenen *Interessen* und b) danach, ob sie *äußerlich* oder *internalisiert* sind, unterscheidet. Die Unterscheidung nach Interessen führt zu 1) *Ideen-* und *Glaubenssystemen* – im Vordergrund stehen kognitive Interessen –, zu 2) *expressiven Symbolen* (Kunstformen, Stile) und zu *Wertorientierungen*, die immer Handlungsalternativen implizieren. Die Klassifizierung von Kulturmustern danach, ob lediglich Objekt der Situation oder internalisierte Handlungsorientierung, thematisiert die Art der Betroffenheit des Handelnden. Kultur als Objekt der Situation kann *kognitive*, *kathektische* oder *evaluative* Stellungnahmen provozieren, in internalisierter Form ist sie indes Teil der Persönlichkeit, konstitutiver Teil des individuellen Orientierungssystems.

In der Klassifizierung von Kultur unter dem Aspekt der Interessen streicht Parsons die Signifikanz von Wertorientierungen (value-orientations) für die Stabilität von Handlungssystemen heraus, weil sie die *Standards* zur Lösung von *Selektionsproblemen* in sozialen Interaktionen stützen. In diesem Zusammenhang diskutiert er auch kurz das Problem der *Konsistenz* von Kulturmustern ("consistency of patterns"). Darunter versteht er für die einzelnen Bereiche von Kultur je etwas anderes: für Ideensysteme *logische* Widerspruchslosigkeit, für die Kunst *stilistische* Harmonie und für die Moral *rationale* Kompatibilität ihrer Regeln. Parsons bemerkt, dass kulturelle Konsistenz nicht immer vollständig erreicht werden kann und in vielen Fällen auch schwer nachzuweisen ist. Grundsätzlich aber bleibt sie für die *Integration* von Handlungssystemen essentiell. Ähnliches wird für die Internalisierung von Wertorientierungen angenommen. Offen bleibt, welche Persönlichkeitstypen und welche Gesellschaften welche Arten von Kultur internalisieren respektive institutionalisieren können. Dies deutet auf Fragen der Kreativität (Persönlichkeitsebene) und

---

[4] Allerdings ist auch diese Position nicht ganz eindeutig, wie folgendes Zitat zeigt: "Culture is not only transmitted from generation to generation through teaching and learning; it can be embodied in externalized symbols, for example, works of art, the printed page, or storage devices such as computer tapes" (Parsons/Shils 1973, S. 16).

Innovation (Gesellschaft) hin. Im Verhältnis des Kultursystems zum Persönlichkeits- (Internalisierung) und Sozialsystem (Institutionalisierung), verbunden mit dem Konsistenzproblem sieht Parsons einen Ansatz zu einer "dynamic theory of culture" (Parsons/Shils 1951, S. 20 ff.).

In Abschnitt 2 ("Values, Motives and Systems of Action") von *Toward a General Theory of Action* holt Parsons (gemeinsam mit Edward A. Shils) zu einer Vertiefung seines Kulturbegriffs aus. Wieder geht es ihm um die Abgrenzung des *Kultursystems* vom *Persönlichkeits-* und *Sozialsystem*. Er fasst zusammen: "Thus a cultural system is a pattern of culture whose different parts are interrelated to form value systems, belief systems, and systems of expressive symbols" (Parsons/Shils 1951, S. 55). Nachdem er vorher nochmals spezifiziert hat, dass dieses System im Unterschied zu den beiden anderen nicht aus Interaktionen und Handlungen besteht, sondern vielmehr eine Art Abstraktion dieser Elemente ist. Als physisches Symbol kann Kultur jedoch getrennt von diesen Elementen existieren und von einem empirischen Handlungssystem zum anderen übertragen werden. Außerdem unterstreicht Parsons nochmals, dass kulturelle Elemente in einem empirischen Handlungssystem nicht zufällig und unzusammenhängend existieren können, sondern einer gewissen inneren Konsistenz bedürfen.

Ein weiterer Aspekt ist, dass Parsons Kultur im Referenzrahmen *Handelnder-Situation-Orientierung* nicht nur als Objekt der Situation (siehe oben), sondern auch als Bestandteil der Orientierung des Handelnden definiert, die er wieder nach *Motivorientierungen* (Wünsche, Pläne etc.) und *Wertorientierungen* unterteilt. "Value-orientation refers to those aspects of the actor's orientation which commit him to the observance of certain norms, standards, criteria of selection, whenever he is in a contingent situation which allows (and requires) him to make a choice" (Parsons/Shils 1951, S. 59). In einer Fußnote schränkt Parsons ein, dass Wertorientierungen selbstverständlich nicht die Gesamtheit der kulturellen Orientierungen ausmachen, strategisch allerdings deren wichtigster Teil für das Handlungssystem sind. Der Handelnde (hier das Individuum) wird durch Wertorientierungen auf bestimmte Regeln festgelegt, die ihm zu befolgen auf diese Weise zum Bedürfnis werden. Auf der analytischen Ebene *Kultur* nennt Parsons diese Regeln *Standards* ("Thus a culture includes a set of *standards*"). Analog zur Klassifizierung kultureller Objekte (siehe oben) unterscheidet er zwischen *kognitiven*, *appreziativen* und *moralischen* Modi von Wertorientierungen, je nachdem welche Standards involviert sind.

Parsons kommt in *Toward a General Theory of Action* zu der Auffassung, dass Wertorientierungen die entscheidendsten kulturellen Elemente in der Organisation von Handlungssystemen sind, auch wenn sie nur einen Aspekt seines Kulturbegriffs ausmachen (vgl. Parsons/Shils 1951, S. 159). Im Unterschied zu Bedürfnisdispositionen (Persönlichkeitssystem) und Rollenerwartungen (Sozialsystem) sind sie diesen äußerlich, symbolisch provoziert (vgl. Parsons/Shils 1951, S. 160). Anders formuliert, die Symbolsysteme (kulturelle Objekte) von denen sich Wertorientierungen herleiten, sind von konkreten Handlungssystemen separierbar. Sie können anders als diese gespeichert, übertragen und revitalisiert (z. B. alte Bräuche oder Sprachen) werden. Parsons sieht Wertorientierungen als Synthese *kognitiver* und *kathektischer* Bewertungen. Worüber die kognitive Orientierung dem Handelnden Entscheidungsalternativen vor Augen führt, während sich die kathektische Komponente auf das Gratifikationspotential der Alternativen bezieht. "Value-orientations become organized into systems of generalized, normative patterns which require consistency of cognitive-cathectic and consequently evaluative orientation from one particular situation to another" (Parsons/Shils 1951, S. 165).

Nach dieser *situativen* Definition von Kultur sucht Parsons in seinem *strukturfunktionalen* Ansatz nach Möglichkeiten der Klassifizierung von Wert- bzw. kulturellen Orientierungen im Allgemeinen. Dabei greift er auf die in Zusammenhang mit der Analyse der Variabilität von Handlungssystemen entwickelten *Mustervariablen* ("pattern variables") zurück.[5] Mit den Mustervariablen werden grundsätzliche Dilemmata angesprochen, vor denen der Handelnde in der Situation steht. Für die Klassifikation von Wertorientierungen auf der kulturellen Ebene sieht er vor allem die Paare *universalism-particularism* und *ascription-achievement* als geeignet an, besonders im makroskopischen Bereich von *Vergleichen*. Das erste Paar bezieht sich auf das Dilemma *Transzendenz/Immanenz*: Soll der Handelnde Objekte in einer Situation nach einer generellen Norm, die Ausnahmen vermeidet ("universalism") oder nach einer eventuell besonderen Beziehung zu ihm ("particularism") behandeln. Das Dilemma der *Modalität*, zweites Paar, stellt hingegen den Handelnden vor die Frage, ob er sich an dem orientieren soll, was ein Objekt ist ("ascription") oder nach dem was es kann ("achievement"). Die Kombination der beiden Paare ergibt vier logische Möglichkeiten von Typen von Wertorientierungen. Parsons versucht diese durch empirische Beispiele zu illustrieren. Typ 1: Der amerikanische *achievement complex*, in dem universalistischen Bewertungen/ Zielsetzungen sowie dem Leistungsaspekt von Objekten in Handlungsorientierungen der Vorrang gegeben wird. Typ 2: Das klassische chinesische Wertsystem. Der *Beziehungsaspekt* eines Objekts geht vor einer eventuell anwendbaren allgemeinen Norm. Gleichzeitig werden aber auch hohe Leistungsanforderungen gestellt. Streben nach Harmonie und Verantwortung. Typ 3: Das kaiserliche Deutschland – *Status* zählt vor Leistung. Gleichzeitig werden universalistische Klassifizierungen (z. B. Bürokratie) immanenten partikulären Lösungen (z. B. Nepotismus) vorgezogen. Typ 4: Das latein-

---

5 Wie bekannt, hatte Parsons ursprünglich zwischen fünf "pattern variables" (Parsons/Shils 1951, S. 80 ff.) unterschieden: 1) self- versus collective-orientation, 2) affectivity-neutrality, 3) specificity-diffuseness, 4) universalism-particularism und 5) ascription-achievement. Bereits für die Klassifizierung des Persönlichkeits- und Sozialsystem hat er aber self- versus collectivity-orientation wieder aufgegeben.

amerikanische Wertesystem. Auch hier gilt, dass Objekte in einer Situation vor allem nach ihrer *Qualität* und nicht nach Leistungskriterien beurteilt werden. Gleichzeitig wird ihm eher in seiner Beziehung zum Handelnden als in einer normativ-objektiven Form begegnet.

Wie schon erwähnt, hat Parsons in der Folge beim Umbau seiner *Allgemeinen Handlungstheorie* einen zweiten Definitionsbrennpunkt für den Kulturbegriff definiert. Der Grundtenor des Umbaus ist Ausdifferenzierung und zunehmende Abstraktion. Dabei werden die vier Mustervariablen als Klassifizierungsinstrument von Systemen durch ein *Funktionsparadigma* abgelöst. Dies wird als die *systemfunktionalistische* bzw. kybernetische Wende bei Parsons bezeichnet. Sein Interesse schwenkt von *Orientierungsdilemmata* ("pattern-variables") zu *Systemerfordernissen*, von Integration des Systems nach innen zu seiner Anpassung nach außen.[6] Aus der Kreuztabellierung der Achsen *Raum* (innen/außen) und Zeit (instrumentell/konsumtiv) ergibt sich ein Vier-Funktionen Paradigma der Differenzierung von Systemen.[7] Diese Funktionen sind *Anpassung* (Adaptation, A), *Zielerreichung* (Goal-attainment, G), *Integration* (Integration, I) und (latente) *Strukturerhaltung* (Latent pattern-maintenance, L) – abgekürzt: AGIL. An dieser Stelle ist vor allem die Funktion *Strukturerhaltung* interessant (Parsons/Platt 1973, S. 13). Diese Funktion versorgt das System mit *Identität* und ermöglicht damit seine Unterscheidung von anderen Systemen (Raumachse). Gleichzeitig wirkt sie in Richtung von *Kontinuität* in der Entwicklung (Zeitachse). Im Bezugsrahmen *Allgemeines Handlungssystem* erfüllt diese Funktion das *Kultursystem* ("Cultural system"), das zusammen mit dem *Persönlichkeitssystem* (Zielerreichung, G) und dem *Verhaltenssystem* (Anpassung, A) als Umwelt des *Sozialsystems* (Integration, I) definiert wird.

Nach der Logik des AGIL-Paradigmas zerfällt selbstverständlich auch das Kultursystem wieder in vier Subsysteme, die von Parsons als *kognitiver Symbolismus* (A), *expressiver Symbolismus* (G), *moralischer Symbolismus* (I) und *konstitutiver Symbolismus* (L) bezeichnet werden. In seinen eigenen Worten: "In cybernetic terms the cultural system is grounded in *constitutive symbolism* which centers in that part of *religious symbolism oriented* to problems of ultimate concern; this is the pattern-maintenance subsystem of culture. *Moral-evaluative symbols* play an integrative role; at the cultural level, moral-evaluative symbols are the focus of societal values including cognitive rationality. *Expressive symbolization* is oriented toward goal-attainment at the cultural level with special links to the personalities of individuals.

---

[6] Genaueres dazu siehe Staubmann 1995, S. 196 ff.; Wenzel 1990; Parsons/Platt 1973 (Einleitung).
[7] Zu Kulturtheorie und dem Problem der Innen-Außen-Differenzierung siehe allgemein Reckwitz 1997.

Finally, *cognitive symbolization* (knowledge) is oriented to adaptive cultural functions"(Parsons/Platt 1973, S. 313).

Dieser zweite, systemfunktionale Brennpunkt in Parsons' Auseinandersetzung mit dem Thema Kultur ergänzt einerseits den ersten, situationszentrierten bzw. strukturfunktionalen[8], scheint dazu andererseits aber auch in Widerspruch zu stehen. Der Widerspruch ergibt sich vor allem aus der Sicht von Kultur als einem eigenen Subsystem im Bezugsrahmen *Allgemeines Handlungssystem* (Parsons/Shils 1973, S. 17). Kultur wird hier nicht nur als *handlungsbezogenes* Symbolsystem verstanden, sondern ist selbst Handlungssystem. Der Widerspruch sticht auch deshalb so ins Auge, weil Parsons diese Deutung von Kultur im älteren, situationszentrierten Ansatz, wie wir gesehen haben, ausdrücklich ausgeschlossen hat.[9] Unproblematischere Ergänzungen sind die Verbindung des Kulturbegriffs mit einem erweiterten Konzept von *Interpenetration*, mit Überlegungen aus der Kybernetik und die Einbeziehung des *Medien*begriffs. All das sind Ergänzungen insofern, als sie den Kulturbegriff auf einer *makro*theoretischen Ebene reformulieren. Der frühere situationszentrierte, eher sozialpsychologische Zugang ist damit aber nicht aufgegeben worden. Ich spreche hier deshalb auch nicht von *Phasen* in der Entwicklung des Begriffs, sondern von *Brennpunkten* in den theoretischen Anstrengungen Parsons.

Die Analogien zur *Kybernetik* kommen vor allem ins Spiel, wenn es Parsons um die Beziehung der Handlungssysteme untereinander geht. Er spricht hier von "cybernetic relations" (Parsons/Platt 1973, S. 31), in denen das Kultursystem den Pol mit hoher *Information* und niedriger *Energie* einnimmt. Das Verhaltenssystem befindet sich am anderen Ende des Spektrums – hohe Energie, niedrige Information. Parsons deutet an, dass dazwischen *Kontroll-* und *Konditionierungsprozesse* ablaufen. Konditionierung vom Verhaltenssystem in Richtung Kultur und Kontrolle auf dem umgekehrten Weg, jeweils mit abnehmendem Potential. Um mit dem semantischen Nebeneinander von Kultur als Symbolsystem und Kultur als Handlungssystem zurechtzukommen, braucht Parsons das Konzept der *Interpenetration*. "Interpenetration means that the cognate subsystems at each of the four-system levels

---

[8] Zur Entwicklung von Parsons' Werk von einer voluntaristischen über die strukturfunktionale zur systemfunktionalen Phase siehe Wenzel 1990.

[9] Dass Parsons selbst diesen Widerspruch offenbar bis zum Schluss toleriert, vielleicht sogar bewusst will, zeigen verschiedene *fuzzy* Argumentationen in *The American University*, wo mit dem neuen Begriff am ausführlichsten gearbeitet wurde. So bleibt in der schon erwähnten Unterscheidung zwischen "cultural objects" und "cultural system" (Parsons/Platt 1973, S. 17) unerwähnt, dass er an anderer Stelle (Parsons/Shils 1951) unter "cultural system" Kultur als Symbolsystem gemeint hat. In *The American University* bleibt auch meistens unklar, ob gerade über die eine oder die andere Bedeutung gesprochen wird. Eine ausführlichere Kritik dieser Konstruktion findet man bei Schluchter 1980.

constitute zones of 'overlap' and thus affect each other across these boundaries" (Parsons/Platt 1973, S. 36). Anders gesagt, ist damit gemeint, dass mit zunehmender Ausdifferenzierung und damit einhergehender Autonomisierung von Systemen, Zonen der Interpenetration entstehen, in denen Systeme einander überlappen und durchdringen können. Eine typische Interpenetrationszone existiert nach Parsons zwischen dem *Kultursystem* und dem *Treuhandsystem* ("fiduciary subsystem"), seiner unmittelbaren Nachbarschaft ("cognate subsystem") im Sozialsystem. Unmittelbar deshalb, weil dieses Subsystem funktional auf die Vertretung kultureller Interessen ausgerichtet ist.[10]

Diese *Interpenetrationszonen* sollen *Austausch* zwischen den Systemen erleichtern. Das Kultursystem verfügt als Austauschmedium über die *Definition der Situation*[11], die sich etwa über bestimmte kognitive Interessen oder moralische Autorität, zum Beispiel auf das Sozialsystem, auswirken kann. Meines Erachtens kann man sich Kultur als eigenes Handlungssystem nur an solchen Interpenetrationszonen vorstellen (vgl. Parsons/Platt 1973, S. 8). In *The American University* ist die Universität selbst ein Beispiel dafür. Die Universität ist eine Institution mit Personen und Gruppen, deren Handeln explizit kulturelle Objekte zum Gegenstand hat, insofern existiert hier ein *kulturelles Handlungssystem*. Im Unterschied dazu kann zum Beispiel ein Wirtschaftsunternehmen zwar auch aus der Perspektive des kulturellen Systems analysiert werden, es ist auch eine Institutionalisierung von bestimmten Wertstandards (vgl. Parsons/Platt 1973, S. 9), die es schließlich realisieren soll, aber diese zu reflektieren und zu bearbeiten, gehört nicht zu seinen Agenden.

Damit glaube ich, Parsons' Kulturkonzeption ausreichend dargelegt zu haben, um auf die Frage ihres möglichen Beitrags zum Verständnis der neueren Entwicklungen in Europa eingehen zu können. Nochmals kurz: Für Parsons ist Kultur a) Objekt in einer Handlungssituation, b) ein symbolisches System, c) (Wert-) Orientierung, d) (analytischer) Aspekt einer Handlung und e) eigenes Handlungssystem. Selbstverständlich würde es sich auch lohnen, auf Spuren dieser Konzeption in Theorien, die bei Parsons anknüpfen, wie der Systemtheorie von Niklas Luhmann, bzw. in postmodernen Theoriediskursen (Alexander 1994; Wimmer 1996), einzugehen. Luhmann zum Beispiel, der mit seiner Systemtheorie in vielerlei Weise an Parsons anschließt, radikalisiert seine Vorstellung von Kultur als Handlungssystem, indem er unter Kultur nur mehr "eine Perspektive für die Beobachtung von

---

[10] "The fiduciary subsystem of a society acts as a trustee of some interests in the society" (Parsons/Platt 1973, S. 8). Mit "some interests" können im Kontext der Theorie nur kulturelle Interessen gemeint sein.

[11] "Definition of the situation" ist eines von vier Austauschmedien auf der Ebene des "Allgemeinen Handlungssystems". Die anderen sind "Affect" (Sozialsystem), "Performance capacity" (Persönlichkeitssystem) und "Intelligence" (Verhaltenssystem) (z. B. Parsons/Platt 1973, S. 439).

Beobachtern" (Luhmann 1995, S. 54) versteht. Er argumentiert aber nicht in die Richtung weiter, dass damit Kultur systemfähig wird, sondern streicht heraus, dass "der Begriff aus dem Operationsbereich der Beobachtung erster Ordnung in den Operationsbereich der Beobachtung zweiter Ordnung" (Luhmann 1995a, S. 32) gehört. Insgesamt lässt sich sagen, dass er den Begriff Kultur zwar nicht fallen lässt, ihn aber eher mit einer ablehnenden Haltung verbindet, in der einige negativen Sentiments gegenüber seiner Ideengeschichte zu erkennen sind (siehe dazu auch Baecker 1999). Wie gesagt, möchte ich mich damit hier nicht weiter beschäftigen, sondern mich jetzt der Frage zuwenden, wie und ob man aus Parsons Theorie Nutzen für kultursoziologische Analysen der gegenwärtigen Entwicklung in Europa ziehen kann. Dazu möchte ich im nächsten Schritt die Themen identifizieren, die immanent oder aus der Sicht der Theorie überhaupt als kulturelle Probleme definiert werden können.

Der Hauptantrieb der europäischen Integration war und ist immer noch die Wirtschaft bzw. der Wunsch, den Wohlstand in den Mitgliedsstaaten der Europäischen Union zu mehren. Wichtigstes Instrument ist dabei die kontinuierliche Verbesserung des allgemeinen Handlungsrahmens für das kapitalistische Unternehmen. Der Nachdruck liegt auf *Modernisierung* im Sinne steigender ökonomischer Effizienz. In den ersten beiden Jahrzehnten nach dem 2. Weltkrieg gab es dabei allerdings einen ernst zu nehmenden Konkurrenten: das kommunistische System sowjetischer Prägung. Interessanterweise waren aber zeitweise die Auswirkungen dieser Konkurrenz eher im kulturellen als im wirtschaftlichen Bereich zu spüren. Dies gilt insbesondere für die sechziger Jahre. Die nachwachsende Intelligenz in Westeuropa sah damals ihre Gesellschaften verstärkt unter dem Gesichtspunkt von Gruppenantagonismen und sozialer Polarisierung. Mitbestimmungsmodelle und Fragen individueller wie kollektiver Emanzipation waren beliebte Seminarthemen. Es war eine Zeit, in der die Forderung nach *Demokratisierung* aller Lebensbereiche breite öffentliche Unterstützung fand. Demokratie sollte vor den Fabrikstoren nicht halt machen müssen und auch die Universitäten revolutionieren. Modelle wie der jugoslawische *Selbstverwaltungssozialismus* oder die kollektivistische Lebensweise der *Kibbuzniks* in Israel fanden zum Teil auch in Westeuropa begeisterte Anhänger.

Entgegen dem universalistischen Impetus der dominanten Themen jener Zeit, inklusive einiger internationaler Dimensionen (z. B. Vietnamkrieg, Solidarität mit den Entwicklungsländern), spielte sich diese Begleitmusik der Systemkonkurrenz hauptsächlich im Rahmen nationaler Kulturen ab. Der Nationalstaat blieb aus dieser Richtung unangefochten. Ähnliches gilt für die *Parallelaktion* "europäische Integration", die sich mit einer Verbesserung der *terms of trade* im Rahmen der Europäischen Wirtschaftsgemeinschaft (EWG) und der Europäischen Freihandelszone (EFTA) begnügte. Keine von beiden artikulierte irgendwelche Ansprüche auf kulturelle Themen. Auch innerhalb des Sowjetblocks blieb Kultur, trotz aller internationalistischen Rhetorik, eine Angelegenheit der einzelnen Volksrepubliken (siehe Csepeli 1997). Es war nicht vor den achtziger Jahren, dass Kultur zu einer Dimension der europäischen Integration wurde. Den intellektuellen Rahmen dazu bot die Verschiebung der Diskurse von strukturemanzipatorischen Themen zu solchen der Identität. Diese Verschiebung hat sich seit der Implosion des Sowjetsystems und der einhergehenden westeuropäischen Integration beschleunigt. Daraus sind ein halbes Dutzend kultureller Diskurse entstanden, die die kritischen Punkte der europäischen Entwicklung offen legen, aber auch noch selbst einer Interpretation bedürfen. Diese Diskurse sollen in der Folge kurz skizziert werden, um dann abschließend nochmals Parsons' Kulturtheorie aufzunehmen, wieweit sie in diesem Zusammenhang neue Sichtweisen und Analyseansätze bieten kann.

Aus einer Vielzahl von Kulturthemen, die in letzter Zeit über den Rahmen des Nationalstaates hinaus Aufmerksamkeit erweckt haben, möchte ich folgende wegen ihrer *strategischen Qualität* für Europa kurz beschreiben: Das "gemeinsame Erbe", die großen Trennlinien, die Erfindung der Region, Hoffnung in die Nation, postkommunistische Transformation, Globalisierung: Der europäische Weg.

– *Das "gemeinsame Erbe"*

Analysiert man Veröffentlichungen zur kollektiven Identität, dann fällt in den achtziger Jahren für Europa ein deutlicher Sprung von *additiven* zu *integrativen* Sichtweisen auf. Zuvor war dieses Genre fast durchwegs nationenzentriert. Auch amerikanische Publikationen über Europa enthielten in der Regel nur eine mehr oder weniger systematische Beschreibung einer kleinen Zahl europäischer Länder. Obgleich die Europäer, sofern sie sich damit überhaupt beschäftigten, meist einen ähnlich additiven Zugang wählten (siehe Enzensberger 1987), produzierten sie zunehmend auch Texte, in denen Europa als eine kohärente kulturelle Einheit verstanden wird. Gelegentlich diente die Geografie, die bisher den Begriff ganz auszufüllen schien, als Ausgangspunkt, um Hypothesen wie die von einer besonderen kulturellen Produktivität dieses Kontinents zu formulieren.[12] Trotz verschiedener Denkansätze, schimmert hinter solchen Texten immer auch die Suche nach gemeinsamen kulturellen Prinzipien hervor. Das ist besonders dann der Fall, wenn es sich bei den Autoren um Sozialwissenschafter handelt. Griechische, römische und christliche Antike werden als Zeugen einer gemeinsamen Basis bemüht. Werte wie Individualismus, Freiheit der Person, Autonomie, Rationalität und Menschenrechte, aber auch die Fähigkeit Geschichte neu zu bewerten (Renaissance), transnationale Stile (Gotik, Barock, Art Nouveau etc.) zu entwickeln, sozial mobil zu sein, Allianzen (Empires)

---

12 Rolf Edberg (1985) zum Beispiel streicht die lange Küstenlinie hervor, die für die kulturelle Entwicklung Europas vorteilhaft gewesen sein soll. Obwohl eine dreimal so lange Küste als Afrika, hat Europa nur ein Drittel seiner Fläche.

zu knüpfen, demokratisches Verhalten zu zeigen usw., werden als typisch europäisch identifiziert (Lipp 1991). Die unübersehbare Vielfalt, die zum Teil extreme Gegensätze und Verfall werden in diesem Argumentationsstrang entweder als nur temporär oder selbst als Kennzeichen einer gemeinsamen europäischen Kultur interpretiert. Was gelegentlich konzidiert wird, ist die Notwendigkeit eines neuen Diskurses um die *Identität* Europas (Glotz 1999).

– *Die großen Trennlinien*
Solche kulturellen Gemeinsamkeiten Europas hervorzuheben, ist erst wieder in den letzten beiden Jahrzehnten zu einer ernstgenommenen sozialwissenschaftlichen Position geworden. Im Normalfall hatte man zuvor, falls überhaupt über den Nationalstaat hinausgedacht wurde, seine kulturellen Bruch- und Trennlinien betont. Als Kriterien dafür dienten die Zugehörigkeit zu unterschiedlichen Sprachgruppen (Germanisch, Slawisch, Romanisch) oder Religionen (protestantisch/katholisch/ orthodox), die Lösung der Machtfrage (demokratisch/autoritär), der Typus der Rechtsordnung (angelsächsisch/kontinental), Stand der Modernisierung, historische Ungleichzeitigkeit in der Entwicklung etc. (siehe Rokkan 1980; Haller 1990; Huntington 1996; Szücs 1990). Auch implizierte die Unterscheidung von "kapitalistisch" und "sozialistisch" während des *Kalten Krieges* nicht nur politökonomische, sondern auch kulturelle Aspekte. Diese Sichtweise setzt sich heute in der Vorstellung von einer *post-kommunistischen* Kultur in den sogenannten Reformländern Mittel- und Osteuropas fort. Möglicherweise eine neue Trennlinie.

– *Die Erfindung der Region*
Beim Wort "Region" fällt auf, wie es seit Mitte der siebziger Jahre unter dem Titel "Europa der Regionen" identitätspolitisch gegen den Nationalstaat eingesetzt wird. Identitätspolitisch heißt, dass an den kulturellen Traditionen eines geographischen Raumes angeknüpft wird, um ihn von den Bindungen des Nationalstaates zu "befreien". Erst dann kommen politische und raumplanerische Aspekte. Anders als bei der Vorstellung von kulturellen Großräumen, in denen universalistische Kriterien bestimmend sind, versuchen sich Regionen kulturell vor allem durch ethnische und folkloristische Elemente zu definieren. "... jedes Regionalkonzept impliziert Elemente eines Kulturkonzepts" (Bausinger 1993, S. 483). Das dazugehörige Assoziationsfeld birgt Begriffe wie Heimat, Volkskultur, Minoritäten, Vertrautheit, Mentalität, Autonomie und regionaler Habitus. Gerade weil es sich hier fast durchwegs um schillernde bzw. diffuse Konzepte handelt, sind sie von großer politischer Attraktivität. Anders als der Nationalstaat, der sich gerade gegen die historischen Regionen durchgesetzt hat, signalisiert der *EU-Komplex* den Regionen (und denen, die es werden wollen) Unterstützung und Interesse an ihrer kulturellen Identität. Das bringt beide in einen mehr oder weniger offenen Gegensatz zum Nationalstaat, der seit seiner Existenz auf kulturelle Homogenität hinwirkt. Nun ist es gerade dieser kultu-

relle Aspekt, der die Region zu einem wichtigen Faktor im europäischen Integrationsprozess macht.

Ein Subdiskurs bezieht sich in diesem Rahmen auf das Thema *Grenze*. In der Regel richtet er sich gegen die Grenzziehungen der Nationalstaaten, welche als Hindernis für die Entwicklung des Wohlstands der Region empfunden werden. Auch hier ist die Kultur vielfach der Ansatzpunkt, um Potentiale grenzüberschreitender Kooperationen zu suggerieren bzw., wenn vorhanden, freizumachen. Kultur kann in diesem Zusammenhang sowohl als Hindernis als auch als Triebkraft grenzüberschreitender Regionalisierung identifiziert werden (Eskelinen/Liikanen/Oksa 1998). Der Diskurs über Grenzen ist indes nicht auf das Thema Region beschränkt, sondern führt auch zum *gemeinsamen Europa* und zur Nation (Mlinar 1996). Wo sind die kulturellen Grenzen Europas? Wie können innerhalb der europäischen Integration die Mitglieder der nationalen Subkulturen kommunizieren und gemeinsam handeln (Häyrynen 1996)? Wieweit festigen Staatsgrenzen Identität (Eger/Langer 1996)? Können Kulturgrenzen politische Grenzen überdauern?

– *Hoffnung in die Nation*
Über Charakter und Zukunft des Nationalstaates gibt es widersprüchliche Vorstellungen (Haller 1996; Kriesi et al. 1999). Neben den diffus anmutenden Prozessen der Globalisierung (Meyer u.a. 1997) ist es in Europa vor allem die Europäische Union, die den Nationalstaat verändert. Der Transfer von Souveränität auf die supranationale Ebene ist hier unübersehbar. Dies spricht für jene theoretischen Positionen, die dem National*staat* ein nahes Ende voraussagen. Sollte der europäische Integrationsprozess institutionell tatsächlich unumkehrbar sein, bleibt aber immer noch die Frage, ob nicht die *Nation* den Staat, der in einem Größeren aufgeht, überdauern könnte. Die Nation ist aber in erster Linie ein kulturelles Verhältnis, auch dort, wo sie – wie in Westeuropa und Nordamerika – bevorzugt über Mitgliedschaft oder verfassungsrechtlich definiert wird.[13] Es gibt wohl keinen Nationalstaat, der nicht versucht, "seine" Bevölkerung auf die eine oder andere Weise kulturell zu homogenisieren. Allein schon die Durchsetzung einheitlicher Rechtsnormen wirkt in diese Richtung.

Die Frage ist nun, wenn auch gerne verdrängt, ob die von den europäischen Nationalstaaten geschaffenen Nationalkulturen unter den Bedingungen einer vollintegrierten Europäischen Union weiterbestehen können. Nachdem die meisten dieser Staaten kulturell über eine Landessprache integriert sind, wird diese Frage von der Politik vorerst kaum ernst genommen. Heißt es doch: "Wir werden auch in einer EU Österreicher etc. bleiben". Wenn man aber berücksichtigt, dass das hohe Niveau der

---

13 Man denke nur an die Entschlossenheit, mit der die Franzosen ihre Sprache zu behaupten versuchen oder wie schwer vorstellbar eine USA ohne den "American Way of Life" ist.

kulturellen Homogenität von Nationalstaaten zu einem guten Teil auf institutionelle Maßnahmen zurückzuführen ist, dann sollte die Schwächung der nationalstaatlichen Institutionen auch Konsequenzen für die Kultur haben. Insbesondere dort, wo der Nationalstaat Zwang eingesetzt hat bzw. nationalstaatliche Identität gegen Widerstand durchgesetzt wurde, ist mit relativ raschen Erosionen der nationalstaatlichen Kultur zu rechnen (Langer 1999). Was könnte sie ersetzen? Eine europäische Identität (Haller 1999)?

– *Post-kommunistische Transformation*
Seit der sogenannten "Wende" Ende der achtziger Jahre nimmt der früher "Ostblock" genannte Teil Europas neue Konturen an. Aus dem roten Fleck auf der Weltkarte aus der Zeit des Kalten Krieges sind vielgestaltige Gesellschaften und Orte mit konkreten Namen aufgetaucht, die im Bewusstsein des Westens erst neu vermessen werden müssen. Bislang geschah dies vorwiegend in Kategorien der Wirtschaftswissenschaften. Stichwort: Transformationsforschung.[14] Fragen der Kultur wurden entweder vernachlässigt oder affirmativ beantwortet. Affirmativ heißt hier, dass angenommen wird, bei "Ostmitteleuropa" – übrigens ein neuer geopolitischer Begriff – handle es sich um Gesellschaften, die, wenn auch nur als Peripherie, kulturell dem Westen zuzurechnen sind (Hadas/Vörös 1996; Langer 1998a). Daraus begründen sich eine Reihe von Vereinnahmungsdiskursen. Zum Beispiel wird argumentiert, dass in Deutschland oder Österreich, die mit ihrer Kultur einmal weit in den Osten ausgegriffen haben, noch immer eine besondere *Ostkompetenz* existiere. Mit dem kulturellen Argument wird aber auch für die Mitgliedschaft dieser Länder in der Europäischen Union geworben.

Durch die Fixierung des Blicks allein auf die ökonomischen Prozesse blieb bislang leider völlig unklar, welche kulturelle Gestalt die post-kommunistischen Gesellschaften heute haben bzw. in Zukunft annehmen könnten. Jedenfalls wird keine ernst zu nehmende Analyse die Erfahrungen der kommunistischen Epoche in diesen Gesellschaften negieren können. Der Vorwurf "zivilisatorischer Inkompetenz" (Sztompka 1993) wäre darin ebenso zu prüfen wie das erstaunliche Faktum, dass diese Gesellschaften einen relativ gewaltlosen Weg von einem Einparteiensystem zu politischen und wirtschaftlichen Institutionen nach westlichem Muster eingeschlagen haben. Bekommt hier Europa aber nicht auch ein neues kulturelles Segment, mit dem es sich auseinandersetzen wird müssen? An den auf allen Ebenen von der Politik bis zur Wirtschaft wieder einsetzenden Beziehungen sollte man feststellen können, welche Konturen die *post-kommunistische* Kultur annimmt (Langer 1998b). Wenn es sie gibt, was theoretisch und empirisch zu klären wäre, dann könnte sie, im

---

14 Zu den Ausnahmen siehe Srubar 1994.

Falle einer Osterweiterung, die bereits umstrittenen ökonomischen Auswirkungen mit zusätzlichen Überraschungen belegen.

– *Globalisierung: Der europäische Weg*
Globalisierung ist ein schillerndes Wort. Man könnte darunter ortsunabhängige Lebensformen verstehen, die über weltumspannende soziale Beziehungen entstehen. Schlagwort: *Weltgesellschaft*. "Fremd" und von "außen" kommend sind begleitende Konnotationen. Für manche verdeckt Globalisierung auch nur die imperiale Durchsetzung des *American Way of Life*. Auch wenn vielleicht nur ein kleiner Teil der Menschheit weltweit kommuniziert, so ist doch jeder in seiner Lebensweise davon betroffen. Globalisierung ist deshalb zur Zeit vor allem ein kulturelles Phänomen. Sichtbar wird sie besonders bei der Jugend, im Entertainment und in den neuen elektronischen Medien. Insbesondere die selbstbewussteren Nationalstaaten müssen sich davon in ihren kulturellen Autonomiebestrebungen konterkariert fühlen. Interessanterweise bezieht sich aber auch ein guter Teil dessen, was sich bisher als Kulturpolitik der Europäischen Union herausgebildet hat, auf dieses Problem. Protektionistische Interessen der Mitgliedsländer scheinen sich mit dem Versuch zu verbinden, der Union insgesamt mehr Einfluss innerhalb der weltweiten Kulturkonkurrenz zu verschaffen. Auf Grund des Primats kommerzieller Interessen in der Union wird hingegen kaum beachtet, dass dieser Prozess vor allem Grundlagen der nationalen Identität wegbrechen lässt (Wintle 1996; Gießhaber 1998). Eine Frage ist deshalb, ob Globalisierung den Integrationsprozess in Europa unterstützt oder eher behindert. Interessieren sollte aber auch, ob Europa diesen Prozess strategisch beeinflussen kann.

Talcott Parsons war ein amerikanischer Soziologe. Mehr noch: Richard Münch, einer seiner erfolgreichsten Interpreten in der deutschsprachigen Soziologie, nannte ihn sogar in einem Atemzug mit der Hegemonie der USA nach dem Zweiten Weltkrieg. Er fügt aber auch etwas über seine Verstrickung in die europäische Geistesgeschichte hinzu: "Parsons ... not only discovered but also constructed a synthesis of the European traditions of positivism and idealism ..." (Münch 1993a, S. 45 f.). Auch wenn diese Synthese unter spezifisch amerikanischen Bedingungen zustande kam, sollte seiner Theorie die europäische Entwicklung nicht fremd sein. Deshalb überrascht auch nicht, dass Parsons die Einleitung seines letzten großen Werkes (gemeinsam mit Gerald Platt) *The American University* mit einer Referenz auf Europa eröffnet, nachdem er die Motivation zu dieser Arbeit mit seinem Interesse an den Entwicklungen in der westlichen Gesellschaft begründet hatte: "What is thought of as modern society took shape in the seventeenth century in the northwestern corner of the European system of societies, in Great Britain, Holland, and France" (Parsons/Platt 1973, S. 1). Diesem "northwestern corner", aus Parsons' Sicht die Wiege der modernen Entwicklung, kontrastiert er an anderer Stelle den zurückgebliebenen "southern tire", das katholische Europa. Genaueres indes wird man bei Parsons über Europa nicht oft finden. Es sei denn, man berücksichtigt die gelegentlichen Exkurse in die Geschichte zur Untermauerung seiner Modernisierungstheorie, denn Nordamerika, um das es ihm empirisch immer geht, kann ohne seine europäische Erbschaft (Antike, Christentum) nicht verstanden werden.

Das zeitgenössische Europa sieht er indes vorwiegend unter der Perspektive der Nation (Buxton 1985). Nur vereinzelt findet man übergreifende Versuche, wenn er zum Beispiel in den sechziger Jahren den damals noch nicht inflationär gebrauchten Ausdruck "Neues Europa" verwendet. Parsons bezeichnete damit jene Ordnung auf dem Alten Kontinent, die als Ergebnis von zwei Weltkriegen zustandegekommen war. Charakterisiert sah er diese Ordnung durch eine Schwächung des europäischen Kerns der modernen Entwicklung, zu dem er Frankreich und England, zum Teil aber auch Deutschland zählte, durch Verlagerung imperialer Macht zur Sowjetunion und den USA, die so als "Flügelmächte" erscheinen.

Unter "Neues Europa" muss klarerweise nach dem Zusammenbruch des unter der Führung der Sowjetunion gestandenen kommunistischen Weltsystems heute etwas anderes verstanden werden. Ob das Machtzentrum mit der Etablierung der Europäischen Union vorerst in den Westen des Kontinents zurückgekehrt ist, also das Parsonssche Europabild einer wesentlichen Korrektur bedarf, kann meiner Ansicht noch nicht beantwortet werden. In Hinblick auf Kultur hingegen wird man ihm eine gewisse Voraussicht nicht absprechen können. Er hat nämlich für sein "Neues Europa" als Hauptentwicklungslinie dessen "Amerikanisierung" ausgemacht (Parsons 1972, S. 164). Darunter verstand er positiv die Steigerung und Ergänzung der industriellen Entwicklung in den europäischen Gesellschaften durch *Demokratie* und *Massenbildung*. Man könnte dabei auch an einen neuen Modernisierungsschub oder aus heutiger Sicht an Globalisierung denken. Wobei Parsons unter letzterem wahrscheinlich "Amerikanisierung" im Weltmaßstab verstehen würde. Die Frage ist, auch für ihn, "wie viele Veränderungen das Ergebnis des amerikanischen 'Einflusses' sind und wie viele Veränderungen aus den jeweiligen Ländern selbst kommen" (Parsons 1972, S. 164). Verständlicherweise kann er diese Anteile nicht exakt bestimmen. Er begnügt sich deshalb damit, die "Amerikanisierung" in Europa mit den Auswirkungen der Reformation und der Französischen Revolution zu vergleichen.

In *Das System moderner Gesellschaften* (1972) versucht Parsons offensichtlich auch seine Theorie, die sonst bevorzugt in Vier-Felder-Tafeln dargestellt wird, auf historisch empirische Analyse anzuwenden. Dies gelingt meiner Ansicht hauptsächlich bei der Identifikation von gesellschaftlichen Bereichen (Subsystemen). Wenn es um Erklärung und Interpretation geht, verflüchtigt sich die Theorie hingegen zu Gunsten einfacher historischer Beschreibungen und Spekulation. Genauer: Die Komplexität der Theorie bzw. ihre Kategorien lassen sich in Parsons' historischen Studien kaum mehr erkennen. Das gilt übrigens *grosso modo* auch für jene, deren

Arbeiten heute an Parsons' Theorie anschließen. Als Beispiel möchte ich hier wieder Richard Münch erwähnen. In diesem Zusammenhang vor allem sein Buch *Das Projekt Europa* (Münch 1993b). Zwar folgt Münch mit der Einteilung der Arbeit in die Hauptkapitel "Identität", "Ökonomie", "Politik", "Solidarität" und "Kultur" ziemlich genau dem AGIL-Paradigma, wenn man "Identität" der "Kultur" als strukturerhaltendes System zurechnet, ansonsten sind im Text aber wenig Anschlüsse zu den Kategorien von Parsons zu entdecken, außer dass er die Amerikanisierungsthese voll übernimmt. Während er das Kapitel "Identität" hauptsächlich unter Gesichtspunkten politikwissenschaftlicher Nationentheorien abhandelt, werden bei "Kultur" Theorien der gesellschaftlichen Intelligenz und der Medien ("europäische Kultur im globalen Kampf um Marktanteile") herangezogen. Kulturelle Gemeinsamkeiten sieht Münch in Europa vor allem dort entstehen, wo die von den USA dominierten Globalisierungsprozesse (Hollywood, Coca Cola, Popmusik, McDonalds etc.) wirksam werden, während die europäischen Nationalkulturen mit ihrer prononcierten Öffentlichkeit und intellektuellen Schulen weiterbestehen. Statt eines expliziten Kulturbegriffs, werden immer wieder empirische Daten zur Unterstützung verschiedener *ad hoc* Thesen ausgebreitet.

Während Münch den Kulturansatz von Parsons stehen lässt (Münch 1984), ohne ihn empirisch-praktisch umzusetzen – worin er sich durchaus mit ihm trifft –, geht Niklas Luhmann, der sonst, wie bereits erwähnt, theoretisch eng an Parsons anschließt, noch weiter. Auch wenn er den Begriff Kultur als "soziales Gedächtnis", "Strategie (ethnozentrischen) Vergleichs" oder einer Realität auf der Ebene der "Beobachtung 2. Ordnung" theoretisch noch mitschleppt (Luhmann 1995a; Luhmann 1998, S. 584 ff.), bei Anwendungsanalysen lässt er ihn ganz fallen. So in einem Beitrag über besondere Strukturen und Probleme des "Mezzogiorno" Italiens, in dem er jene Studien kritisiert, die diese Tatsachen auf die Feststellung von Unterschieden in der "Kultur" oder "Mentalität" der Bevölkerung des Südens zurückführen.

> Kultur scheint es immer und überall gegeben zu haben, solange und soweit es Menschen gibt. Theoretisch hat dieser Begriff jedoch wenig erbracht. Vor allem ist unklar geblieben, wovon sich Kultur unterscheidet, wenn alle Artefakte, einschließlich Texte, einschließlich sogar der jeweiligen Vorstellung von 'Natur' als 'Kultur' zu verstehen sind ... Wenn aber ein Begriff nicht klarstellen kann, was durch ihn ausgeschlossen wird, was also die andere, nicht bezeichnete Seite seiner Form ist, sind wissenschaftliche Erträge nicht zu erwarten (Luhmann 1995b, S. 7).

In seiner eigenen Analyse gibt er der Wissenschaft wenig Chancen, der Politik Instrumente für die Entwicklung von peripheren Regionen zur Verfügung stellen zu können.

Ist es nun mit dem Kulturbegriff im Allgemeinen sowie seiner Version bei Parsons erkenntnistheoretisch und forschungspraktisch wirklich so schlecht bestellt? Was Parsons betrifft, möchte ich an die bisherige Darstellung und Diskussion anschließend sagen, dass mir sein Ansatz nicht so überholt erscheint, wie immer wieder behauptet wird. Zuerst bietet er eine a) *Klassifizierung* von *Funktionssystemen* und *Forschungsfragen* (siehe Münch), die erkenntnisleitend und hypothesenkreierend wirken kann. Dadurch wird dem heute in Europa spürbaren Druck, den Blick auf Fragen von Wirtschaft und Technologie zu verengen, entgegengewirkt. Politik, Gemeinschaft und Kultur erscheinen zumindest theoretisch als "gleichwertige" Handlungssysteme. Die Theorie fördert b) auch das Denken in *Zusammenhängen*. Dies kommt unter anderem im Konzept der "Interpenetration" zum Ausdruck, über das in bezug auf Kultur erschlossen werden kann, wie sich diese mit Politik, Wirtschaft und dem sozialen System überlappt bzw. auf welche Weise sich die Systeme gegenseitig durchdringen. Der "analytische Realismus" von Parsons impliziert auch für seinen Kulturbegriff die Möglichkeit des c) *Perspektivenwechsels*. Kultur kann darin sowohl als Objekt einer Situation, Formaspekt von Beziehungen, Wertorientierung von Handlungssystemen (Person, Organisation) als auch als eigenes Handlungssystem studiert werden. Schließlich ermöglicht Parsons Kulturbegriff d) mehr oder weniger eindeutige *analytische Unterscheidungen*. Hier wird nicht wie zum Beispiel vielfach in den sogenannten "cultural studies" alles und jedes mit Kultur gleichgesetzt und in post-moderner Beliebigkeit kommentiert.

Was lässt sich daraus für die aufgezählten und für Europa als "strategisch" bezeichneten Kulturprobleme ableiten? Meiner Ansicht ist Parsons' Kulturbegriff so vielschichtig und flexibel, gleichzeitig aber auch ausreichend trennscharf, um bei jedem der aufgezählten Themen eine Erweiterung des Blicks gegenüber den heute gängigen Diskursen zu bewirken. Dazu zwei Beispiele:

Wie erwähnt hat Luhmann die *kulturvergleichende Regionalforschung* in Europa als politisch unbrauchbar kritisiert. Ich bin zwar nicht dieser Auffassung, würde aber doch zugestehen, dass sie als *Mentalitäts*forschung oft auch nur Vorurteile bestätigt, wenn nicht erst erzeugt. Die Politik wird sich unter dem Gesichtspunkt der Stimmenmaximierung eher anpassen als Mentalitäten zu verändern suchen. Für die Wirtschaft sieht es schon wieder anders aus. Sie muss sich bei ihren Entscheidungen auf die Art der Leistungsorientierung der Mitarbeiter stützen können, aber auch die Präferenzen der potentiellen Kunden berücksichtigen. Der Begriff der (Wert-)Orientierung bei Parsons kann das abdecken. Dies betrifft aber hauptsächlich das Persönlichkeitssystem. Im sozialen System erscheint Kultur als *normative Standards* und als *Beziehungsform*, denn jede Beziehung hat in diesem Begriffsverständnis neben ihrem sozialen auch einen kulturellen Aspekt. Die Theorie richtet die Aufmerksamkeit deshalb auch auf die soziale Begrenzung (Patronage, Netzwerke etc.) von Rationalität und Freiheit. Neue Anstöße für die Regionalforschung könnte daneben das Konzept der *Interpenetration* bzw. der *Interpenetrationszonen* liefern. Ich denke hier an das Problemfeld der grenzüberschreitenden *Euroregionen* und den Versuchen, zwischen den Nationalstaaten und der EU megaregionale Beziehungen (z. B. Ostseeraum, Alpen-Adria) zu etablieren.

Die *post-kommunistischen* Gesellschaften sind ein anderes europäisches Problemfeld (Müller 1995), in dem Parsons' Theorie getestet werden könnte. Für den durchschnittlichen Westeuropäer sind diese Gesellschaften erst 1989 wieder in die Geschichte zurückgekehrt. Sie tragen deshalb immer noch das Stigma des Fremden, Unberechenbaren und Gefährlichen an sich. Es gibt mittlerweile über sie Tausende – wenn auch oft nicht sehr zuverlässige – ökonomische Daten und Analysen, weiters eine ganze Reihe von empirischen Untersuchungen zum Verhalten und Bewusstsein ihrer Bevölkerung. Was man hingegen selten findet, sind profunde theoretische Analysen, aus denen man etwas über den Gesamtzustand und die Entwicklungsrichtungen dieser Gesellschaften entnehmen könnte. Dafür gibt es umso mehr Mythen, Vorurteile und *ad hoc* Thesen. Ich möchte hier in bezug auf Kultur zwei herausgreifen, die aus der Sicht von Parsons' Theorie wahrscheinlich aufgegeben bzw. revidiert werden müssten. Das eine ist der Mythos der "Ostkompetenz" bestimmter westlicher Nachbarn des früheren Sowjetblocks, das andere die These von einem "post-communist mind". In Ländern wie Österreich, Deutschland oder Finnland wird die Vorstellung über "Ostkompetenz" zu verfügen besonders in der Wirtschaft gepflegt, teilweise wird sie auch von den Medien verbreitet. Es gibt auch wissenschaftliche Untersuchungen, die diese These zu belegen versuchen.[15] In Österreich findet sich dazu noch ein spezieller Hintergrund, den man als "Mitteleuropatheorie" bezeichnen könnte. Einer der Eckpfeiler dieser Theorie ist die Vorstellung, dass es in dem Raum, der bis 1918 die Österreichisch-Ungarische Monarchie ausgemacht hat, eine kulturelle Kontinuität gibt, die gleichsam die Grundlage der "Ostkompetenz" österreichischer Manager ist.

Diesem positiven Bild steht eine ebenfalls im Westen kreierte Vorstellung von einem *post-kommunistischen Bewusstsein* gegenüber, das praktisch allen Idealen demokratisch-marktwirtschaftlicher Orientierungen widerspricht und als böse Erbschaft des kommunistischen Totalitarismus verstanden wird.[16] Nach dieser Theorie hat man es hier mit Gesellschaften zu tun, in denen Autoritätshörigkeit, Apathie, Zynismus, Xenophobie und Anomie vorherrschen. Diese Orientierungen konterkarieren den *Transformationsprozess*, indem neu geschaffene demokratische Institutionen nach alten Prinzipien betrieben werden, kein kritisches öffentliches Bewusstsein entsteht, der Wirtschaft die hochmotivierten und verlässlichen Mitarbeiter fehlen, Familien sich nach außen abschließen usw. Diese Orientierungen und

---

15 Siehe dazu z. B. die Publikationen des Instituts für Europaforschung an der Wirtschaftsuniversität Wien oder des Instituts für den Donauraum und Mitteleuropa, Wien.
16 Siehe dazu u.a. Feichtinger/Fink 1998 und die dort zitierte Literatur. Jiri S. Melich, auf den der Begriff "post-communist mind" wahrscheinlich zurückgeht, hat kürzlich einen ähnlich provokanten Text über den wirtschaftlichen Transformationsprozess vorgelegt (Melich 1999), in dem diese Bezeichnung nicht mehr aufscheint, obwohl ihr alle dort beschriebenen Phänomene subsumiert werden können.

Verhaltensweisen werden so beschrieben, als ob die Kultur des *Totalitarismus* in den nach 1989 zweifellos entstandenen Organisationen und Institutionen ungebrochen weiter besteht. Der Bevölkerung wird gleichzeitig ein *Kulturschock* attestiert, der sie vielleicht noch Jahre, wenn nicht Jahrzehnte in Bann halten wird (Feichtinger/Fink 1998). Angesichts der Tatsache, dass der beidseitige Wille bekundet wurde, diese Gesellschaften über kurz oder lang in die Europäische Union (Evers 1994) aufzunehmen, ist eine solche These ernst zu nehmen, wenn man noch größeren Problemen zuvorkommen will.

Was kann man aus Sicht von Parsons' Kulturbegriff dazu sagen? Eine kulturell fundierte "Ostkompetenz" würde voraussetzen, dass es in dem besagten Raum nach wie vor ein gemeinsames System *konstitutiver Symbolisierungen* gibt. Damit sind die letzten Werte der Religion gemeint, ob transzendental legitimiert oder in säkularisierter Form. Zwar lebten die Gesellschaften der Donaumonarchie überwiegend nach der Habsburgischen Variante des Katholizismus, doch ist unwahrscheinlich, dass diese gemeinsame Wertbasis heute noch existiert. Zum Beispiel ist nach Umfragen die Atheismusrate in diesen Ländern weit höher als bei ihren westlichen Nachbarn. Die kommunistischen Gesellschaften haben bewusst mit der gemeinsamen Wertebasis gebrochen, indem sie eine eigene Moral und Ästhetik förderten. Selbstverständlich kann man diskutieren, ob nicht die sozialistischen Werte nur eine säkularisierte Form des Christentums darstellen und sich vielleicht gar nicht so sehr von denen im Westen unterscheiden.

Noch gravierender erscheint mir ein anderer von Parsons herleitbarer Einwand, dass nämlich der Sozialismus praktisch alle *gesellschaftlichen Beziehungen* neu gestaltet hat und dadurch gerade auf der Ebene des Miteinander-Umgehens, die für die "Ostkompetenz" so wichtig ist, andere kulturelle Formen entstanden sind als im kapitalistischen Teil des ehemaligen Donauraums. Dass gelegentlich dennoch Gemeinsamkeit empfunden wird, hängt am ehesten mit dem zusammen, was Parsons als *kognitive* und *kathektische Orientierung* in Situationen bezeichnet hat. Wer in die post-kommunistischen Länder reist, trifft nach wie vor auf Artefakte, die ihm aus Österreich, Süddeutschland oder Norditalien vertraut sind. In der Regel handelt es sich dabei um architektonische Objekte aus der Habsburgerzeit oder Kostbarkeiten der mitteleuropäischen Küche. Beides ist hier wie dort vorhanden und kann über Vertrautheit Kompetenz suggerieren. Für die beschworene "Ostkompetenz" reicht das aber wohl nicht. Dass aus der Nähe Österreichs (räumlich, politisch, wirtschaftlich etc.) zum ehemaligen Ostblock einige Personen in die Lage kamen, sich aus Erfahrung mit den Nachbarn besondere Kompetenzen anzueignen, ist ebenfalls eine ganz andere Sache, die mit Kultur nicht viel zu tun hat. Auch die Kompetenzen, die durch Verlagerung von Osteuropazentralen nach Österreich ins Land gekommen sind, fallen in diese Kategorie. Hier geht es um Lernen und Erfahrung.

Auch die These von der angeblichen Dominanz eines post-kommunistischen Bewusstseins kann meiner Ansicht Parsons' Kulturbegriff nicht standhalten. Die aufgezählten Orientierungen und Verhaltensweisen entsprechen weder "westlichen" noch "sozialistischen" Grundwerten. Vielmehr sind sie individuelle Überbleibsel aus dem "realen Sozialismus" und Abwehrreaktionen gegenüber der über Nacht hereingebrochenen neuen Situation. Dort, wo die sozialen Beziehungen entschlossen und mit Nachdruck neu organisiert werden, wie das in der Regel bei den westlichen Unternehmen, die sich in diesen Ländern eingekauft haben, der Fall ist, kommt es zu einer relativ schnellen Stabilisierung der Orientierungen und Verhaltensweisen im Sinne moderner Arbeitsgesellschaften. Die These vom post-kommunistischen Bewusstsein übersieht aber auch die unterschiedlichen kulturellen Verhältnisse in den einzelnen gesellschaftlichen Subsystemen und Funktionsbereichen. So wird man in vielen Familien bzw. im Verwandtschaftssystem Orientierungen und Verhaltensweisen finden, die eher mit *vorsozialistischen* Verhältnissen zu tun haben. Das betrifft zum Teil das Verhältnis zwischen den Geschlechtern, das Essen, allgemeine Umgangsformen u.ä. Ebenfalls außerhalb des Konzepts von einem *post-communist mind* liegt die Entschlossenheit, mit der die Bevölkerung die westliche Konsumkultur angenommen hat, sofern sie für sie finanziell erreichbar ist. Die post-kommunistischen Gesellschaften sind zweifellos in einer kulturellen Situation, die sie von Westeuropa deutlich unterscheidet, diese kann aber nicht auf ein *post-communist mind* Syndrom reduziert werden, sondern muss mehrere Systeme von Formen und Orientierungen berücksichtigen. Bezeichnend ist die oft nur lose *Kopplung* zwischen den dem Westen formal nachmodellierten Institutionen/Organisationen und dem tatsächlichen Verhalten der Akteure. Aufmerksamkeit wird man in Zukunft auch den Fragen der *Interpenetration* widmen müssen, wenn die östlichen und westlichen Gesellschaften in Europa zusammenwachsen sollen.

Auch wenn jede Theorie eine Eigenlogik hat und ihr Wert nicht unbedingt davon abhängt, ob sie exakte Aussagen über Sinn und Funktion eines konkreten historischen Ereignisses treffen kann, wird man sie letztlich doch immer an ihrem Erkenntniswert messen. Unter diesen Voraussetzungen kann man Parsons' Kulturkonzept eine gewisse praktische Relevanz nicht abstreiten. So impliziert zum Beispiel seine Modernisierungstheorie in der Tradition von Max Weber (Säkularisierung, Rationalisierung) eine Annäherung der Kulturen an das Muster des westlichen Kerns der Moderne. Allerdings ist Parsons meines Wissens nicht soweit gegangen, daraus auch ein Ende des sowjet-kommunistischen Systems vorherzusagen. Die politischen Realitäten seiner Zeit waren offensichtlich stärker als der theoretische Impetus. Vielleicht ist es aber auch, dass man diese Theorie sowohl dynamisch als auch statisch lesen kann. Welche Variante sich jeweils durchsetzt, hängt vom Zeitgeist ab. Auch das kann dazu beigetragen haben, warum trotz sichtbarer kultureller und ökonomischer Veränderungen im kommunistischen Weltsystem, sein politischer Zusammenbruch Ende der achtziger Jahre auch aus der Perspektive dieser Theorie nicht erwartet worden ist.

Das sich heute weltpolitisch und gesellschaftlich neu formierende Europa ist eine ähnliche Herausforderung für die Sozialwissenschaften. In diesem Zusammenhang sollte man auf Parsons' Ansatz, der immerhin die Synthese der Ideen von einigen der bekanntesten europäischen Denker (Durkheim, Pareto, Weber, Freud) über die moderne Gesellschaft ist, nicht verzichten. Zwar kommt das zeitgenössische Europa in Parsons Arbeiten wenig vor, das sollte aber niemanden daran hindern, seinen Theorien wieder mehr Beachtung zu schenken. Dies wird auch dadurch gefördert, dass die mittlerweile stattgefundene Verschiebung des öffentlichen Interesses von der sozial- zur wirtschaftswissenschaftlichen Perspektive und dann in den Sozialwissenschaften noch einmal von Gesellschaft zur Kultur, zunehmend von vielen als defizitär empfunden wird. Die wirtschaftliche Transformation Europas lässt neue Probleme und Fragen aufkommen, die zeitgeistgemäß nicht selten als solche der Kultur identifiziert werden. Parsons' Kulturbegriff kann hier dadurch, dass er Teil einer allgemeinen Handlungstheorie ist, die Perspektive erweitern. Auf diese Weise rückt vor allem die Gesellschaft mit ihren sozialen Beziehungen und systemischen Ausdifferenzierung wieder stärker ins Blickfeld. Das heißt nicht, dass deshalb auf den Kulturbegriff verzichtet werden kann, aber er könnte über Parsons wieder in einen größeren Zusammenhang geführt werden. Eine simple, aber keineswegs selbstverständliche Einsicht daraus: Eine gemeinsame Kultur kann sich nur dort entfalten, wo es eine gemeinsame Gesellschaft gibt.

Literatur

Alexander, Jeffrey C. (1994): Modern, Post, Neo – How Social Theories Have Tried to Understand the "New World" of "Our Times". Zeitschrift für Soziologie, 23, S. 165-197.
Alexander, Jeffrey C. / Smith, Philip (1993): The Discourse of American Civil Society: A New Proposal for Cultural Studies. Theory and Society, 22, S. 151-207.
Alexander, Jeffrey C. / Seidman, Steven (eds.) (1990): Culture and Society: Contemporary Debates. Cambridge: Cambridge University Press.
Archer, Margaret S. (1985): The Myth of Cultural Integration. The British Journal of Sociology, 3, S. 333-353.
Bauman, Zygmunt (1999): Culture as Praxis. London: Sage.
Bausinger, Hermann (1993): Europa der Regionen: Kulturelle Perspektiven. Leviathan, 4, S. 271-92.
Baecker, Dirk (1999): Gesellschaft als Kultur. Lettre International, 45, S. 56-58.
Buxton, William (1985): Talcott Parsons and the Capitalist Nation-State. Toronto: University of Toronto Press.
Csepeli, György (1997): National Identity in Contemporary Hungary. New York: Columbia University Press.
Edberg, Rolf (1985): ... und sie segelten weiter. Stuttgart: Klett-Cotta.
Eger, György / Langer, Josef (eds.) (1996): Border, Region and Ethnicity in Central Europe. Klagenfurt: Norea.
Enzensberger, Hans Magnus (1987): Ach Europa. Frankfurt/M.: Suhrkamp.

Eskelinen, Heikki / Liikanen, Ilkka / Oksa, Jukka (1998): Curtains of Iron and Gold. Aldershot: Ashgate.
Evers, Tilman (1994): Supranationale Staatlichkeit am Beispiel der Europäischen Union: Civitas civitatum oder Monster? Leviathan, 1, S. 115-34.
Feichtinger, Claudia / Fink, Gerhard (1998): Post-Communist Management. Journal of Cross-Cultural Competence & Management, 1, S. 35-59.
Glotz, Peter (1999): Europäische Identität – Eine Spekulation. Die Neue Gesellschaft, March, S. 209-216.
Grießhaber, Christoph (1998): Zum Problem der kulturellen Einigung Europas: Frankfurt/M.: Lang.
Hadas, Miklos / Vörös, Miklos (eds.) (1996): Colonisation or Partnership? Eastern Europe and Western Social Sciences. Special issue of Replika, Budapest.
Hall, Edward T. / Reed-Hall, Mildred (1990): Understanding cultural differences. Yarmouth: Intercultural Press.
Haller, Max (1999): Voiceless Submission or Deliberate Choice? European Integration and the Relation between National and European Identity. Kriesi, H./K. Armingeon/H. Siegrist/A. Wimmer (eds.), Nation and National Identity – The European Experience in Perspective. Chur: Rüegger, S. 263-296.
Haller, Max (1996): Identität und Nationalstolz der Österreicher. Wien: Böhlau.
Haller, Max (1990): The Challenge for Comparative Sociology in the Transformation of Europe. International Sociology, 2, S. 183-204.
Haller, Max / Hoffmann-Nowottny, Hans-Jürgen / Zapf, Wolfgang (eds.) (1989): Kultur und Gesellschaft. Frankfurt am Main: Campus.
Häyrynen, Yrjö-Paavo (1996): Borders as psychological factors in Europe. G. Eger/J. Langer (eds), Border, Region and Ethnicity in Central Europe. Klagenfurt: Norea, S. 69-90.
Herzog, Roman (1999a): Europe – A Culture of Shared Causes? Bulletin, 11. Bonn: Presse- und Informationsamt der Bundesregierung, S. 117-118.
Herzog, Roman (1999b): Kulturdialog als neue Dimension einer Außenpolitik der Zukunft, Bulletin, 23. Bonn: Presse- und Informationsamt der Bundesregierung, S. 217-219.
Hofstede, Geert (1984): Culture's Consequences. London: Sage.
Huntington, Samuel P. (1996): The Clashes of Civilization and the Remaking of World Order. New York: Schuster.
Kriesi, Hanspeter / Armingeon, Klaus / Siegrist, Hannes / Wimmer, Andreas (eds.) (1999): Nation and National Identity – The European Experience in Perspective. Chur: Rüegger.
Langer, Josef (1999): Last in, First Out? – Austria's Place in the Transformation of National Identity. Kriesi, H./K. Armingeon/H. Siegrist/A. Wimmer (eds.), Nation and National Identity – The European Experience in Perspective. Chur: Rüegger, S. 153-173.
Langer, Josef (1998a): Colonization or Partnership? Sozialwissenschaften in Osteuropa. September, S. 38-40.
Langer, Josef (1998b): Culture in an Era of Accelerated Social Change. Journal of Cross-Cultural Competence & Management, 1, S. 241-269.
Lipp, Wolfgang (1991): Europa als Kulturprozeß, Verhandlungen des 25. Deutschen Soziologentages. Frankfurt/M.: Campus, S. 349-356.
Luhmann, Niklas (1998): Die Gesellschaft der Gesellschaft. Frankfurt/M.: Suhrkamp.
Luhmann, Niklas (1995a): Gesellschaftsstruktur und Semantik. Frankfurt/M.: Suhrkamp.
Luhmann, Niklas (1995b): Kausalität im Süden. Soziale Systeme, 1, S. 7-28.
Luhmann, Niklas (1980): Talcott Parsons – Zur Zukunft eines Theorieprogramms. Zeitschrift für Soziologie, Jg. 9, 1, S. 5-17.

Meyer, John W./ Boli, John / Thomas, George M. / Ramirez, Francisco O. (1997): World Society and the Nation State. American Journal of Sociology, 1, S. 144-81.
Mlinar, Zdravko (1996): New states and open borders – Slovenia between the Balkans and the European Union. L. O'Dowd/Th. M. Wilson (eds.), Borders, Nations and States. Aldershot: Avebury, S. 135-153.
Müller, Klaus (1995): Vom Postkommunismus zur Postmodernität? Kölner Zeitschrift für Soziologie und Sozialpsychologie, 1, S. 37-64.
Münch, Richard (1993a): The Contribution of German Social Theory to European Sociology. B. Nedelmann/P. Sztompka (eds.), Sociology in Europe. Berlin/New York: de Gruyter, S. 45-66.
Münch, Richard (1993b): Das Projekt Europa. Frankfurt/M.: Suhrkamp.
Münch, Richard (1989): Gesellschaftsanalyse und Kulturdeutung. Haller, M./H.-J. Hoffmann-Nowottny/W. Zapf (eds.) (1989), Kultur und Gesellschaft. Frankfurt am Main: Campus, S. 696-702.
Münch, Richard (1984): Die Strukturen der Moderne. Frankfurt/M.: Suhrkamp.
Parsons, Talcott (1951/1967): The Social System. London: Routledge & Kegan.
Parsons, Talcott (1972): Das System moderner Gesellschaften: München: Juventa.
Parsons, Talcott / Shils, Edward (eds.) (1951): Toward a General Theory of Action. Cambridge/M.: Harvard University Press.
Parsons, Talcott / Smelser, Neil J. (1956/1972): Economy and Society. London: Routledge & Kegan.
Parsons, Talcott / Platt, Gerald M. (1973): The American University. Cambridge/M.: Harvard University Press.
Reckwitz, Andreas (1997): Kulturtheorie, Systemtheorie und das sozialtheoretische Muster der Innen-Außen-Differenzierung. Zeitschrift für Soziologie, 5, S. 317-336.
Rehberg, Karl-Siegbert (1986): Kultur versus Gesellschaft? Anmerkungen zu einer Streitfrage in der deutschen Soziologie. Kölner Zeitschrift für Soziologie und Sozialpsychologie, Sonderheft 27, S. 92-115.
Rokkan, Stein (1980): Eine Familie von Modellen für die vergleichende Geschichte Europas. Zeitschrift für Soziologie, Jg. 9, Heft 2, S. 118-128.
Schluchter, Wolfgang (1980): Gesellschaft und Kultur – Überlegungen zu einer Theorie institutioneller Differenzierung, W. Schluchter (ed.), Verhalten, Handeln und System. Frankfurt/M.: Suhrkamp, S. 106-149.
Srubar, Ilja (1994): Variants of the Transformation Process in Central Europe: A Comparative Assessment. Zeitschrift für Soziologie, 3, S. 198-221.
Staubmann, Helmut (1995): Die Kommunikation von Gefühlen. Berlin: Duncker&Humblot.
Sztompka, Piotr (1993): Civilizational Incompetence: The Trap of Post-Communist Societies. Zeitschrift für Soziologie, 2, S. 85-95.
Szücs, Jenö (1990): Die drei historischen Regionen Europas. Frankfurt/M.: verlag neue kritik.
Thomas, Alexander (ed.) (1996): Psychologie interkulturellen Handelns. Göttingen: Hogrefe.
Wallerstein, Immanuel (1990): Culture as the Ideological Battleground of the Modern World-System. M. Featherstone (ed.), Global Culture. London: Sage, S. 31-55.
Wenzel, Harald (1990): Die Ordnung des Handelns. Frankfurt/M.: Suhrkamp.
Wimmer, Andreas (1996): Kultur. Zur Reformulierung eines sozialanthropologischen Grundbegriffs. Kölner Zeitschrift für Soziologie und Sozialpsychologie, 3, 48, S. 401-425.
Wintle, Michael (1996): Culture and Identity in Europe. Aldershot: Avebury.

The Body, Expressive Culture and Social Interaction
Integrating Art History and Action Theory*
Jeremy Tanner

Parsons' writings on art are amongst the least well understood and least widely appreciated of his contributions to sociology.[1] My aim in this essay is to show that Parsons developed a framework for the sociology of art which provides the basis for a successful integration of sociological and art-historical approaches to art in exactly the way that has been called for in recent work in the sociology of art.[2] In the first section of this paper, I shall sketch Parsons' treatment of art against the context of earlier and more recent attempts at synthesizing sociological and art historical approaches to art. In particular, I shall show how Parsons both grounds expressive symbolism in the context of systems of social interaction and recognises its autonomy as a cultural system in its own right. In the core of the paper (section 2), I shall seek to build upon Parsons' legacy, by elaborating his initial and tentative attempt to integrate some of the core concerns and concepts of the idealist tradition of art-history writing within a much more determinate account of art as a cultural system, embedded within the general action system. I shall draw upon recent strands of pragmatist semiotics and material culture theory to address the significance of the sensuousness of artistic signs, their place in social interaction, and sociological ac-

---

[*] This article has been greatly improved by the comments and criticisms of Harold Bershady, Jas Elsner, Danae Fiore, Christopher Kelly, Victor Lidz, Stephen Shennan, Helmut Staubmann, Peter Ucko and Harald Wenzel. I am particularly grateful to Helmut Staubmann for all his help in bringing this essay to publication. Address all correspondence to the author at: j.tanner@ucl.ac.uk

[1] As within other fields of sociology, it is commonplace to define the beginning of the recent history of the field in terms of the escape from manifestly inadequate Parsonian approaches, not always on the basis of having read the relevant parts of Parsons oeuvre. See for example Zolberg (1990, 46), arguing that Parsons, conflated culture and psychology within the pattern-maintenance subsystem and did not develop any serious discussion of the aesthetic aspects of art, citing the essay "An Outline of the Social System", apparently unaware that Parsons' treatment of art as a cultural system differentiated from particular contexts of interaction is to be found the essay "Culture and the social system", in the same volume (1961). Peterson (1994, 164) criticises the inadequacy of Parsons' view of culture as "a reflection of social structure". It should become clear during the course of this paper that Petersons' criticism is misplaced.

[2] For example Zolberg 1990, x and 12; Bowler1994 – although both advocate an eclectic juxtaposition of the two perspectives, rather than a genuine synthesis.

counts of the nature of aesthetic experience and its entailments. Integrating pragmatist semiotics with Parsons' AGIL schema on the level of general action analysis permits a non-reductionist grounding of the cultural analysis of the German idealist tradition in the functional environments of the behavioral, personality and social systems. The interpenetration of expressive culture with those environments produces new emergent patterns of organisation of action processes. I conclude by deploying this framework in a brief case study of Roman portraiture (section III) to show how an action theoretic approach to art can allow a sociologically consequential interpretation and explanation of aesthetic innovation in one particular artistic system.

Sociology and Art History: The Struggle for Synthesis

The intellectual history of both the social history of art and the sociology of art may be seen as a series of failed attempts at interdisciplinary synthesis. Karl Mannheim argued that intuitive links between art and its environments - articulated in terms of ethos, Weltanschauung and Kunstwollen, by art historians in the German idealist tradition like Panofsky[3] – should be formulated more rigorously in terms of such conceptions as correspondence, parallelism, function, causality or reciprocity.[4] Meyer Schapiro criticised the empiricist adduction of "piecemeal political or economic facts to account for single traits of style or subject matter". He advocated a more systematic theoretical approach which integrated the analysis of style, as an open system, with the psychological and social environments in which it functioned, in place of the "purely analogical character" of the parallels drawn between style and thought already critcised by Mannheim.[5] Neither scholar, however, produced the synthesis which they advocated. More recent attempts at synthesis have proven one sided. The theoretical project of reception theory ultimately took on a strongly formalist character, arising out of the indeterminacy of its key concept, the "horizon of expectation" which was in practice reconstructed on the basis of textual linguistics and assumed the institutional autonomy of art and literature.[6] The epistemological presuppositions of post-structuralist theory conflate the social and political dimensions of societal organisation back into culture.[7] Correspondingly, in practice, the "new art history" is still centered on the explication of objects at the expense of

---

[3] Panofsky 1980 (o.v. 1920); 1939; with Alpers 1979.
[4] Mannheim 1993 (ov 1922).
[5] Schapiro 1951, 299-311; quotations from p. 311.
[6] Holub 1984, 59ff.
[7] Bowler 1994, 257-8; Jones, 1996 293ff.

analytic theory and causal explanation.8 From the sociological side of the divide, Bourdieu and Witkin have both sought to integrate art history and sociology by invoking a mechanism of homology between artistic structure and social structures. This effectively inverts the idealism of art historians like Panofsky, whose iconological perspective they seek to extend. Habitus performs for Bourdieu's sociological theory the same function as Kunstwollen for Panofsky's art history, in so far as it provides a purely sociological principle for the explanation of the production, reproduction and transformation of social structure, without any need to invoke autonomous traditions of culture or the functional exigencies of the personality as a system of action.9 Correspondingly, art is a residual category within Bourdieu's conceptual framework, and is continually folded back into social structure. Integrating as it does, the idealistic art historical tradition of Panofsky and Riegl, the perceptual psychology of J.J. Gibson, and Piaget's cognitive psychology, all embedded within an evolutionary account of the relationship between social struture and human-environment relations, Witkin's sociology of art is a theoretical tour-de-force.10 Nevertheless, his concept of art remains a residual category, indeterminate in relation to his theory of social systems and social relations, and given a strongly cognitive slant, as the sensuous means by which the values which animate a social system are "thought" through.11 Moreover, the whole theory has a somewhat reductionist slant in so far as the relationship connecting systems of social relationships and systems of visual forms is conceived as a functionally and semiotically neccessary correspondence.12 In neither case, are the functionally distinctive contributions of art to the reproduction and transformation of social systems adequately grasped. For both Bourdieu and Wiktin art functions merely as a repeater – if in highly mediated form – of already given social relations.

In the context of this continued oscillation between idealism and materialism, Parsons' intellectual project has an obvious relevance to the construction of a genuinely synthetic historical sociology of art. His first major work, *The Structure of Social Action*, was concerned with establishing the basis on which a viable synthesis might be realised between the German idealist tradition – in which art history is

---

8   Preziosi 1981, 1ff, esp. pp. 16, 31ff. See Bourdieu (1996, 184ff) for an excellent discussion of "literary doxa" and the elective affinity between new art or literary histories in the tradition of Saussure and Foucault and the established disciplinary habitus of *explication de text*.
9   Bourdieu 1996, 179 for the connection with Panofsky; ibid passim for reductionism. The problems of Bourdieu's sociology of art are entailed by the shortcomings of his theoretical programme as a whole, on which see the devastating criticisms of Alexander 1995.
10 Witkin 1995.
11 Witkin 1995, esp. pp. 12, 168.
12 Witkin 1995, 11-12.

founded[13] – and traditions of thought like utilitarianism, Marxism and Durkheimian sociology which recognised the reality of material and social constraint.[14] Parsons' major discussion of art developed out of his Freud-Durkheim synthesis in the middle, structural-functional, phase of the development of action theory.[15] In this period, Parsons developed an analytic conception of art as expressive symbolism, parallel to cognitive and moral-evaluative symbolism, through an analysis of the structural components and properties neccesarily implicated in a system of interaction as an ongoing system. Whilst expressive culture is a component of any interaction system, its distinctive bases and functions are perhaps most easily understood in terms of the development of the mother-infant relationship.[16] At birth, an infant is an organism with a biologically given potentiality for social and cultural levels of behaviour, but whose current relationship to its environment is primarily organic, and whose primary needs are organic. The mother is merely the source of discrete concrete gratifications of these organic needs: warmth, milk, cleansing of bodily waste products etc. The baby cries as an instinctive response to the physiological discomfort of being cold or hungry. The mother's intervention to feed the infant – although obviously motivated sociologically and psychologically on her part through a commitment to caring for the baby as its mother – is, on the level of the infant-mother system, a purely instrumental measure, which adjusts the infant organism's relationship to its environment to a more satisfactory state. These discrete gratifications come to share a common meaning for the baby owing to three factors. First, the gratification of needs is patterned, by virtue of the regular response of the mother to the baby's instinctive expression of his organic needs. Second, the infant is predisposed by human biological make up to perceive such patterning. Third, the gratifications share a common tone – rooted in the sensuous responsiveness of the human body – of pleasurable erotic stimulation, associated with feeding (oral pleasures), cleaning (stimulation of the anal and genital regions) and other acts of care. This organic-sensorily based, temporally organised, structure of experience grounds a process of symbolic generalisation. The infant comes to anticipate or expect gratification of its needs. Certain acts preparatory and conditional to the gratification of those needs – food preparation, or the unveiling of the mother's breast for example –

---

[13] Podro 1982.
[14] Parsons 1937. On Parsons' treatment of art in *Structure*, Staubmann 1997, 739-43.
[15] On the development of Parsons' theory in its middle period as a specification of the multidimensional argument of the *Structure of Social Action*, see Alexander 1983, 51ff; 122ff on Parsons and Freud. Staubmann 1997, 743-755 for the development of Parsons' thought on aesthetics during this phase.
[16] Parsons 1951, 384ff; esp. 386-7; 1952/1964, esp. 26ff; 1953, esp. 39-42. Trevarthen 1995 for a comparable emphasis in contemporary child-psychology on mother-infant interaction in the development of expressive orientations in individuals.

come to be interpreted as signs of the forthcoming gratification and invested with a secondary cathexis, which extends the pleasurable meaning of the primary gratifications to these associated acts.[17] These signs tend in turn to be integrated by the infant into a single symbolic complex by virtue of their common authorship in the person of the mother. Through the generalisation of expectations and of meaning of a set of actions (feeding, cleaning etc.), to the instrumentalities through which those actions are performed (the breast and other parts of the mother's body), and to the single object in the infant's environment who organises them, the infant becomes affectively attached to the mother. Each particular act is then interpreted by the infant within this more generalised frame of reference, as indicating the attitude of the mother towards the infant. An expressive symbol is thus any such act or object which stands for the feelings or attitude of an ego towards an alter and which thereby mediates the affective component of interaction.[18]

The development of expressive symbolism significantly transforms both the structure of the mother-child relationship and the structure of the child's personality, which is formed as part and parcel of the process of expressive generalisation. The mother is "internalised" as a motivationally significant alter. Since it is now not simply her physical interventions which are gratifying to the infant, but the signs of her attitude which are motivationally significant to the affective economy of his emergent personality, the mother is able to control the infant's behaviour through symbolic means. The child can be induced to act in accordance with the mother's wishes through his or her desire to secure gratifying symbols of the mother's love and approval, as a "good boy" who learns to do things for himself in order to please "mummy".[19]

The logic of the mother-child interaction can be extended to other interaction systems, where the development of an expressive dimension to the interaction serves to stabilise patterns of interaction, through what Parsons calls "the institutional integration of motivation", beyond the parameters possible solely on the basis of the purely instrumental interests of the two actors. Expressive symbols thus control motivation of actors to realise the goals and conform with the norms which constitute a collectivity. They also mediate the identification of actors with each other and the collectivity of which they are a component, so that pleasing each other and participating in the collectivity become gratifying, motivationally significant, activities in themselves, quite apart from the short term instrumental interests in participation. In such a context, the stabilisation of expressive interaction requires the elaboration of shared normative standards, conventions defining what counts as an adequate

---

[17] Parsons, 1953, 38ff; 1956, 63ff.
[18] Parsons, 1953, 38ff.
[19] Parsons 1952, 26ff; 1956, 63ff, 69ff.

expression of, for example, love or approval, and the circumstances in which an actor has the right to expect to receive such an expression from another.[20] As systems of interaction become increasingly complex, the expressive strands of action may become increasingly differentiated from the instrumental or the evaluative. Some actions may have a purely expressive meaning, and there may even be specialisation of action in the creation of particular kinds of facilities, expressive forms, specifically designed for the communication of expressive meanings. A work of art is simply a highly differentiated expressive symbol, an object created with the primary purpose of communicating expressive or affective meanings – for example an altarpiece with a painting of a Madonna and Child, used as a focus of attention in prayer in order to construct an appropriate attitude or feeling towards the mediators of the deity's favours who are the objects of prayer. The emergence of a distinct role of "artist" represents an extremely specialised concern with the expressive culture of a highly differentiated social system.[21]

Action Theory and Artistic Expression: A Pragmatist Synthesis

Parsons recognised that the properly cultural aspect of expressive symbolism was a central concern of art historians, and that systematisation of the structural or pattern aspect of expressive culture required an integration of the concepts of art history with those of action theory.[22] In his essay on "Culture and the social system", he sketched a synthesis of art historical and sociological concepts, by suggesting that concepts such as techniques, content, and style could be seen as elements of a cybernetic hierarchy analogous to that of facts, problem solutions, theory and presuppositions in science as a cultural system. Surprisingly, this interesting beginning of a

---

[20] Parsons 1953, 41; 1951, 417ff. On a theoretical level, much of Hochschild's empirically interesting work on emotion work and feeling rules (1979, 1983), particularly her discussion of feeling rules and social exchange (1979, 568ff) simply reinvents a wheel already created by Parsons, whose work on the social construction and regulation of the emotions she largely ignores.

[21] Parsons 1951, 399ff; esp. 408ff.

[22] 1951, 427 on the importance of systematisation of the theory of expressive symbolism on the cultural level, addressing the structure of expressive symbolic systems in addition to their functional interdependencies with personality and social systems; 1961, 964 on the pattern aspect of culture as the task area of "formal disciplines: logic, mathematics, structural linguistics, systematics of stylistic form, purely logical structure of a theological system, and the formal analysis of legal norms"; 1970 on the humanities' concern with the interpretation of cultural patterns as such. Contrast 1937, 601 for the principle that valid conceptual schemes dealing with the problem of human action ought to be translateable in terms of each other or of a wider scheme.

synthesis of sociological and art historical conceptual schemes has been neither developed theoretically, nor used empirically. Within sociology, its development has been blocked by the positivistic turn of sociology of art in the production of culture movement, which was formulated in specifically anti-Parsonian and anti-art-historical terms.[23] Conversely the strongly idealist turn taken within post-structuralist "new" art history has cut apart questions of the cultural patterning or organisation of aesthetic culture from its behavioral-sensory and interactional groundings.[24] Consequently, it is not at all immediately clear how the components of art – motifs, composition, style etc. – accomplish the kind of expressive work that is relatively transparent in the case of mother-child interaction.

In the following paragraphs, I wish to draw out the bodily bases of expressive culture drawn attention to by Parsons, their role in expressive generalisation, and to go beyond Parsons by showing how the components of artistic culture – techniques, style etc. – accomplish a precisely homologous function on a higher level of cultural abstraction, constructing affective experience on the basis of cultural level codifications of sensuous form. Art appropriates the motivational energies of the personality system for commitments to its social and cultural (e.g. religious culture, moral culture) environments by engaging the capacity of the human behavioral organism for sensuous response. This potentiality is given in the biological nature of the human organism, but the biological organism is itself culturally and socially organised to constitute the behavioral system, which is the adaptive basis of the general action system. The beauty of the Parsonian schema is that it reintegrates the insight of empathy theory – and from within the German idealist tradition of art history, the early work of Wölfflin – that expressive form is grounded in our sensuous embodiment, without resorting to the kind of crude biological reductionism that sometimes characterised such early work.[25] On the contrary it opens up the genuinely cultural level of art analysis, insisted on by Panofsky and the critical German idealist tradition in art history more generally, but replaces the free floating idealism of that tradition with the possibility of specifying new emergent patterns of the organisation of action processes. These arise from the interpenetration of the cultural with the

---

[23] For example L. Coser, 1978, "Introduction" pp. 225-6 in *Social Research* 45.2, a special number on *The Production of Culture*. The immediately preceding issue was a special number celebrating and reviewing the work of Meyer Schapiro on the social history of art – entirely written by art historians. It is a nice indication of the extraordinarily strong boundaries between the disciplines that neither issue has been taken notice of outside its home discipline.

[24] Wolff 1992.

[25] Wölfflin 1966 (o.v. 1888). On Wölfflin and empathy theory: Podro 1982,100ff; Dissanayake 1992, 140-193.

social and personality levels, through internalisation and institutionalisation of expressive culture.

The sensuous basis of expressive symbolism

Parsons' concept of the artistic sign is an implicitly pragmatic one, standing in strong contrast to structuralist and post-structuralist theories of art modelled on Saussure's account of the diacritical and radically arbitrary nature of the sign.[26] Expressive symbolism is "grounded" in the structure and potentialities of the human organism. It realises its specific "significe effects" on the basis of the "qualitative possibilities" of sensuous expression and response, built into the body and elaborated through the socialisation and enculturation of the human organism in the production of the behavioral system, the adaptive basis of the general action system.[27]

Where eroticism is the basis of the generalisation of affect and expressive meaning in the case of the infant-mother relationship, sensuous form, anchored in indexical and iconic relationships to the body, is the medium through which expressive meaning is generalised in more differentiated systems of social relations.[28] The socialised and enculturated body is differentially responsive to the variable expressive-sensuous or aesthetic patterning of stimuli encountered in its environment.[29] The proper significe effects of the dance-patterns used as compositional principles in some Renaissance paintings, for example, are realised not simply through per-

---

[26] Cf. Mukerji 1994 for a powerful critique of post-structuralist assumption that the material gains its "authority" or efficacy through "its relation to language categories" – most notably manifest in the idealism of Foucault's *Discipline and Punish* – at the expense of the recognition of "the forms of [material] practice that can mobilise language categories.... handwork, crafts of material manipulation, traditions of working with materials, ways of designing objects and using them to reach social goals"; quotation p. 160. More generally, see Joas 1985, 114ff for the pragmatist account of the situation of language in the context of body related expressions, and the emergence of language from the human organism.

[27] Lidz and Lidz 1976 on the behavioral system, p. 132 on behavioral bases of symbol-processing, in particular binocular vision and imaginative envisioning. Rochberg-Halton 1982, 459ff on Peirce's conception of the ground of a sign as representing "through its own qualitative possibility, rather than through opposition". Zeman, 1977 for the clearest general introduction to Peirce's theory of signs, commenting primarily on Peirce 1955.

[28] Parsons 1956, 66ff, 97ff on the special significance of erotic pleasure as a vehicle of generalisation; cf. idem 1974, 316 on erotic pleasure as the "security base" of the generalised medium of affect.

[29] McCarthy 1984 for a development of Mead's account of the "resistance of the world to our perception of it", and " the meaning of the physical thing" as constituted by "the organism's selective sensitvity and response to it"; quotation p. 112.

ceptual recognition on the part of the viewer of these patterns and an appropriate decoding, but through the bodily responsiveness of the properly socialised viewer. Such a viewer's behavioral capacities are indexically engaged by such compositions, providing the ground for a structure of affective involvement in the scene represented or affective relating to (for example positive or negative identifications) the types or figures (representatives of particular social or religious roles for example) represented.[30]

Interaction and the genesis of expressive culture

Whilst expressive symbolism has a behavioral grounding, the expressive potentialities of the human organism are, like language, only produced and realised through processes of interaction. Symbols or patterns of symbolic organisation with apparently "natural" expressive meanings – like Jung's archetypes – may be seen as rooted in and drawing their power from certain fundamental exigencies of the socialisation process. Perhaps the best example is Barry Schwartz's account of vertical classification, although others like the subjective and objective status of frontal and profile faces could be interpreted in similar terms.[31] Schwartz argues that the apparently universal use of the vertical axis of up and down to describe social "hierarchy", and the positive valency of "high" status, ultimately derives from the interactional dynamics of child socialisation: the physical inferiority of the infant in relation to its carer; the gratifications involved in being raised up, in order to be nursed, and their contrast with the frustrating deprivation of maternal nurturance when the infant is put down. This produces a libidinisation of the vertical axis, manifested in

---

[30] Baxandall 1972, 56ff, esp. 77-81 for dance patterns in Boticelli's "Pallas and the Centaur". Far from it being the case that it is the well-socialised viewer whose engagement meets no resistance to the play of the habitus, it is by virtue of the viewer's socialisation, and in this particular case his embodiment of certain dispositions, that he is sensitive to the material patterning of the painting, and that the particular resistance it arouses releases a particular, behaviorally grounded, pattern of response, which has its own entailments – contrast Bourdieu's reading of the same passage of Baxandall in terms of structural homologies spinning narcissistically together (1996, 315-321). It is the viewer without the appropriate equipment who cannot locate himself in the material texture of the painting, but whose eyes simply skate over the surface, unable to encounter the resistances through which expressive meaning arises as a particular pattern of response. Cf. Jones 1996, 306, again building on Mead, on describing the "self as an attribute of a physical object, a body moving and acting on a field of perceptible resistances", accomplishing "a culturally mediated reading of the meanings that material resistances arouse as they come to presence in human experience."

[31] Schapiro 1973; Trevarthen 1995.

the attested tendency of respondents to attribute an exaggerated height to persons of high status and the widespread use of vertical classification as an iconographic schema in visual art.32

Again, in practice, such a potentiality built up in socialisation processes is only made use of and generalised to specific relational contexts through interaction. A predisposition to exaggerate the height of those in authority over one is elaborated into gestures of self-abasement, perhaps nothing more than a scarcely self-conscious, barely perceptible bow, on the part of the powerless, designed to express a sense of self-subordination and call out a corresponding attitude of condescension on the part of the powerful.33 Any such adjustment of an actors gestural repertoire involves labour on the primary "expressive continuum", the human body, shaping it to resonate with or fit the particular expressive-affective meanings being communicated in a process of interaction.34

Specifically artistic labour simply involves a more differentiated form of work on the expressive continuum – the physical medium in which expressive meanings are instantiated – sometimes differentiated to the point of role-specialisation. The abstraction of the production of such expressive symbolisation from the immediate exigencies of interaction, the physical limitations of the human body as a means of expression, and the limitations of cultural expertise presupposed by a restricted division of labour permits enhanced possibilities in the communication of aesthetic-expressive meanings.

---

32 Schwartz 1981, 100ff, esp. 104 on the visual mediation of social roles.
33 Goffmann is, of course, the finest observer of such miniscule interaction rituals in patterns of everyday life – although his analytical framework lacks either the behavioral embedding of the sensuous-expressive dimensions of such rituals, or an understanding of their elaboration into cultural conventions which may stand behind and give shape to particular patterns of interaction; see, for example, Goffmann, 1963.
34 Cf. Hochschild 1979 and 1983 for the development of an interactionist approach to such "feeling work". Mannheim (1993; o.v. 1922) makes much of the of the sensuous grounding of expressive meanings, esp. pp. 155f: simply saying 'I am sorry for you' does not express a feeling, it merely "refers" to it; it is the gesture, or – one might add – the *tone* of voice (or a particular stylisation in the choice and composition of words to communicate the sentiment) which accompanies the statement that expresses and communicates the feeling. Interestingly, this whole dimension of sensuous stylisation and its affective significance is eliminated in Panofsky's (1939) appropriation of Mannheim, in which style is primarily a distortion of reality through which one must get in order to identify what is represented on the pre-iconographical level of interpretation. The concept of an expressive continuum is familiar from work in semiotics, see for example Eco 1976, 151ff on the labour of producing a signal, performed on the expression continuum.

The components of artistic culture

Effort or will *per se* is not sufficient to shape an expressive continuum – whether the body, pigments on a canvass, or a block of marble – to fit the affective meanings it is intended to communicate. That effort must be controlled in terms of certain pattern components. Conversely, even if the structural components of artistic patterning can sometimes loosely be said to be homologous with the patterns of social structure from which they emerge (for example, a king being represented on a larger scale than his subjects), or to have a natural basis (as in the case of response to frontal and profile faces), that patterning is never a simple emanation from or epiphenomemon of social structure or human nature, but involves the creation of specific cultural resources consisting in a capacity for aesthetic objectification. This permits the production and organisation of the relevant visual field or expressive continuum in terms of the relevant schemata of vertical classification, or of frontal and profile arrangements of faces.

The components of aesthetic-expressive culture as a cultural system, that is abstracted from its functional prehensions with social, personality and behavioral systems, can be classified in terms of Parsons AGIL schema of four functions, defining the necessary functions which must be performed if a system is to reproduce itself as a system over time. I follow here Parsons' classification – somewhat elaborated and clarified by replacing "content" (not actually a pattern component of expressive culture), with "motif" as the goal-attainment component of the artistic cultural system. Parsons conflates the specifically artistic and the cognitive components of an artistic symbol, following the model of Panofsky's iconographical analysis: thus the specifically artistic contribution to a concrete symbolisation of the Madonna and Child is not the content, "Madonna and Child", which is classified cognitively as part of the Christian belief system, but the particular visual motif used to represent the theme and through which the viewer encounters the theme as one with a particular expressive meaning.[35]

The adaptive sub-system (A) of an action system is concerned with the provision of the generalised facilities which an action system needs as a prerequisite to performing the tasks of that system. In the case of the artistic system, the primary facilities are techniques and technical devices, which provide the means of working upon and manipulating the expressive continuum: the generalised capacity for transforming marble, for example, through the use of sculptural tools and techniques, or

---

[35] Parsons 1961, 183. The components I include correspond to those identified by Schapiro as "form motifs", "ways of combining", "qualities" and "material technical determinants" (1953, 289), although he sees all these as components of "style", where I use that term to refer to what he calls "quality".

a canvass-support through the controlled application of paint with brushes. This is a generalised capacity which is controlled through rules of composition and stylistic formation which represent higher level components in a cybernetic hierarchy.

The goal attainment sub-system (G) is concerned with performance of systemic goals, which put or maintain the system in the optimal state in relation to its environment. In the case of the artistic system, the primary goal of artistic production is the creation of effective expressive-symbolic forms, which meet the expressive needs of the groups and personalities that use them. The minimal effective-expressive form is the motif, built up on the basis of technical devices – brush strokes, blows of the chisel or whatever – but recognisable as an expressively meaningful symbolic representation in its own right.

The integrative subsystem (I) of an action system co-ordinates the relationship among the components of the system. The integrative components of an artistic system are the syntactical rules which regulate the combination of technical devices into motifs, and the combination of motifs into larger compositional patterns. This combination and ordering of distinct motifs in ways more intense and powerful than normally found in real-life – where other factors than aesthetic-expressive principles often control, for example, the sensuous ordering of two people's interaction – is what Freud referred to as "condensation" in his analysis of dream symbolism. It is this which allows art to intensify the motivational meaning of the contents it represents.

These distinctions are analytical: what at one level is a motif, at another level is a device or facility in the building up of larger motifs. Correspondingly there are many different levels on which devices and motifs are integrated or organised into larger wholes, from the building up of brush strokes into a motif such as a hand, through articulation of the hand into a broader figure composition, and the integration of that into a whole group, interacting in a narrative representation, on the basis of certain principles of composition. Conversely, the technical device – the culturally directed sweep of the brush – may in some traditions, notably Chinese painting, constitute a motif in its own right.

The pattern-maintenance sub-system (L) of an action system functions to maintain the stability over time of the constitutive patterns which define a system as a structured system. The pattern maintenance component of artistic culture is style. Style stands behind and regulates in terms of certain fundamental expressive-aesthetic principles the use of techniques, the way they are built up into motifs, the patterns of compositional or syntactic combination into larger wholes.

These components become fully differentiated from each other only in complex societies. In simple societies they may be fused in the motor habits elaborated from technical means for the production of, for example, woven-baskets or bone-carvings into principles of formal organisation and style.36 The existence of style as a structurally distinct level of organisation from technique or compositional patterns may be characteristic of the axial age societies, and even here it remains fused with heteronomous religious-evaluative components of culture. The principles of rationality that inform the construction of motifs and their organisation in compositions in classical and later Greek art, and the principles of balance and harmony that perform the same role in classical Chinese art, are obviously derived from the religious conceptions of ultimate reality of the Greek philosophers and the Confucian literati respectively. The wide-ranging civilizational stylisation of the lives of the ancient Greek intellectual and social elites in accordance with principles of rationality, and of the Confucian literati in accordance with principles of harmonious balance, and sponsorship of the production of works of art which were informed by such principles, was not simply the expression of a Kunstwollen (or a marker of social distinction). It served to infuse every aspect of life with motivational meaning, constructing the ground for affective commitment to a wide range of roles and life-involvements in terms integrated with the moral-evaluative culture of the respective religions. This expressive ground of motivational involvement endured over an extent of time co-extensive with the existence of these civilisations, alongside multiple small-scale shifts in content, favoured genres, and details of aesthetic organisation within this generalised frame, corresponding to more subtle shifts in social structure and motivational requirements. This classification of these components of art as a cultural system thus provides the basis for the systematic cross cultural comparison of the levels of differentiatedness of artistic systems, as well as a sense of the relative importance or consequentiality of change in artistic systems at these different levels of the cybernetic hierarchy.

Expressive culture in its functional environments

Such cultural eleboration of expressive meanings, on whatever level of differentiation, may serve both to intensify levels of affective investment in roles and relationships, and to communicate affective meanings with a greater level of precision, thus enhancing the degree of social and cultural control over motivation. Cultural forms *per se*, however, are not capable of controlling expressivity, except through being interwoven with other components of action systems. In addition to the cultural level, the expressive process requires organisation on both the social system and the personality system levels if it is to maximise control of motivational commitments.

---

36 Boas 1955; Schapiro 1953, 303-4.

Institutionalising aesthetic culture: culture/society interpenetration

In return for the motivational commitments attracted by expressive culture to the performance of social roles and participation in collectivities, the social system supports and stabilises the relevant components of expressive culture, by institutionalising them as conventions, socially mandated means of expressing certain attitudes, subject to sanctions if they are not used appropriately.

The increase in degrees of freedom, and upgrading of the expressive power of artistic symbolisation, potentially realised through the abstraction of the production of the symbol from the processes of interaction in which it is used, however, increases the level of contingency affecting the realisation of the desired expressive affect. First, the immediate sanctions that might be applied in face to face interaction to ensure conformity with expectations are obviously suspended. Second, the creation of a specialised artistic role engenders pressures for purely aesthetic rationalisation of form, to some degree independent of, and perhaps even in tension with, the substantive expressive functions of art within the particular institutional contexts where it is used.

Genre rules reduce these contingencies. They may be seen as normative codifications of expressive expectations, articulating the function of artistic symbolism in expressive interaction within a particular institutional domain, with the codification of rules regulating the production of expressive symbols within the artistic system itself. They exist at the zone of interpenetration between the integrative subsystem of the artistic system and the integrative subsystem of the social system, and function to stabilise the relation between social system and a differentiated artistic system. The expressive expectations codified in genre rules may also, of course, be internalised in personalities, creating genuine need-dispositions to respond expressively in particular ways, and predisposing viewers to respond in particular predictable ways to appropriately patterned works of art, thereby strengthening culturally codified control of motivation, structured in ways integrated with the exigencies of the functioning of systems of social interaction.

Viewing, response, and the internalisation of expressive culture: culture/personality interpenetration

The viewer's share in the production of meaning has been an increasing preoccupation in recent work in art history and the sociology of culture. Early work in reception theory tended to fold viewing/reading back into formal analysis, by taking the institutionalisation of "literature" and associated modes of reading for granted, and presupposing an "ideal" reader who had effectively already internalised the rules of the genre of the work in question.37 This produces exactly the thin connoisseurial decoding characteristic of literary criticism and art history as academic genres, and in effect endorsed by Bourdieu and Witkin in their conceptualisation of the relationship between personality structures and cultural forms in terms of homology. More recent work has complicated this picture in two respects. First, ethnographic work has shown in a structured way how the different interpretative strategies of different "communities of interpretation" give rise to systematically differing attributions of meaning to ostensibly the same cultural objects.38 Consequently, the horizon of expectation can no longer be read out of the object alone, or reconstructed simply in terms of the genre rules of a group of objects. Second, it is increasingly recognised that the "meaning" attributed to a cultural object by a viewer, may extend considerably beyond the arbitrary verbal concepts identified by Saussure as the signifieds of signifiers, or the underlying texts of Panofskian iconography. Peirce's more dynamic account of interpretants identifies the meaning of a cultural object with the responses it elicits, which may be behavioral and affective, as well as verbal and cognitive.39 Parsons' framework suggests possibilities for offering a theoretically compelling synthesis of these approaches. It provides an analytically more differentiated account of what the phenomenological school would call "concretisation". Peirce's "interpretants" can be specified in terms of the functional environments of action. Viewing and the consumption of art may be analysed as a structured and multilevelled process, occuring in time and with determinate functional entailments.

What kind of process in action takes place when a viewer is engaged by a work of art? The ground of viewing is behavioral and perceptual (A). Not only can there be no meaning effect without their being a sensuously formed object to elicit it, but the capacity for aesthetic-sensuous response presupposes a behavioral capacity to perceive the relevant sensuous differences. Parameters are obviously set by human biology (a red-green contrast does not have much meaning for a colour blind person, and the range and sensitivity of human capacity for making perceptual discriminations is limited). But within these parameters, there is a considerable role for the cultural organisation and elaboration of such behavioral sensitivity, and variable social distribution of such sensitivities in a population. It is only on the basis of such perceptual capacities that Baxandall's ideal (i.e. bourgeois) viewer is able to discriminate the reproduction of iconographic conventions based on dance movements or structures of pictorial organisation linked to practices of weighing and measure-

---

[37] Holub 1984, 60ff.
[38] Press 1994.
[39] Rochberg-Halton 1982; De Lauretis 1983. Zeman 1977 is the best brief introduction to the complexities of Peirce's semiotics.

ment, let alone attribute motivational, social or cultural meaning to them.[40] Such a sensitivity is the condition for any kind of gearing of the viewer with the forms presented by the work of art. It is what allows the "material resistance" encountered by the viewer in engaging with the aesthetic object, that is to say the *work* of viewing, to be meaningful or *productive*, to generate determinate effects within a process of action, as opposed to the empty skating on the surface, the perceptual chaos and perecieved lack of determinate organisation of a painting for the viewer not possessed of the appropriate behavioral-perceptual equipment.[41]

Viewing an expressive symbol also involves a distinctive pattern of involvement on a personality level. Looking at a map, for example, is a very different kind of experience, at least ideal-typically, than looking at a landscape painting of the same area represented by the map.[42] A viewer's engagement with and response to a map is normally structured in cognitive-instrumental terms: a good map is one that allows you to master the environment represented, to move from A to B with minimal fuss. A work of art like a landscape, by contrast, is designed to elicit an affective-expressive response, to enhance or intensify the projection of cathexis by the viewer onto the landscape whether real or imaginary. It accomplishes this by virtue of visually transforming the same object (the landscape) expressively – on the basis of patterns of composition, style, condensation of contents, textural effects – in such a way as to seem intrinsically relevant to the personality motivations of the viewer. Affect, therefore, is the primary interpretant of a work of art, as of any expressive symbol. By virtue of the cultural patterning of an expressive symbol, that affect can be organised quite precisely in terms of its structure and in terms of the objects – social, cultural or whatever – to which it is attached.

In the short term - the immediate response of a viewer to a work of art – expressive symbols elicit (or fail to elicit) affect by virtue of a contingent congruence between their patterning and the motivational dispositions of viewers.[43] In the longer term, expressive symbolism, and in particular the codes in terms of which it is ar-

---

[40] Baxandall 1972.
[41] On the resistance of the world to our perception of it, and "the meaning of the thing" being found in "the organism's selective sensitivity and response to it", see McCarthy 1984. On the "culturally mediated reading of meanings" to which "material resistances" give rise, see Jones 1996, esp. 300ff. For a sophisticated action theoretic account of the behavioral system, Lidz and Lidz 1976, pp. 220ff on expressive symbolism.
[42] But cf. Alpers 1983 on the expressive significance of maps within Dutch artistic culture of the 17th century.
[43] The motivational meaning of an expressive symbol may also be negative, generating fear, anxiety or hate – negative affects – and attaching it to particular objects. Congruence need not imply positive expressive meanings: it is simply the condition of their being any expressive meaning at all. Such congruence is contingent and has functional implications, it is not a neccessary given, as Bourdieu and Witkin imply.

ticulated, may also reach into the personality, through internalisation, and reorganise the motivational dispositions of viewers. Conforming with certain style patterns in one's behaviour becomes in itself motivationally meaningful, quite apart from the particular contents those patterns might be used to communicate in specific works of art. The possibility of such internalisation is implicit, but presented in a radically conflated manner, in Wölfflin's insistence that the categories of pictorial organisation that he analyses are at one and the same time modes of "beholding" or viewing.[44] In place of their reification as Kantian transcendental categories of mind, as suggested by Panofsky[45], Parsons' scheme allows us to analyse such dimensions of expressive-aesthetic culture in a more differentiated way – first as produced technologies of aesthetic representation and now as ways of organising response which may be internalised in the personality – with functionally productive entailments. Fromm's account of the importance of the motivational appeal of Protestant doctrines to their adherents, and conversely the way in which those doctrines – once internalised – rationalised, systematised and intensified the affective dispositions of their berarers, offers a helpful model of analysis here.[46] Recent work on the classical tradition in German art, for example, may be interpreted to suggest that the production and stylisation of affective commitment to Nazism and anti-semitism in prewar Germany was grounded not only in distinctive patterns of family structure (and the styles of relating to which they gave rise), and in the religious traditions so well analysed by Fromm, but also in long standing aesthetic traditions which formed the sensuous ground for affective commitment to an "Aryan" vision and loathing for all those who did not conform, or could be represented as not conforming, to a strongly classicising racial aesthetic. The classicism of Nazi art both depended on the motivational meaning of this style for German viewers, and was the aesthetic means for organising, systematising and intensifying love for Führer and Fatherland, and hate for the Jews.[47]

Viewing and the consumption of art, as an action process, is of course also subject to potential controls on social and cultural levels. There are institutionalised expectations about practices of aesthetic reception. A member of a congregation in a church at a performance of a Bach mass is expected to join in the chorales, and applause would not be an appropriate response to the completion of the Mass. In a concert performance, the audience is expected to listen, not to join in, and applause is the appropriate expression of appreciation, if one appreciated the performance; if

---

[44] Wölfflin 1950, 226.
[45] Panofsky 1981.
[46] Fromm 1942.
[47] Mossé 1978, 1-34; 1996. Adam (1992) is the most accessible picture book; chapter 9 on classicising sculpture.

not, on occassions the audience may even whistle or jeer.[48] Such differences in patterns of control shape the way the viewer/listener engages with and processes the material resistances of the aesthetic symbol in question. In former case, a certain pattern of expressive orientation on the part of the listener is insisted on and inculcated as a concomitant of membership of the religious community, and from time to time reenforced by compulsary participation in certain expressive activities as a way of controlling motivational commitment to the church and its teachings. In the latter case, it is the artistic pattern component of the Bach Mass, not its Christian content which is the primary object of response. This is the arrangement institutionalised in modern high culture, whereby a variety of expressive patterns are made available to viewers/listeners, who are free to choose for themselves whether to repeat exposure to these particular paintings or musical compositions, in order to organise their expressive orientation to their lifeworld in terms of the particular patterns offered by these cultural objects. The enormous proliferation of artistic styles and the variety of themes represented through them is not simply an epiphenomenon of the structure of the art market. On the contrary, it is a functionally significant structural component of the institutionalised individualism of the modern world, greatly increasing the probability that viewers of diverse background and social situation will be able to find some artistic forms that help them to make sense of the motivational meanings of their life world, and through internalisation construct the affective ground for participation in a vastly more complexely structured social and cultural world than that of the great civilisations of ancient Greece and China.

The shape of an explanation

It is by placing these conceptual elements in the context of the cybernetic hierarchy represented by the AGIL schema (both within art as a cultural system, and placing art within the context of the general action system), and specifying the inputs and outputs of the different systems to each other, that one is able consistently to interrelate the key conceptual elements of sociological and art historical theory, define the variable modes of articulation of such elements in concrete processes of action, and understand their consequences for the reproduction and transformation of action systems. This stands in contrast to the schemes of Bourdieu and Witkin in which the synthesis of art historical and sociological theory remains indeterminate (residual status of key categories such as art, sensuous etc). Their reliance on the concept of homology gives their accounts of art a strongly reductionist cast, unable to show the value-added contributions that artistic innovation can make to action processes when

---

[48] Parsons 1951, 411.

integrated with relevant social and psychological mechanisms. The interpenetrations between systems presupposed by Parsons are contingent, and, if realised at all, only realised as a result of action processes occurring over time. A functional theory of art as a particular component of the human action system, allows one to specify the consequences of, for example, the institutionalisation of a new aesthetic-expressive convention within a particular system of interaction, or conversely the withdrawal of aesthetic-expressive resources from a particular institutional domain, for example from the established church during the iconoclasm of the English reformation.[49] An action theoretic analysis of artistic innovation will, therefore, involve several consecutive and interwoven modes of analysis: 1) structural interpretation of the patterning of a complex of expressive symbolism on cultural and social levels as appropriate, 2) functional analysis of the interpenetrations between cultural, social, personality and behavioral systems, and their entailments for the reproduction and transformation of relevant action systems, 3) explanation of the innovation in question in terms of structures and agency, involving a mixture of teleological, practical and quasi-causal arguments.[50]

---

[49] See Gould 1991, 94-8 on the logic of functional explanation. The action of the European community to ban cigarette advertising, and in particular the sponsorship of sports by cigarette manufacturers, rests on an implicit functional theory: the association between sport (energy, youth, attractiveness) and cigarettes in advertising and the placing of promotional signs on sports-equipment (football-players' jerseys, formula-one cars) makes smoking motivationally attractive to young people, and thereby encourages them to smoke. The withdrawal – through censorship – of such expressive resources will reduce the proclivity of young people to take up smoking. The cultural patterning of the symbolism and the structure of the mechanisms involved is considerably more complicated in the case of, for example, interpreting, explaining and elucidating the functional significance of changing patterns of style and content in Renaissance altar pieces, but the logic of explanation is not fundamentally different. For an implicitly functional account of the patterning and use (for philosophical recruitment) of Epicurus' portrait in antiquity, see the fascinating study of Frischer, 1982. Cf. also Meiss 1951, for a study (of stylistic and iconographic changes in late 14th century Florence, responding to and shaping attitudes to religion, wealth and social status in the period after the Black Death) that lends itself very nicely to reformulation in action theoretic terms.

[50] On the logical structure of explanation in action theory, see Bershady 1973, esp. pp. 158-64, p. 163 for "a mixture of quasi-causal statements and practical arguments". Cf. Parsons 1954, 36 – for a brief summary of the relevant levels of analysis and their interrelation.

Case Study: Portraits, Power and Clientelae in the Late Roman Republic – An Action Theoretic Interpretation

In order to illustrate how such an action theoretic sociology of art might operate in practice, I wish to conclude by sketching a case study.[51] In the middle to late second century BC a new type of portrait was created in the Roman world. The Museo Torlonia patrician (PLATE 1) is a quintessential example of late republican "veristic" portraiture. The head is deliberately unideal. It is asymetrical, with a bulging left cranium, and projecting ears. A zig-zag of creases intersects with a line under the eye and a deeply engraved naso-labial furrow cuts into the left face of a heavy, protuberant nose. The cheeks are sunken and hollow. The aging flesh hanging from prominent cheek bones in folds creased with a patchwork of wrinkles. The thin-lipped mouth turns down at the corners. Heavy bags hang under the eyes, whilst folds dip down from the brow over them. Crow's-feet fan out from their corners. A patternless play of wrinkles deeply engraved in the forehead, concentrating on the root of the nose, completes this study in senescence – at least as it appears to us.[52] The Torlonia patrician, conventionally dated to the middle of the first century BC, represents one extreme of the range of mid first century Roman portraits. Other portraits, like that of the Tivoli general (PLATE 2) seem softer in their treatment and less "unsympathetic": the cheeks are not sunken and the furrows of the brow less deeply gouged; the mouth is full and the upper lip takes the form of a cupid-bow. Nevertheless, the crow's-feet, the hooded eyes, the furrows across the cheek and the box around the mouth defined by the deeply engraved naso-labial furrows and the folds of a fleshy chin, all serve to set apart the general as a Roman Republican portrait from potentially related Hellenistic Greek portrait types, such as images of intellectuals, kings or members of civic elites.

Hellenistic kings are almost always represented as being youthful, seldom older than thirty-five to forty. The lines and wrinkles of aging are very lightly modelled, smoothed out to the point of vanishing even on relatively "mature" portraits like that of Seleukos I from the Villa of the Papyri (PLATE 3). Although Hellenistic civic benefactor portraits are considerably more aged than their royal counterparts, the model they follow is that of the Hellenistic philosophers like Carneades with wide-

---

[51] This is a very much simplifed version of my article "Portraits, Power and Patronage in the Late Roman Republic", forthcoming 2000, *Journal of Roman Studies* vol. XC. This contains a full discussion of the relevant primary evidence and secondary literature. For the purposes of the present article my major concern are the problems of theoretical logic involved in creating a determinate, logically integrated and non-reductionist account of the problems raised by late Republican portraits.

[52] The Torlonia patrician is chosen as the type-example of Roman veristic portraits in Bianchi Bandinelli 1969, pp. 71ff; Nodelman 1975, 10ff.

open eyes and raised brows echoed and emphasized by symmetrical wavy worry lines, all set on heads which still retain in their structure (overall proportions and facial symmetry) and modelling the characteristics of classical ideal portraiture (PLATE 4).[53] The treatment of the face in Roman Republican portraits is distinctly different from most Hellenistic civic portraits, notably in the way the eyes are often hooded and the brows pulled down over the eyes towards the roots of the nose, as on both the Tivoli general and the Torlonia patrician, to create a concentrated, somewhat austere, expression in contrast to the more mild reflectiveness of contemporary portraits of Greek civic elites.[54]

Art historical accounts of these portraits have oscillated between explanations in terms of "Greek influences" and "Roman values". The Greek influence argument suggests that this genre of Roman art should be understood as the direct unfolding of the naturalistic tradition in Greek aesthetics, albeit applied to a very different kind of subject, Roman politicians. It is characteristically supported by showing that all the distinctive aesthetic features can be found in Greek sculpture of an earlier date.[55] Most notably the technical sculptural devices underlying verism are anticipated in "genre figures", representing peasants or fishermen, and probably created as garden sculptures and objects of derision for members of the Hellenistic Greek elite (PLATE 5).[56] Alternatively, it is suggested that the veristic style "is a direct reflection" of the Romans high valuation of old age and thus corresponds to a "structural element" in the Roman gerontocratic constitution, according to which senior magistracies were age-graded.[57]

Both these answers represent straightforward examples of idealist theoretical logic, making art a simple epiphenomenon of broader cultural traditions: an emanation of Roman values, or the unfolding of the immanent logic of Greek art. These theoretical shortcomings also entail inadequacies of the explanations to the empirical data. If art reflects cultural values, why are earlier Roman portraits not veristic but "idealising"? Why is it only in the second century that Greek "influence" gives rise to this particular kind of portrait at Rome, although the Romans had been both producing portraits and commissioning Greek artists for at least two centuries?[58] Furthermore, a considerable group of Roman veristic portraits are combined with naked or semi-naked body types, based on classical Greek statues of gods and heroes (PLATES 6, 7). Nudity distinguishes these Roman portraits from their prede-

---

[53] Zanker, 1995 180-188 on Carneades, 188-194 on "The intellectualisation of the citizen portrait".
[54] Cf. for example, Vessberg 1941 plates LV.1-2, LVI, LXI. LXV, LXVIII, LXVIII.
[55] Richter 1955; Zanker 1983.
[56] Pollitt 1986, 141-147.
[57] Breckenridge1968; Smith 1981, esp. 37-8; Giuliani 1986, 190-199, quotation p. 197.
[58] Hölscher 1978, esp. 344ff on early Roman art and patronage.

cessors in the middle Republic, and from civic portraits within the Greek Hellenistic world, where togate and mantel statues were the convention. It also distinguishes them from their putative peasant prototypes, whose decrepit, hunched bodies, generally less than 2/3 life size, stand in clear contrast to the muscled *cuirasse-ideal* of the Roman portraits, standing upright and well-over life size. Public nudity was perceived by the Romans to be a Greek vice, hardly an appropriate expression of Roman values. The combination of extreme realism – with its technical foundations in representations of peasants – with ideal nudity, based on divine and heroic prototypes hardly represents a simple unfolding of traditions in Greek art. On the contrary it combines elements from quite discrepant genres within Greek art, and presupposes a reorganisation of form that cannot be understood in purely internalist terms.

Parsons' theory of expressive symbolism indicates a different approach. The components of art works, including iconography and style, as elements of a system of expressive symbolism are organised about "the attitudinal structure of the relationship" which they are used to construct, and "the cathectic interests involved in it".[59] Cultural analysis of the distinctive formal structures of portraits must be supplemented by reference to their relational implications.

When embedded in ongoing systems of interaction, expressive symbols, as expressions of ego's attitude to alter, are "relational possessions" which "ego can give or withhold".[60] "Possessions are rewards in so far as their significance is expressive, that is in so far as they constitute objects of direct gratification without regard to their instrumental uses."[61] The transfer of such relational possessions is normatively regulated. I may have a "legitimised expectation" that someone for whom I perform a favour should show a positive attitude towards me. Conversely, the conditions under which such relational possessions may be withheld or withdrawn, under which "alter may legitimately change his attitude towards ego" are institutionally defined.[62] Portraits in the late Roman Republic, I shall argue, were produced as reward symbols. As such, their allocation, use and form were regulated by a number of institutional rules. On each of these levels – cultural choices of form and social regulation of use – this system of expressive symbolism was "integrated with the cathectic interests" in each others' attitudes of the parties to these relationships. The creation of the new genre represented by our portraits intensified the production of affect within a particular system of relationships, with significant consequences for the integration of the Roman state in the late Republic.

---

[59] Parsons 1951, 391.
[60] Ibid. 414ff
[61] Ibid.
[62] Ibid. 415

The Body, Expressive Culture and Social Interaction

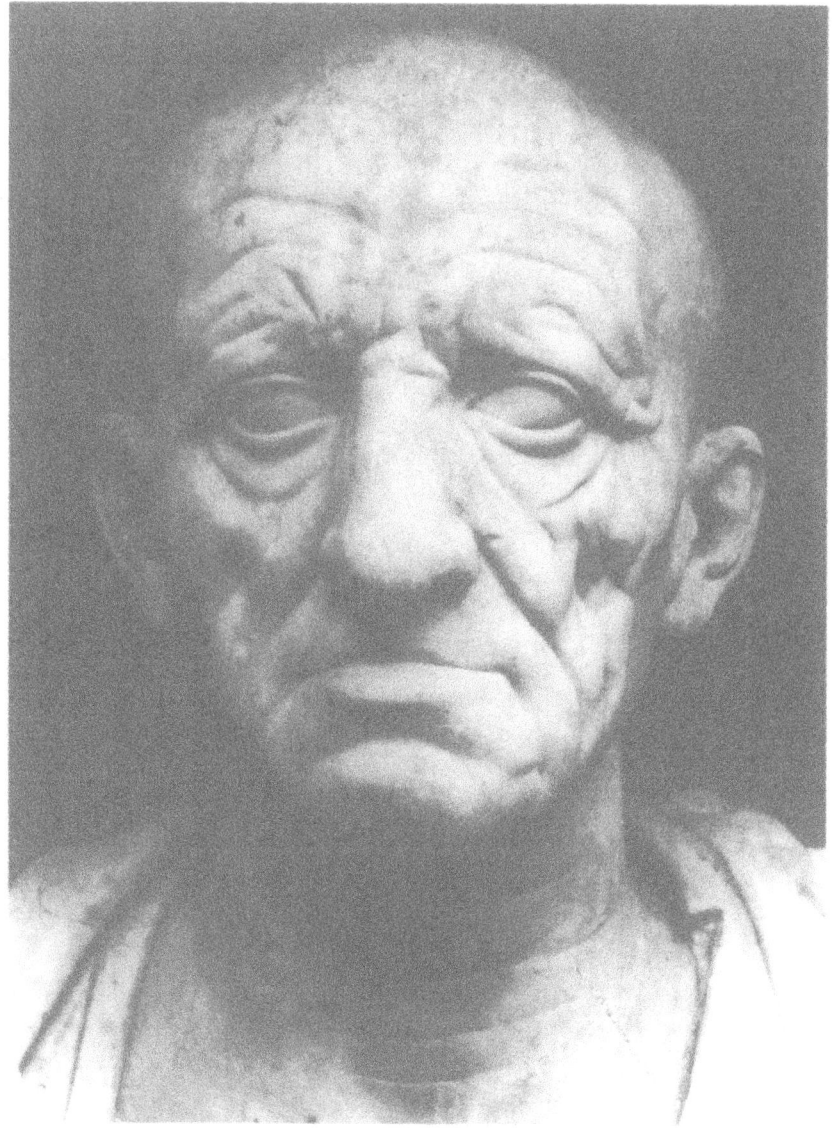

PLATE 1: Portrait of a "patrician", Museo Torlonia, 1st century BC.
(Source: DAI-Rome 33.58)

PLATE 2: Head from portrait of a general, from Tivoli, 1st century BC.
(Source DAI-Rome 32.415)

PLATE 3: Portrait of Seleukos I, Roman copy of a 3rd century BC Greek original.

PLATE 4: Portrait of a man, from Delos, 2nd century BC.
(Source: DAI-Athens 70.1010)

PLATE 5: Statue of an old fisherman. Roman copy of Hellenistic Greek original of 3rd century BC. (Source: DAI-Rome 65.1733)

PLATE 6: Portrait of a general, from Tivoli, 1st century BC.
(Source: Alinari/Anderson 28853)

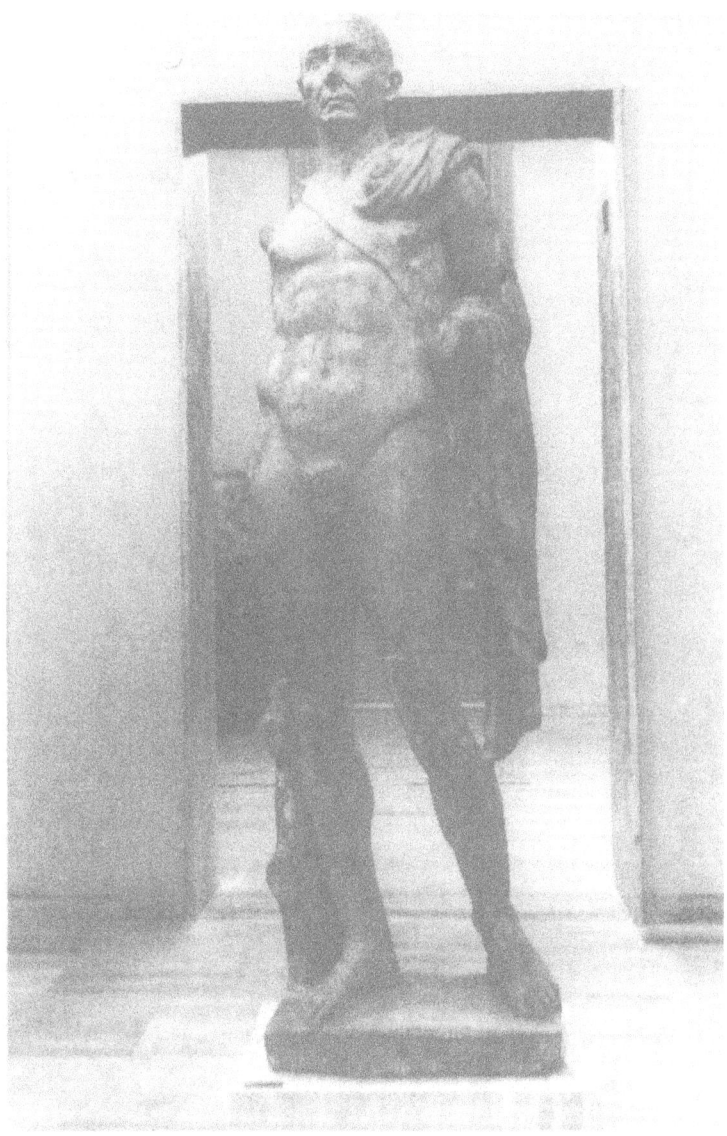

PLATE 7: Statue of a general, from Foruli, 1st century BC.
(Source: DAI-Rome 60.32)

PLATE 8: Theseus and the Minotaur. Wall-paintings from Pompeii, Roman copy of the 1st century AD, after a classical Greek original. (Source: Alinari/Anderson

Literary evidence points to two patterns of the social regulation of the use of portraits in the late Republic, public honorific portraits erected by the state, and portraits of patrons erected by client communities in those communities and at Rome itself. The rules regulating public honorific portraiture can be inferred from the terms of the decrees passed by the paramount governing collectivity in the Roman state, the Senate, in order to set up such portraits.[63] The award of public honorific portraits to stand in civic space was at the disposition of the Senate and People, as was the particular location of the statue. The award of a portrait statue is not only a token of honour, expressing the esteem in which the receipient is held, but also a gift. As a gift, it creates obligations on the part of the recipient to reciprocate with an attitude of gratitude towards the Senate and People, manifested by respect for the authority of the Senate and continued meritorious action in service of the Senate and People. Failure to reciprocate could provoke condemnation, and withdrawal of the symbol of the Senate's esteem, through demolition of the statue. The iconography of the portrait – whether for example it should be equestrian or pedestrian – was also controlled by the senate, because there was an internal relationship between the form of the portrait and the precise definition of the relationship between giver and receiver constituted by setting up the portrait. Public honorific portraiture, however, does not allow us to explain the emergence of verism. The institution was established two centuries before the earliest veristic portraits. Public honorific portraits were always in bronze, not marble, and never naked before the imperial period. The practice was designed to bind the recipient in closer loyalty to senate and people, and seems unlikely to have stressed the personal authority of the person represented, let alone assimilated them to gods and heroes.

In the late Republic, however, the practice of portrait giving was taken up in the context of relationships of *clientela*. In such relationships, a "patron" from an elite family provided physical and legal protection for his clients in return for political support and the performance of acts expressive of respect which enhanced the prestige of the patron within the community as a whole – for example attending the patron in the morning or during his public business in the forum. The moral ideology which informed such relationships was explicitly patriarchal, modelled on a father's authority over his children and the reciprocal duties which characterised familial solidarity.[64] The ideal patron was characterised by a cluster of moral and personal qualities encapsulated in the concepts of *fides*, *gravitas* and *severitas*, all of

---

[63] For example, Cicero *Phillipic* IX, 15-17.
[64] Badian 1958, pp. 1-14,163-5 on the ideology of patronage and the reciprocal services; Gelzer 1969, pp. 62-70 on the personalistic and hierarchical character of patrocinium. The classic statement of the moral ideology of clientela is Dionysius Halicarnassus, II.10.

which expressed the hierarchical relationship of the patronus to his clientes.[65] The core concept was the *fides* of the patronus, his trustworthiness and reliability in the fulfilment of his obligations as patronus.[66] The patronus in whom one could have such confidence was characterised by *gravitas*, a weightiness which was once exterior and physical as well as intellectual and moral, manifested in reduced emotional expression and constancy (*constantia*) in all circumstances in one's dealings with clients, gravity in style of speaking (*graviter dicere, sententia gravis*), and a certain moral rigour or *severitas*, both in one's personal conduct and in one's dealing with clients.[67] These qualities were a prerogative of age. Severity of visage combined with weightiness of stature and a certain stateliness of movement represented the physical expression of the moral qualities of the ideal patron.[68] The ideal client responded to such a patron with the pious respect a son might be expected to show his father, manifested in particular dutifulness in supporting his patron in times of need and manifesting gratitude for *beneficia* rendered by the *officia* of attendance upon his patron in his house and in the forum.

Portrait-giving seems to have been a late innovation in this institution, possibly initiated by Greek cities in the expanding Roman empire, seeking the favour and protection of members of the Roman elite. To give a portrait in return for benefactions received and in anticipation of benefactions to come was tantamount to entering into a relationship of clientela with the recipient as patron. As in the case of public honorific portraits, the client community who made the gift of the portrait was free to chose whether or not to give a portrait, as well as to determine the precise character of its form, materials and location. But where in public honorific portraiture, the person given the portrait owed *gratia* as a particularly honoured individual to the larger community of which he was a member, in clientela relationships the portrait itself was an expression of gratitude in return for benefactions received from the powerful patronus who stood in a patriarchal and authoritarian relationship to his clients. The strongly inegalitarian nature of the relationship between Roman patrons and their Greek clients became increasingly marked over time. The religious honours that had been enjoyed by the Hellenistic kings displaced

---

[65] Hellegouarc'h 1963, pp. 275-94 "Les virtues du Patronus". Cf. Giuliani, 1986, 125 ff for a discussion of the same concepts in their relation to verism, but as I suggested above, unable to explain the timing of their manifestation in portraiture (only in the second centry BC), or the combination of verism with ideal nudity, partly because he does not, as Hellegouarc'h, see their particular connection of these value concepts to patronage, partly because he has no institutional account of the functioning of portraiture as relational symbolism rather than simply a reflection of values.

[66] Hellgouarc'h 1963, 275.

[67] Ibid. 275-85.

[68] Ibid; Giuliani 1986,125ff.

by the Romans were extended to Roman magistrates, and we find patrons being accorded the cultic title "soter", saviour, inscribed on the bases for portrait statues.

Moving from a structural analysis of the cultural patterning of works of art, and of patterns of interaction in social relations, we can now integrate these levels of analysis in terms of their functional interdependencies with the psychological and the behavioral levels. This allows us to understand the iconographic and stylistic patterning of these late Republican portraits, like the Tivoli general, as the sensuous-aesthetic basis for the production and generalisation of forms of affect appropriate to and sustaining of the attitudes and values which animated the relationship of client and patron-soter.

The veristic style of the portrait heads, stressing the age, gravity and severity of the sitter functions as a visual metaphor which invokes the moral contract, *fides*, the shared normative culture, between the two parties to the relationship. It is the sensuous, material basis which makes possible the generalisation of meanings and sentiments proper to the relationship of clientela from the relationship and its parties to the portrait as a sign that stands for the relationship.[69] An image dedicated at Rome by a client community of their patron calls out in the patron a pleasurable feeling of authoritarian benevolence for them as clients which is his response to their self-subjection manifested in the gift of the portrait. For the clients, gazing on a portrait of their patron in the forum or senate house of their home community, the veristic style of the portrait allows them, as they gaze upon it, to project and elaborate affect-laden fantasies of their patron as ideal patron, fantasies of his *constantia* and *fides*, fantasies which generate a pleasurable sense of personal security rooted in personal subjection to the masterly patron.[70]

This structure of feeling was amplified and adjusted by other material attributes of these statues. Whilst most public honorific statues were of bronze, many patronal statues were of marble, a material normally used only for *agalmata*, cult-statues of both gods and Hellenistic kings. Their colossal format and nudity also set them apart from standard honorific portraits, and evoked images of heroes and kings. "Superi-

---

[69] Cf. Parsons 1953, 33 on the cognitive basis of association between sign object and principle object as one of the conditions of the genealisation of meaning and the transfer of cathexis. Ibid. 36 for the principle that, in so far as a system of expressive culture is shared by participants in interaction, its sign objects "should have a primary or secondary cathexis by both in such a way that each may 'feel' its significance to each other. It must arouse either the same feelings, that is expectations of gratification or deprivation, or at least complementary feelings in both. It must, that is, be cathected by both in ways that are integrated with the motivational system of each vis-a-vis that of the other".

[70] On response, when expressed, as a symbolisation of attitude, and ego's expression of attitude as a "focus of gratification" or pleasure for alter "if it indicates the attitude for which alter hopes", see Parsons 1951, 385-7.

ority in appearance... as well as in the actions, movements and attitudes of the body" were the visual counterpart of the Hellenistic king's superiority of the soul, and as such were supposed to "put in order those who looked upon him, amazed at his majesty", which was in turn held to be "a godlike thing (*theomimon pragma*), [which] can make him admired and honoured by the multitiude".[71] The particular iconographic types chosen for portraits of persons may have been selected on occasion with the specific intention of enhancing the sense of awe generated in the first place by a superiorly powerful and beautiful body. These recall classical images of saviour-heroes like that copied in the house of Gavius Rufus at Pompeii (PLATE 8), showing Theseus receiving the grateful thanks of the Athenian children he has saved from the minotaur, manifested in acts of self-negation such as *proskynesis*, grovelling at the feet of Theseus, and kissing his hand.[72] The material, scale and body-imagery of our group of statues all point towards a desire to evoke the idea of "saviour", expressing the corresponding attitudes of humble dependence on the part of those who set up the statue, inducing respectful subordination on the part of their primary viewers and seeking to call out an attitude of concern and readiness for intervention *in extremis* on the part of the patron thus portrayed. Both in the exchange of portraits and in the repeated viewing of them, patron and client are socialised into a language of emotional communication, which shapes the feelings of the two parties to that communication in terms of the moral culture which underpins the institution of patronage. They become sensitised to, and increasingly affectively invested in, their relationship to each other, the reciprocal attitudes and expectations which constitute that relationship and the moral values which legitimate those attitudes and expectations.[73]

Such a functional contextualisation of veristic portraiture in its immediate cultural, social and psychological environments, does not in itself amount to a full historical explanation. It represents simply a more multidimensional account of the construction of meaning than earlier efforts, and one which at least intimates how art feeds back into the contexts out of which it was created rather than being solely an epiphenomenon of them. What is the special motivation during this period on the part of both clients and patrons for developing this new practice in the context of

---

[71] Diotogenes, ap. Stob. *Anth.* iv 7.62 = 266ff. [Hense], transl. in Goodenough 1928, 71ff. Smith 1989, 50-3.

[72] Brilliant 1963, p. 14 for the paintings from Herculaneum and from the house of Gavius Rufus, esp. on the frontality of the hero, and the worshipful "adulation" of the "hero who is greater than life, as the saved humiliate themselves before their savior". For convenient illustrations: Ling 1991, p. 120, fig. 121 – Theseus and the Minotaur, Villa Imperiale, Oecus A; ditto, Pompeii VII.2.16 (House of Gavius Rufus), c. 70 AD. On proskynesis: Sittl 1890.

[73] Parsons 1951, 387ff on the internalisation of expressive symbolism.

clientela relationships, which required, in addition to the expenditure of resources on statues, the considerable cultural investment represented by the creation of the new artistic language of these images, abstracting the cultural techniques used in the creation of peasant images, using them to build up the characteristic motifs of the veristic portrait, and integrating them in a novel way with traditional body iconography of gods and heroes to create this new portrait genre? What are the broader ramifiactions of the heightened level of mutual affective investment on the part of clients and patrons?

We first encounter these portraits in the second century BC. The second century marked the climax of Rome's early territorial expansion, when she acquired her first overseas provinces. One of the problems faced by the Roman elite as a result of the expansion of their city-state into an empire was how to include the conquered within Roman patterns of social and political organisation. The privilege of citizenship was jealously guarded. Extending individual aristocratic families' clientela beyond the immediate enviorns of Rome was an alternative, less radical mechanism of inclusion. The increased spatial distancing of clientela relationships cannot, however, have been unproblematic. The traditional expressive acts of morning attendance and donation of food doles presupposed the mutual presence of client and patron in order to sustain the sense of mutual affective investment or solidarity which underlay the relationship. The creation and display of these new portrait types, with their characteristic style and iconography, was a means whereby the Roman elite and their new foreign clients sought to upgrade the expressive symbolic system which was part of the institution of clientela. But for this innovation, the ties of solidarity between patrons and clients would have been weaker, and the capacity of patrons to mobilise their clients for political and military purposes correspondingly eroded. The strength of these ties was crucial to the important role played by the Republican dynasts' vast networks of clients in the break down of centralised state control of violence during the Roman revolution.

Conclusions

My reconstruction and elaboration of Parsons' sociology of art offers a genuine synthesis of social theory and art history. First, it has used the four-function schema to formalise the relationship between key concepts from the critical tradition in German art history, showing that they can be understood as components of a cultural system, standing in relationships of cybernetic hierarchy to each other. Second, it has drawn upon the differentiated account of types of signs and semiotic processes in pragmatist thought to integrate aesthetic analysis of expressive culture with the Parsonian schema for general action analysis. Such an analytic framework transcends both the essentialism of formalist approaches opposing art as culture to society or biology or the reductionism of many sociological approaches to art. It is not, however, a muddled or compromised middle way, merely adding humanistic methods to an unchanged structural sociology.[74] On the contrary, an action theoretic framework both allows and requires the analyst to explore the relative balance of behavioral, psychological, social and cultural components in particular aesthetic-expressive practices and processes, and to assess the degree to which cultural level components are emergent from, and autonomous of – even whilst interpenetrating with – lower level components in the hierarchy of the general action schema.

Such approach to art has a general value for the sociology of art. First, it is sensitive to the aesthetic structure of the art object, whilst not making a fetish of it. It facilitates the integration of the cultural analysis of works of art with general sociological theory without reducing art to an epiphenomenon of its social environment. Functional theory as an analytic frame of reference allows one to formulate relatively determinate propositions about the social consequences of modifying an element in a system of expressive symbolism or of continuing to use an unchanged system in a changed environment. This enables the sociologist to make sense of artistic change in the context of broader social and historical processes without reducing that change to an inevitable consequence of that process. More generally, action theory offers the possibility of integrating into the sociology of art the rich cross civilizational tradition of cultural analysis characteristic of the German historical school, but without the historicism that characterised both this work and that of its heirs in contemporary art history. Action theory's analytic framework is sufficiently differentiated to be able to be sensitive to the extraordinary variety of artistic expression characteristic of world history, but sufficiently integrated to show how such differences are generated by variant combinations and interrelationships of fundamentally constant underlying components. A research programme which promises to combine the interpretative sensitivity of art history with the strong comparative and explanatory thrust of sociology is surely worth further development.

Bibliography

Adam, P. (1992): *The Arts of the Third Reich*. London, Thames and Hudson.
Alexander, J. (1983): *Theoretical Logic in Sociology vol IV: The Modern Recnstruction of Classical Thought – Talcott Parsons*. Berkeley, University of California Press.
Alexander, J. (1995): The reality of reduction: the failed synthesis of Pierre Bourdieu, pp. 128-217. In: idem *Fin de Siècle Social Theory: Relativism, Reduction and the Problem of Reason*. London, Verso.

---

[74] As advocated by Zolberg 1990, x and 12; Bowler1994

Alpers, S. (1979): Style is what you make it, pp. 95-107. In: B. Lang ed. *The Concept of Style*. Philadelphia, University of Pennsylvania Press.
Alpers, S. (1983): *The Art of Describing*. Chicago, University of Chicago Press.
Badian, E. (1958): *Foreign Clientelae 264-70 BC*. Cambridge, Cambridge University Press.
Baum, R.C. and F.J. Lechner (1981): National socialism: towards an action theoretical interpretation. In: *Sociological Inquiry* 51, 281-308.
Baxandall, M. (1972): *Painting and Experience in Fifteenth Century Italy*. Oxford, Oxford University Press.
Becker, H.S. (1982): *Art Worlds*. Berkeley, University of California Press.
Bershady, H.J. (1973): *Ideology and Social Knowledge*. Oxford, Basil Blackwell.
Bianchi Bandinelli, R. (1969): *Rome: the Centre of Power. Roman Art to AD 200*. London, Thames and Hudson.
Boas, F. (1955): (ov 1928) *Primitive Art*. New York: Dover.
Bourdieu, P. (1984): *Distinction: a Social Critique of the Judgement of Taste*. Cambridge, Mass; Harvard University Press.
Bourdieu, P. (1996): *The Rules of Art: Genesis and Structure of the Literary Field*. Cambridge, Polity Press.
Bowler, A. (1994): Methodological dilemmas in the sociology of art, pp. 247-266. In D. Crane ed. *The Sociology of Culture: Emerging Theoretical Perspectives*. Oxford, Basil Blackwell.
Breckenridge, J.D. (1968): The Roman portrait, pp. 143-186. In: idem *Likeness: a Conceptual History of Portraiture*. Evanston, Northwestern University Press.
Brilliant, R. (1963): *Gesture and Rank in Roman Art.*. New Haven, Connecticut Academy of Arts and Sciences.
Bryson, N. (1992): Art in context, pp. 18-42. In: R. Cohen ed. *Studies in Historical Change*. Charlottesville, University of Virginia Press.
Crane, D. ed. (1994): *The Sociology of Culture: Emerging Theoretical Perspectives*. Oxford, Basil Backwell.
De Lauretis, T. (1981): Semiotics and experience, pp. 158-186. In: idem. *Alice Doesn't: Feminism, Semiotics, Cinema*. London, Macmillan.
Dissanayake, E. (1992): *Homo Aestheticus: Where Art Comes from and Why*. Seattle, University of washington Press.
Eco, U. (1976): *A Theory of Semiotics*. Bloomington, Indiana.
Frischer, B. (1982): *The Sculpted Word: Epicureanism and Philosophical Recruitment in Ancient Greece*. Berkeley, University of California Press.
Fromm, E. (1942): *The Fear of Freedom*. Routledge, London.
Gelzer M. (1969): *The Roman Nobility*. Oxford, Oxford University Press.
Giuliani, L. (1986): *Bildnis und Botschaft: Hermeneutische Untersuchungen zur Bildniskunst der Römischen Republik*. Frankfurt.
Goffmann, E. (1963): *Behaviour in Public Places: Notes on the Social Organisation of Gatherings*. New York, Free Press.
Goodenough, E.R. (1928): The political philosophy of Hellenistic kingship. In: *Yale Classical Studies* 1: 55-104.
Gould, M. (1991): The Structure of Social Action: at least sixty years ahead of its time, pp. 85-107. In: R. Robertson, B.S. Turner eds. *Talcott Parsons: Theorist of Modernity*.
Griswold, W. (1985): *Renaissance Revivals: City Comedy and Revenge Tragedy in the London Theatre 1576-1980*. Chicago, University of Chicago Press.
Hellegouarc'h, J. (1963): *Le vocabulaire Latin des relations et des partis politiques sous la République*.

Hochschild, A.R. (1979): Emotion work, feeling rules and social structure. In: *American Journal of Sociology* 85: 551-575.
Hochschild, A.R. (1983): *The Managed Heart: Commercialisation of Human Feeling*. Berkeley, University of California Press.
Hölscher, T. (1978): Die Anfänge Römischer Repräsentationskunst. In: *Mitteilungen des Deutschen Archäologischen Instituts* 85.2: 315-357
Holub, R.C. (1984): *Reception Theory: a Critical Introduction*. London, Methuen.
Joas, H. (1985): *G.H. Mead: a Contemporary Re-examination of his Thought*. Cambridge, Polity Press.
Jones, M.P. (1996): Post-human agency: between theoretical traditions. In: *Sociological Theory* 14.3, 290-309.
Lidz, C.W. and V. Lidz. (1976): Piaget's psychology of the intelligence and the theory of action, pp. 195-239. In: Loubser et al. eds. 1976.
Ling, R. (1991): *Roman Painting*. Cambridge, Cambridge University Press.
Loubser, J.J., A. Effrat, R.C. Baum and V. Lidz eds. (1976): *Explorations in General Theory in Social Science*. New York, The Free Press.
Mannheim, K. (1993) (o.v. 1922): On the interpretation of Weltanschauung, pp. 136-186. In: K. Wolff ed. *From Karl Mannheim*. London, Transaction Books.
McCarthy, E.D. (1984): Toward a sociology of the physical world: George Herbert Mead on physical objects. In: *Studies in Symbolic Interaction* 5, 105-121.
Meiss, M. (1951): *Painting in Florence and Sienna after the Black Death*. Princeton, Princeton University Press.
Mosse, G.L. (1978): *Towards the Final Solution*.
Mosse, G.L. (1996): *The Image of Man: The Creation of Modern Masculinity*. Oxford: Oxford University Press.
Mukerji, C. (1994): Toward a sociology of material culture: science studies, cultural studies and the meaning of things, pp. 143-162. In: Crane ed. 1994.
Nodelman, S. (1975): How to read a Roman portrait. In: *Art in America* 63, 26-33; repr. in and cited from E. D' Ambra 1993 *Roman Art in Context* pp. 10-26.
Panofsky, E. (1939): Introductory, pp. 3-17. In: idem *Studies in Iconology: Humanistic Themes in the Art of the Renaissance*. Oxford, Oxford University Press.
Panofsky, E. (1981) (o.v. 1920): The concept of artistic volition. In: *Critical Inquiry* 8: 17-34.
Parsons, T. (1937): *The Structure of Social Action*. New York, McGraw Hill.
Parsons, T. (1951): Expressive symbols and the social system: the communication of affect, pp. 384-427. In: idem *The Social System*, New York, The Free Press.
Parsons, T. (1952): The super-ego and the theory of social systems. In: *Psychiatry* vol. 15. no. 1. Repr. in and cited from idem 1964, pp. 17-33.
Parsons, T. (1953): The theory of symbolism in relation to action, pp. 31-62. In: T. Parsons, F. Bales and E. Shils eds. *Working Papers in the Theory of Action*. New York, The Free Press.
Parsons, T. (1954): The father symbol: an appraisal in the light of psychoanalytic and sociological theory. Repr. in and cited from idem 1964, pp. 34-56.
Parsons, T. (1956): Family structure and the socialisation of the child, pp. 35-132. In: T. Parsons and R.F. Bales eds. *Family, Socialisation and Interaction Process*. New York, The Free Press.
Parsons, T. (1961): Culture and the social system: an introduction, pp. 963-993. In: T. Parsons, E. Shils, K. Naegele and J. Pitts eds. *Theories of Society*. New York, The Free Press.
Parsons, T. (1964): *Social Structure and Personality*. New York, The Free Press.

Parsons, T. (1970): Theory in the humanities and sociology. In: *Daedalus* 99.2, 495-523.
Parsons, T. (1974): Religion in post-industrial America: the problem of secularisation. In: *Social Research* 41, 193-225. Repr. in and cited from idem 1978 *Action Theory and the Human Condition*, pp. 300-322
Parsons, T. and Platt, G. (1973): *The American University*. Cambridge Mass; Harvard University Press.
Parsons, T. and W. White (1961): The link between character and social structure. Reprinted in and cited from Parsons 1964, 183-235.
Peirce, C.S. (1955): Logic as semiotic: the theory of signs, pp. 98-119. In: *Philosophical Writings*, ed. J. Buckler. New York, Dover Books.
Peterson, R. (1994): Culture studies through the production perspective: progress and prospects, pp. 163-189. In: D. Crane ed. 1994.
Podro, M. (1982): *The Critical Historians of Art*. New Haven, Yale University Press.
Pollitt, J.J. (1986): *Art in the Hellenistic Age*. Cambridge, Cambridge University Press.
Press, A. L. (1994): The sociology of cultural reception: notes towards an emerging paradigm, pp. 221-245. In: D. Crane ed. 1994.
Preziosi, D. (1981): *Rethinking Art History: Meditations on a Coy Science*. New Haven and London, Yale University Press.
Richter, G. (1955): The origins of verism in Roman portraits. In: *Journal of Roman Studies* 45, 39-46.
Rochberg-Halton, E. (1982): Situation, structure and context of meaning. In: *Sociological Quarterly* 23, 455-476.
Schapiro, M. (1953): Style, pp. 287-312. In: A.L. Kroeber ed. *Anthropology Today*. Chicago, University of Chicago Press.
Schapiro, M. (1973): Frontal and profile as symbolic form, pp. 37-47. In: idem*Words and Pictures: on the Literal and the Symbolic in the Illustration of a Text*. The Hague: Mouton.
Schwartz, B. (1981): *Vertical Classification: A Study in Structuralism and the Sociology of Knowledge*. Chicago, University of Chicago Press.
Sittl, C. (1890): *Die Gebärden der Griechen und Römer*. Teubner, Leipzig.
Smith, R.R.R. (1981): Greeks, foreigners and Roman Republican portraits. In: *Journal of Roman Studies* LXXI: 24-38.
Smith, R.R.R. (1989): *Hellenistic Royal Portraits*. Oxford, Oxford University Press.
Staubmann, H.M. (1997): Action theory and aesthetics: the place of the affective-cathectic action dimension in Talcott Parsons' general theory of action. In: *European Journal for Semiotic Studies* 9: 735-768.
Trevarthen, C. (1995): Mother and baby seeing artfully eye to eye, pp. 157-200. In: R. Gregory ed. *The Artful Eye*. Oxford, Oxford University Press.
Vessberg, O. (1941): *Studien zur Kunstgeschichte der Römischen Republik*. Lund.
Witkin, R.W. (1995): *Art and Social Structure*. Cambridge, Polity Press.
Witkin, R.W. (1997): Constructing a sociology for an icon of aesthetic modernity.In: *Sociological Theory* 15.2, 101-125.
Wolff, J. (1992): Excess and inhibition: interdisciplinarity in the study of art, pp. 706-16. In: L. Grossberg et al eds. *Cultural Studies*. London, Routledge.
Wölfflin, H. (1950) (o.v. 1922): *Principles of Art History: the Problem of the Development of Style in Later Art*. New York, Dover.
Wölfflin, H. (1966) (ov 1888). *Renaissance and Baroque*. Ithaca: Cornell University Press.
Zanker P. (1983): Zur Bildnisrepräsentation Führender Männer in Mittelitalischen und Campanischen Städten zur Zeit der später Republik und der Iulisch-Claudischen Kaiser,

pp. 251-266. In: *Les "Bourgeoises" Municipales Italiennes au IIe et Ier Siecles av. J.C.* Naples.

Zanker P. (1995): *The Mask of Socrates: the Image of the Intellectual.* Berkeley, University of California Press.

Zeman, J.J. (1977): Peirce's theory of signs, pp. 22-39. In: T.A. Sebeok ed. *A Perfusion of Signs.* Bloomington, Indiana University Press.

Zolberg, V.L. (1990): *Constructing a Sociology of the Arts.* Cambridge, Cambridge University Press.

Autorinnen und Autoren

Andreas Balog, Prof., Verwaltungsakademie des Bundes, Mauerbachstraße 43, A-1140 Wien. (andreas.balog@mauer.vab.vab.gv.at)
Keith Doubt, Prof., Chair, Sociology Department, Wittenberg University, Springfield, Ohio 45501-0720. (kdoubt@wittenberg.edu)
Harold J. Bershady, Prof., Sociology Department, University of Pennsylvania, 3718 Locust Walk, Philadelphia, PA 19104-6299. (hbershad@sas.upenn.edu)
Renée Fox, Prof., Sociology Department, University of Pennsylvania, 3718 Locust Walk, Philadelphia, PA 19104-6299.
Max Haller, Prof., Institut für Soziologie, Karl-Franzens-Universität Graz, Universitätsstraße 15/G4, A-8010 Graz. (max.haller@kfunigraz.ac.at)
Josef Langer, Prof., Institut für Soziologie, Universität Klagenfurt, Universitätsstraße 65-67, A-9020 Klagenfurt. (josef.langer@uin-klu.ac.at)
Victor M. Lidz, Prof., Department of Psychiatry, MCP Hahnemann University, 1427 Vine Street, MS 984, Philadelphia, PA 19102-1192. (Victor.Lidz@drexel.edu)
Tamás Meleghy, Prof. Institut für Soziologie, Leopold-Franzens-Universität Innsbruck, Universitätsstraße 15, A-6020 Innsbruck. (Tamas.Meleghy@uibk.ac.at)
Gerald Mozetič, Prof., Institut für Soziologie, Karl-Franzens-Universität Graz, Universitätsstraße 15/G4, A-8010 Graz. (gerald.mozetic@kfunigraz.ac.at)
Dénes Némedi, Prof., ELTE, Szociologia, Pollák Mihály tér, H-1088 Budapest. (h9096nem@ella.hu)
Helmut Staubmann, Prof., Institut für Soziologie, Leopold-Franzens-Universität Innsbruck, Universitätsstraße 15, A-6020 Innsbruck. (Helmut.Staubmann@uibk.ac.at)
Jeremy Tanner, Prof., Institute of Archaeology, University College London, 31-34 Gordon Square, London WC1 H 0PY. (j.tanner@ucl.ac.uk)
Bryan S. Turner, Prof., Chair, Faculty of Social and Politcal Science, Free School Lane, Cambridge CB2 3RQ. (bst22@cam.ac.uk)
Harald Wenzel, Prof., Abteilung Soziologie, J. F. Kennedy-Institut für Nord-Amerika-Studien, FU-Berlin, Lansstraße 5-9, D-14195 Berlin. (wenzelha@zedat.fu-berlin.de)

Niklas Luhmann
Organisation und Entscheidung
2000. 479 S. Geb. mit SU DM 68,00
ISBN 3-531-13451-5

35 Jahre nach der erstmaligen Veröffentlichung von „Funktionen und Folgen formaler Organisation" schließt „Organisation und Entscheidung" das Gesamtwerk Niklas Luhmanns mit einem weiteren Grundlagenwerk zur soziologischen Theorie formaler Organisationen ab.

Klaus Türk (Hrsg.)
Hauptwerke der Organisationstheorie
2000. 346 S. wv studium, Bd. 186. Geb. DM 49,80
ISBN 3-531-22186-8

Dieses Lehrbuch behandelt 139 ausgewählte Hauptwerke der Organisationstheorie alphabetisch nach Autorennamen sortiert. Jede einzelne Besprechung folgt einem einheitlichen Muster: Zunächst wird das jeweilige Werk in der Originalsprache genannt, dann in einer (wenn vorhanden) deutschen Übersetzung. Im weiteren geben die Beitragsautoren eine dichte Beschreibung der Entstehung, des Gehalts des Hauptwerkes sowie seiner werkgeschichtlichen Bedeutung sowie Rezeptions- und Wirkungsgeschichte. Angefügt werden bibliographische Hinweise auf aktuelle Ausgaben und weiterführende Literatur.

Günther Ortmann, Jörg Sydow, Klaus Türk (Hrsg.)
Theorien der Organisation
Die Rückkehr der Gesellschaft
2. Aufl. 2000. 661 S. Br. DM 78,00
ISBN 3-531-32945-6

„(...) eine der wichtigsten Publikationen dieses Jahrzehnts (...)"
Organisationsentwicklung 2/99

ZUM THEMA

Organisation

www.westdeutschervlg.de

Abraham-Lincoln-Str.46
65189 Wiesbaden
Tel. 06 11. 78 78 - 285
Fax. 06 11. 78 78 - 400

Erhältlich im Buchhandel oder beim Verlag.
Änderungen vorbehalten. Stand: April 2000.

Westdeutscher Verlag

AUS DEM PROGRAMM

Soziologie

Werner Fuchs-Heinritz, Rüdiger Lautmann,
Otthein Rammstedt (Hrsg.)
Lexikon zur Soziologie
3., völlig neubearb. und erw. Aufl. 1994. 763 S. Br. DM 78,00
ISBN 3-531-11417-4

Das Lexikon zur Soziologie ist das umfassendste Nachschlagewerk für die sozialwissenschaftliche Fachsprache. Es bietet aktuelle, zuverlässige Erklärungen von Begriffen aus der Soziologie sowie aus Sozialphilosophie, Politikwissenschaft und Politischer Ökonomie, Sozialpsychologie, Psychoanalyse und allgemeiner Psychologie, Anthropologie und Verhaltensforschung, Wissenschaftstheorie und Statistik.

Jürgen Friedrichs
Methoden empirischer Sozialforschung
14. Aufl. 1990. 430 S. wv studium, Bd. 28. Br. DM 26,80
ISBN 3-531-22028-4

Dieses Buch ist eine Einführung in Methodologie, Methoden und Praxis der empirischen Sozialforschung. Die Methoden werden ausführlich dargestellt und an zahlreichen Beispielen aus der Forschung erläutert. Damit leitet das Buch nicht nur zur kritischen Lektüre vorhandener Untersuchungen, sondern ebenso zu eigener Forschung an.

Rüdiger Jacob
Wissenschaftliches Arbeiten
Eine praxisorientierte Einführung für Studierende
der Sozial- und Wirtschaftswissenschaften
1997. 146 S. wv studium, Bd. 176. Br. DM 22,80
ISBN 3-531-22176-0

Voraussetzung für ein erfolgreiches wissenschaftliches Studium ist das souveräne Beherrschen der Techniken wissenschaftlichen Arbeitens. Dazu zählen nebem dem Umgang mit wissenschaftlicher Literatur, der Archivierung gelesenen Materials und der Erstellung von Manuskripten und wissenschaftlicher Abhandlungen auch Präsentationstechniken und die Moderation von Arbeitsgruppen. Dies ist die erste kompakte Einführung für Studienanfänger und Studierende im Grundstudium.

www.westdeutschervlg.de

Erhältlich im Buchhandel oder beim Verlag.
Änderungen vorbehalten. Stand: April 2000.

Abraham-Lincoln-Str. 46
65189 Wiesbaden
Tel. 06 11. 78 78 - 285
Fax. 06 11. 78 78 - 400

Westdeutscher Verlag

Österreichische Zeitschrift für Soziologie
Vierteljahresschrift der Österreichischen Gesellschaft für Soziologie

Westdeutscher Verlag GmbH, Abraham-Lincoln-Straße 46, D-65189 Wiesbaden
Geschäftsführer: Dr. Hans-Dieter Haenel   www.westdeutschervlg.de
Verlagsleitung: Dr. Heinz Weinheimer
Gesamtleitung Produktion: Reinhard van den Hövel
Gesamtleitung Vertrieb: Heinz Detering
Gesamtleitung Anzeigen: Thomas Werner

Herausgeber: Vorstand der Österreichischen Gesellschaft für Soziologie: Josef Gunz, Sabine Blaschke, Max Preglau, Franz Wagner, Gerald Angermann-Mozetic, Franz Gschwandtner, Petra Murauer, Renate Gerstl

Redaktion: Gerda Bohmann, Eva Cyba, Jörg Flecker, Ulrike Froschauer, Manfred Gabriel, Walburga Gáspár-Ruppert, Peter Gasser-Steiner, Joachim Gerich, Evelyn Gröbl-Steinbach, Wolfgang Holzinger, Helmut Staubmann, Meinrat Ziegler.

Redaktionssprecher: Manfred Gabriel (Universität Salzburg, Institut für Kultursoziologie, Rudolfskai 42, A-5020 Salzburg)

Redaktionelle Zuschriften bitte nur an die Redaktion senden. Unverlangt eingesandte Rezensionsexemplare können nicht zurückgeschickt werden.

Leserservice: Tatjana Hellwig, Telefon (0611) 7878-151; Telefax (0611) 7878-423;
E-mail: wv.service@bertelsmann.de
Abonnentenverwaltung: Ursula Müller, Telefon (0 5241) 80 1965; Telefax (0 5241) 80 9620;
E-mail: Ursula.Mueller@bertelsmann.de
Marketing: Ronald Schmidt-Serrière M.A., Telefon (0611) 7878-280; Telefax (0611) 7878-439;
E-mail: Ronald.Schmidt-Serriere@bertelsmann.de
Anzeigenleitung: Björn Jagnow, Telefon (0611) 7878-398; Telefax (0611) 7878-430;
E-mail: bjoern.jagnow@bertelsmann.de
Anzeigendisposition: Alexa Michopoulos M. A., Telefon (0611) 7878-149;
Telefax (0611) 7878-443; E-mail: Alexa.Michopoulos@bertelsmann.de
Es gilt die Anzeigenpreisliste vom 1. Januar 1998.
Produktion/Layout: Gabriele McLemore, Telefon (0611) 7878-174; Telefax (0611) 7878-468;
E-mail: Gabriele.McLemore@bertelsmann.de

Bezugsbedingungen: Jährlich erscheinen 4 Hefte.
Jahresabonnement 2000: DM 72,– / öS 526,– / sFr 65,50,–, für Studenten gegen Studienbescheinigung DM 56,– / öS 409,– / sFr 50,50. Einzelheft DM 27,– / öS 197,– / sFr 25,–, jeweils inkl. MwSt. (Versandkosten Inland DM 27,– / öS 197,– / sFr 25,–).
Alle Bezugspreise und Versandkosten unterliegen der Preisbindung. Abbestellungen müssen spätestens 3 Monate vor Ende des Kalenderjahres schriftlich beim Verlag erfolgen.

© 2000 Westdeutscher Verlag GmbH, Opladen/Wiesbaden
Der Westdeutsche Verlag ist ein Unternehmen der Fachverlagsgruppe BertelsmannSpringer.
Alle Rechte vorbehalten. Kein Teil dieser Zeitschrift darf ohne schriftliche Genehmigung des Verlages vervielfältigt oder verbreitet werden. Unter dieses Vorbehalt fällt insbesondere die gewerbliche Vervielfältigung per Kopie, die Aufnahme in elektronischen Datenbanken und die Vervielfältigung auf CD-ROM und allen anderen elektronischen Datenträgern.

Satz: Laudenbach, Sigmundsgasse 14, A-1070 Wien
Druck und buchbinderische Verarbeitung: Rosch-Buch, Scheßlitz
Gedruckt auf säurefreiem und chlorfrei gebleichtem Papier.
Printed in Germany
ISSN 1011-0070

Gedruckt mit Förderung des Bundesministeriums für Wissenschaft, Bildung und Kultur in Wien.

GPSR Compliance

The European Union's (EU) General Product Safety Regulation (GPSR) is a set of rules that requires consumer products to be safe and our obligations to ensure this.

If you have any concerns about our products, you can contact us on

ProductSafety@springernature.com

In case Publisher is established outside the EU, the EU authorized representative is:

Springer Nature Customer Service Center GmbH
Europaplatz 3
69115 Heidelberg, Germany

www.ingramcontent.com/pod-product-compliance
Lightning Source LLC
LaVergne TN
LVHW010337260326
834688LV00036B/744